The
TRAVEL
Writer's
Handbook

5TH EDITION

How to Write—and Sell—
Your Own Travel Experiences

Louise Purwin Zobel

SURREY BOOKS
Chicago

To my wonderful family

THE TRAVEL WRITER'S HANDBOOK, 5th Edition, is published by
Surrey Books, Inc., 230 E. Ohio St., Suite 120, Chicago, IL 60611.

Fifth edition: 2 3 4 5

This book is manufactured in the United States of America.

Library of Congress Cataloging-in-Publication Data

  Zobel, Louise Purwin
  The travel writer's handbook : how to write and sell your own travel experiences /
  Louise Purwin Zobel.—5th ed.
    p. cm.
  ISBN 1-57284-044-7
  1. Travel writing—Handbooks, manuals, etc. I. Title.

  G151.Z62 2002
  808'.06691—dc21

                                                          2002008710

For prices on quantity purchases or for a free book catalog, contact Surrey Books
at the above address.

Distributed to the trade by Publishers Group West

ACKNOWLEDGMENTS

Twenty-two years ago, when I was preparing the original edition of *The Travel Writer's Handbook*, this is how I began the Acknowledgments:

> No venture ever succeeds alone, but is always reinforced and strengthened by the contributions of many people. I have been especially fortunate in the planning and writing of this book to find such a wealth of helpful allies who have enriched it, and in this modest way I wish to thank them.

What I wrote in March, 1980, is equally true today. Many people shared in the success of that first hard cover edition and the subsequent paperback editions and numerous printings. And many have made it possible for me to offer this completely updated and revised Fifth Edition. I scarcely know where to begin to say "thank you." I do want to express my sincere appreciation to:

My thousands of students, both in-person and online, whose successes have proved the value of these concepts, and whose ongoing quest for learning keeps me searching for better and better answers.

The program directors at the 40 universities, colleges and online learning institutions where I present travel writing seminars, the program chairmen of the many national and international writers' conferences I attend as a faculty member, and the program planners who ask me to speak on various occasions—all of whom have enabled me to fine-tune my ideas.

The reference librarians, too numerous to name, at the various public and university libraries, where answers to my questions and assistance in tracing elusive details proved invaluable.

The dozens of editors I deal with, who have taught me so much about the articles they've bought—and about the articles they haven't bought. And a special thanks to those whose astute assistance and gracious permission to quote have provided enhancement.

My agents, Michael Larsen and Elizabeth Pomada, my publisher, Susan Schwartz, as well as my editor, Leona Pitej, managing editor Gene DeRoin, and other members of the Surrey Books staff, all of whom have helped to breathe life into this new revision of *The Travel Writer's Handbook*.

Members of the various national and regional writing and travel groups to which I belong, who have contributed to my growth and development as a writer. I've learned so much from all of them.

The numerous people named in the body of the book who are allowing me to share their ideas, experiences and expertise with my readers. The many friends, relatives, consultants, colleagues, and assistants who have contributed in myriad ways, both before-the-scenes and behind-the-scenes. It would be impossible to name them all, but I believe they know the sincerity of my gratitude. A special word of thanks to Lee Foster, Terry Shuchat, and Tom and Michelle Grimm.

And, far from least, I'm grateful to my children, Thomas and Lenore Harris, Jan Zobel, Robert and Karen Zobel, and Todd and Audrey Dollinger, for all of their help. To them, and to their children, Rahbeka, Josh, Grant, Rachael, Lauren, Kevin, Sara, and Seth, my thanks for their stimulating company on the wonderful trips we've enjoyed together.

I cannot end these acknowledgments without a word of appreciation to the spirit of my favorite travel companion, Dr. Jerome Zobel, who provided a lifetime of support, encouragement, and devotion.

Louise Purwin Zobel
Summer, 2002

CONTENTS

INTRODUCTION

Although the travel writing profession is seeing some difficult times this spring and summer, this does not, by any means, indicate an end to the power and pleasure of the written word.

While some publications—both in print and online—as well as some cruise lines and some tours with international clientele—have quietly shut up operations, that neither forecasts the end of travel nor the end of the written word. Even when the popularity of some destinations changes as a result of world events, travel, itself, remains a constant. The desire to see and experience what others have enjoyed remains a desire of the reader. Yes, there is a need for travel writers in 2002 and beyond.

Some of you reading this book may already be travel writers, hoping to discover useful tips and shortcuts. You will discover them. Some of you are probably successful writers in other fields, yearning to move in a different direction, trying to find the tools that will help you. You will find them. Doubtless some of you are writing-relatives—English teachers, advertising copywriters, newsletter editors, and others who feel they can become successful travel writers by learning how to move in the right direction. You will learn how. Certainly some of you are travel writers, writers of exciting letters, tellers of inviting tales. You want to professionalize your product. You can do it. And some of you, with no background at all in writing or traveling, are reading this book because you think it sounds like fun to be a travel writer. It is.

This book is for each of you. If you've ever had anyone say, "You write such wonderful letters—you ought to publish them," or "When you tell about that trip, it sounds simply fantastic—why don't you write it all down?" or "We loved looking at your pictures and your videos—you made it all so interesting"—this is the book you need.

While not a book on basic writing techniques (it assumes you already know how to write grammatical English sentences, and that what you don't know about punctuation, you'll look up), it does offer helpful avenues to organizing and writing travel articles, both print and electronic. It explains the importance of market research and subject research before, during, and after you travel. It suggests successful approaches to editors and online content managers. It tells you how to write the most popular types of travel articles and gives you an in-depth look at the business of being a travel writer, including such diverse subjects as how to use the query as a sales tool, where to obtain illustrations, and what to take off your income tax.

While not exactly a book on travel, either (it assumes a basic familiarity with traveling, whether around the corner or around the world), the advice you will find here on preparing for the trip, as well as profiting from it, should be welcome to any traveler. It's important to remember, too, that the travel-oriented article may just as well be about your own neighborhood—an exciting, faraway destination to others.

I have taught travel writing to college and university students of all ages, as well as to cruise ship passengers of many nationalities, and to online participants around the world. I have served on the faculty of many writers' conferences and published in many kinds of media. I've traveled from the Cape of Good Hope and the Straits of Magellan to the Midnight Sun and the Inland Sea, crisscrossing the equator and the international date line too many times to count. Much of my travel has been by plane, train, bus, streetcar, automobile, ship, subway, gondola, launch, taxicab, rowboat, cable car, and safari bus; much of it has been by shoe leather. I have enjoyed sharing my travels with my readers, and I hope you will enjoy sharing your travels with your readers. That is what this book is about—writing good travel copy that other people will want to read.

Though writing of itself should please and satisfy the writer, and may even have some therapeutic value, here we are talking about writing as a public profession—writing about your travel experiences for the enjoyment and the edification of your readers. Professionalism leads to pleasure *and* profit for the travel writer. The trip is more enjoyable when you know you'll be writing about it. And it is possible to make your vacation pay for itself.

The ideas expressed in *The Travel Writer's Handbook* have, in my experience, proved helpful, and I hope they will prove helpful to you. But, of course, there is no assurance that all the pieces of the puzzle will always fit together advantageously. In the end, each of us must find our own way to satisfaction.

As a travel writer you will feel a great responsibility—the writer's responsibility to the reader. Later travelers see what you have seen, not only in the setting of your words but also within the framework of the emotional responses you transfer. The need for truth and accuracy in both hard facts and intangibles can never be emphasized enough.

While successful travel writers never forget the importance of accurate detail, they also know that equally important is how the writer—and the reader—feel about that detail. For no matter how literal your piece may be—counting the miles to every turnoff and the dollars for every dinner—

in travel writing, as in most kinds of writing, it is the people and the emotions that matter. How did you *feel* about the experience? Without the *feeling*, your reader might as well look up "Paris" in the encyclopedia.

Emotions are awakened by the travel itself; and the desire to write is stimulated by new faces and new places. Travel and writing complement each other, and the travel writer finds that thinking about the reader and trying to increase the reader's enjoyment enhances his own excitement in the adventure.

The travel writer's success is determined by how precisely he defines his audience. All good writers know that the reader is not only a partner in the writing but is the ultimate boss. The travel writer has to *care* about the reader enough to break though the barrier of ink to the magic of shared feeling—*I* care about *you*.

PART ONE

Travel Writing Is Alive and Well

Cars skidded on the damp street and pedestrians huddled in their overcoats as I scooted into the drugstore. I grabbed some sunscreen and a sun shade and thrust them at the clerk. "Please hurry. I'm catching a plane."

"Where to?" she asked.

"Hawaii. I have an assignment. . . ."

"Ha-wa-ii!" She fairly breathed the word. "Lucky *you*! Ha-wa-ii—instead of shivering here!"

"Well, I have this job. . . ."

"*Job!*" she gulped. "A job that takes you to Hawaii in February—you must have been a saint in a previous life!"

I don't know much about sainthood. But I do know that a travel writer's job can take you to Hawaii in February, to New Orleans in August, to India in time for the monsoon. If you like to write and you like to travel, if you're the kind of person who's continually captivated by new places, new ideas, new faces, you may find that this job sometimes seems less like work than play. But it's always more work than it seems.

Depending on how you look at it, the travel writer never takes a vacation—or lives in the vacuum of perpetual vacation. The hours are flexible, so you end up working most of them. I was amused by a letter from a program chairman thanking me for accepting a Saturday speaking engagement. "Such a nice day for relaxing," she wrote. "Appreciate your giving up your Saturday for this talk." To me, Saturday is a working day. So is Sunday.

So is every day, 365 or 366 days a year. The travel writer's job is ongoing and demanding. It's also intriguing and rewarding.

What Makes You a Travel Writer?

Anybody can be a Tourist. A Travel Writer needs instinct, insight, imagination, and enthusiasm. As a travel writer, you not only see and hear, you investigate and interpret and try to understand. You meet people of different colors and different backgrounds. You learn new customs, embrace new thoughts, absorb new knowledge.

Not satisfied only to ask *what*, the travel writer wants to know *who* and *how* and, more important, *why*. He or she recreates the travel experience, lending it relevance and perspective. In his desire to enhance his reader's enjoyment, he draws on his own spirit of adventure, rousing senses that tend to lie dormant and discovering that, as Herman Hesse says, "The true profession of man is finding his way to himself."

New places and new faces stimulate perception, encouraging you to delve more deeply, observe more carefully, and focus more clearly.

As a travel writer, you will never be lonely, never be bored, as you share with your readers the people and places, adventures and activities of your trips.

You'll find yourself behind the scenes in search of stories, and you'll come across areas and information the average person has no access to. Tell people you're a travel writer, and nothing's too much trouble for them to show you or to take you to. Again and again, you'll be led to a front seat instead of a back one; picked up and chauffeured by someone assigned to show you around; or provided with a meal, a briefing, and a ticket to an event you didn't even know existed. It's always more fun to be on the inside looking out.

While travel writing, of itself, is not a notably lucrative field—not in the same ballpark as, say, electrical contracting or dentistry—its fringe benefits are irresistible. As we'll see later in this book, the travel writer can sometimes accept exotic hospitality, sometimes deduct expenses from his income tax, and often arrange lecture engagements and other related professional activities. You'll know the gratification of seeing your name in print, and your byline may lead to professional advancement in other fields. You'll appreciate comments of friends and colleagues; enjoy letters and phone calls from strangers.

For many of us, a special advantage of being a travel writer is the feeling of doing meaningful work, even on vacation. Raised in the Puritan ethic of "keep busy," we sometimes feel uncomfortable in a state of complete relaxation for more than a few days. It seems as though we *should* be learning, absorbing, taking notes, becoming expert. Being a travel writer gives you a legitimate motive for listening and learning. You know that later you'll use this information in some meaningful manner.

One prolific writer replies to questions about how long it took him to write this article or that book with, "How long did it take me? All my life." He goes on to explain, "Everything I've ever been or done or thought or known or experienced somehow went into the writing of this particular piece. I couldn't have written it exactly this way a year ago, and if I were to write it a year from now, it would be still different." The most successful travel writers use everything they've ever been and done, thought and known and experienced, as their jumping-off point.

Travel Writers Come in Many Flavors

The term "travel writer" is all-inclusive. It encompasses newspaper and magazine travel editors, staff writers, columnists, and freelancers, as well as public relations and advertising practitioners, writers of radio and television scripts, art reviewers, compilers of cookbooks, publishers of travel newsletters, producers of armchair travel books, audiovisual materials and travel videos. It includes those who deliver "content" to online travel programs, write for e-zines, and contribute to their own websites or those posted by others.

It includes, also, the guidebook writers, whether nuts and bolts or literary and mystical, and writers who need an exotic background for other work—anything from juvenile stories and whodunits to historical novels and musical comedies.

This book will speak to all types of travel writers but will focus on the freelancer who provides travel material for newspapers and magazines in print and online.

For some of you, travel writing will be a full-time occupation, for others a part-time profession. Some of you part-timers may also write other types of material, and much of the information in this book applies, of course, to other types of writing as well.

If you can't be a full-time freelance travel writer, is it better to work at a writing-related job so you're primed to sit down at your home keyboard, or should you work at a task completely unrelated to writing so all your creative energy is hoarded for your freelancing? That debate probably goes back to Caesar and Cicero and has no "right" resolution.

Because readers vary—in their needs and desires, age and financial position, level of education and travel experience, temperament and lifestyle— a varied group of travel writers will succeed. It's hard to draw a profile of the successful travel writer, but there are certain qualities every travel writer needs.

In addition to instinct, that spontaneous impulse that moves you to the right place at the right time, and insight, that quality of discernment that apprehends the inner nature of things, the travel writer also needs imagination, the creative ability to visualize something not currently present. Add to this great quantities of enthusiasm, the force that propels the writer forward and carries the reader along.

A travel writer should also cultivate the characteristic of curiosity (nosiness, if you wish), the readiness to observe, to eavesdrop, to look figuratively through the keyhole, always wondering what's waiting around the bend in the road. You have to be active, eager to see new places, and alert to simple pleasures.

You need to be energetic and willing to work hard. You need to be healthy, as well as a good sport, ready to accept inconvenience. You should be a good listener, sensitive and perceptive, good at drawing people out, and interested in and knowledgeable about a variety of matters. If you know another language, that's super. But even if you don't, you should learn the basic words and mores of your target area. You have to be good at understanding unfamiliar accents and prepared to make conversation through pantomime, crudely drawn pictures, and fingers pointing to words in the dictionary.

To be a travel writer you need faith in yourself and in your opinions.

Trust Yourself

You won't be the passive tourist who always eats at the name restaurant because "everybody goes there." You'll seek out your own adventures and feel confident that what you have to say about them will prove valuable to others. One of my favorite cartoons shows a couple standing on the rim of the Grand Canyon, with the wife saying to the husband, "This can't be so very attractive. We're the only ones here."

If *you* think it's attractive, you don't need to have anyone else there admiring it. If *you* think it's worth writing about, it's worth writing about.

You must be observant, conscious of small details, accurate in recording them, and prepared to undertake any amount of work to verify existing particulars or to uncover new ones.

Because both traveling and writing are things everybody wishes to do "if I ever found the time," the travel writer must *make* the time. If you want to be successful you must learn to use your "thinking time" to best advantage, so that your writing times is used for writing. Thinking about what you'll write while you're standing in line, stopped at the signal, or waiting in the departure lounge means your time at the keyboard will be spent writing. You need self-discipline and the conviction that waiting for ideal working conditions will never put a word on paper.

You also need to be an aggressive salesman, knowledgeable about markets, confident of your own abilities, and aware that a manuscript in the desk drawer has no chance of selling.

You Need "Plus Value" for Success

To make your work salable in today's competitive world, the most important characteristic you need is "plus value," that special something that makes your piece better than the next person's. It exists, but it's hard to define. Yet all successful manuscripts have it.

Plus value, that patina of excellence that triggers a positive response in the editor and, later, the reader, may result from any of several advantages: a universality that communicates clearly; a strong connection with a topic of current interest; a personal background that lends depth to the experience; a theme so true we can't fail to recognize it; a conviction so firm it's only logical to listen; research so extensive it's impossible to discredit; information so relevant we can't ignore it; or writing so polished that reading is effortless.

Of all the characteristics a travel writer should have, this is the most essential: to be a successful travel writer today you must produce stories of higher quality than the editor specifies or than the reader anticipates. You need plus value.

When we speak of "success," we're equating it with publication, preferably publication with pay. While you never want to be caught in the trap of writing *only* for the money, money *is* the yardstick of professionalism. When somebody's willing to pay for what you write, you have, in a sense, succeeded.

On the other hand, the principles of effective travel writing applied to the standard trip postcard or Christmas newsletter can only improve them. What the traditional "Having a wonderful time—wish you were here" is really saying is, "*I'm* having a wonderful time. Don't *you* wish you were here? I'll bet you're jealous. I sure hope so." Whether it's a postcard or a bestseller, the writer's concern for the reader is the difference between failure and success. When you write on your postcard:

> I thought of you when the outboard refused to catch this morning—
> how many balky outboards have we coped with! I can hardly wait for
> you to see this place—you'll love the sandy beach and the gentle waves
> and the fishing—well, I'll tell you all about it when we get home. . . .

your reader's jealousy is mitigated by the fact that you wrote to *him*, specifically and concernedly.

This creative relationship to the reader, this feeling of kinship with him, should always predominate in the travel writer's mind.

I used to wonder about that reader. With so many people on wheels, waves, and wings these days, could there possibly be enough stay-at-homes to provide a reading audience for all the travel material being published? And when I came across a slim booklet, "The Moon on $5 a Day," I began to think of the time when earthbound travel writing would be obsolete. But even since Moon Publications published *Moon Handbook: A 21st Century Travel Guide*, I have sold, and my students have sold, so many down-to-earth travel pieces that I *know* there is a market out there for today's travel writer.

Do You Know Your Reader?

Do you know your reader and what interests her? You should.

There is no such thing as writing "generally." Good travel writing is always addressed to a specific reader, and it's essential to visualize that reader. Market research tells us who our reader is; the travel writer tries to anticipate and answer her questions. For some articles and some destinations the questions may be: What is it like to take that trip? Where are the best places to stay, eat, shop? What sights should I see? What time of year is best? What shall I wear? How much will it cost? Under other circumstances, they may be: What kind of people live there? What are they like? How can I meet them? What and where are the flora and fauna? How can I see it? For still other pieces, the reader's questions might be: How can I get there? What special training do I need? How long should I stay? And some readers may be saying, "Why should I stay away from there?" or, "If I go, what precautions must I take?"

Whether your reader is an active or an armchair traveler, whether he's planning a similar trip or reminiscing about one he's taken or simply enjoying a vicarious view of the world, it's up to you, the writer, to give him the kind of story he wants. You bring to life reminiscence and breathe possibility into planning. You pave the way for later travelers by telling them what it's like so they see it in the setting of your words and within the framework of the emotional responses you have developed.

This saddles the writer with tremendous responsibility. Your opinion has great influence on others. A bad word from you, and the restaurant will lose customers. Recommend a delightful, out-of-the-way Paris hotel full of charming French customers, and a year later it's so full of American tourists there's no room for the French.

Whether you're going around the world or around the corner, you must take this responsibility seriously. You must know what you're saying and be sure you're telling it exactly as it is. You may be surprised at how much this book emphasizes research. But don't let it frighten you. Many activities you've never thought of as *research* are continually adding to your store of knowledge. Research, remember, is an exchange of ideas. Often it's done on the ski slopes or at the theater or at a sidewalk café. *Research!* Of course! So sit down and order some refreshment. Look around you. Listen. Ask questions. Take notes. Record how it feels, tastes, and smells. If you've already gone on the trip you plan to write about, and you didn't take all the steps this book advises, don't despair. You can still write a travel article. But it will be harder to develop the plus value without the preliminaries.

Your Reader Has Great Expectations

Today's readers expect a lot of plus value in a travel story because they're sophisticated. They've probably traveled a good deal themselves, and, with the twenty-first century communication systems, they're as familiar with an opera at the Baths of Caracalla as they are with a song in the shower. Travel is one of the most important facts of modern life. And today it's big business. Travel is now one of the largest industries in the United States, and seers predict that it will continue to grow.

Travel has a long history. Remains of caravansaries and entertainment centers that catered to visitors have been discovered at the most ancient archaeological sites. Over two thousand years ago the goddess Artemis/Diana lured pilgrims to her new temple at Ephesus, one of the ancient world's Seven Wonders. The goddess had a very efficient public relations organization, with branches on three continents. They used every inducement to encourage tourists to visit Ephesus, sign up for the temple sightseeing tour, and take home a silver souvenir. (Some scholars think they probably offered charter rates on the express galleys, but so far no advertisements for this have been uncovered!)

Are people today interested in travel? A national magazine offering a free brochure on an upcoming festival had five thousand requests in the first twenty-four hours. When Fielding mentioned Ethiopia in a travel talk, officials had to close the Ethiopian tourist office for three days to get caught up with the backlog of visas for travelers headed there. One of my students, Owen Johnson, had a brief article in the *Los Angeles Times* Travel Section about a tiny town in Germany. Within a week the town's chamber of commerce had fielded sixty phone calls from people in California requesting information about how to get there. Each travel article published finds new readers, thus building an ever-increasing audience for future travel articles, by that author or by others.

You don't have to travel to exotic places to be a travel writer. What's "down home" to you may be glamorously distant to others. It may not seem like *travel writing* when you tell about the haunted house that's a big attraction in your neighborhood, the new lodge at a nearby ski slope, or the local farmer's market. But that's what travel writing *is*—telling readers about something interesting beyond *their* own backyards.

If it's in *your* backyard, celebrate. If your own milieu is in the backwater, you can be first to tout its attractions. But even well-traveled areas can provide new angles of interpretation. How about inspiration from the homes of all the writers who've lived on Long Island? Backyard barbecues in Las Vegas? Touring California's wine country with a teetotaling relative? Palm Springs in summer?

Wherever you live, wherever you travel, there's a story somebody wants to read. Whether you go around the world or around the corner, when you discover the plus values of the travel experience, you'll be ready to share your pleasure with your readers.

Some people, of course, travel around the world but never leave home. They follow Michelin's advice for weeks, but don't find anything as good as Sally's Creamery at First and Main. The Black Forest isn't as pretty as Turner Woods at home, Arlington Cemetery is only a larger version of their own church graveyard, and Saks Fifth Avenue doesn't have a thing better than their own Emporium at Second and Elm. Listen to them talk a minute and you're likely to hear somebody say, "We went around the world last year—but didn't like it."

The travel writer *celebrates* the differences in manners and customs. While he's interested in seeing temples and museums, he's more interested in learning lifestyles.

Travel should have an important purpose. It should result in meaningful experience. As Thoreau says, "It's not worthwhile to go around the world to count the cats in Zanzibar." The travel writer needs to be excited about his trips, so plan destinations and activities that intrigue you. Expand your horizons. Cultivate the urge to see, know, enjoy so you can inform, entertain, and motivate your reader.

As a travel writer you'll find that your own attitude is intrinsic to the value of the trip. In the words of Emerson, "Though we travel the world over to find the beautiful, we must carry it with us or we find it not." Travel writing encourages deeper insights and a gratifying sense of belonging. While we welcome the travel experience, we realize that we have to take something to the experience as well as bring something away from it.

If you're already a vital, sparkling, positive person, travel writing becomes you.

Begin at the Beginning–
With Research

While it may seem as though the trip, itself, is the story and pre-trip research is unnecessary, "being there" is never enough. To write successfully about travel, we need to begin at the beginning and learn all we can before we leave.

Travel research is a subtle skill. You may consciously say to yourself, "Today I'm going to the library and read up on Yellowstone," or "I'm going to call the Tollivers and ask about their trip to Yellowstone." But more likely you'll research Yellowstone when you run into Laura Tolliver at the drugstore or pick up a consumer magazine that's running an in-depth issue on national parks or come across a "Yellowstone" link online when you're looking for something else.

Research is done in libraries, yes. It's done at computer terminals, yes. It's also done in face-to-face interviews, on the telephone, and through "snail mail" or e-mail. Still more often it's done on the golf course, at parties, during coffee breaks, or while eavesdropping on the bus. Many informal encounters you never thought of as research turn out to be more helpful than the fattest guidebook.

Research helps you decide where to travel in the first place. You may be wondering about that—how the travel writer decides on a destination. People often ask which comes first, the assignment or the desire to visit a particular place. Does an editor ever suggest you go to Blanketyville and do a story? The answer is, sometimes. Or, do you indulge a lifelong dream of seeing Blanketyville—and then decide to write about it later? Again, the answer is, sometimes. Most often, though, the impetus for exploring a particular place begins with the research that makes that place seem an attractive one to write about. And the research usually starts with an informal encounter or casual reading—things we'll be talking about in this chapter.

Research not only helps you decide where to go, it tells you how to get there, where to stay, where to eat, what to see, what to do, what to buy, and what's likely to prove valuable to the travel writer. Pre-trip research saves you time, because you're sure to see the things that most interest you, and you'll know what you're seeing when you arrive at your destination. You'll be familiar with the lifestyle you'll find; you'll be able to add to your store of knowledge without beginning at the beginning. You've probably already discovered some of the aspects you want to write about, and you're already thinking about a fresh approach to some of the others. Your theme and your angle are defined. With pre-trip research you're in a good position to ask the right questions, and you're more likely to find yourself behind the scenes, where you want to be.

"Carry Knowledge With You"

Samuel Johnson quotes an old Spanish proverb that says, "He who would bring home the wealth of the Indies must carry the wealth of the Indies with him. So it is with travel," says Johnson. "A man must carry knowledge with him if he would bring knowledge home." The travel writer with pre-researched knowledge will bring home the stories with plus value.

The successful travel writer subscribes to the iceberg theory—know ten times as much as you're telling. The part that's unseen beneath the surface gives you the voice of authority that makes your readers sit up and take notice. An information overload enables you to choose which materials to use, rather than simply using whatever you happen to have; and doing lots of research helps you to assimilate, understand, and enhance the parts you do use. When you produce a well-researched travel article, editors respect you. Readers respect you. You respect yourself.

Also, as we'll discover later, the travel writer has to do enough preliminary research to write a descriptive query letter.

Research always becomes easier the more you do it. Some pushbutton mechanism in the brain starts sending out signals: "Yes, this goes with and enriches something I'm now beginning to understand," or "No, I already know all about that—I won't bother with this piece of research."

Research: Live and Library, Offline and Online

We used to divide subject research into *live* and *library*, but in this computerized world we need to consider additional resources. However, we still find the various research opportunities so intertwined that we need them all. Your friend Jim tells you Pennsylvania is the most fascinating place he's ever seen. He shows you the pictures he took on his last vacation at the national recreation area in the Poconos. You ask questions and he answers them. That's live research. If he also brings over a book on Pennsylvania he wants you to read, and you read it, that's library research. If you query your online search engine about Pennsylvania, and the computer comes up with useable results, that's a combination of both.

You then scan your own bookshelves and go to your public library to find materials to guide you in deciding which parts of Pennsylvania to see and how you'll get to your gateway city and what kind of transportation you'll use from there. Perhaps you'll go to a travel website that gives you a quick fix on Pennsylvania prices or check out the Pennsylvania home page. You may point your browser to www.ipl.org, which is the Internet Public Library. Then you'll visit a travel agent and ask for answers.

Next you contact the Philadelphia Convention and Visitors Bureau, the National Park Service, the Gettysburg Travel Council, and the Pennsylvania Dutch Visitors Bureau. You study the brochures, booklets, and maps they show you and send you. You e-mail the Pennsylvania Bureau of Travel Development, asking specific questions. Then you call Cousin Susie, who honeymooned in the Poconos and lives in Pittsburgh.

You call the local reference librarian with a quick question and go down to the automobile club to pick up the *Mideastern States Camping Book*. You rent a video on "The Beautiful Key Stone State." By now you've decided which facets of Pennsylvania are likely to have the most plus value for articles you will write. Back to the library or back to the Internet you go for specific information on Valley Forge, the Amish Farm Home, the U.S.S. Olympia at Penn's Landing, and the Philadelphia Zoo.

You can see how pre-trip research is a combination of writer and written word, and writer and other human beings.

Live research includes observation and interviews, both of which we'll discuss in more detail in Chapters 7 and 14. Less formal than interviews are encounters—your conversation with Jim and your visit to the travel agent, for instance. The encounter is less structured than the interview—often because it's just the kind of casual give-and-take the travel writer needs. You absorb easily what the other person has to offer, using the information to fill up the chinks in your own knowledge. Somehow this comes through in your finished story, making you sound less didactic because it isn't only *you* speaking to the reader—it's you along with your reference sources.

As soon as you've done enough preliminary research to ask sensible questions, talk to everybody you think can help you—airline representatives, steamship company representatives, government officials, other travel writers and editors, college students from far away, friends and friends of friends, and anybody else who has already been where you plan to go. Rent, borrow, or buy appropriate CD-ROM disks, videos, and audio tapes.

Attend community college courses and illustrated lectures, as well as films about the area you plan to visit. Log-on to information sources and chat rooms. And don't hesitate to ask questions.

Prepare yourself in advance, for instance, for visiting a town in a developing country. What will you look for? Does that country claim free, compulsory education? But will you see school-age children playing in the street during school hours? Do the houses have electricity? Plumbing? Privacy? What are the residents like? Do they have radios, books, mirrors, ice, newspapers? If you've done your homework, you'll know what you're looking at and what it means.

If it's a ruin you'll be visiting, do enough homework to people it—with those who lived there; worked and played; made love, made war. Picture them relaxing in their atrium, fountains playing on a warm summer evening, or poring over their clay tablets as they discuss the inflationary spiral of household expenses. If you get to know the *people*, a ruin is more than a pile of old stones.

Travel agents are usually generous with information, but don't impose on them. When I gave a travel-related assignment to my class of university students, I soon discovered that every travel agent in the area was furious with me. It turned out that all my students, instead of using the university library or a handy modem to research the information I required, were calling local travel agents for quick and easy answers.

It's almost impossible to conduct live research until you've laid a foundation of library or online research. You have to know the right questions to ask—you have to already be familiar with the subject before composing a questionnaire or conducting an interview or even taking advantage of an encounter. So let's consider, in addition to informal live research, some of the less formal research you can conduct in your home library.

Again, some of your best sources will be those you really don't think of as research. Your home bookshelves doubtless already contain an up-to-date dictionary, a thesaurus of some sort, and a style manual such as Strunk and White's *The Elements of Style*, as well as a recent edition of *Writer's Market* or some other marketing manual. You probably subscribe to at least a Sunday newspaper and at least one travel-oriented periodical, such as *National Geographic*, in addition to at least one writing-oriented periodical, such as *Writer's Digest*.

What else does the travel writer need at home? That depends partly on your computer skills and equipment and how much information you can download. It depends also on how close you live to a public library, how good the library is, how often you go there, and how much it means to you to *own* the book or magazine and to be able to mark it up, cut it out, put it aside to read next week, or take it along. And don't forget to begin your *futures* file early—stockpiling information you may need at some future time. When you *do* get ready to visit the places described in your files, you'll find the clippings and bibliographic notes invaluable.

The Travel Writer's Home Library

A quick sampling of my own overstuffed travel shelves reveals a diversity of books, ranging from *A Traveller's Guide to Caribbean History* to the *Insight Guides* to the *Waterways of Europe*; from *Adventures in Japan* to *Let's Go Turkey*. Travel advice ranges from *Lonely Planet Travel with Children* to *The Curmudgeon's Guide to Child-Free Travel*. The many books on business travel include the *Berlitz Business Travel Guides, Alternative Travel Directory,* and *Volunteer Vacations.*

There are all kinds of books on "how to get there"—from motorcycles to tramp steamers, and a myriad of information on places to stay, places to eat, places to shop, learning opportunities, and sightseeing of all types. *The Frugal Traveler* (2000) tells "How to see more of the world for less." There are classics like Paul Theroux's *The Pillars of Hercules*, and books of travel tales by ancient travelers—from Herodotus to Marco Polo. A book of *Travelers Tales*, compiled by Eric Newby, a literary travel writer of no small stature, gives the reader a taste of the past—from Anthony Trollope to John Charles Fremont. Several volumes of *Literary Trips* transport readers from Franz Kafka's Prague to John Steinbeck's Cannery Row. The *Chronicles Abroad* series covers great cities, according to Somerset Maugham, Thomas Mann, Jean Paul Sartre, Orson Wells, Benjamin Disraeli, Leo Tolstoy, Lawrence of Arabia, and other travelers inclined toward literary reporting.

This book, in its original first edition, was the first book ever directed specifically to the would-be travel writer, and it has been judged the definitive book on the subject. But in addition to *The Travel Writer's Handbook* in this brand new, updated version, there are many excellent books that provide insights into nonfiction writing in general.

Books on Writing

Rudolf Flesch, Henry Fowler, Jacques Barzun, and Theodore Bernstein stand ready to advise on the niceties of the writing process itself. Such books as Bartlett's *Familiar Quotations*, the *Home Book of Quotations*, or the *Oxford Dictionary of Quotations* belong on the travel writer's bookshelves or on easy electronic access. The *Oxford English Dictionary* (OED) contains nearly half a million words and two million quotations. The *American Thesaurus of Slang* and the *Acronyms and Initialisms Dictionary* help keep your language up to date, and *The Travellers' Dictionary of Quotation*, edited by Peter Yapp, is sometimes just what you need.

Bartleby.com has an excellent site for answering questions about English usage (www.bartleby.com/usage), and even has the full text of Strunk's *Elements of Style*. Many other language aids reside online, including Merriam-Webster OnLine (www.m-w.com), with its dictionary, and Thesaurus.com, with synonyms and antonyms, as well as a daily crossword puzzle.

Searching for special tips, shortcuts, and hints from the pros? Look for *Tools of the Writer's Trade*, written by members of the American Society of Journalists and Authors. Although not brand new, it's still helpful when some of the most experienced writers in the world tell how they handle their computers, their phone lines, their financial arrangements, and what books they refer to for their special needs. They reveal how to treat reluctant interviewees, how to promote a book on television, how to get help with your research, and how to find envelopes at bargain prices. *Travel Smarts*, written by the editors of the newsletter of that name, talks about how to get the most bang for your travel dollar—everything from being a cruise ship host to which side of the train to select for a scenic journey.

Books on Photography

Since awareness of photographic techniques, sources, prices, and markets is part of the travel writer's essential knowledge, you'll want to read several books on photography.

Photographer's Market, published annually, not only gives advice on setting up a business, preparing a portfolio, and "How to Package and Mail Your Work" but also provides a comprehensive, up-to-date list of photography buyers. Buyers range from advertising agencies to audiovisual firms and include consumer magazines, trade journals, and company publications. The listings tell you the name of the buyer, what each publication needs in the way of photographs, and what it will pay for them.

Kodak produces many kinds of books and booklets and their home page (www.kodak.com) offers valuable information, too.

"Traveling with a Camera" is an especially helpful chapter in the fourth edition of *The Basic Book of Photography* by Tom and Michelle Grimm. Traveling photojournalists, the Grimms have authored several photography-oriented books. Rohn Engh and others provide authoritative advice for the camera carrier. Additional books about the digital world, as well as magazines and online advice, can help you over the rough spots, if that's the route you decide to take. (More on photography in Chapter 15.)

Books on Using Computers

There are a number of books about online writing and marketing for writers, such as *Writer's Online Marketplace*.

Dummies books have inundated the market with simplified information on everything from *Internet for Dummies* to *Starting an Ebay Business for Dummies*. If you're past the "Dummies" stage, try a title in the "Bibles" series.

Probably the most current written electronic information is available in magazines, and there are dozens—maybe hundreds—available at newsstands and bookstores, as well as everywhere computer equipment is sold. Magazines such as *MacAddict*, *PC World*, and *Wired Magazine* cater to the knowledgeable users. Other publications are pitched to owners of specific hardware or specific software, users in certain geographic areas—from San Diego to Vancouver—or people who use computers for particular purposes, such as archaeology or genealogy.

Guidebooks

You'll surely want to read at least one guidebook on where you think you might like to go—or several guidebooks while you're deciding what your destination will be. But consider the different types of guides so you can make a sensible selection. You can often purchase guidebooks for less than half of their marked price at bookstores' end-of-year sales. You can buy used guidebooks for a few cents from Friends of the Library sales or rummage sales or thrift shops.

If you're using a previous year's guide, be sure to update it from the public library's current copy. Restaurant and hotel information becomes obsolete quickly. And while sight-seeing information on Old Faithful or Pike's Peak doesn't change much with the years, still, we all know that Niagara Falls was turned off for a while, Yellowstone had a devastating fire, and currently you can't always enter the Parthenon or the stone circle at Stonehenge.

When buying guidebooks for your home library, select those most appropriate for your own writing. Just as *you* have in mind *your* reader as you research and write, so do guidebook writers visualize *their* readers. Ask yourself what kind of traveler your guidebook is written for—the shaggy teenager in blue jeans or the little old lady with blue hair.

Temple Fielding said he originally wrote his guides for the small-town real-estate agent or dentist who is afraid he'll be in a situation he can't control when he gets to Europe. If the small-town real-estate agent or dentist can stand Fielding's baroque prose, he'll be able to easily select a hotel and restaurant. Fielding emphasizes creature comforts—if you want culture, look elsewhere—and he's super-candid about these creature comforts. Brief tips inserted randomly tell the reader how to avoid unpleasantness and warn of "local rackets."

Baedeker, the doyen of guidebooks, devotes twenty-five pages of its *London* guide to the British Museum, while covering hotels and restaurants in a page or two. But many long-out-of-date Baedekers are superior resources for finding out how things once were, and libraries keep them around for that purpose.

The *Blue Guides* are nearly as detailed as Baedeker's and cover the same ground—a plethora of historical background and not much for the night-club hopper.

There's a guidebook series directed to just about any type of traveler. *The Sierra Club Adventure Travel Guides* are, logically, devoted to adventuring as well as to ecological concerns. The *Lonely Planet Guides*, although strong on adventure, too, usually cover less developed countries, as explored by the budget-minded traveler. *Moon Publications* provides thoroughly researched information on every aspect of travel within an area, and while they, too, lean toward the budget traveler, they contain lots of good hints for the big spender. *Insight Guides* are well-illustrated cultural experiences that give you an excellent background for the country but not too much on everyday arrangements.

Cadogan guides are easy to read and give you some local lore, along with hotel and restaurant listings and the address of American Express. It might be useful to know that the lovely elm trees of the Alhambra were planted by the Duke of Wellington or the early history of Monaco and how the Grimaldi family first came there.

Guidebooks I heartily recommend are Robert Bone's *Maverick Guides* to Hawaii, Australia, and New Zealand. They give an overall view, then history, airports, transportation, hotels, restaurants, sight-seeing, guided tours and cruises, water sports, other sports, shopping, nightlife, and an address list. The books are well balanced in their presentation of history, sight-seeing, and everyday details.

Several publishers specialize in very small take-along guides—the kind that fit in a shirt pocket. They may be limited in scope and printed in hard-to-read type, but their niche is an important one.

On the other hand, the gigantic (over 700 pages) *Texas: A Guide to the Lone Star State* covers in a matter-of-fact way the history, government, agriculture, folklore, and social life of the state. Then it describes the fifteen largest cities, giving brief information about accommodations, airlines, and annual events. Then comes specific information about the history of the city and its points of interest. Another section gives detailed highway tours with interesting historical notes interspersed. Excellent maps and illustrations abound.

So far, all the guides we've spoken of, with the exception of Fielding's, are continuously updated. They are revised at random intervals, as author, publisher, or readership demands. You have to look at the copyright date to tell when the book was published. Many dated guides do come out annually; but because of research and writing time and traditional publication schedules, much of their material is two years old by the time we're ready to use it. So update guidebook information yourself whenever you can.

Annual Guidebooks

Two of the best-known dated annual guidebook series are Fodor and Frommer. Fodor publishes regional guides to the United States, area guides, foreign country guides, city guides, and such specialized books as *Plan and Enjoy Your Cruise* and *Travel with Your Family*. The format is a mixture of enrichment material for the entire area, followed by descriptions of the state, province or canton, and specific city, interspersed with "Facts at Your Fingertips" for the area and each of its subdivisions. "Historic Sights," "Seasonal Events," "What to See," "What to Do with the Children," and other helpful sections are accompanied by practical information on hotels, restaurants, and such.

Fodor guides appeal to the middleclass traveler who wants to stay at a good, if not deluxe, hotel and eat sometimes at a fancy restaurant, sometimes at the nearest coffee shop. This traveler will probably arrive by plane or car (rather than cruise ship or bicycle) and wants to see the major sights and be amused in the most typical fashion but doesn't feel compulsive about examining every case in the museum.

Arthur Frommer, who has been advising his readers for over two decades on how to enjoy travel, first on five dollars a day, then ten, fifteen, twenty-five, fifty dollars, and now just "Dollar Wise," visualizes a traveler young at heart, if not in years. His language is informal—"Before doing anything hop over to the helpful tourist office and pick up brochures." Frommer's books are sometimes filled with readers' suggestions. I have two objections to this system. First, as a traveler, since I know nothing about these readers, their tastes, their travel backgrounds and knowledge, I'm disinclined to follow their suggestions. I would rather hear from Frommer's experienced researchers, even though I realize they may miss some of the goodies that readers can fill in. Second, as a writer, I object to Frommer's form of payment for published suggestions—a copy of the book that contains the suggestion. *As a travel writer, don't ever give away your good ideas this way.* If you discover some little-known facet of the travel experience, some plus value, blow it up into an article of your own and get paid for it— in *cash*!

Frommer emphasizes accommodations and meals in addition to telling you where to go and what to see. His books court the economy minded crowd but include suggestions for those who want to splurge occasionally.

Frommer's books do give a lot of information, such as where to find Dr. Scholl's or the nearest launderette. But his seventeen lines on the British Museum only mention the Rosetta Stone, the Magna Carta, and the Elgin Marbles.

Some travel writers would rather see the research sources on screen and others would rather hold it in their hands, but in tomorrow's world we'll need both ways.

Online Guides

Both *Fodor* and *Frommer,* as well as *Travel + Leisure* magazine have an online presence. Their sites offer a wide array of travel information, including excerpts from their publications and news features, as well as links to reserve flights, hotels, and rental cars and order traveler's checks.

What else can the travel writer find online? You are only limited by your imagination and your favorite search engine.

Forums and chat rooms accessed through the various Internet providers can be invaluable resources for the travel writer. A variety of websites, as well as online writers' newsletters and magazines, such as *Writer's Resource* (www.writersresource.net), *Bookwire* (www.bookwire.com), *WritersOnLine* (www.writersonline.com), *Writers Write* (www.writerswrite.com), *Poets and Writers* (www.pw.org), and others, provide information about writing and marketing, as well as answers to copyright questions, conferences, and contests. *ShawGuides* (www.shawguides.com) has switched from print to Internet editions of Guides to Writers Conferences, Photography Workshops & Schools, Language Vacations, and other gatherings.

Special Interest Guidebooks

Many guidebooks, while seemingly of interest only to a specific group of travelers, contain material of widespread value. Globe Pequot Press' *Europe by Eurail,* while addressed primarily to the train traveler, and overflowing with authoritative worldwide railroad information, also discusses jet lag, hotel reservations, and what to do if you lose your passport. Its country-by-country section includes maps and sight-seeing material, as well as plans for one-day train excursions and scenic rail trips.

There are a number of good guides to trains around the world, and a number of good guides to cruising, as well. The Berlitz *Complete Handbook to Cruising* not only rates 269 cruise ships in great detail but also gives 100-odd pages of advice about shipboard life in general—everything from "The Shopping Scene" to "Adventure Cruising," from "Going Ashore" to "Cruising for the Physically Challenged."

Guidebooks such as *The Grown Up's Guide to Retiring Abroad* usually appeal to those with more time than money but occasionally offer a good universal idea. As the number of traveling retirees grows, and as we writers become increasingly aware of senior citizens as a potential audience for travel material, more and more guidebooks will be addressed to them. Do we need to be reminded that the Baby Boomers are fiftyish and sixtyish now and looking for AARP travel experiences?

Lets Go: The Student Guide to Europe, on the other hand, is intended for the young and adventurous. Although some will be traveling by car, this book assumes many will be biking, walking, or hitchhiking. It gives the rundown on student accommodations, food, and sight-seeing. Its advice for England: "The drinking age is eighteen, but this isn't strictly enforced."

Other long-time favorites are *Cook's Timetables* for the railroad buff, guides to religious shrines of various denominations, advice for the would-be healthy traveler, and insights into faraway spas for the fitness seeker. Bed and breakfast books proliferate.

One worthwhile series is *America's Favorite Inns, B&Bs & Small Hotels* by Sandra Soule. The books divide the country into six regions and are quite complete.

Today's guidebooks often advise on particular activities—biking, hiking, camping, fishing, sailing, etc. Even guides to shopping and finding outlet stores tell their readers how to do it. Family adventures and travel activities to share with children attract a very important audience. Background guides for environmental tourism, a major interest of many readers, abound. Not only do a number of guidebooks concentrate on weddings and honeymoons, but Globe Pequot Press publishes a series of *Romantic Days and Nights* in some of America's largest cities. And readers of Linnea Lundgren have been so successful—or so unsuccessful—that their book *Best Places to Kiss in Northern California* is in its "completely revised and updated third edition."

Omnigraphics publishes oversized, expensive but excellent books such as *Parks Directory of the United States* and *Holidays, Festivals, and Celebrations of the World Dictionary*.

Motoring Guidebooks

The *Michelin Guides* are intended for the knowledgeable and sophisticated motorist. Their red and black symbols of quality have long been a report card the traveler can trust. Michelin has plenty of maps and city plans and includes "plain but adequate" hotels and "good food at moderate prices," as well as more deluxe suggestions. If I need a CD-ROM, my library will lend me one.

Within the United States, Mobil's regional travel guides and the AAA's individual state or regional tour books are geared to the driving traveler accompanied by children. The AAA's books are set up with a brief "What to See" in each city in the state, arranged alphabetically, and then a chart and information on the recreational possibilities. About three-fourths of the book deals with specific accommodations and restaurants, again in alphabetical order by city. These digest-size books are distributed free to AAA members, as are maps, camping books, and special tour guides.

This barely scratches the surface of available guidebooks. Whether you're a youth hosteler, a garden lover, a tombstone viewer, or a bird watcher, you'll find a travel guide to help you do your thing. If it's not completely current, you can usually update it on the Internet. But before you invest too much time in too many general guides, be sure they're the ones whose approach and orientation will really help you and the audience you write for.

Reference Works

At home I use a multi-volume encyclopedia, purchased when our children were very young and updated annually. It explains most of the things I want to know clearly and reliably, if sparsely and simply. I also occasionally use the encyclopedia *my* parents bought when *I* was very young. But I'm more likely to look up what I need at my local library or on the Internet. If I need a CD-ROM my library will lend anything from *The Silk Road* or *The Yukon Trail* to the *Encyclopedia of Endangered Species*.

Two books I find indispensable are *Webster's Geographical Dictionary* and *Webster's Biographical Dictionary*, both published by G. & C. Merriam, both thumb-indexed and packed with valuable information. *The Columbia Lippincott Gazatteer of the World* is good, too. The *Toll-Free Phone Book* or one of the other directories of 800 numbers, as well as a zip code directory, are essential tools in today's world.

You probably already own a current almanac. Librarians say nearly 90 percent of reference questions can be answered from an almanac, and I have found this the most important reference book to take along when working as a Cruise Enrichment Lecturer. The *World Almanac and Book of Facts*, *Information Please Almanac*, and others are all produced annually and all arranged slightly differently, with different emphases. You might want to own more than one—or search online for the one that suits you best. Outside the United States, the *Canadian Almanac and Directory* and *Whitaker's Almanac* (for Britain) serve the same function.

You can't be a travel writer without an atlas, either print or electronic. True, boundaries and political entries change so fast you need to update your maps almost hourly, but a good basic atlas or two—or three or four— is essential for general geographical information. There's nothing like an atlas to help you decide where to go. Whether your travel writing specialty is literature, genealogy, history, or biblical scholarship, you'll find an atlas designed especially for your needs. Are you a treasure hunter? The *Atlas of*

Treasure Maps shows three hundred locations of buried treasure in the Western Hemisphere, but there is no guarantee of a *find*.

Finding map information on the Internet can sometimes be almost a "lifesaver." Sometimes, though, I have felt that the instructions took me "the long way." I did, however, yearn for a GPS (Global Positioning System) in the car. But one day, when my car was in the shop, the car rental agent called me four times for directions during his five-mile journey to my house—which isn't particularly hard to find. When I discovered that the rental car he was delivering contained one of those GPS treasures, I stopped yearning.

Specialty Publications

Depending on the kind of travel writing you're doing, you'll want to have the most helpful reference materials within arm's reach. A writer who concentrates on the historical aspects of travel needs an historical atlas. This would be supplemented by a book on mythology, handbooks on art and architecture, and several standard volumes of world history. Other travel writers might find it more helpful to invest in or power up guides to sports, airplanes, antiques, wild animals, music, stamps, botany, or the *New York Times International Cookbook*. I have a friend who's under contract for a book on ferryboats of the United States, and he was delighted when I told him about a book on ferryboats in my area. As we focus more sharply on special facets of traveling, we need more and more background material to digest.

Don't forget those beautiful coffee table books, from *Amalfi: Italy's Divine Coast* and *A Luminous Land of Greece* to *America A to Z* and the beautifully illustrated *Brazil—Places and History*. Expensive, yes, but they give background that makes destination decisions easy. *Seven Centuries of Sea Travel: From the Crusaders to the Cruises*, for instance, shows the development of sea travel from the thirteenth to twentieth centuries. Its profuse illustrations begin with a scene from the story of Tristan in a fourteenth-century French manuscript and continue with watercolor sketches of nineteenth-century cruise-ship cabins, sectional plans of emigrant ships, paintings of paddlewheel steamers, and menus from the *Lusitania*. Illustrations of hovercraft, hydrofoils, car ferries, and modern cruise ships, with explanatory text, bring the reader's knowledge up to the present.

Ancient Egypt: Discovering Its Splendors tells, in words and illustrations, of the Nile, the pyramids, the tombs, the ancient gods, as well as the pleasures of life in ancient Egypt and the invention of writing. *New Mexico: A Pictorial History* shows the state from the time of the conquistadors, with wars, revolts, banditos, ghost towns, Indians, and Billy the Kid. The Sierra Club's *On the Loose* is a medley of poetry and photography that explores human freedom and the great outdoors.

All these books, with their emphases on the lasting and memorable, provide special insights. I even know someone who's found a desperate need for a numbered copy of the limited edition of the *Pictorial Supplement to the Denver South Park and Pacific*. A railroad buff's treasure, it contains maps, timetables, and full-color paintings relating to this narrow-gauge mountain railway.

Classics and Sources

Have you longed to see Alexandria after reading Lawrence Durrell? Or promised yourself a trip to Spain with a copy of *Don Quixote* on your lap? Are you considering a visit to Colleen McCullough's Thorn Bird country or Nathaniel Hawthorne's New England or James Michener's Hawaii? Some of the world's best travel guides are Charles Dickens and Mark Twain, Ernest Hemingway and Joseph Conrad, Robert Louis Stevenson and Pearl Buck, Somerset Maugham, Charles Darwin, Rudyard Kipling, Jack London, Herman Melville, and John Steinbeck.

More and more special travel bookstores are springing up in every city and hamlet, as well as online. If you need a guide to the next town or a language lesson for the next continent, you are very likely to find it. And if the booksellers don't have it, they'll order it. As the travel industry becomes the second largest in the U.S., it spawns more and more shops devoted to *everything* the traveler needs—including reference books. So you're in a good position to take advantage of the pre-trip learning period.

Handy Brochures

Touring maps of all kinds are the travel writer's tools. As the free ones become ever harder to come by, hoard what you have. Automobile clubs sometimes distribute, in addition to their tour guides, maps and such helpful books as Triple A's *Travel Tips* and *A Guide to California's Gold Country*. The British Automobile Association gives facts and figures for hundreds of hostelries in its low-priced *Guide to Guesthouses, Farmhouses, and Inns of Britain* and its *Guide to Guesthouses, Farmhouses, and Inns on the Continent*.

For your travels by car, both the AAA and National Automobile Club provide custom-made trip kits and strip maps for its members.

CD-ROMs are strong on maps and travel information, and, of course, a vast amount of material can be downloaded from the World Wide Web.

Touring materials also include museum guidebooks, which I usually order before my trip. I've learned to order in English. When I wrote to the Louvre in my best high-school French, the director replied, in expert English, that he was sending me a Louvre guidebook in "*le français facile.*" It turned out to be such "easy French" that it was a guidebook for young children.

If you plan a foreign trip in the fall, the English language tours may be finished, and the government tourist offices have probably run out of travel literature. Experienced travel writers suggest writing in the spring to tourist offices of the places you expect to visit, asking them to send you all their English-language information as soon as they have it.

Periodicals

You'll surely want easy access to the newspapers and magazines you expect to write for. You'll doubtless subscribe to or send for samples of many travel-oriented publications, not only the big ones—*Travel + Leisure, Condé Nast Traveler, Travel America*, etc.—but everything from *Family Motor Coaching* to *Endless Vacation*, from *Northeast Outdoors* to *Transitions Abroad* and *Caribbean Travel and Life*. Again, depending on your own specialized interests, you may turn to *Gourmet Fare* and *Bon Appétit* or to *Lakeland Boating and Yachting*.

Don't forget to subscribe, if only briefly, or at least look up at the library or online, a newspaper in the area you're planning to visit. The Philadelphia *Inquirer*, for example, gives you the *feel* of the city, an overview of what it's like, and alerts you to the colorful New Year's Day Mummers Parade, the Little League World Series, or the June celebration when the colonially costumed people of Elfreth's Alley, the oldest continually occupied residential street in the United States, hold their annual fete.

Other local papers tell you about special activities, so you can plan your vacation or weekend jaunt around the Oyster Shucking Championships in Leonardtown, Maryland; the World Championship Inner Tube Race in Yuma, Arizona; or the Fishworm Judging Contest in Sterling, Colorado.

In this climate of exploding city and regional magazines, try to buy the magazine(s) of the area you'll be visiting, such as *Cascades East* or *Texas Highways*. This is the kind of background information you need to pursue the live research you'll do on the trip itself and there's always the possibility that this periodical will become a market for *your* story.

Don't be timid about requesting photocopies of newspaper and magazine articles published long ago, when you hear of something that might provide just the research pivot you need. I've found periodicals remarkably generous in filling requests for copies of special stories. Another writer once asked, without much hope, for a copy of a magazine article on camels written 116 years ago. Within an amazingly short time, this treasure appeared in her mailbox. Usually this service is free; if not, the cost is only a few cents.

As the flood tide of printed material threatens to engulf us, it becomes increasingly important to know what information is where. Bless the magazines that provide annual or semi-annual indexes. Some still provide printed ones, but most magazine indexes are online.

U.S. Government Publications

The U.S. government is one of the world's biggest publishers. Take advantage of it. The government even puts out several publications to help you discover what is available:

▲ *Consumers Guide to Federal Publications* gives 300-odd subject lists from architecture and automobile insurance to surveying and mapping, and Spanish publications.

▲ *Selected List of U.S. Government Publications* gives 130–150 publications with wide appeal. Issued biweekly—ask to be placed on the mailing list.

▲ *List of Government Bookstores*

▲ *List of Depository Libraries*

▲ *Government Periodicals and Subscription Services* lists periodicals by various government agencies, from the bimonthly Cultural Post, published by the National Endowment for the Arts, to the quarterly Outdoor Recreation Action, published by the Department of the Interior.

There are a number of other aids to finding your way around in the maze of federal publications. Either visit the U.S. Government Online Bookstore (http://bookstore.gpo.gov/), write to the U.S. Government Printing Office, Washington DC 20402, or contact the U.S. Government bookstore nearest you to order. Material is free or modestly priced.

Several other lists and compendiums are especially valuable to the travel writer. *Maps (United States and Foreign)* not only includes weather maps and distribution of various segments of the population but also lists general reference maps of foreign countries—from Cambodia and Cyprus to Yemen and Yugoslavia. The lists of miscellaneous and special purpose navigational charts, sheets, and tables are helpful, too.

Background Notes are short, factual pamphlets (usually eight pages) written by State Department officers for about 160 countries. The pamphlets, which are invaluable for taking along on your trip, cover the country's land, people, history, government, political conditions, economy, and foreign relations. They also include a profile, brief travel notes, a map, a list of government officials, and an excellent reading list.

Much more detailed, the Defense Department's *Area Handbooks* for 105 countries, from Afghanistan to Zambia, are just about the best guidebooks you can buy.

The government also publishes a directory of 1,500 industrial plants and federal installations, including copper mines, breweries, and newspapers, all of which offer free tours.

The U.S. Travel Service of the Department of Commerce has issued free booklets ranging from *Getting the Best Value for Your Vacation Dollar* to

Your Rights and Responsibilities—Know Before You Go. Its publications include helpful hints for the older traveler, the handicapped traveler, the health-seeking traveler, and others. You can order these from:

Consumer Information
United States Travel Service
U.S. Department of Commerce
Washington, DC 20230

If you're traveling near a president's boyhood home, send for the hardcover *Presidents. Ducks at a Distance,* a colorfully illustrated waterfowl identification guide, is a bargain. So is the *Guide to Genealogical Records in the National Archives. Key Officers of Foreign Service Posts* is a good buy if you think you'll get overseas and need to know the name of your ambassador. The Civil Aeronautics Board will send the free *Fly-Rights: A Guide to Air Travel in the U.S.,* and the U.S. Customs Service will send, also free, booklets on customs hints and on the generalized system of preferences for 101 nations and 36 dependent territories where you're likely to buy certain items. Customs will also help the writer with material on smuggling, tariff laws, and what people try to get away with.

The Bureau of Consular Affairs of the Department of State produces *Your Trip Abroad,* a good roundup for the beginning traveler.

If your readers will be interested in camping in national parks, travel accommodations for the handicapped, international relations, backpacking, Indian ceremonials, or outdoor sports, send for the government booklet that gives you all the details.

If you like to vacation away from crowds, request information on lesser-used national parks from:

National Park Service		U.S. Forest Service
Department of the Interior	or	Department of Agriculture
Washington, DC 20240		Washington, DC 20250

The National Park Service publishes reams of helpful information and also presents the visitor with special leaflets at most of the attractions it administers, such as Valley Forge National Historical Park, San Francisco's Fort Point, and Washington's John F. Kennedy Center for the Performing Arts. The Park Service's *Guide to the Historic Places of the American Revolution* is a gem.

Next time you're in Washington, DC, visit the Library of Congress—it's fascinating. If you're visiting Washington, be sure to write or call your congressman for help in securing tickets to special attractions. Allow plenty of time. Ask your congressman, too, for assistance in finding information about anything connected with the federal government.

The Library of Congress Reference and Bibliographic Service will help those outside the Washington area find material for a small fee. You can obtain a copy of anything there unless it's restricted or needs copyright clearance. One writer, doing a roundup of Civil War battlefields, asked for—and received—the Reports of the Secretary of War to the 33rd and 34th Congresses in the 1850s. For this kind of help, get in touch with:

Chief, General Reference and Bibliography Division
Library of Congress
Washington, DC 20540

or visit:

Services for Researchers online at www.loc.gov/rr

Local Government Publications

Various agencies of state governments also print free or low-cost material valuable for the travel writer, from a beautifully complete, 879-page *California Historical Landmarks* to a leaflet on *Three Lincoln Shrines in Illinois.* South Dakota booklets tell all about the Black Hills and the Badlands, Delaware emphasizes its coastal vacationland, and Oregon has all sorts of literature on forests, trees, and parks, as well as on the Lewis and Clark Trail. *I Love New York* is a comprehensive guide to the state, while the quarterly leaflets, *New York in Summer, New York in Winter*, etc., concentrate on the Big Apple itself. Philadelphia also publishes seasonal booklets, as well as *Philadelphia: A City for All Seasons!* Unsurprisingly, California's Department of Transportation issues a *Safety Roadside Rest Area Report*. North Carolina's *One Day At a Time* details eleven different tours for visitors.

You can also write to individual areas for information. Denver publishes *Mile-Highlights*, Fort Lauderdale recommends the Everglades, and the El Paso Convention and Visitors Bureau publishes *El Paso-Juarez*. Islands, from Martha's Vineyard to Guam, call themselves to your attention.

Worldwide, 382 areas are affiliated with the International Association of Convention and Visitors Bureaus, many of which issue seasonal calendars listing special events. Look up the events online or send a postcard requesting the calendar to:

International Association of Convention and Visitors Bureaus
P.O. Box 758
Champaign, IL 61824

Don't forget historical societies as a source of pre-trip research material. The Mount Vernon Ladies Association of the Union will inform you about Mount Vernon, and the Preservation Society of Newport County, Rhode Island, will send you a booklet on six mansions located there. San Francisco's

Chinese Culture Foundation has information on the Chinese Heritage Walk and the Chinese Culinary Walk, and the Nevada County Historical Society will bring you up-to-date on Gold Country restorations.

Sometimes several political entities join together to promote their joint travel-recreation area. They publish huge amounts of material. Pennsylvania Dutch country, Cape Cod, the Redwood Empire, and the Shenandoah Valley all do their best to lure visitors. So do the East African Wild Life Society, the Caribbean Travel Association, the Organization of American States, and the Pacific Asia Travel Association.

Literature from Other Areas

Early in your subject research write to the travel promotion bureaus of the countries you'll be visiting. Every country wants to present—aggressively— its most attractive features. From Australia's *Queensland Explorer* and *Kenya: A Land of Contrasts* to *Japan's Tourist Handbook*, and the *Traveller's Encyclopedia of Ontario*, tourist office publications do a fantastic job of telling the rest of the world what they have to offer. Read the literature carefully. A single line reference may produce an idea that will produce sales. A.R. Roalman, for instance, contemplating a trip to Japan, found in the tourist-office literature a single sentence about the oldest wooden building in the world. Queries to *Popular Mechanics* and *American Forest* netted pre-trip assignments, and on-scene research developed additional noncompetitive stories.

If you read the travel folders—either government or commercial—it's hard to believe there is anything but sandy beaches with girls in bikinis and majestic, snow-covered slopes. Everybody seems to live in picturesque thatch-roofed cottages and picnic in sylvan settings.

To get a more realistic picture and to plan intelligently, first cross out all the adjectives in the promotional brochure. Then read the last page for the straight facts. The relationship of one day to another, one country to another, within the tour framework, gives you an idea of what the tour people consider important about the area. Look for the words "We stop at" or "We visit."

One of the travel writer's most important skills is learning to read *between* the lines. A European tour that offers half a day in Florence and during its day and a half in Paris provides half a day of city sight-seeing and a trip to Versailles plus "an afternoon free for relaxing or perhaps a visit to the famous Louvre museum" is *not* a tour for art lovers. If you're writing an art-oriented article, don't bother reading *that* tour brochure.

Miscellaneous Freebies

Online forums can provide all kinds of useful knowledge to the travel writer, and there are many other areas of free information. Don't spurn public-relations handouts. As a matter of fact, when you're beginning your research, *ask* for handouts. In addition to writing to tourist offices, a good technique is to place free ads in newsletters that go to hundreds of PR people. An excellent resource is:

Betty Yarmon, Managing Editor
Party Line
35 Sutton Place
New York, NY 10022

Another super help is:

Frank Scott
Travel Publicity Leads
Scott American Corporation
P.O. Box 88
West Redding, CT 06896
Fax and phone: (203) 938-2955
e-mail: scottamerican@msn.com

These weekly or biweekly newsletters are sent to PR specialists who buy subscriptions for the privilege of sending materials to writers like you. Replies to you from these PR specialists often result in useful information, great ideas, and welcome hospitality.

Sometimes you can even inquire in a book section, such as that in the *New York Times*, or on an online bulletin board for the information you need. You'll soon be inundated with news about anything remotely related to the subject you've asked for.

Inflight magazines, those publications you find in the seat pocket in front of you as you struggle into your seat belt, and in-room magazines, which you find on your desk in many hotels, are valuable sources of information for pre-trip subject research. When you make your plane and hotel reservations, ask for copies to be sent to you in advance.

Although some of the airlines' extensive literature requires a modest payment or is only handed out on the plane, most will appear in response to a postcard from you. Here's a small sample of what's available: United Airlines publishes a detailed *Guide to the Pacific* that includes everything from hints on metric conversion to sketches of various airports, with directions to the United desk. KLM provides a *Motoring Guide to Europe* and Air France offers several extremely helpful booklets, such as *Inexpensive Restaurants Near Famous Monuments* and *Business Traveler's Guide to Paris*. Continental's *Wings Over Paradise* is a beautifully illustrated history of Micronesia, and Quantas sends prospective tourists a variety of literature, ranging from *100 Things to See and Do in Australia* to a pocket-size *Understanding Down Under*. Japan Airlines, SAS, and others pass out very helpful city guides to their various destinations.

A booklet put out by the American Society of Travel Agents (ASTA) reminds you that your homeowner's insurance may not cover your cameras and tape recorders and offers a number of other good, basic suggestions. The Institute of Certified Travel Agents explains, in the booklet *Let's Talk Travel*, everything from ITX (an Independent Tour Excursion Airfare) to Open Jaw (where the round trip has different points of origin and return).

Ecology Is Here to Stay

The travel writer needs to be aware of upcoming and ongoing trends. While the reader may still be interested in rooting around for his ancestors or advice on how to dress for a successful national convention, a couple of major trends today are adventure travel and "green" travel. Even sedentary grandparents are taking up ballooning, scuba diving, snowmobiling, windsurfing, and white-water rafting. The more adventurous go dog-sledding on the arctic wastes, kayak exploring in Thailand, paragliding into dormant volcanoes, and tracking the Bengal tiger in India.

If you feel that adventure travel will lead you to a story you can't bear not to tell, there are many books to help you with before-trip research. *Ultimate Adventure: National Geographic Ultimate Adventure Sourcebook* is one of the best.

The Green-Travel Sourcebook, which Daniel and Sally Grotta have subtitled "A Guide for the Physically Active, the Intellectually Curious, or the Socially Aware," speaks to a slightly different audience. They think of the green traveler as one who welcomes the physically challenging adventure, as well as the one who explores the natural environment and the entire ecosystem. They also include the green traveler who delves deeply into the learning experience, the one who travels to underdeveloped countries to help the people in some way, and the one who volunteers to dig at an archaeological site or take underwater photographs to document marine activity. With the goal of preserving the environment, of "taking nothing but photographs and leaving nothing but footprints," Green Travelers are also concerned with humanitarian matters and cultural interchange.

Environmental Vacations by Stephanie Ocko emphasizes the kinds of volunteer vacations that save the planet and benefit mankind. She points out that tourism has been around since Neanderthal man crossed a river to track down mammoths, but the newest trend is to combine the vacation with a worthwhile purpose—a purpose that does not insult the environment.

Eco-Journeys by Stephen Foehr leans more toward the wilderness adventure, but wants the traveler to be environmentally aware from beginning to end.

The Sierra Club, of course, publishes many books that enhance the pleasure of the wilderness experience, always keeping in mind the importance of preserving and improving the natural state. The pocket-sized Totebooks the club publishes range from *Starr's Guide to the JMT and High Sierra* to *Hiker's Guide to the Great Basin*, and all are wonderfully detailed guides.

Outward Bound challenges, expedition cruises, special ecotours, greater interaction with native populations, and other occasions to experience new adventures and a stronger relationship with the worldwide environment are becoming an ever-more important facet of travel. Opportunities for joining such organizations as Earthwatch, where volunteers observe and record facts about earth's natural state, are increasingly popular.

Much pre-trip research material is available to the traveler who plans to write about adventure and ecology. The Galapagos Islands, for instance, have become such a popular destination that the visitor goes well prepared with information. And upon returning, that same visitor can become a sought after supplier of interesting material for an entire galaxy of environmentally oriented magazines, e-zines, CD-ROMs, and other outlets.

As more and more readers realize the effects of tourism on the environment, the travel writer should show awareness of plans to protect and enrich our planet, in ways both large and small.

Use Discretion

Although travel writing resources proliferate, they aren't all necessarily helpful and accurate. The travel writer has to approach pre-trip research with discretion. Some of what you read is good—some of it is garbage. For instance, I read a book for women cruise travelers that advised those with children to try to engage the children's counselors as babysitters in the evening. If this is not possible, suggested the author, perhaps you could persuade your room steward or the purser to sit with your children. *The purser!* I knew instantly that author had never been on a cruise and immediately lost faith in anything else the book said.

However, the more involved you become with travel writing, the more convinced you will be that you can never do *too much* research. As you learn to use what you glean from both formal and informal sources, you'll realize that the information overload makes destination decisions easy and constitutes unmistakable plus value.

As we consider what to do before your trip, while traveling, and after your return, we'll look into other forms of research, such as online information, telephone interviews, face-to-face encounters, questionnaires, and on-the-scene observation. But in the next chapter let's consider some of the valuable aids the travel writer can find on library shelves or in cyberspace.

THREE

"Being There" Is Never Enough

"LIBRARY RESEARCH!" My friend threw up her hands in amazement. "What do you mean—*library research!* You're *going there*, aren't you? Isn't that enough?"

Going there is seldom enough for the travel writer. Nobody but another writer seems to realize that travel articles require subject and market research before you go, while you're traveling, and after you return home.

Subject research is the glue that holds your story together. It's the credibility you achieve by presenting someone else's opinion along with your own. It's the way to understand what you're seeing before you see it, while you're seeing it, and after you've seen it. Subject research is the keystone of the writer's craft; it's a big part of the plus value.

The danger is that the research will become an end in itself. The writer becomes so enamored of the research materials that he or she keeps postponing the actual sitting down at that keyboard. It isn't enough to *do* the research—you have to *plan* the research. First, decide in a general way at least what you hope to achieve by the research you are doing. Then, decide how much time you have to get it all together. Spend your time researching in the most likely places for the most important information. When you are looking for the "most likely," ask yourself, "Who would know?" and "Who would care enough to pursue it?"

Are you beginning to think the travel writer spends a lot of time on research? You're right. Does it all sound formidable? Really it's not. A lot of the topics we'll cover you've probably known about for a long time—you just never thought of them as research. This chapter introduces you to the research that provides a firm framework for other library, online, or face-to-face quests for information.

Entire books are devoted to the description and use of research resources, but this is only a quick guide to finding what the travel writer needs.

Ask Your Friendly Librarian

Our most valuable resource is still the reference librarian. Librarians exist to provide information. They are delighted to provide that information. I have researched in many libraries—public, university, and special, in the United States and abroad—and I've always found librarians helpful and eager to supply whatever I requested. First introduce yourself to the librarian. Explain that you are a writer. You'll find that nothing is too good for you. You're important to the library—you create library material.

Often a phone call to the reference desk will answer a simple question. Are you interested, for instance, in how your own money lines up with the cruzeiro, krone, rupee, or baht? If your local paper doesn't have a complete foreign-exchange column and you don't subscribe to the *Wall Street Journal*, the reference librarian may look it up for you. Be sure your question is specific. *Not* "Tell me about Thailand" or "Tell me about polygamy," but "Does the present king of Thailand have more than one wife?" Here's a sample of some of the questions I've asked over the years:

What are the opening words of Sweden's national anthem?

Which is bigger—Disneyland or Disney World?

How does the travel industry rank in importance among U.S. industries?

What is the weather like in Trieste in January?

Which airlines serve Sun Valley?

What do they call the schools where Muslim boys study the Koran?

Where was the world's first travel agency established?

Who originally built Tree Tops in Kenya?

Was it sunny or cloudy on May 14, 1607, when Captain John Smith landed at Jamestown, Virginia?

Once the entire library staff spent a week trying to find out for me what the ancient Greeks used for theater tickets.

If you're not familiar with the Vertical File, ask your librarian where it is. The file may or may not be physically vertical, but it will surely contain maps, guidebooks, menus, museum catalogs, photographs, theater programs, and hundreds of nonbook items that will help in your pre-trip research.

You probably know that most libraries file their materials according to either the Dewey Decimal system or the Library of Congress system. At the main library in Moscow, however, when one of my daughters asked the librarian whether they use Dewey, the reply was, "No, the Russians have something better than the Dewey Decimal system." We later found out that most of their filing is by size. Unwilling to waste a twelve-inch shelf on a nine-inch book, they arrange their closed stacks according to the book's size and shape. It takes hours to page a book from the loan desk.

Sometimes even in this country you have to be a super-sleuth to find what you seek. If the catalog, card-oriented or electronic, doesn't show what you're looking for, turn to the multi-volume *Books in Print*, print or electronic, to see if the book exists. You may have difficulty finding the heading the library cataloger used for the subject you're trying to find. Will it be under "archaeology" or "history" or "ancient history" or "European history"? Ideally, it will be under all of them, each with a "see also" reference. But sometimes you have to work hard to come up with a classification that you and the cataloger agree is what you're looking for. Consulting *Subject Headings Used in the Dictionary Catalogs of the Library of Congress* may send you off in the right direction, but even so, it's confusing.

Do you need something on the Peace Corps, for instance? Don't give up too easily. Try "United States—Peace Corps." Sometimes there'll be a cross-reference card telling you to see a different or additional subject heading. Persistence pays off.

If the book is not held by your local library, check with your librarian to discover what an interlibrary loan can do for you. I once found a book in Sydney, Australia's main library that I later wanted to refer to at home. My local library queried regional libraries, the California State Library in Sacramento, and the Library of Congress. Nobody had the book. But the local library finally found it and borrowed it from a special library in Toronto.

When the author Hayes Jacobs wrote in the 1960s, "If a writer lives near a good library, he is especially blessed, if he lives near a poor one, he ought to think about moving," he did not, of course, visualize today's Internet.

Computers Speed Research

Although some libraries still retain their traditional card catalogs, the list of those who have completely computerized their collections grows longer every day. What replaces the banks of alphabetized index cards, filed by subject, title, and author? Comfortable chairs in front of computer screens, with directions for dialing up. You can look up the library's holdings by author, exact title, subject, series, or call number. Or you can browse among subjects and titles by inserting a key word. It's like browsing among the stacks, as your electronic servant brings related topics to the screen. Not only will your screen tell you which branch and location contains your selection, but it will also indicate whether or not your selection has been checked out, and if it has been, when it's due back.

You don't even have to go to the library to obtain this information. If you have a computer and a modem, a few keystrokes and a password will put you online to the library's catalog. This service is free. Additionally, hundreds of database vendors of thousands of online databases await your subscription. Some of these databases will give you titles, some will give you abstracts, some will give you full text—or all three. Ideally, you will select a few from all the titles available and ask for abstracts; then select a very few abstracts and ask for full text. You can have the text printed out and mailed or faxed to you, have it appear on your computer screen, or listen to it over a telephone line.

Online Information Abounds

Newspapers, magazines, books, encyclopedias, official records—practically anything is available online somewhere. Do you want to scan all the Yellow Pages directories in America for an all-inclusive picture of travel services? Do you want to compare winter weather in Miami and Cancun or to compile the geographical distribution of Mrs. Field's chocolate chip cookies? Just ask. For instance, Sacramento writer Michele McCormick was preparing a speech she was scheduled to give at a lawyer's conference, so she looked online for some lawyer jokes. By using newsgroups, listservs, and message boards, you can put all kinds of questions to perfect strangers. "Has anybody traveled across the Atlantic on a Russian ship? How was it?" "Looking for male non-smoker to share hunting camp in Idaho last week in November." "What's the rock-bottom price to rent a car for a month in Tahiti?"

Travel agents, of course, use several programs that search, book, and confirm airline reservations, hotels, and other services. You, too, can access these programs, and sometimes your careful perusal will spot a bargain.

If, however, you feel unable to cope with "Enter," "Ctrl," "Alt," and "Esc," you can have somebody else do the search for you. Some libraries will do it free, depending on the question. If this service is not available from your library, look in your phone book under "Information Retrieval Services & Research." Costs of subscribing to an information service may be monthly or by the amount of use or a combination of both. An information broker charges for out-of-pocket expenses plus a search sum.

Whichever way you conduct your search—either personally, with an individual computer maven, or through an information broker—give considerable thought to framing your search question. Will you ask for background material on the Japanese drink *sake*? Or will you just say, "*sake*"— and come up with screens full of information that include all instances of people exclaiming, "For heaven's *sake!*" Do you want a census of all the English-speaking countries of the world—or just the ones where English is the *first* language? Use the thesaurus on your computer to select the perfect search words. Keep your search question as brief and simple as possible, and be sure to seek the kernel that counts.

Almost Everything Is Indexed

Whether online, hard copy, or microfiche, one of the travel writer's most valuable tools is the *New York Times Index*. This multi-volume, frequently indexed series gives you the exact date, page, and column for articles on your subject in the *New York Times*. It also gives a synopsis of the article that may answer your question, so you don't have to look up the newspaper itself. I didn't have to look through months of newspapers to find out, for instance, exactly when the Pope visited Ephesus—information I needed for half a sentence of a major travel article.

If you need a national or international story from your unindexed local newspaper, you can assume the story appeared approximately the same day it appeared in the *New York Times*. So once you have the date, you can find the paper in the file at your library or local newspaper office or from an online service. The *Wall Street Journal* and other periodicals also publish helpful indexes, so whether it's online or on the shelf, voluminous amounts of data are available.

Large library newspaper rooms keep back issues of the world's leading papers, either physical copies, microfilm or microfiche, or online collections for many years. That's how my husband and I found out about the *Frank H. Buck*. Our research on the Standard Oil tanker *Lyman K. Stewart* that collided with the freighter *Walter A. Luckenbach* and sank in San Francisco Bay in 1922 turned up information about the *Stewart's* sister ship, the *Frank H. Buck*. After some digging we discovered that she, also, met her end on a foggy Saturday afternoon in San Francisco Bay. The *Buck* collided with the luxury liner *President Coolidge* at nearly the exact spot where the *Stewart* had met the *Luckenbach* fifteen years earlier. Both ships spilled oil all over the bay as they were buffeted against the Land's End rocks, where their remains rust today. We did most of the research in newspapers published at the time, and the story turned out to be bigger than we expected.

City directories, both old and new, in addition to the telephone books, help you track down the exact fact you're missing. They not only give information about each household but often include listings by addresses and by telephone numbers, supplemented by maps and general facts about the area.

William Rivers tells of a researcher trying to retrace the steps of Mark Twain in Hawaii:

In one of his "Letters from the Sandwich Islands"...Twain mentions a wonderful party at "Sam Brannon's bungalow." The problem: Where was Brannon's bungalow? A hundred years had passed, Honolulu had changed, and everyone living in Brannon's time was dead...If he [the researcher] had been looking for a living resident of Honolulu, he would have needed only a City Directory and a city map. He needed no more to fix the location of Sam Brannon's bungalow. The City Directory of Honolulu for 1865 lists Brannon and his address, and a map shows the precise location.

Google or one of the other online search engines can help you find names and addresses for practically anything.

Another travel writer's tool, *Facts on File: A Weekly World News Digest with Cumulative Index*, a classified loose-leaf digest of news arranged under broad subject headings, is an index I always consult when I begin an article on a country I haven't done for some time, just to be sure I've kept up with what's been going on in that country.

Facts on File has another advantage—it's more accurate than the daily newspaper, put together at top deadline pressure, can hope to be. We all know that newspapers give us many clues but are usually not scholarly authorities. Books, on the other hand, present a problem to the library in many fast-changing fields. They're obsolete almost as soon as they're printed. For this reason, libraries tend to spend greater and greater proportions of their budgets for periodicals, where the time lag is not so great. Books on some subjects, however, provide valuable information even when their copyright dates aren't current. The rule of thumb for accuracy is: if three people say it's true, it's likely to be.

There's a Reference Book for Every Subject

Some books, of course, are definitive, regardless of their age. Need to know anything about food? *Larousse Gastronomique* should give you the word, and they say if you need to ask what it is, you aren't ready to use it. The thirteen-volume *Mythology of All Races* is well illustrated and what you want is easily located therein. Helen Gardner's *Art Through the Ages* is an old standby. One of the world's best reference books for the travel writer is the *World Travel Directory*. It not only lists travel agencies, wholesale tour operators, and local sight-seeing companies all over the world but tells you, state by state and city by city, about newspaper travel sections, hotel and travel media, and all sorts of people and companies connected with the travel industry. Other useful books include:

▲ Alden Todd's *Finding Facts Fast*, with its several levels of aid to the researcher.

▲ *The Directory of Directories* that can help you identify which directory you need.

▲ *Statistical Abstract of the United States* and its various supplements are published by the U.S. Bureau of the Census and provide statistics on political, social, and economic aspects of the United States.

▲ *The Guinness Book of World Records.*

▲ *Chase's Calendar of Annual Events* tells what's happening when, and gives days, weeks, and months of special events.

▲ Field guides to birds, wildflowers, and trees.

Want to know something about specific people? Perhaps the address of someone still alive? Try the British *Who's Who* or the Canadian *Who's Who* or *Who's Who in Canada. Who's Who in America* is supplemented by *Who's Who in the West, East, Midwest,* etc., and *Who's Who in American Law, Government, Religion,* etc., as well as the *Directory of Medical Specialists* and *Who's Who of American Women* and other biographical directories.

While not as useful when it comes to contacting research sources, there are several directories of notable Americans, Britons, and Canadians of the past. *Who Was When? A Dictionary of Contemporaries* places subjects in historical perspective. It may come in handy to know that Abraham Lincoln lived at the same time as Emperor Maximilian.

Some libraries are full or partial depositories for federal or state publications, and these materials may be cataloged and shelved like other library books or may be classified as government publications and arranged alphabetically or numerically in a separate place.

Of course you're not going to read *all* of this literature for any one article or even any one subject. Yet, here at the library, the "memory of the human race," you're bound to find, among the morass of superfluous and useless information, the kernel of a fresh idea, the perfect quote, the reference to the authority you didn't know existed, the very special something that provides the plus value for your story.

Naturally, our online searching will uncover many of the materials we need, but there's something about actually handling the book, itself, that makes us doubt the imminent obsolescence of libraries.

Quickly finding exactly what you need is an art that comes with practice. Soon you'll learn how to flip through an index and see if there's anything you want, look over an entire section of books and pull out only the single most authoritative one. You learn, too, to skip over material that's unwanted *now*, while making a mental note (perhaps also a physical one) about where to find it in case that's the very thing you need next month or next year.

If you want a guide to the reference works at the library, Eugene P. Sheehy's *Guide to Reference Books (with Supplement)* is the one librarians use.

Obviously the travel writer's reference books I'm mentioning here are merely a sample—materials I've found especially helpful, and a guide to further exploration. Some of them you'll find you use so much you'll want a copy at home if you can't access it online. If your nearby library has periodic sales of used books, sometimes you can buy a useful reference book that's a year or two old for a small sum. If you use information from it, check to make sure that information is still current.

Encyclopedias Are Specialized, Too

Encyclopedias we all know about—or at least we think we do. Most libraries have both the *Encyclopedia Britannica* and the *Encyclopedia Americana*. The *Britannica*, especially, has changed greatly in its newer editions, with the facility for quick answers to quick questions in the Micropaedia, more complete answers in the Macropaedia. These are general encyclopedias, as are the single-volume *New Columbia Encyclopedia* and the multi-volume *Collier's, Chamber's, Compton's, Academic American,* and *World Book* encyclopedias. However, with CD-ROMs, an entire encyclopedia, along with an index of every word, can be contained on a single disk. As the software proliferates, the travel writer will be acquiring new tools, both at home and at the library.

Special Libraries for Special Research

Did you know there are entire libraries devoted to sailing ships or Shakespeare, American Indians or American wine, insects or international trade? These special libraries are maintained by professional organizations, charitable foundations, trade associations, consulates, labor unions, and sometimes by the estates of private individuals. From the Folger Shakespeare Library in Washington to the Joseph Conrad Library at the Seamen's Church Institute in New York, special libraries are a windfall for the travel writer. If you live near one, it's usually not too hard to secure permission to inspect its treasures.

Sometimes, too, you can obtain special privileges at a nearby university library, or perhaps at the morgue of your local newspaper. In any of those circumstances, be sure to express your appreciation for the opportunity and try to be as little trouble as possible.

How to Organize Your Research

Once you begin your online and library research you have to decide how to arrange the information you're accumulating. If it's a borrowed book, you're not going to mark it up, of course; but develop the habit of reading with pen in hand. Insert paper bookmarks with directions to yourself to send for or look up additional information, or to photocopy the page or make a special note for a special article. Try to include all pertinent information—dates, call numbers, authors' names—to make re-finding the material as painless as possible.

Be sure to indicate whether the gem of information you're jotting down is a direct quote from someone else or has been paraphrased into your own words. Even paraphrased, you may need to give credit if what you're using is a proprietary fact—something which that particular author dug out for himself, something nobody else knew about, as opposed to a common fact, which can be found in many places and is known to many people.

Whether you outline your story first, then key in the various fragments of research material, or collect the fragments in separate file folders, or color-code with a rainbow of pens, or make a separate file card for each fact, or devise some more acceptable system of your own, getting your research together is a hard job. A number of travel writers admit, "I do a lot of filing on the floor while I'm working on a project!"

You'll find extensive cross-indexing worthwhile if you want to find all the information you've squirreled away. Never be tempted to file anything under "miscellaneous." If it's worth noting, it's worth labeling.

None of the travel writers I interviewed for this chapter seemed thoroughly satisfied with their present methods of accumulating and arranging information. Each one said, "If you find a good way, please let me know!"

Magazine Articles Are a Great Resource

Do you now feel as though you know everything you need to know about researching your subject? Wait! Don't leave the library yet! Not until we discuss the value of the *Reader's Guide to Periodical Literature* in print or online, which tells you where to find magazine articles on your subject. The *Reader's Guide* does three things for you: it tells you what else has been published on your subject and where and when; it tells you whether or not your target market has published anything on your subject recently (which we'll discuss with market research in Chapter 4); and it provides additional research resources by showing you where to find articles that may teach you something about your subject. As a footnote to the advantages of magazine articles as research sources, let's not forget that the authors are often available to provide additional information or fresh quotations.

In looking for magazine articles you'll have to define your subject in the same terms the cataloger uses, but there are hints in the *Guide's* cross-references. If you find nothing in *Reader's Guide*, even after you've considered several synonyms for your subject, you may need a different guide. Is your subject very scholarly? The *Social Sciences and Humanities Index* covers the scholarly journals. If your subject is more likely to be found in specialized periodicals, try the indexes that list articles about science, art, music, business, psychology, or engineering. Another indexing service covers such popular publications as *Women's Day* and *Weight Watcher's Magazine*.

A newer indexing service at the library, the *Magazine Index*, is a computerized arrangement of hundreds of periodicals, including major newspapers, which covers many more publications than *Reader's Guide*. However, its history is short, and if you need something published 30 years ago, the information may not be available.

Send to the H. W. Wilson Company, 950 University Ave., Bronx, NY 10452, for a free pamphlet on using the *Reader's Guide*. Other indexes are handled so similarly that the information is universal.

These guides for readers are also tremendously important in market research. There's no doubt that the quantity and quality of the market research and the subject research differentiate the amateur, who says, "Some day I must get around to writing up the story of my wonderful trip to Paris and send it to one of the big magazines—I'm sure they'll buy it," from the professional, who says, "I want to be sure I have all my facts straight on the Paris Sewer trip—what time it leaves, how much it costs, and the other details. Then I'll search the electronic *Magazine Index* to see who's published what about the Paris Sewers lately."

The professional's reasoning might contemplate a negative market list—don't try *XYZ Magazine* because they just ran a Paris sewer story—but it might also uncover an "Underground Barcelona" article published recently. Wouldn't they like a companion piece? The *Magazine Index* and the electronic card catalog are bound to yield some historical background for a Paris sewer story, and they may provide clues about people to contact for anecdotes or quotes to sandwich between the bare facts. Additionally, the vertical file might contain a program from the New York production of "Les Miserables"—would that be any help?

Smart Marketing Leads to Satisfying Publishing

"Amateurs talk about writing; professionals talk about marketing" is a cliché well known to writers—well known because it's true.

Again and again I've heard one professional writer respond to another's description of a project with, "Good idea. Where are you going to send it *first*?" And again and again I've heard one pro respond to another pro's tale of rejection with, "Too bad. Where are you going to send it *next*?"

Ask an amateur who he's writing the article for, and he's likely to reply, "Oh, nobody special. I'm just writing it kind of generally." *There is no such thing as writing generally*. Successful writing is always for somebody. It's for a particular publication, a particular reader. Successful writing is aimed and slanted, facts astutely selected to appeal to a well-defined segment of the reading public.

One of the travel writer's best friends is the *Travelwriter Marketletter* (www.travelwriterml.com). Travel writer Bob Milne established the newsletter some years ago, and it always seems as though whatever I read about travel writing, it always seems I read it in the *Travelwriter Marketletter* first. Send editorial correspondence to:

Mimi Backhausen
Travelwriter Marketletter
P.O. Box 1782
Springfield, VA 22151
fax (208) 988-7672
e-mail mimi@travelwriterml.com.

For subscriptions and payments inquire to:

Travelwriter Marketletter
tel/fax (253) 399-6270
e-mail reikko@travelwriterml.com.

We need to be aware, too, that practically any publication will be receptive to travel material if the material is geared to its *specific* audience. In a minute we'll take a typical travel experience and consider where it might sell. But first—how do you go about finding that audience? You begin with marketing manuals. Study them at the library before deciding which is most convenient and complete for your needs.

Two Major Marketing Guides

Writer's Market and *The Writer's Handbook* are the marketing manuals most familiar to freelancers.

Writer's Market contains listings for more than 4,000 periodicals, publishers, and organizations that are potential buyers of freelance material. Travel material can be packaged and presented in a multitude of forms, but the most familiar is the newspaper or magazine feature. Potential travel-article buyers appear in *Writer's Market* every year under the basic headings of consumer publications and trade, technical, and professional journals. The market lists are updated via the monthly magazine *Writer's Digest*. Each listing gives the publication's address, the name of at least one editor (sometimes several in charge of different types of material), the publication's emphasis, and its readership. The listing also mentions the number of freelance manuscripts used, the kind of material the publication will consider buying, rights purchased, normal reporting time, connection, if any, with an electronic publication, and how the freelancer should get in touch. The book also tells about agents, syndicates, scripts, contests, and other outlets for writing.

Writer's Market Online has all the resources of the print edition combined with a year-long subscription to their online database. It has excellent search capacity, enabling you to search for publications in a particular genre, subject category, or location; or those with particular pay rates, those that buy reprints, pay on acceptance, and don't demand all rights.

Merely browsing through market manuals will give you many ideas for articles, as well as introduce you to hundreds of publications you're unaware of. You'll find many pleasant surprises as you thumb through them. They will give you a springboard, a jumping-off place, to marketing ideas of your own, as well as ideas for shaping and writing the piece, itself. If one of these publications should not happen to work well for you, still it catalyzes the recognition of another that may turn out to work better.

The Writer's Handbook, published annually by *The Writer* magazine and updated through monthly market lists in the magazine, has a slightly different format. Its hundred-odd articles on various types of writing fill two-thirds of the book. The rest deals with specific markets, categorized by type of material, such as "Fiction Markets," "Article Markets," "Reprint Magazines," etc.

Other Guides to the Freelance Market

The annual *Literary Marketplace*, published in two volumes, gives all sorts of information about book publishing, literary agents, and related topics, but not much on periodical publication. It does, however, include a section on electronic publishing that answers such questions as, "Where can I find someone to convert a manuscript into machine-readable form by optical scanning?" or "How can I take an image from a video camera and reproduce it as an illustration?"

The *International Literary Marketplace* is arranged alphabetically by country, with information on each about public holidays, mailing requirements, literary agents, major libraries, translation agencies, and a vast amount of material.

Both *Ulrich's International Periodicals Directory* and the *Standard Periodical Directory* list their 60,000-odd entries under about 250 "field of interest" classifications. Browse through them next time you're at the library. Look over the *Gale Directory of Publications and Broadcast Media*, the *Directory of Publishing Opportunities*, and the *Editor & Publisher International Year Book*, too. Each approaches its periodical listings from a different direction and includes different information.

The multi-volume *Working Press of the Nation* is designed for publicists, but it can be extremely helpful to freelancers. It covers newspapers, magazines, newsletters, and internal publications, as well as TV and radio.

Most of these manuals can be accessed online.

Be Sure to Study Your Target Magazines

With thousands of periodicals publishing all sorts of material, whatever kind of travel story you write, there's a market for it *somewhere*. As you pore over the various marketing aids, jot down the names (and page references) of the likeliest prospects for the subject(s) you have in mind. Then read copies of the publications themselves.

There is simply no substitute for studying at least three or four recent issues of each of your target markets, either in print or online. This not only tells you whether or not this publication is a likely buyer for your idea, but actually helps you shape the idea. Read each issue from cover to cover, including the ads. The ads, often designed by professional readership analysts, provide strong clues. Are these readers more interested in saving money or in having the best? Are they in need of more tax shelters or more ways to fix a hamburger? Are they tennis players or wheelchair users? Scrutinizing the advertisements and editorial material is the best way of judging what each market is likely to want.

Wooden Horse Publishing's website, a wonderful online resource, www.woodenhorsepub.com, keeps track of who wants what in print and electronic publications.

Some of the online media delineate their readership very frankly in their zines or on their web pages, and they expect the writer to pay attention. The Robb Report (www.robbreport.com) which describes itself as the "Bible of Luxury," indicates that most of its readers can afford to buy anything they want, and nothing but the best of travel circumstances will do for them.

Big World (www.bigworld.com) on the contrary, calls itself a "magazine for people who like their travel on the cheap and down-to-earth. . . people who prefer to spend their traveling time. . . discovering, exploring, and learning, in touch with local people. . ."

Gorp.com talks about "planning an active vacation," and wants articles on paragliding, horseback riding, fly fishing, and other strenuous activities. An article on finding adventure in Japan provided a myriad of details about climbing Mount Fuji.

Many of these magazines are available at the library. Others can be purchased at the newsstand. Still others appear on the Internet. But how can you obtain copies of the more obscure publications?

There are a number of ways. One is by studying the *Writer's Market* listings that say "Free sample copy on request." I underline those as I go through the book, then have a helper address postcards to the seven or eight hundred I want, pressing onto the other side of the postcard a label with the message, "Please send a sample copy and information on your requirements as suggested in *Writer's Market.* Thank you." I sign them. For publications that charge for sample copies, I write a letter with a similar message, adding $1.50 enclosed," or whatever. If a magazine doesn't say anything in its listing about sample copies, I send a form letter requesting them, which usually results in their arrival. (If you're thinking only of yourself—not classrooms full of students—your sample copy needs might be more like seventy or eighty, or even seven or eight.)

What are some of the other ways to find obscure magazines not generally available at the library or the newsstand?

From Trash Cans to Flea Markets

Tell everybody, "Never throw away a magazine. Whatever it is, please let me look at it first." My mother used to live in a large apartment house where residents placed their old magazines on a shelf beside the incinerator. Every time she heard the incinerator door closing, Mother dashed out to look for treasures. That's how she happened to bring me *Aramco World*, published by Arabian American Oil Company for libraries and researchers, as well as for Aramco's friends. When I saw they used in-depth articles on the Middle East, along the lines of what I was writing, I checked into it further, and *Aramco* proved a good market for me. Ask your barber, your hairdresser, your dentist, your doctor—anybody—to save magazines for you. Ask friends to give you their old trade journals, company publications, religious magazines, hobby periodicals, and club association magazines. You'll be surprised at some of the unusual markets you'll find.

Never pass up a rummage sale, thrift shop, or flea market. Your traveling companion may tease you about hoarding for paper drives but when you think of those old magazines as potential *markets*, you're glad to give them a little space. Don't overlook the Friends of the Library sale or the Post Office distribution of undeliverable magazines. There are other places to look for discards, too. As we stood on a Los Angeles street corner awaiting the bus to take us to the Rose Bowl game, I glanced at the mesh trash can beside me. When I saw three hard-to-find magazines in a paper bag, I fished them out. (I won't tell you what my husband had to say about *that*!)

Look for Other Opportunities

Always search for hidden markets. You'll build up an "old boy/old girl" network as you move along in freelancing, but meanwhile take advantage of whatever you can find—from chat rooms and message boards to the local newspaper. When the British American Magazine advertised in the newspaper classifieds for writers, I called it to the attention of a student who had just returned from England. When the editor of *Guest Informant* (which you often find in your hotel room) told me how desperately she needed writers in a couple of cities, I was able to give her the name of a friend in one of them, which was the beginning of a mutually satisfactory literary relationship for them. There are markets and there are ways to find them.

Market research not only helps you find the obvious and hidden markets and shows you what else has been written on your subject, it helps you know *how* you should write for your target markets. Your final target will determine your *exact* focus and slant, but you'll be doing your general planning well in advance. Will your piece be in first person, in third person, in a combination "I-you," or in a hidden viewpoint that takes the reader right on-scene without revealing who is giving the information? Will your lan-

guage be formal or informal? Your tone serious, helpful, nostalgic, humorous? Will you use quotes, anecdotes, fictional techniques? Do the markets
you have in mind require more research than you will be able to complete?
Is the approach you intend to take appropriate for the age, sex, political inclination, financial condition, and educational level of the audience you seek?

Plan Your Article Itinerary

Analyze the stories in your sample publications and begin preparing an itinerary for your manuscript. Where will you send it *first*? Then where will you
send it *next*?

Psychologically, an itinerary for each story you're contemplating is one
of the travel writer's most valuable supports. When you have all possible
markets listed on your itinerary sheet, if your query or your story gets a
"Sorry, no thanks," you already know where you're going to send it *next*.
This is not only an important time-saver for a datable subject—you just
type out a fresh title sheet, put the package in a fresh envelope, and drop it
back in the mailbox—but it alleviates the "I'm not much of a writer, they
didn't like it, after all, nobody's ever going to buy anything from me" blues.

After arranging your preliminary itinerary, return to your magazine
indexes. How recently have your target markets covered your subject? Is it
too soon to suggest that subject again? If there have been a great many stories, you may feel the marketplace has been saturated, unless you have some
new, absolutely irresistible angle. If you find *nothing* on your subject, you
may wonder whether for some reason that subject is too taboo among
major media or whether you've looked it up incorrectly and should search
for a synonym for the heading you're looking under. Or this may be a lucky
accident for you to be first with the story.

Sometimes it's harder to research your subject's recent publication history on websites or in zines, but it's helpful if you can do it, either online
or in print. Then you can plan a firmer itinerary.

There are several ways of devising an itinerary. If money is your primary goal, the first publication you would try for would be *Reader's Digest*,
perhaps, or *Playboy* or *Women's Day*. Your descending order would list
lower-paying markets, on down through the cent-a-word possibilities.
However, there's another factor to consider: does the magazine pay on
acceptance or on publication? *On acceptance* means you'll get your check a
couple of weeks after you get the "Yes, we want it." *On publication* means
you'll get paid when and if your piece appears in print. Some editors are
very fair about this and only accept material they know they'll be using in
the near future. Others are tempted by the opportunity to build up a free
inventory, and your story may sit "in inventory" for months or years. In
general, an editor is more likely to publish promptly something he's already

paid for. Sometimes a periodical will pay immediately for the article but will hold all the photographs you've sent until the staff is actually laying out the issue. Then they'll return the unused photos and send a check for those they use. That seems reasonable, doesn't it? But if you're the kind of writer who doesn't really believe it's *sold* until it's *paid for*, beware of pay-on-publication involvements.

If prestige and the respect of colleagues and peers would please you most, you'll begin your article's travels by sending it to the *Journal of Archaeology, American Heritage, Scientific American*, or some other prestigious publication, whether or not they pay you at all, then move on to more popular markets.

If, on the other hand, you want to sell the piece quickly, you might begin your itinerary with the publication that seems to you a most likely market for this particular story. After you've done your market research, read several copies of your selected targets, and eliminated those that have recently used your subject, you should be in a position to judge which publication would most want what you have to offer, and which market would be the next most probable, on down to the long shots and the lucky accidents. Your individual itinerary will show some combination of these.

Consider the Hundreds of Markets Before You Go

Let's take a mythical trip and see what we can do about finding candidates for a marketing itinerary. In thumbing through *Writer's Market*, don't merely turn to one section and stop there. *Every* section lists publications likely to buy travel material. From *Baby Talk* to *Modern Maturity*, hundreds of periodicals are potential markets for your work. So study *Writer's Market* carefully and creatively. Study the print possibilities and search out the online mentions, as well as the information in *Writer's Online Marketplace, Online Markets for Writers, writers.net*, and similar reference books. Begin to identify all the possible audiences for your trip story as soon as you know you will be traveling.

Say you're scheduled to take a trip on the Mississippi Queen—fourteen days on the Ohio and Mississippi Rivers, from Cincinnati, Ohio, to Minneapolis/St. Paul, Minnesota. Traveling with you and your spouse will be your three children: Mike, a high school football player; Melanie, an inquisitive nine-year-old; and Brucie, a toddler in diapers. You will also be accompanied by your eighty-four-year-old mother-in-law and your recently divorced thirty-two-year-old sister Sue, a bank executive in training. You will *not* be accompanied by Butterball, your Siamese cat, whom you've left in a kennel, or the tank of tropical fish a neighbor boy is supposed to feed.

When doubts arose about the departure of any Mississippi river boats, you decided to take the trip anyway—by road.

Both you and your spouse get three weeks' vacation, so you'll travel a thousand miles to Cincinnati in your RV, taking six days to see the sights along the way. After the trip, some members of your party will fly home on a commercial plane from the Twin Cities while some of you will fly in a friend's private plane back to Cincinnati.

How many periodicals would be interested in some kind of story related to your trip? Hundreds! Let's do this systematically. Turn first to the Consumer Publications section in the latest edition of *Writer's Market*.

Animal publications such as *Cat Fancy* or *Cats Magazine* might be interested in your efforts to find the perfect kennel for Butterball while you're traveling. Is there a story in the neighbor boy and the tropical fish for *Tropical Fish Hobbyist*—either in print or online?

Art publications like *The American Art Journal* or *Art Papers* would be likely to publish something on Cincinnati's Taft Museum, the Walker Museum of Art in Minneapolis, or Carl Milles's thirty-six-foot onyx Indian statue in St. Paul.

Associations, clubs, and fraternal magazines are very concerned with the ideals, projects, and activities of their sponsoring clubs or organizations. Any of these become excellent markets for the freelancer familiar with the area where the organization will be holding its next convention or the area where the group sponsors a particular project.

Even stories on the environs of the convention city are popular with association editors. If the Elks or the Lions, members of Kiwanis or Rotary or one of the other associations happen to be planning a convention or trade show in Cincinnati, Louisville, St. Louis, St. Paul, Minneapolis, or even some nearby city, wouldn't some of its members be interested in extending their convention trip with a vacation in the area? Aren't you the logical one to tell them all about it in the association publication?

Automotive and motorcycle sections mainly list those publications concerned with the vehicle as a hobby or sport. (Publications in the travel, camping, and trailer section deal with the vehicle as transportation or shelter.)

Is the friend with the private plane an aviation personality? Or will the trip be an especially interesting or unusual experience? If so, perhaps *Air Line Pilot* or *Private Pilot* would take a story. The latter says, as do many of these magazines, "the online magazine carries original content not found in the print edition."

Banking publications should be considered. Often these are addresses to those senior enough to have optional income. And what are most of these people saving for—travel, of course!

Black publications might like to hear about your trip, especially if you're black.

Business and finance publications—eight pages of them—might need a special angle.

Child care and parental guidance magazines might find travels with a toddler a worthy story. *Home Life*, *Parents Magazine*—many of them would welcome your advice.

Company publications (also known as house organs) are sponsored by a particular company to keep employees, customers, stockholders, salesmen, and dealers aware of what's going on in the organization. Some companies publish several magazines—one for customers, one for stockholders, and another for employees, for instance—while others distribute the same periodical to everybody. Does the organization you or your spouse work for publish a house organ? Would the story of your trip find a good home at one of them?

The emphasis varies tremendously. Some insist on every word being company-related, while others barely mention the sponsor. Volkswagen's *Small World* steers a middle course—the editor says he wants "interesting stories on people using Volkswagens. Our approach is subtle, however, and we try to avoid obvious product puffery." Was a VW the star in any of the stories you saw in route?

Consumer service and business opportunity publications should not be overlooked. Actually, money is such a universal subject—everybody wants to know how to make it, save it, spend it to best advantage—that a financially oriented travel article is likely to sell almost anywhere.

Education publications? Select one that looks for travel articles that show the educational value of the experience for the child.

Entertainment? You should be able to find a periodical that will take a story on old-fashioned melodrama, Dixieland Bands, or Mardi Gras Night.

Food and drink is another lucrative category. Perhaps your meal experiences will be appropriate for inclusion in *Gourmet Magazine* or *Bon Apetit*—or maybe *Veggie Life* or *Home Cooking*.

General interest and miscellaneous publications run the full gamut of reading material. And practically all of them publish travel stories in one form or another. *Friendly Exchange*, for instance, is distributed to policyholders of Farmers Insurance and prefers destinations west of Ohio. Editor Adele Malott says its articles "offer a service to readers and encourage them to take some positive action such as taking a trip. . . tell us about the people, activities, or events that make the location special. We prefer to go for a small slice rather than the whole pie. . . .Concentrate on what families can do together."

What segment of your adventure would interest the *Friendly Exchange* reader? Probably not the same part you would write about for *Diversion's* "eclectic mix beyond medicine" for its audience of physicians or the luxury lifestyle travel trends you'd need to consider for the *Robb Report*.

Travel-sophisticated readers of the "Big Three"—*Travel + Leisure, Travel Holiday*, and *Conde Nast Traveler*—need an entirely different focus and tone from the focus and tone for readers of *Reunions Magazine*, which, as the name implies, is primarily interested in reunions of families, classes, military groups, etc., and whose online content is somewhat different. The estate oriented reader of *Town and Country* is a very different person from the small-town reader of *Grit* and the rural reader of *Capper's Weekly*. It's up to you, the writer, to discern these differences and pinpoint ideas that will appeal to the specific audience. *Smithsonian Magazine*, an intellectual monthly, might be interested in your tale. So might *Open Spaces*. But they would want quite different stories.

National Geographic tells the writer not to worry about submitting photos, as these are handled by professional photographers. On the other hand, its listing suggests that photographers submit a generous selection of transparencies. "The use of many clear, sharp color photographs. . . makes lengthy word descriptions unnecessary," warns the *Geographic*, indicating also that historical background be kept to a minimum. The magazine is, it says, " seeking short American place pieces with a strong regional 'people' flavor." Doesn't that sound like a natural for a travel writer like you?

Another natural could be a story relating to contemporary American life—something that is upbeat and positive. Many publications look for "narrow scope" destination stories, similar to the type of thing Don McLeese did in "New Orleans; We're Playing Its Song." The story really wasn't about New Orleans at all, but about the music of Bourbon Street. What will you find on your trip that will give you the sharp focus you need for a story like that?

Reader's Digest, at the top of the pay scale, sometimes runs original "armchair travelogues." But most *Digest* articles, whether original or reprints, have a message far beyond "My Trip." When Charles Kuralt's "Prettiest Places I've Ever Seen" appeared, the description of a fantastic summer night on an Alaskan glacier, with the Northern Lights putting on a memorable show, was appealing. But toward the end of the article he speaks of the pilot who took him there, perhaps accidentally: "He sized us up as a couple of guys in a hurry who would benefit from a night to slow down and look around."

While this is a personal experience, written in first person, an earlier piece, "Take a *Real* Vacation!" is an advice article, where "I," the author, am telling "you," the reader, what you should do. The message is similar—take time to slow down and have fun—but it's more strictly structured. Steps one to five, describing common vacation problems and their solutions, and eight additional tips result in a final message clearly stated: "When you get right down to it, you *do* have time for a good vacation, and you *can* afford to take one. So let yourself go!" Is there something in your travel experience that will help your reader? Can you share that experience with him, either as a personal narrative or as good advice?

Health publications? Well, if your mother-in-law is even slightly incapacitated, *Accent on Living*, or *Arthritis Today*, under **Disabilities**, might be interested in how she gets along. *American Health and Fitness, Natural Health*, and others, all have something special to say to the reader. Can you help them say it? All kinds of articles on health and fitness are very popular right now—a trend likely to stay. A whole covey of fitness magazines, from *Intouch* or *Shape* to *Vim & Vigor* and *Weight Watchers' Magazine*, will encourage you to tell about the fitness equipment and health and fitness classes you come across on your trip. The *Healthy Living Series Webzines* (*Healthy Woman, Healthy Man, Healthy Parenting, Healthy Eating, Healthy Sexuality, Healthy Mind, Healthy Athlete, Alternative Medicine, Healthy Over 50, Healthy Traveler*, and *Healthy Rx*) demand a still different kind of content. You could probably find something to fit each one.

History publications are another possibility. *American History* welcomes suggestions for illustrations, but usually doesn't buy photographs. *True West* limits its coverage to "anything west of the Mississippi River," so you'll have to be careful which riverbank you're talking about if you try to do a historical piece for them. The western part of the United States seems to interest many of the publications in this group, but *Traces of Indiana* and *Midwestern History* might be receptive to your ideas. What about the Nauvoo, Illinois, Mormon community or the Indian battles at Dubuque, Iowa, or the Indian games in Lacrosse, Wisconsin, or other vignettes of history encountered on your trip. Would *Military History* be a possibility? How about periodicals dedicated to antiques?

Hobby and craft publications occupy 22 pages in *Writer's Market* and include many unexpected titles. *Treasure Chest* and *Lost Treasure* would be interested in the history of Cave-In-Rock, Illinois, if there's even the slightest hint that some of the unsavory characters who once peopled the rock left some hidden treasure behind. *Early American Life* is an excellent market for stories about visits to historic sites.

Home and garden publications (of which there are many) run some kind of travel article every month. Each travel article is, naturally, geared to that publication's readers, so the same idea wouldn't work for *Home and Condo, Flower and Garden Magazine*, and *House Beautiful*. While *Better Homes and Gardens* frequently runs travel stories, they are always family oriented, fact-filled, and related to something the reader can imitate. A recent fall issue juxtaposed two possibilities for winter vacations: "Some Like It Hot," a roundup of warm weather possibilities, from Palm Springs to Freeport, and "Some Like It Cold," with best tips for skiers, snowmobilers, and ice skaters. Both articles give advice on how to get the most for the money. Could you work out something around a theme like "It wasn't so expensive, after all" or "How to cut costs on a family vacation?"

Inflight magazines have been affected by the shake-up in airline carriers. They still provide an excellent mid-range market for the travel writer, though, *if* you can figure out who the players are and what they are playing. What we call inflights—and their advertisers—court the affluent business travelers, who make up over 50 percent of the plane's load, so it's a special kind of travel material. No first-person accounts, no camping out with the children, no long-winded sagas for what may be a fifty-minute ride. Naturally, inflights try to appeal to the reader who *flies* to his destination—unlike auto magazines, which extend friendship to the reader who *drives*; *Hertz No. 1*, which includes sight-seeing information for the reader who *rents* and drives; and *Go Greyhound*, which features historic, scenic, or entertainment attractions accessible to the reader who leaves the driving to *them*.

While the trend is toward shorter stories, they don't ignore the fact that people who fly to a destination sometimes use other means of transportation once they get there. United Airlines' *Hemispheres*, for instance, did an extensive feature on "Walking England, A Coast-to-Coast Trek Across a Land of Love and Legend." *Hemispheres*, like many other inflights, has regular departments that cover business and investments, art and entertainment, food and golf, shopping and personal growth. And every month they publish a feature, "Three Perfect Days" in various cities, which purports to be an insider's guide to what and where to see, do, eat, stay, and enjoy. How about "Three Perfect Days" in Minneapolis or Cincinnati?

Even commuter airlines have their own inflights these days, and a publication called *Frequent Flyer* is distributed to those who fly so frequently and so unexpectedly that they have need for an *Official Airline Guide*. A recent cover story, "Getting a Handle on Baggage!" delves into the sophisticated mechanics of airlines' luggage problems and is probably *not* the kind of story you would research on *this* trip.

In-rooms, magazines similar to inflights, are produced by many large hotel chains, both in the U.S. and abroad, and we often see other in-transit publications, such as *Amtrack Express*. From time to time, waterborne inflights have appeared, produced by various cruise lines—this is something to check into. Nothing too "heavy" in any of these, and nothing too blatantly commercial. Just pleasant reading as you relax on a plane or train, in a room, or aboard ship. You could probably find a dozen subjects that would work into short pieces for this market.

Juvenile publications use travel material in two ways—stories introduce young people to the experience of traveling; and they teach about children from other countries and other cultures. Many of them emphasize the values in other cultures, helping young people to realize that other people are *different* but not *inferior*. *Cricket, Highlights for Children, Touch,* and any of the *Scholastic* magazines would be good candidates for the travel experience from the child's viewpoint. Flora and Fauna around the River, History of the Area, What Would Mark Twain Say if He Could See Us Now? would all make good themes. So would caring for vacationers' pets. Try your story out on Melanie, and see if *she* likes it.

Literary and little publications take up over 30 pages of listings, many of them initialed, beginning with *AGNI* and ending with *ZYZZYVA*. These, along with their online companions, provide a number of opportunities for self-expression and recounting of personal experiences. Many, however, pay only in contributors' copies. The writer who feels a desperate need to get his or her travel thoughts in print might consider these as beginning markets.

Men's publications still thrive. With the right angle to your trip story, you should be able to market it at *Heartland USA* or *Men's Journal.* Could you find some aspect for *Esquire?*

Military publications? In addition to the purely professional periodicals, a number of these are interested in historical pieces, like features on little-known battles, ancient warfare, and weapons of war. How about something on those Indian battles in Dubuque? The *Retired Officer Magazine* reaches a slightly different group and often is similar in content to other retirement magazines.

Music in this area is often spectacular and may inspire you to search for one of the music publications or one of the theater, movie, TV, and entertainment publications as markets for your stories. In music, especially, you have a wide choice for reviewing the entertainment or interviewing the entertainers, from *Bluegrass Unlimited* to *Modern Drummer* and *Guitar Player Magazine.*

The Nature, conservation, and ecology section—popular topics right now—features many publications. Some such as *Seasons, Appalachian Trailway News, High Country News,* and *Nature Canada,* are environmentally oriented. Others, like *Audubon/Bird Watcher's Digest* and *The Atlantic Salmon Journal,* are concerned with particular wildlife, while *National Wildlife, American Forests, International Wildlife,* and *Wildlife Conservation Magazine* are more generalized. *Sierra, The Environmental Magazine,* and *The Amicus Journal* often publish well-documented exposes on environmental issues of national importance, while *Summit* is more literary and *Natural History* emphasizes the biological sciences and anthropology. All, of course, publish materials that interest their readers.

What ecology-oriented events and adventures are you finding on your vacation? Do you see groups of people walking along the riverbank picking up trash? Have you spotted, and photographed, a rare bird? Are developers cutting down fruit trees to build houses? Does one of the lecturers point out the wildlife in the water and along the banks? What is the history of the levees—good or bad? How do ships dispose of garbage and minimize the environmental impact of passage along the river? You can probably think of a dozen other article ideas that would fit into one of the ecology magazines.

Pacific Discovery, a quarterly journal, says it publishes articles whose subjects include "behavior and natural history of animals and plants, ecology, anthropology, indigenous cultures, geology, paleontology, biography, taxonomy, and related topics in the natural sciences." One of the best travel stories I have ever read appeared in *Pacific Discovery*, when zoologist Steven Anderson wrote of an afternoon in a Persian garden. He described in detail the historic people and animals marching in marble-carved relief down the Apadana Stairway in Persepolis in Iran.

Newspapers and weekly magazine sections are among the best travel markets in terms of volume, although their pay is often modest. You can, however, usually sell the same piece over and over again, marking it "exclusive for your circulation area," and sometimes it builds up quite a nest egg. Better still would be to make an arrangement with a syndicate, but that's sometimes harder than it appears. Newspapers will often have special theme issues, such as the *Los Angeles Times* with its annual issues for International and Europe; Alaska; Canada and the Pacific Northwest; Summer Vacations; Hawaii and the Pacific; Mexico; Cruises; and Caribbean. Many weekly travel sections run annual vacation issues. The travel writer can ask for a schedule of the issues planned, and act accordingly.

Magazine supplements and Sunday supplements often produce a travel edition in early spring and a vacation-resort edition shortly before school closes. Often the editorial material has some connection with the areas, accommodations, or means of transportation being advertised. If you have file cabinets bulging with travel research and photographs, let your local editors know where they can call you when they need to cover a particular area. Or find out when they're likely to be ready for a story you would be able to produce.

Many newspaper editors insist on a degree of exclusivity, notwithstanding the fact that their checks may be disappointing. However, appearance in some publications adds to your reputation. For instance, publication in the travel section of the *New York Times* is very prestigious (they want all rights, by the way). At the *Times* they say, "Write what you have to, and then get out," but most newspapers insist that a writer keep under their maximum word length, usually about eight hundred words, hardly ever more than fifteen hundred, sometimes as short as three hundred. More and more newspapers are accepting color photographs now (for discussion of photography, see Chapter 15), but all prefer some kind of photos, either color or black and white, to accompany the story.

Monthly and bimonthly magazines, incidentally, have in-depth issues on specific themes, too—a certain area of the world and all its various charms, or a certain activity, like skiing or golf, and all the places it can be pursued. If the area, the site, or the activity is familiar, find out about these in-depth or theme issues ahead of time and see if you can fit what you know into what they want. Get in touch with suggestions before you begin your trip. It's highly likely that some editor will be planning an in-depth issue or a complete roundup of recreational activities in the area you'll be traveling.

Photography publications might also welcome your story if you're clever with a camera. Photographs are an important plus value for any story, so keep your camera handy. Perhaps the picture-taking possibilities will give you ideas for writing, too.

Poetry and puzzle sections are so specialized you'll have to work extra hard to tempt them. Wouldn't it be fun, though, to drift through a somnolent afternoon, sitting in the shade composing verse or constructing a crossword puzzle?

Regional and city publications, have, as you know, been booming, multiplying and expanding. They're sorted by states, but they don't always stick precisely to their own areas in the stories they publish. They do, however, try to publish articles that will interest their readers. So your trip might make an intriguing story for the "affluent, luxurious" readers of *Palm Springs Life*, published in California, or the "upwardly mobile" readers of *Jacksonville*, published in Florida.

By carefully reading the *Writer's Market* listings, we discover that *Bend of the River, Cincinnati Magazine,* and *Ohio Magazine* sound like good markets for your trip story. *Kentucky Living* and *Back Home in Kentucky* are likely prospects, too. Don't overlook the geographically related areas served by publications in Indiana, Louisiana, Tennessee, Pennsylvania, and Minnesota.

Would an article on choosing a kennel appeal to all of them?

Bend of the River specializes in Ohio history and antiques, and, indeed, seems to be living in an historical era, offering as does only $10 to $75, on publication, for an exclusive 1,500-word article, and $1 per black-and-white photo, with caption. Other magazines in these two groups pay more, some of them much more. Practically all of them say they want history, nostalgia, humor, and travel pieces, and many would like photo essays. Understandably, *Chicago Magazine* has a more urban outlook than *Wisconsin Trails*, but most of them speak of their readers as upper-middle income, college educated, interested in the arts and in travel to nearby areas.

Religious publications include magazines of all denominations. The material doesn't have to be *too* religious in theme, but it can't be *anti*-religious. Here again, each periodical is especially concerned with its convention site or the area of a special project. Some of the religious magazines pay very modestly, others are competitive with general publications.

Saint Paul's Cathedral, styled after Saint Peter's Basilica; the Mormon buildings in Nauvoo, Illinois, built by Joseph Smith and his followers; the buildings of the communal society at New Harmony, Indiana—all would fit into a religious publication. I have sold articles to religious magazines of all denominations on such subjects as: Olvera Street, the Mexican quarter of Los Angeles; the Junior Museum of Palo Alto, California; the largest all-women's college in the world, Ewha University of Korea; and "How Far Does Your Dollar Travel?"

Another travel writer says he has revised some of his nonselling travel articles to emphasize the religious peg, thereby making them appealing to this group of magazines. He wrote about religious statues adorning an Arizona site that were built by a man fulfilling a World War I vow, and an Indian pueblo once destroyed because its inhabitants professed Christianity. Study the religious markets. You'll get lots of ideas from your travels for stories that might appeal to them.

Retirement publications, as we have said, gain in importance as the average lifespan increases. More and more citizens retire earlier and live productive and interesting lives for longer periods of time. Travel is an important part of those lives. The "Cadillac" of retirement magazines, *Modern Maturity*, the voice of the American Association of Retired Persons, has a huge circulation and pays very substantially. They publish separate issues for younger and older retirees. While there's considerable emphasis on promoting AARP trips, other travel material also appears in every issue. What travel-related stories could you write for them? Previous issues have contained nature-related articles about life along India's River Ganges; another article is entitled "Can We Afford the Wilderness?"; and a photographic roundup of bridges, called "Magnificent Links," is featured in still another issue.

New Choices, Plus, Senior Living Newspaper, and dozens of other publications, many of them church sponsored, welcome travel material that is slanted to those over 50. These are not for rocking-chair seniors but for people with a desire to enjoy their well-earned retirement or pre-retirement or semi-retirement in an active way.

Additionally, newspapers addressed to seniors proliferate in all parts of the country. Some are weekly, some monthly, some quarterly, but they all accept freelance material, and they are all interested in travel. Pay here is often low and slow, but it's something to keep in mind.

This true story bears out today's awareness of seniors. On a recent Alaska cruise I thought I was very original in deciding to focus on what a great trip this would be for the over-50 set. As the cruise line's public relations director polled the travel writers, many of them in their early 20s, about their intended focus and markets, I was lucky to be the last one to speak—and had time to rearrange my thinking. Every one of the others expected to write about some facet of the senior experience on a cruise to Alaska! People of all ages are writing for seniors these days.

Rural publications like *Mother Earth News, Country Folk,* and *Ruralite* are interested in organic gardening, rural living, homesteading, natural foods. Will you see stories along the way that would be suitable for one of them? Perhaps you'll buy eggs at a dilapidated farm just purchased by a young couple beginning to restore it, or you'll notice a hundred miles of roadside vegetable stands with signs advertising their wares as organically grown, and you'll stop to interview several of the farmer-greengrocers.

Sports and outdoor publications (over 200 of them) beckon, with everything from bow hunting to baseball, from water sports to wrestling, each snug in its own category. There are even publications that whisper of privileged information, like *Triathlete Magazine* under Running, *Blackjack Forum* under Gambling, and *Inside Kung-fu* under Martial Arts.

Field and Stream, Outdoor Life, or *Sports Etc.* are excellent targets for your travel experiences. En route did you encounter any unusual hunting and fishing laws? Did you, yourself, have an extremely successful fishing session with new or unusual equipment? A *Silent Sports* editor, who uses original articles and reprints for both the print magazine and the web page, says, "Our readers are participants—from rank amateur weekend athletes to highly competitive racers." He emphasizes that his audience is people who will be going out and doing it—not the armchair athlete with the coffee table magazine.

Sports Illustrated is a wonderful market because of its *weekliness*—it uses four times as much material as a monthly! Sometimes what it uses it amazing—everything from "Sail a Slow Boat to See," a charmingly illustrated journey along the canals of France, to an early-in-this-century story of two small boys who crossed the continent on horseback, to the origin of Australia's theme song, "Waltzing Matilda," to "America is Formed for Happiness," a story from the diaries and letters of British travelers who toured the colonies before the Revolution. A history teacher friend says *Sports Illustrated* publishes "some of the best history articles around."

In that same sports section, many of the boating magazines, from *Heartland Boating* to *Sailing Magazine,* would be good markets for a *Mississippi River* story. Readers—and editors—who are interested in boating are interested in any type of waterborne holiday.

Other sports categories might tie in, also, and son Mike might have ideas about good angles, especially game-related.

If your travels take you where some sport will be holding a championship meet, you may have a story. The idea is, of course, to urge those interested in the sport to attend the championship event. *Skating*, for instance, began its story "On the Oregon Trail" with:

> Portland, Oregon, host to the United States National Figure Skating Championships next February, is more than just a city, it is an idea, an experience. Portland is a potpourri, spiced by variety. But Portland has something else undefinable but perhaps best called personality.

It doesn't take much insight to figure out that this was written by the Portland Chamber of Commerce—but it does prompt the freelancer to look out for future championship areas. Naturally, you'll have such events as the Olympic Games, the World Series, the Boston Marathon, and other major sports events calendared in early. Perhaps next year one of them will be part of your travels.

Teen and Young Adult publications are for teenagers 13–19, and many have a religious orientation.

Some of them, however, are good markets for travel material "from a student's angle": how to budget, what to take, where to go, etc. Could you adapt your material with son Mike's help? *Seventeen* likes to advise female teenagers on travel. *Ranger Rick's Nature Magazine*, published by the National Wildlife Federation, would certainly consider a story on the Upper Mississippi River Wildlife and Fish Refuge, a 196,000-acre preserve where Canadian geese, blue herons, bald eagles, beaver, and deer can be seen. *National Geographic World*, published for young readers, would like this type of story, as well as a host of other stories you might get out of this trip.

Trade, technical, and professional journals (*Writer's Market* has 125 pages of them) offer a huge number of possible markets, too. These publications are produced for people in a certain trade, industry, or profession, and while their emphasis is on technical expertise, many of them fill their pages with interesting, only slightly related stories as well. Does your trade or profession publish a journal? Some education magazines, for instance, like travel stories the teacher can use in the classroom and those that help the teacher plan her own vacation. Your story could work either way, couldn't it?

Photography trade journals are good markets for the travel writer-photographer. Trade journals within the travel industry rely heavily on freelance material to help the travel agent find—and sell—the best possible vacations. Travel, camping, and trailer publications, on the other hand, appeal to the buyers of those vacations. They cover a broad range. In addition to the AAA publications, other automobile clubs, both U.S. and Canadian, publish similar magazines. Insurance companies and oil companies vie for the traveler's attention. There are several newsletters of travel advice, and a whole host of possibilities among the RV and camping publications. As one editor states, "Freelancers are very important to national special interest publications, since it is economically unfeasible for magazines to have staff writers cover such a broad geographical area." He says that in addition to articles written by experts, he also needs travel pieces with an enthusiastic approach. During your RV trips to and from Cincinnati, will you find something to approach enthusiastically?

Travel + Leisure, one of the biggies, buys 200 travel pieces a year—all geared to the upper-middleclass traveler, who is too rich and too old for the pack-on-the-back crowd but too poor and too young for the Mercedes and 5-star hotel. With the good photographs you're going to take and the lively story you'll promise to write, you're likely to get an expression of interest here.

Many of the travel publications appeal to those with special needs and desires. The *ASU Travel Guide*, for instance, is a quarterly designed for airline personnel. While its stories highlight the destination, they give no information on flights, tours, or hotels—those are arranged in a special way. But they might take something impersonal on your trip.

Accent, on the other hand, appeals to a very general audience since it is a house magazine, purchased by various businesses to distribute to employees, customers, and friends. Its editors like lively travel vignettes that are short but informative and of lasting interest. They prefer stories about U.S. destinations and might be a good prospect for your travel article.

Don't overlook those house magazines, purchased in bulk by travel agents to send to their best customers. They need stories that lure the frequent traveler into planning yet another trip; and the trip has to be of the type to generate travel agents' commissions. These periodicals come and go, but while they're publishing they make good markets, so seek them out. Contributions to travel newsletters can be winners too!

Since some travel magazines are geographically oriented—the North, the South, the East, the West, Mexico, Canada, the Caribbean, etc.—your adventures would have to fit in with the area they cover. *Islands* is a wonderful magazine, and even if you can't create an article for them this trip, keep them in mind for another time.

Conde Nast Traveler says its service information is presented in a "tip-sheet style," but its destination stories are literary. It thinks of its readers as "affluent, well-educated, and sophisticated about travel." What part of your experience might interest those readers?

In general, travel writers may find the competition severe at the more sophisticated travel magazines. On the whole, it's probably easier to sell a travel story with national exposure and payment in the dollar-a-word range or more.

Women's magazines present probably the greatest diversity within a category. You doubtless know the big traditional publications, all of which use travel stories sometimes.

For some, though, the focus has greatly changed, and it's especially important to read several current issues before formulating your ideas for a travel article for one of them. *Woman's World* is a weekly, and it uses a lot of material. But it's a different kind of material than you'll find in *The Ladies' Home Journal.* The pitch to *Cosmopolitan* would be quite different from the pitch to *Family Circle*, and the pitch to *Country Woman* would be still different. *Rosie* wouldn't use the kind of story you're preparing for *Woman's Day*, and *Vanity Fair* is entirely different from *Good Housekeeping*.

Essence is addressed to the African-American woman, *Chatelaine* speaks to the Canadian woman, *Radiance* is written for the large woman. Many women's publications, both online and off, cultivate business women or religious women. *Bridal Guide* and *Modern Bride* use a lot of material on possible honeymoon destinations. So does a magazine called *Bride Again*, where they seek ideas for unusual wedding venues and honeymoon trips for the encore bride. *Redbook*, no longer one of the biggest buyers of travel material, has changed its focus slightly. The *Redbook* "Young Mother" may be in her late forties, and their other special sections are geared to the mother past thirty, as well as the mother under thirty. But if you think your family's vacation would interest other families, it's worth an inquiry.

Although these women's magazines are very different, all of them might be interested in a unique version of how to save money while traveling, how to pack, how to select accommodations, how to make your sight-seeing arrangements, and other general themes that can be slanted specifically.

Whether you travel closer to home or farther away, the travel story you write can be published. Nearly all the publications I've mentioned here are listed in *Writer's Market*. And practically all of them pay *something*. I'm not really mercenary, and I don't feel a writer's soul should have a price tag, but on the other hand, a travel writer is a professional and is entitled to be paid a fair price for a job well done. The trick, of course, is finding the right periodical for your particular story and studying the markets before you mold your material. This will pay big dividends in terms of selling what you write. Recognizing the wide world of travel writing markets can turn the story you write into the story you publish.

We'll explore marketing in more detail in Chapter 10. Then, after you've completed your preliminary market research and your itinerary, you'll be ready to tackle the ultimate sales tool, the query letter, which we'll discuss in Chapters 11 and 12.

The Online Market

In today's world "publish" may refer to an electronic outlet as well as to the printed page. And there *are* writers out there "publishing" in cyberspace for money. The potential is tremendous. Again and again the current explosion of computer "content" is compared to Gutenberg's invention of movable type.

A pioneer in electronic travel writing, Lee Foster insists it's possible to make a good living traveling and writing about it today. "My overall trajectory," he says, "has been to go out into the world, live out the raw travel experiences, then come back and publish them profitably. . . in congenial print or electronic situations."

Foster and other online writers suggest several directions for the freelance travel writer to explore. One way is to approach the Travel Product Manager at a commercial online service, such as CompuServe and America Online, with an appealing proposal showing content you are prepared to provide. If accepted, you will receive a percentage of the revenue that the online provider collects from viewers of your material. It is possible, of course, to also prepare and collect examples of this content on a computer disk, which can then be sold in the same manner as a travel book.

Although CD-ROMs are becoming less and less popular as travel resources you may still find a CD-ROM a good outlet for your travel experiences. If you have enough to say, with photographs and graphics to illustrate, you can publish your own CD-ROM and either distribute it yourself or find a national distributor. It's more likely, perhaps, that you'll hope to sell content to some other publisher of travel-related CD-ROMs, such as Topics Entertainment. Study a CD-ROM catalog at the library to see what has already been published and who is publishing what. Then you can get together the facets of your adventure to try to fill an electronic void.

Another opportunity for profitable publishing involves an information database service on the World Wide Web. This kind of arrangement gives free browsing to the viewer with payment to the writer only when his or her article is downloaded.

Arranging for a home page on the Internet provides infinite possibilities, many of them as yet unexplored. You can fill your website with your own travel material, permitting viewers to browse, then download for a fee, payable to you directly. You can also use the site to advertise and sell other materials you have available, such as books, disks, or CD-ROMs; or promote yourself as a writer, speaker, or professional in another capacity. And you can sell advertising space to "outsiders" whose goals don't conflict with or compete with yours.

Still another Web connection offers you the opportunity to provide content for online publications. Some of these, which proliferate daily, are stand-alone electronic magazines, like *Slate*. The *Air Affair*, for instance, focuses on recreational aviation, while *Tropi-Ties* caters to people who love tropical places. Others are electronic extensions of print publications such as *Conde Nast Traveler* or *Outside*. Your agreement with the commercial site organizer will either result in outright purchase of your material or will provide you with a percentage of the revenue from every viewer.

Writing an ongoing online travel column is a money maker, and every once in awhile a writer's publication will contain an item like, "America Online is looking for writers and illustrators to submit original humorous columns."

A number of travel writers report on assignments they have received or resales of previously published articles resulting from their participation in appropriate online forums or chat rooms.

Unfortunately, not every writer is being recompensed for the exposure of reused material online. This entire issue of copyright and contract law is sometimes a murky area, as technological advances introduce new problems. As time goes by, more and more travel writers may think in terms of licensing their work rather than selling it, and all of them will become increasingly aware of what rights they are actually offering.

While we know that books, magazines, and newspapers are here to stay, the travel writer cannot afford to overlook the additional possibilities of online publication.

Getting Ready to Go

You'd think those who travel for a living would always be on their toes about what they'll need: letter-perfect in their preparations, and ready for the summons to adventure. They would think so, too—but they know better.

Georgia Hesse, then travel editor of the *San Francisco Examiner*, wrote a bittersweet column about meeting her friend the travel editor of the *Chicago Tribune* in Sri Lanka. His arm was red and swollen. Why? Because he had delayed too long in arranging for a necessary shot. Georgia was amused at the time, but admitted she found the situation less amusing a few days later, when she arose at three a.m. for a trip across the island of Mauritius to make a six a.m. flight to the Malagasy Republic. Authorities refused to let her board the plane. Why? Because she had no visa for Malagasy. When she'd looked up the requirements in San Francisco a week earlier it seems she'd mistaken Malagasy for Mali.

Whether you're going to Malagasy or Mali, whether your journey is to the next town or across nine time zones, do as much homework as you can when you're getting ready to go. Otherwise you're likely to be disappointed in dozens of wretched little ways—and plenty of big ways, too.

Using a Travel Agency

If your "getting ready" involves planning with a travel agent—and there are those who think this is wise and those who think it's foolhardy—be honest with him. How much money and how much time do you really have to spend? What do you really want to see, and how do you want to see it?

And insist that the travel agent be honest with you. Ask "What is the 'half day of sight-seeing'—is it four hours or only two and a half? What is a 'transfer' supposed to do—meet me at the plane and assist me through customs and immigration, or meet me at the taxi stand and put me in a cab? Does this price include all gratuities? Will my sight-seeing tours be in English *only*? Does a 'driver guide' know enough to help me with my research? Would reversing the itinerary be desirable?" (Always request separate vouchers for each person and each item, so if you decide not to do something it will be easy to obtain a refund.)

Traveling with a group is usually the easiest, in terms of planning and executing. Traveling on an FIT (Foreign Independent Tour) arranged by a travel agent also features prepaid arrangements tailored to suit you with more freedom and responsibility. Giving you still more freedom and more responsibility for taking care of yourself is the kind of trip with no prepaid reservations, no arrangements made for you—you go as you please each day.

With so much travel material online these days, it becomes easier and easier to plan your own trip. But whether you use a travel agent, accept a hosted trip, or do it yourself; whether you have assignments, go-aheads, or just something you want to see, always consider your sight-seeing plan very carefully. It is the single most important feature of any trip. Sight-seeing can be dull and dreary, hurried and half-baked; or, with intelligent arranging, it can provide maximum writing and research value as well as personal pleasure and enrichment.

Your sight-seeing program is not something to arrange casually, trusting to luck that you will see the best things in the easiest way at the cheapest price. Too many people select the wrong trip for the wrong reasons. They ruin any chance of writing about their travels because they don't ask the right questions when they're getting ready to go. Sight-seeing plans are geared toward particular people, particular places, and particular pocketbooks. If you know the full range of what's available, you'll be able to select your own ideal plan, whether solo or in a group.

Get Your Objectives Straight

Ask yourself, "Why am I traveling? For adventure and discovery? Or for relaxation and diversion? What kind of readers will my stories appeal to? Why will *they* be traveling?"

There are other questions: is the getting there or the being there more important to you? Are you traveling to find new ideas for your writing, or to give your ideas a rest? As Lawrence Durrell says, travel is "one of the most rewarding forms of introspection."

Are you pursuing the Holy Grail of some long-cherished dream? Will you be satisfied only if you see London's Old Curiosity Shop or the Mark Twain Museum in Hannibal, Missouri?

Do you want to know how people live in other parts of the world? Are you hoping to make new friends? Or mere acquaintances for the duration?

Do you want to travel with other writers? With other photographers? There are a few tours geared especially toward writers and/or photographers (usually listed in spring issues of writers' magazines), as well as many work-play conferences. If well run, these can be stimulating and rewarding. As at a writers' conference, the shop talk is valuable in itself and the entire trip is slanted to your purposes.

Perhaps you've already arrived at that lofty peak where the editor calls *you* for a story on the new Robert Trent Jones golf course at Xanadu, scheduled for the next issue. Can you make it to the airport by five? Your first-class air tickets and hotel vouchers await you there. At Xanadu's capital you'll be met by the press charge d'affaires, who will conduct you, via camelback, to the third, sixth, and seventeenth tees. Send the story by Friday.

In such cases, your travel plan has selected you. Sit back and enjoy it. But if you're the one choosing what you will see and how and with whom you'll see it, be sure to consider what kind of person you are.

Gear Your Plans to Your Personality

Take into consideration your habits and your characteristics. *Your* sight-seeing choice, if you like to get up early and be on your way by eight, will be different from that of someone who prefers to review the nightclub circuit. If you are compulsive about eating at definite times or need to rest after lunch in hot weather, you must take this into consideration. If you feel lonesome unless lots of other people are sharing your experience, or you're out of sorts when you have time on your hands, *your* sight-seeing program won't resemble that of the person who's bored hearing someone else's opinion and gets disgruntled when every minute's arranged for. Do you like to laze in the sun, ride a horse, dress for dinner? Do you like to drive or be driven? Are you impulsive, eager to do what you want to do, when you want to do it? Do you detest regimentation? Remember what *you* are like when you plan your sight-seeing program.

Two writers comparing trip notes discovered that each had had a wonderful time traveling to the same area—although one covered every cathedral and museum and spent evenings at the theater, while the other shunned cities and tramped backcountry roads, staying at country inns in medieval villages. Each had planned a sight-seeing program that covered exactly what she considered a good time and liked to write about.

Each of these women traveled alone, because each was very sure of what she wanted to do and unwilling to make compromises. If you're an independent kind of person, never bored by your own company, consider solo traveling. Going alone, or with a known traveling companion, or perhaps with several well-chosen ones, may work out best for you. If you and your traveling companion(s) don't agree about the ratio of time and money to be spent on various stages of the trip, you'll have to work out compromises. If you want it to be a good trip, negotiate these matters *before* you go. If you intend this to be a business trip for you, what will your traveling companion do while you're tracking down all the facts a travel writer needs? Your traveling companion may or may not feel the benefits are worth the sacrifice of your company, the early morning phone calls, the late-night research and writing sessions. Perhaps you can persuade him or her to become a part of the project—by taking photographs, for instance. If you join some group of congenial traveling companions, such as an alumni tour, you'll have to conduct your own business within the framework of the group arrangements, without inconveniencing anybody else.

No matter how much information you unearth, and no matter how enthusiastic you *try* to be, you'll never convince your readers it's a great place if *you* aren't having a good time. So take into consideration your personality, the things you like to do, your special interests, and your physical condition. Consider, too: is this likely to be your *only* trip to this area? If so, perhaps you'll want to see the "musts." However, don't overlook the advice of Dr. Ralph Crenshaw, who says you should limit your goals and your expectations. "You can't see or do everything there is to see or do in a few days, so focus on some special interest." In the Netherlands, for example, he began with Rembrandt's home in Amsterdam, and "went on trying to visualize the city as it must have appeared to him around 1650. I didn't try to frustrate myself by trying to gulp down the Dutch nation's whole history and cultural development."

As Mildred Martin says, "Travel gives the writer the opportunity of enjoying, in another setting, the same hobbies and activities that are rewarding at home. If you're a garden lover, find out where the spectacular gardens are—you have the background to fully appreciate them and to communicate that appreciation to your readers." She points out, also, that the other side of the coin is the refreshing surprise of the unfamiliar, and that, too, can be a valuable experience for the travel writer.

I once met a charming, sophisticated woman, a buyer for Sears Roebuck, who had traveled throughout the world. "I've probably been in more foreign cities without seeing the most famous landmarks than anybody you've ever known," she said. She spends her free time sunning on beaches and exploring back alleyways. She added, "I'm past the stage where I feel I have to see something just because three generations of travel writers have stamped it with approval."

The Pros and Cons of Tours

Discuss with your travel agent, or with your prospective companion(s), or with yourself whether you want to join a tour group, design an FIT, or just amble unscheduled from day to day. Different traveling writers have different needs.

There's a tour to fit every possible interest or affinity, whether you're a nonsmoker, a wheelchair traveler, or a ballet buff; whether your particular desire is to concentrate on "The Train in American Culture" (a nineteen-day cross-country railroad odyssey), "The European Approach to Policing" (with visits to Interpol and Scotland Yard), or "Surfing in Hawaii."

In choosing a tour, consider not only your assignments and planned stories but also your other interests and hobbies. Do you think you might find interesting and valuable a tour designed for those studying gourmet cooking, international theater, music festivals, local crafts, viticulture, or stamp collecting? Your pre-trip homework will probably be designed by the tour leaders, who will send you informative study material in advance. Then they will take care of most of the everyday arrangements, which the solo traveler has to work out for himself.

Even if your temperament is anti-tour, for certain destinations at certain times a tour may be the best answer. The *Student Travel Catalog*, published by the Council on International Educational Exchange, makes note of the fact that its users may ordinarily "avoid 'tours' like the plague!" It goes on to describe the "unique opportunities" of overland tours from Europe to Asia and throughout Africa but points out bluntly, "If you love your creature comforts, DO NOT BOOK on one of these trips."

Equally candid are brochures encouraging travelers to join excursions to mainland China. They recommend "a little homework before you depart" and "a flexible and positive attitude." One tour discourages the squeamish with:

> The accommodations tend to be adequate to modest. If you find unan-
> ticipated changes unpalatable or cannot accept accommodations consid-
> erably less than you would normally prefer, you may not wish to partic-
> ipate in this program. It requires a sensitivity to the customs of the
> people and a willingness to accept the tour arrangements "as is" regard-
> less of your particular interest or taste.

At least you *know* before you go!

How do you select the best bus tour? Al Stich, a travel photographer, charted the seven most appealing tours for the area he wanted to visit at the time he wanted to go. By listing in graphic form the airlines and equipment used, the number of meals provided, the number of days, the type of hotels, the points of origin and return, the side trip options, the actual cities and areas visited, and the price, he figured out which of the tours would be best for seeing the places he and his wife had in mind, and which would give the most value for the money.

As one travel writer says, "There are no bad tours—only unfortunate marriages of tour and tourer."

Do You Need a Guide?

Your "getting ready" preparation helps you decide on sight-seeing arrangements of all kinds. Aboard ship, for instance, you'll plan whether or not to take the shore excursions. Some ports of call aren't worth a tour—just walking around will show you more than a bus ride would. Others have so much to offer that if the ship is in long enough you would do well to hire a private car and driver.

By yourself with private car and driver is, of course, the most luxurious way to sight-see. If money is no object, you can tour the Rockies in a Cadillac limousine, complete with driver-guide and no worry about route maps or service stations.

Sometimes the money for a private car and guide is money well spent. I was in Milan only once, many years ago, between trains. Yet, I'll never forget *The Last Supper*—thanks to the knowledgeable young man who met our train, whisked us out to the refectory of Santa Maria delle Grazie, and then back to the train for Lake Como. His sensitivity, his awareness, his education in art, his ability to communicate the artistic experience, gave me a lifetime memory of da Vinci's masterpiece. That brief visit to Milan was expensive, but it was a bargain.

If you plan to concentrate on scenery, you won't need a guide, except for reasons of safety in wild and remote areas. Unless you feel compelled to know the height of every mountain and the depth of every sea, you can enjoy the Appalachian Trail or Washington State's San Juan Islands without explanation. You move at your own speed, take all the pictures you want, and stop and eat when you feel like it.

Other times, the guide will be the key to your sight-seeing program. Find out which sites have built-in guidance, such as the Panama Canal, where the "talker" comes aboard your ship and explains everything as you sail through the locks, or the French chateaux, where they hand out mimeographed information in your own language. Allow enough time for Gettysburg, where buses take you on regular guided tours of the battlefields, and Williamsburg, where the buildings are attended by the knowledgeable, costumed hostesses. Today many museums, from Paris to Hiroshima, lend or rent cassette recorders with taped commentary on the exhibits. If you're touring some U.S. or Canadian national parks, or driving from San Francisco to Monterey or from County Cork to County Clare or to and from a variety of other places, you can buy taped tours that run on an ordinary cassette recorder and lead you through all major sights. They set forth the history, culture, and folklore of the area, along with shopping trips and sports advice. There are many suppliers of these tapes; look in your Yellow Pages or ask at your nearest travel store.

Many large cities, as far-flung as Wellington, New Zealand, and Goteborg, Sweden, provide city tours in municipal buses, and Melbourne, Australia, does it with a harbor tour on a city-owned boat. The independent travel writer can build a sight-seeing program around these possibilities.

For developing countries, however, where the language and even the alphabet is often extra-difficult, where all facilities are expensive, where arrangements are complex and time-consuming and distances are vast, you're usually better off with a doorstep-to-doorstep guided tour.

Consider Your Special Interests

Incorporating your special interests always makes travel more meaningful. An amateur genealogist talked for months about his exciting solo trip to study at the National Archives in Washington, DC, and seek out the tombstones of his Virginia ancestors. A couple traveling in the Orient made arrangements to visit the Hong Kong orphanage supported by their church, to which they've been donating for half a lifetime. An artist inspected photographs of the areas she intended to see, so she knew in advance which would be the most interesting scenes to paint. These special interests later contributed to their travel stories.

Do you belong to a national or international organization? Write ahead to find out what's doing along your route. Not only Rotarians and University Women, but kite fliers, square dancers, model airplane builders, fishermen, ham radio operators, quilters, bridge players, and people tied together by practically any concern you can name, have associations with many branches. Get in touch ahead of time for a warm welcome. This kind of "getting ready" homework is not only personally rewarding—it often leads to a story.

Perhaps you'll want to join an organization especially for the trip. Depending upon your age and orientation, such groups as the American Association of Retired Persons, Parents Without Partners, the Union of Polish Women in America, the Society of Painters in Tempera, the Youth Hostels Association, the Sierra Club, the British-American Society, the Irish Georgian Society, as well as your professional or trade association, your alumni group, your church affiliation, and hundreds of other possibilities can lead you to travel friendships, travel discounts, and stories with plus value. Plan far ahead and send for membership information.

71

If you explore the various sight-seeing possibilities, taking into consideration your personal tastes and desires, where you are going, and the type of sights you will be seeing, you can plan an ideal program within the framework of available time and money.

Whether it's your money or your editor's, you'll want to take advantage of financial considerations often given to those under twenty-five, over sixty-five, married, unmarried, teachers, students, doctors, patients, weekday travelers, weekend travelers, skiers, bowlers, joggers, and almost anyone alive and breathing. If it's the off-season, there's a special rate. If it's the right day you can go to the museum without paying. Days of the week and hours of the day can make a difference in the price of transportation, admission, and other travel writing needs. So look out ahead of time for whatever discounts or bonuses you're entitled to. And don't hesitate to ask, "Is this your best rate?"

Line Up Your Informants

As you think about your upcoming trip and what you'll be writing about it, think first: whom do I need to talk to for the stories I'll be working on? Then line up your interviews and appointments. In some countries you'll never get to interview anyone without a letter of introduction. Sometimes consulates and embassies can help you arrange business appointments; other times you can work through a company's branch offices. But it's imperative to search out the local customs and set all the wheels in motion early.

Will the person you need to see be available? Even if you're only traveling to the next town, check on the business days and hours so you'll be able to do what you need to do while you're there. Does an annual May Day parade block downtown traffic and close most business establishments? Is Election Day a legal holiday in that town? Do you need to speak to somebody at the school board office during a week when all school functions are on half-day session? Will the store you need to research be closed for inventory? Have all the farmers you planned to interview taken off for the Apple Butter Festival?

The farther you travel, the more critical the problem becomes because your actual transportation plans grow less flexible. One writer counted his single day in Buenos Aires a total loss because the taking of the census entailed a holiday that prevented him from finding the information to complete his story. Another travel writer, visiting Venice for an assigned photo essay on mosaics, found all the crucial people and places immersed in celebrating the Feast of the Redeemer. More than one surprised journalist has discovered that all of Australia races to a standstill on Melbourne Cup Day. And Japan celebrates a handful of holidays during Golden Week.

Holidays: A Plus or a Minus?

Both national and international holidays, like Papua New Guinea's Thanksgiving Day in August, Japan's Respect for the Aged Day in September, Hawaii's Aloha Week in October, and the "anything goes" Oktoberfest in La Crosse, Wisconsin, can be a plus or a minus for the travel writer. He has to work around the movable feasts, too, like pre-Lenten Mardi Gras in New Orleans, Carnival in Rio, or Charro Days in Brownsville, Texas-Matamoros, Mexico, as well as Ramadan, observed by all Muslim countries with a month of daylight fasting, and Kurban-Bairam, when everything is closed for family festivities. Travel writers may avoid holidays or embrace holidays but should always be aware of their existence.

If you're embracing the holiday—Good Friday in Seville, the Tournament of Roses in Pasadena, Queen Elizabeth's Jubilee visit to the South Pacific—and you want to go there at that time *because* that's the story you want, find out first what will be the best vantage point. Then beg, bribe, or buy your way into that vantage point. Consider, too, that you'll want to take pictures, so if there's a choice of vantage points, pick the one at a good height for picture taking, with the sun in the right direction. Try to ask friends who've been where you're going the best way to see the event. They may tell you that at Copenhagen's Tivoli Gardens you can rent a sort of periscope that lets you look over the crowd to see what's going on. Other friends may tell you to climb the steps to the rooftop restaurant overlooking the Djemaa-el-Fna Square in Marrakesh, where, for the price of a soft drink, you can see all the action. You can look down on and photograph the peddlers, the snake charmers, the storytellers, the water carriers with their tinkling bells and copper cups, and the mobs of fascinated bystanders.

The seasons of the year can be important to the travel writer. Naturally, if your story involves New England's fall color or the show of rhododendrons in San Francisco's Golden Gate Park, you'll have to take pains to be there at the critical moment. Sometimes, it's hard to second guess nature. What week will the cherry trees bloom? What time will the fairy penguins parade up from the sea? Do your best to obtain accurate predictions from tourist offices, chambers of commerce, local residents, and frequent travelers to the area. Human beings, on the other hand, are more predictable. In August, when the French take *their* vacations, most Parisian activities shut down or fold up; during the hot summer months many U.S. East Coast businesses work a four-day week, or shorter hours some days, or different hours.

While off-season travel has many advantages, in cheaper prices, smaller crowds, warmer welcomes, it can have its disadvantages, too. The excursion boats don't travel up the Hudson to West Point or up the Thames to Greenwich; the famous restaurant may be closed; the planes, the trains, the buses will run on different, less frequent schedules. Twice a year the arrival and departure of daylight saving time can change your travel schedule. (Several November homecomings have found me waiting an hour at the airport for a relative to pick me up at the time it said on my daylight saving itinerary.) Nailing down these specifics is part of "getting ready."

Local Customs Can Affect Travel Plans

Even days of the week make a difference. One travel writing team spent three Sunday hours restlessly pacing among the benches of a Paris train station after discovering that the eleven a.m. train to Chartres didn't leave at eleven on *Sundays*. Another couple spent a long, hungry day aboard a Kuala Lumpur-Singapore train. Now they know—the dining car isn't always attached to the train on *Sundays*. In New Zealand and Australia you could starve on a weekend while the waiters and the dishwashers are out surfing and sailing, and if you insist on eating in a restaurant, you're going to pay extra for it. Your pre-trip homework will reveal that in those countries and in many others, as well as many major U.S. cities, sabbath laws regarding the serving of alcoholic beverages dictate what time the restaurants will be open.

What day *is* the sabbath? In Muslim countries it's Friday. In Israel it's Saturday, beginning at sundown on Friday. Not only are all banks, business offices, stores, and restaurants closed, but transportation is limited as well. The wise travel writer confirms this information and takes it into consideration when getting ready to go.

Museums all over the world tend to be closed on Mondays. Except some are closed on Tuesdays. Or Wednesdays. Or Sundays. A California journalist making a trip to New York for a special show at the American Museum of Natural History heard the museum was open Mondays but telephoned ahead to be sure. It was a good thing—the Museum *is* open Mondays, but not until noon.

Will you be doing research at libraries, museums, archaeological digs? These often require letters of introduction before they let you through the gates. Ask the most eminent scholars you know to attest to the excellence of your character and the importance of your mission. (Then write ahead for a built-in welcome.)

The welcome extended to Alice Kennedy by the Shakespearean research area of San Marino's Huntington Library didn't include even her husband. When he started to accompany her into the special room, the receptionist stopped him. "I'm sorry, sir," she said firmly. "You'll have to wait here in the lobby. Only Mrs. Kennedy has permission to enter."

Get Your Tickets Well in Advance

In some countries it's essential to have a "Reader's Ticket" to work at the National Library, the Public Record Office, the National Maritime Museum, or other research source. Save on-trip time by sending ahead for these permissions. An audience with the Pope? It's easier if you write ahead to:

Bishop's Office for United Stated Visitors to the Vatican
Casa Santa Maria
Vis dell'Umilita 30
00187 Rome, Italy
06-670-658

If you're Roman Catholic, include a letter from your priest or bishop, or ask your local parish to help arrange the audience.

Whether it's for a story or just for fun, tickets to a special festival or event can add another dimension to your trip. But the Salzburg and Bayreuth festivals sell out a year in advance, and the every-ten-years Passion play at Oberammergau is reserved long ahead of time. Whether you're going to the opera in Santa Fe, the Mozart Festival in Burlington, Vermont, or the Old Fiddlers' Convention in Galax, Virginia, write for tickets as soon as you know your plans. Enclose a self-addressed, stamped envelope or an international reply coupon to expedite the answer.

Do you want to review a Broadway show? Sometimes you can send a check and an SASE to the theater months in advance. (That's how we happened to have six first class seats for a hit musical. By the time we saw the show, the tickets were selling for many times what we had paid.) Or you can go to the TKTS booth near Times Square for discounted tickets the day of the performance, but be prepared to stand in line. They open at 3 p.m. (earlier on matinee days), but right after breakfast the line straggles out to the street. Occasionally you can go up to the box office a few minutes before showtime and find turned-in tickets at the box office price. Or you can call or show up at a ticket broker's headquarters and pay a surcharge—which may be very substantial.

You Can Communicate Efficiently and Economically

Your telephone can be your passport to efficiency and economy. In big countries like the United States, Canada, and Australia, an off-peak call from west to east or an early-evening call from east to west still catches people during the business day. This often works for country-to-country calls, too, so the writer needing a telephone interview or wanting to make an appointment or check a fact with someone several time zones away can call at the cheapest rate. This is true of fax usage, as well. Send your fax messages at bargain rates whenever possible. Also, collect communications from your answering machine, message center, or voice mail at the cheapest times to call in for them.

Your cell phone may not work outside of North America, but it's possible to make an overseas rental arrangement with other companies such as cellhire (www.cellhire.com).

If your itinerary isn't firmed up, you'll need mail arrangements. The traditional route, both within the United States and abroad, is "Care of American Express." Some Thomas Cook and airline offices also hold mail for their customers. Another way (of venerable tradition) is, of course, *poste restante*, or general delivery. Find out how long mail is likely to take, and instruct your correspondents to mark "hold for arrival" on the envelope.

These offices are closed evenings, weekends, and holidays. But you can usually get your mail at the best hotel in town. You don't have to stay there. Just give that as your address, then ask the concierge or mail clerk what is being held for *your arrival*; slip him a modest tip, and hint of more to come.

Big hotels usually have fax machines for their guests and the general public. In many areas other service facilities and stores also offer fax sending and receiving for a small sum in case you need to communicate with the home base *right now*.

If you take along your laptop, e-mail is the way to go. Even if you don't take your own equipment, you'll find what you need to use at one of the ever-present cybercafes, or possibly at your own hotel or a nearby shop. If you're using "snail mail," don't spend a huge hunk of trip time and money addressing postcards and letters to the folks back home. Always type out gummed address labels before you go so you can just press them onto the postcard or envelope. Going a step further, you can buy the postcards themselves before you go. (Foreign Cards Ltd., Box 123, Guilford, CT 06437, is one place—doubtless there are others.) Stick the gummed labels onto your prebought postcards and, if absolutely necessary, write your preplanned message. (I've never done this, but sometimes I've been tempted!)

Cross the "T" in Document

What kind of documents must you have to travel where you're going? Passport? Visa? Tourist card? Apply for whatever you need in plenty of time, and follow the instructions carefully in filling out the forms. Check and recheck to make sure you have everything you need. Many times I've seen people in the airport prevented from boarding the plane because some "i" wasn't dotted or "t" wasn't crossed on their travel documents—or they had looked up requirements from the wrong country. (Incidentally, allow plenty of time at airports for inspection of those documents when you're traveling internationally.) Jot down the numbers of your travel papers, as well as those of your credit cards, traveler's checks, and airline tickets, and put them in a different place from the originals. You might even wish to photocopy them. If anything is lost or stolen, you'll have an easier time replacing it if you have the number.

When you visit most foreign countries you'll need a passport, and for some you'll need a visa, as well. If you travel a great deal you can apply for a 48-page passport at no additional cost, so you'll have more room for the official stamps of entry and exit. If your plans change en route, don't worry—you can obtain the necessary visas in some other country as long as the one you're planning to visit has representation there.

Throughout your trip you'll often be required to identify yourself on various documents, and the phrasing of the information may be more significant than you think. In some countries, listing yourself as "Journalist" or "Travel Writer" is like waving a red flag. Consider the political situation in some Third World nations. Perhaps it's better to stick with "Businessman," "Housewife," or "Retired." Sometimes this becomes a sexist matter. When we debarked from a ship in Chile a few years ago, the immigration people wanted to know all of the *men's* professions—even those who were retired had to come up with something to satisfy the questioners. But the *women* were never interrogated. On each woman's debarkation card, beside the Spanish word "Ocupacion," was written the English word "Laborer"!

You may wish to describe yourself as a "Student" on your passport. Catherine Elwood did that when she was studying for her Ph.D. at Stanford University. One immigration inspector took a second look at her papers, then a second look at her forty-year-old face. "Student?" he muttered. Then he looked her straight in the eye. "*Still?*" he inquired.

If you can prove you have been a full-time student during the current academic year, regardless of your age, apply for an International Student Identity Card. Bring your current student ID card, a small picture, and a modest fee to a regional office of the Council on International Educational Exchange, available on most college campuses, or send it to the main office at:

C.I.E.E.
205 East 42nd Street
New York, NY 10017-5706
Tel. (212) 661-1414, Fax (212) 972-3231
e-mail: info@ciee.org

Allow at least three weeks for processing.

Identified students become eligible for student-priced charter flights and discounted air, rail, boat, and bus fares, reduced-rate car rentals, museum entries, tours, accommodations at student hostels, welcome services, and special travel insurance, as well as a variety of helpful publications. In Los

Angeles, for instance, students can stay at a desirable, centrally located hotel for seven to fifteen dollars a night. Even New York's venerable Waldorf-Astoria provides dormitory-style rooms at student rates. Many hotels are under five dollars a night—some are free.

If you study only part time and don't qualify for the C.I.E.E. card, you may still find that describing yourself as a student will open many doors. Mature researchers Norm and Rose Grabstein, while working for advanced degrees in archaeology, found that writing in advance for permission to see restricted sites and beginning the letter, "We are students," usually led to the special permission they sought. When they asked to tour France's closed-off Lascaux caves, the French Conservation Service not only granted permission but warned that visitors have to walk through disinfectant to protect the art and suggested they wear expendable shoes and clothing.

Your Appearance Can Be Important

As a travel writer you should *always* plan to wear clothing you don't care too much about. But the *type* of clothes can be important when you're searching for a story abroad. In many countries clothing customs require covering some specific part of the anatomy. In Saudi Arabia, women who do not conceal their arms and legs risk fine, imprisonment, or expulsion. In Jerusalem's ultra-Orthodox Mea Sherarim district they risk stoning and spitting. At the Vatican a Swiss guard refuses admission to women considered immodestly dressed. (Formerly a nun posted at the main door to Saint Peter's lent plastic raincoats to women with bare arms and legs, but too many took the raincoats as souvenirs.)

It's all right for women to wear long pants at the Vatican, but at the Meteora, the cliff-top monasteries of Greece, they must wear skirts or dresses. To enter the African republic of Malawi, those skirts or dresses must cover the knees.

Malawi, incidentally, is one of the many countries that imposes its own grooming standards on the length of male visitors' hair and beards. If immigration officials consider them too long, the airport barber stands ready with the shears.

Golf courses and tennis clubs all over the world are becoming increasingly strict about players' apparel. If you show up in cutoff jeans and a tank top with an advertising message, they won't let you play.

Men must cover their heads at Jerusalem's Wailing Wall, as well as at any Orthodox synagogue, and paper skullcaps are usually provided. Women, however, should come prepared with scarves of their own. At the Wailing Wall married women of all faiths cover their heads, as do all women, married and single, in the churches of many other religions.

You should think ahead, too, to the parts of you that will be uncovered while traveling. At Muslim mosques and Buddhist temples all over the world, as well as many other buildings of the Orient, you'll be required to remove your shoes.

You will, of course, inquire in advance about climate and activities that would influence your clothing choice. Try to take clothes that won't make you too conspicuous and outfits and separates that will do double or triple duty for many kinds of occasions.

Your pre-trip research will not only help you conform to local dress customs but will also alert you to differences in manners and mores you'll want to observe. Whether it's a matter of kissing the hand, kissing on both cheeks, arriving early, arriving late, eating with your fingers, or sending flowers to your hostess, you as a travel writer will want to blend into the local environment.

Attend Carefully to Pre-Trip Details

It shouldn't be necessary, but maybe it is, to remind the travel writer to try out *everything* at home. Break in your new shoes. Run a couple of rolls of film through your camera. Make sure your alarm clock works reliably. Does your laptop do everything it should? How about your palm pilot?

If you plan to do any shopping on your trip, think about which brand of computer, typewriter, photographic lens, binoculars, wristwatch, etc., is most easily serviced back home. Will you really know a good buy when you see one? How much duty will you have to pay? And what time do the shopkeepers take their siesta?

If you'll be driving in another country, get your International Driving Permit from either the American Automobile Association or the National Automobile Club. Valid for one year, the permit costs $10 and requires two passport-size photos. If you don't have any photos, they'll take your picture for a small extra charge. Usually, ten or fifteen minutes takes care of the whole procedure. If you're an auto club member, inquire as to what membership privileges carry over to other countries: Emergency road service? Legal advice? Lists of club offices? Estimates of road conditions? In the British Isles, where U.S. auto club memberships *are* honored, the British Automobile Association not only patrols the highways and byways but also provides the driver with information about what times big trucks and buses jam the narrow, winding roads so you can avoid them.

To guard against a possible fuel shortage, the travel writer at the wheel does all he can to ensure against an empty tank. Find out ahead of time what days, what hours service stations are open so you won't linger watching the sunset while the last gas station is closing.

If you're driving your own car, of course you'll make sure it's in first-rate running condition before you take off.

If you're driving in another state or another country, look into speed limits, traffic rules, etc. Trucks, campers, motorcycles, bicycles (and probably burros) are also subject to certain regulations and restrictions, so find out what they are.

Check with your insurance carrier about what additional auto insurance you may need. Check, too, about health and accident insurance, trip cancellation insurance, baggage insurance, and perhaps a floater on your camera equipment.

At home or abroad, arrange for good maps. But don't be misled by them. Sometimes what appears to be an easy hundred-mile drive is really two hundred miles of winding mountain path. Learn the names of major towns along your route and also your compass directions—your particular destination may not appear on the highway signs. Your CD-ROM and various sites on your computer can boot up multimedia details of attractions along the way as well as a series of maps and driving instructions for each segment of your trip. Try to obtain good city maps and site plans. Then you'll be able to mark the path you took down the mountain at Delphi, the sites of different treasures, and exactly where you were standing when you took that dramatic picture with the wide-angle lens.

About Matters of Money
In addition to your purely professional planning, it's important to know, too, that local customs vary greatly as to when the banks are open. If you arrive in a foreign country when the banks are closed, you may have expensive dealings with a hotel cashier. Instead, buy in advance from your travel agent or foreign exchange broker enough currency to get you through the first few days, and spend some time memorizing what the different denominations look like.

Give thought to how you will handle your travel funds when you're getting ready to go. There are advantages to traveler's checks, and there are advantages to credit cards, which sometimes include automatic insurance, opportunities for securing emergency cash, easy car rental deposits, and other assistance. ATM cards and debit cards can also be very helpful to carry in your wallet, and are useable throughout most of the world.

If you're applying for a new credit card, allow plenty of time. Three trips in a row we applied three months in advance for a particular card, which never arrived until after we had left. If it's an old credit card, and you are suddenly charging expensive air tickets and cruise deposits, even though it's within your credit limit, be sure to call the company and explain. Otherwise, they may think it's a scam and refuse the credit. Mention, also, any foreign countries from which you expect to make charges. Leave some money in your checking account and take along your checkbook, too. Some establishments give discounts for cash or checks.

You can often obtain traveler's checks at no charge from an institution that uses this service as a promotion, and they're a handy way of carrying cash, even if you're only traveling fifty miles. If you're staying more than a few days in a foreign country, you may find it saves time and trouble to buy traveler's checks in *their* currency when you're getting ready to go. In any case, plan to take a handy selection of small-denomination bills. I've never had much sympathy for the travel writer who converted a five-hundred-dollar traveler's check into the currency of a former Iron Curtain country where he was scheduled for two days. Since there were no souvenirs to buy, his trip was prepaid, and tipping was not permitted, by noon of the second day he was trying to trade the currency back into U.S. dollars. He not only spent the entire afternoon at the bank, splitting and splicing red tape, but he missed his dinner and nearly missed his 8 p.m. exit plane.

Can You Learn the Language?

If you're planning an overseas trip, you may want to learn, or brush up on, a foreign language. At least listen to records or tapes as you dress every day, and practice your pronunciation. While every travel advice writer emphasizes the importance of learning "Please" and "Thank you" and "Where is the bathroom?" in all the languages of your itinerary, it's also important to learn the directional words. Although non-English-speaking people may think they know the difference between "right" and "left," it's best to check the directions by repeating them in their language. How do you say "around the corner" in German? "Fourteen kilometers" in French? "Down the hill toward the sea" in Greek? "Back to the Imperial Hotel" in Japanese?

If you'll be interviewing somebody in a foreign country, even if that person speaks English, it's well to look up ahead of time translations for the key words you'll want. Look up words you'll be needing at the post office, at the camera repair shop, at the library. English is a difficult language, and often people who have mastered a few words don't really speak or understand as much as we think they do. The *Eurail Guide* explains that even those who have mastered English sometimes hesitate to speak it—and when they do speak it, sometimes they're hard to understand.

The Eurail Guide Travel Language System involves pointing to the appropriate question in French, Italian, German, or Spanish. The questions are arranged in the book to cover such emergencies as catching the wrong train, *not* finding the porter who took your luggage, or remarking to a fellow passenger, "You are sitting in a seat I reserved." The quotations are designed to enable a "yes" or "no" answer or an appropriate directional gesture or number.

Hal Gieseking suggests also learning the words in every language for "Is the service charge included?" Then you'll know whether to tip the waiter and the housemaid the traditional amount or just leave a little spare change.

You can talk to the waiter with a Berlitz *European Menu Reader* that not only translates and tells you how to pronounce the names of likely dishes but indicates in many languages, from Danish to Serbo-Croatian, how to say: "That's not what I ordered"; "The meat is too tough"; "What's taking you so long?"; "You've made a mistake in this bill"; and a variety of other useful phrases.

Marling Menu-Masters (1330 Polk St., San Francisco, CA 94109) has publications that provide clues in several languages as to what restaurant dishes actually contain and how they are prepared. After consulting Menu-Masters and with the aid of two bilingual nephews, the Italian owner of her local fish market, and a friend in a consulate, freelancer Frances Lilienthal prepared for each country she was visiting a neatly typed list of idiomatic phrases pertaining to food, including such phrases as "My husband is on a diet for his health"; "Low fat"; "Please serve the sauce on the side"; "Does the fruit juice have sugar added?"; "May we have unbuttered toast?" It not only worked, she says, but "responses were invariably pleasant and helpful."

How Healthy Are You?

It would be foolish not to candidly consider your physical condition as you get ready for your trip. Writers are often sedentary people. If you sit at a keyboard day after day, you're likely to have overdeveloped hips and not much stamina in the legs and feet. (One travel writer, incidentally, considers a visit to her podiatrist an important pre-trip ritual.) If you've hardly walked around the block all winter, your heart, lungs, and muscles will protest when you have to hurry between widely separated airline counters. There's a lot of walking involved in any trip—far more than the writer may be accustomed to—so you have to begin early to get ready. Start by walking five or six blocks a day at a good, brisk pace. Increase the distance daily until you've worked up to at least three miles a day for several weeks before you leave. If you intend to carry a heavy purse, camera case, or flight bag, haul it around at home, gradually adding items, so your arm and shoulder muscles won't be screaming with pain your first day of sight-seeing. If you'll be bicycling, dancing, or rock-climbing on your trip, practice before you go.

For really rigorous trips you need rigorous training. Martha Poppy, well-known mountain climber and ski instructor, who, at age fifty, climbs 19,000-foot ice-covered peaks and skis through the Alps and the Sierras with a pack on her back, thinks consistency is the most important factor in building stamina for rugged traveling. "Just running or biking once in awhile won't do it," she says. She runs five or six miles *every* day and bikes fifty or sixty miles *every* week, and feels she couldn't possibly make some of her difficult mountain crossings or undertake her mountaineering ski trips without the kind of stamina she's built up through consistent exercise.

Arrange for a complete physical examination, and obtain all required shots in time to recover by departure day. See your dentist, too. But don't let him fill, extract, or work on a root canal within twelve hours of an air trip. As a Midwestern dentist explains, "Whenever a tooth is opened, a small bubble of air may enter. Then that trapped gas expands as you're airborne. Changes in atmospheric pressure can leave you stifling screams of agony."

Do you worry that you may need a doctor while away from home? In the United States, just look in the phone book for the county medical society—the operator will provide you with the names of several qualified specialists. In foreign countries, American country clubs usually have lists of U.S.-trained doctors and dentists.

If you're visiting a non-English-speaking country, your consulate or embassy may help you. But it's wise to be prepared with a list of well-trained English-speaking physicians on twenty-four hour call. One method of obtaining such a list is a voluntary contribution to the International Association for Medical Assistance to Travelers:

417 Center Street
Lewistown, NY 14092

or

40 Regal Road
Guelph, Ontario N1K 1B5

or

1287 St. Clair Avenue West
Toronto, Ontario, M6E 1B8

or

P.O. Box 5049
Christchurch, New Zealand 5

or

57 Voirets
1212 Grand-Lancy
Geneva, Switzerland

IAMAT not only supplies lists of qualified physicians but its twenty-four climate charts cover the globe, detailing specific climatic conditions throughout the year, advising on clothing, and outlining the state of sanitation in food, water, and milk in 1,440 cities. Its "Traveler Clinical Record," completed by you and your doctor, belongs beside your passport.

Intermedic (777 Third Ave., New York, NY 10017) also provides a list of qualified English-speaking doctors who respond to emergency calls and charge reasonable fees.

Medjet (800-963-3538 or 888-256-5508) will transport you to a hospital near your home in case of medical emergency.

The International SOS Medical Service Program (Neshaminy Interplex, Trevose, PA 19047; phone (800) 523-8930) will help you in major emergencies if you need such services as an ambulance plane or a guarantee of your hospital costs. Travel Assistance International (1133 15th Street NW, Suite 400, Washington, DC 20005) helps with all kinds of problems before, during, and after your trip.

Medic Alert (2323 Colorado Avenue, Turlock, CA 95380; phone (209) 668-3333) protects you by alerting others to information about your special conditions, medications, or allergies. The organization sells identification bracelets and necklaces that specify the wearer has a medical condition that might not be apparent and provides a twenty-four-hour number to call for the patient's medical history.

While it's helpful to know about these and other emergency services, one travel writer suggests, half-humorously, half-seriously, that the most important aid to the health of a pair of museum-hopping travelers is a wheelchair and a plaster cast. "One of you," directs Shepherd Mead, "pops the cast on one leg, sits in the chair and is propelled by the other past the ticket booth. Assume brave and cheerful expressions. . . .If you lean heavily on the chair it is easier and takes some weight off the feet. The other passenger is resting and gathering strength." He recommends a change of passengers every forty minutes or so, with the cast transferred to the other person's leg. "Alternately resting and pushing, you can last for hours," he guarantees.

On a more serious note, a traveling doctor contends that poison ivy, poison oak, and poison sumac have "ruined more vacations than the combined effects of bad weather, missed travel connections, and inconsiderate guests." Learning to recognize—and avoid—these is another precautionary pre-trip preparation. Find out what some of the other botanical hazards may be in the area you'll be visiting. Are there animal and insect hazards, too? Those travel writers who are extremely allergic to the bites of bees, mosquitoes, sand fleas, or other common insects will want to inquire carefully about the area's fauna.

Dealing with Jet Lag
While travel writers often require treatment for itchy eruptions, tired backs, overwalked feet, gastrointestinal disorders, respiratory complaints, heart and blood pressure problems, accidents, sunburn, insect bites, and heat exposure, the complaint you're most likely to have is jet lag.

Although there are many hints on how to prevent jet lag, nobody has really found the answer. If you cross more than two or three time zones, you'll feel it. Dr. Wilbur Mattison says it`s really "jet lag insomnia" that bothers the traveler, and it varies with the length of the trip and other factors. He suggests that sufferers try to avoid napping and, if absolutely necessary, take short-acting drugs to help them sleep or avoid sleep.

Design an easy day after your jet lands, and don't plan anything too important; it takes three days to reset your internal clock. Arrange a stopover if it's a long trip. How long is a long trip? I don't know. But I do know that Johannesburg to San Francisco in one hop is *too long*.

One traveling family always begins changing time zones a week before going overseas, a half-hour each day. The day before they leave they eat breakfast at 4 a.m. and the children go to bed at 5:30 p.m., with the adults following shortly. Thus, they avoid wee hours' hunger pangs and general exhaustion.

Several scientific experiments are presently being conducted to determine the ideal diet for the "jet set," and it appears that particular combinations of foods and a change in eating habits may help.

Don't add boredom to fatigue. Ameliorate the effects of long airport waits and endless rides by bringing books to read, letters to write, work to organize. Survivors of many cases of jet lag and auto ennui advise the traveler to get up or get out and walk around as often as possible. If you're driving, plan to stop every couple of hours, whether anybody's tired or not, and take along some nutritious munchies and something to drink. Don't try to drive more than eight hours a day, and quit before your reactions begin to slow down.

Plan for Your Comfort

The travel writer should consider creature comfort in getting ready to go on a trip. Find out in advance how late your hotel will hold your reservation. Should you guarantee the charges on your credit card? And inquire about checkout time. Does the tropical beach resort shove you out at 9 a.m. so you're sitting all day in your traveling clothes, waiting for your evening plane? Or will your room's previous occupants remain legally staked out until late in the afternoon while you're arriving at dawn, exhausted by jet lag?

You may not have much choice in the selection of a hotel room, but if there is a choice, opt for the quiet one. Spurn the room with a door that connects it to the adjacent room (television and party sounds seep through the cracks) and the room that opens directly on the pool area (you'll hear the night owls swimming at midnight and the early birds trying to beat the dawn).

If swimming and tennis are important to your story, make sure the pool and the courts will be in service while you're there.

Mealtimes are worth knowing. Is seven a normal dinner hour at your destination? In Ireland it's too late. In Spain it's too early. If you're the kind of writer who can't work on an empty stomach, important pre-trip inquiries will be about food service on trains, motels with twenty-four-hour restaurants, and meals served on flights. If you have special food needs, find out in advance what kind of restaurants you should look for.

Let the airlines know your dietary requirements when you make your reservations, then double-check twenty-four hours before you leave. They'll provide you with an ulcer patient's meal, a low-calorie meal, a vegetarian or diabetic meal, hamburgers and hot dogs for your children, or whatever else you need.

Are You a Frequent Flyer?

Be sure you're using your Frequent Flyer miles to your best advantage. Make an overall plan for them. If you belong to several programs, should you consolidate? Do you have some miles that expire this year? Would you have a more comfortable trip if you used your miles to upgrade to business class or first class? It's generally considered that Frequent Flyer miles are worth about two cents each, so act accordingly.

If you are charging expensive travel costs to a credit card that gives Frequent Flyer miles, inquire as to whether there is a limit on the miles that can be awarded for any one purchase. If your credit card has that limit, it may be better to split your charge over several dates or several credit cards.

Do you have a favorite airplane seat? Obtain the chart from the airline and reserve your seat by telephone several weeks in advance, if possible. The window seat is best if you're taking pictures, but the aisle assignment may give you a little more leg room. Try to avoid seats against the bulkhead that don't recline fully. If you occupy a seat in an emergency row, you must be prepared to assist in case of emergency.

Any time you can avoid a connecting flight, do so. The chances of missing your connection, losing your luggage, or just plain hassling escalate each time you change planes. Check and double check whether your flight is "direct" or whether it involves a connection. Airlines often use the same flight number for the connecting planes—but it's a connection, just the same.

Weather, as we know, can be crucial to the traveler. While the weather likely to greet you at your destination is important, it's even more important to find out what the weather is like at your plane's point of origin and at any point where it may touch down en route. Winds in Chicago, snow in Boston, or even an unusually hot day in Los Angeles can cause significant delays, which may affect your ongoing plans.

If you can avoid flying during the busiest flight hours of a holiday weekend, you'll be glad you did. And you'll be glad, too, if you can arrange to leave and arrive at some time other than rush hour on the highway outside a big city airport.

Be Ready to Field Questions

Most places you travel, a brigade of well-wishers stands ready to help the travel writer with personal or professional problems. But sometimes when people discover you're a travel writer, they want *you* to help *them*. They expect you to be expert in many fields and know something about anything they might ask you. Sometimes they have hard questions they've been waiting to ask people for months, and when you show up, they expect you to answer.

So one of the most important pre-trip preparations is getting ready to answer the questions people will ask you. Whether it's in the next room or across nine time zones, the people you meet will be interested in what it's like where *you* came from. A little thought and a little homework will make it possible for you to present logical and informative answers. Some questions, of course, like those about power shortages, First Amendment rights, racial discrimination, inflation, strikes, unemployment, sometimes don't *have* any easy answers. But try to be prepared so you can present the facts without floundering.

Pondering questions to probable questions is part of getting ready for your trip. So is planning your sight-seeing program. And if you set up your business appointments in advance and arrange for your professional and personal comfort when you're getting ready, it will pay off in pleasure and productivity once you start traveling. Preplanning makes it possible for you to find plus values, and when all the pieces fit together for you as a traveler, you can begin to act like a travel writer. So think ahead, get ready, and *go!*

What to Take Along with You

"Get out everything you think you want to take along on your trip; then put half of it back." Experienced travelers have heard this truism so many times they're convinced it's true.

But there are four tools the travel writer must *not* put back: four tools every travel writer must carry—even if you have to leave behind your toothbrush and your clean underwear.

The first necessity is *Something to show you're a writer.* Take along your letters of assignment from editors; go-aheads; tear sheets of your published articles; downloads of online material; printed programs of travel lectures you've presented; newspaper stories and other publicity about you as a writer; membership cards in travel or writing organizations; a press card if you have one.

At the very least, arm yourself with a walletful of printed business cards. If you're going overseas, where business cards are an even more important appurtenance than in North America, have the blank side printed in the language of the country you're visiting. You'll be surprised how many doors those little pasteboards will open—everything from the press box at the horse races to a private tour of a government child-care center. You can print them yourself if you have the right software, or have them printed inexpensively online or at your local copy shop, but be sure the design is attractive and the information appropriate. With professional credentials you take on a professional air and encourage professional respect.

Don't Forget Your Camera

The second essential tool is your camera. Now you may be thinking, "Oh, my camera isn't very good—it doesn't have all those fancy gadgets," or "*I'm* not very good—I'm not much of a photographer," or "I don't have time to take all those pictures—I need to see what's going on!" Carry your camera, anyway. Not only do photographs help you sell what you write, but even if they aren't of salable quality, they'll help you write your story. The very act of taking a picture forces you to focus sharply, to concentrate on what you're looking at, to see it more clearly. And when you get home you'll discover details you'd half forgotten. I didn't remember, for instance, that Indonesian schoolchildren consider it an honor to sweep the schoolroom floor, and sweeping duties are always assigned to the best behaved pupil of the day. I didn't remember, that is, until I saw my picture of the grinning Indonesian boy with the broom.

We've all heard jokes about the photographer who was afraid to look at the Alps with his naked eye, and the lady who took a Polaroid picture of the Pyramids so she'd get to see what they looked like right away. Pay no attention. While you don't want photography to overwhelm the trip experience, the advantages of taking pictures far outweigh the disadvantages.

You needn't be an expert photographer to strengthen your memories of a trip through photographs. Most modern cameras demand only the ability to focus on the subject and hold your breath for an instant to keep the camera still as you shoot. The cameras do the rest.

You don't have to invest thousands of dollars in photographic equipment. A medium-priced camera, operated by a moderately experienced photographer, will provide salable illustrations. And the cheapest disposable camera, operated by a stumblebum, will provide useful pictures to help you recapture the feeling of where you have been. Digital cameras that take photographs without film can have advantages and disadvantages, as we shall see. Even an instant processing camera, although it seldom produces publishable photographs, delivers valuable gifts for new-found friends in outlying areas, where picture taking is still a novelty.

Videos are wonderful, of course, and the cameras are lighter and less expensive than they used to be. I'll never forget the thrill provided by an early video camera owner on our first trip to China when he put today's tape on the ship's television set every night—and there we were at the Great Wall. You will have to decide whether the extra weight and expense will give you enough extra pleasure and enough additional exposure as a first-rate travel writer. But as one who has sat through countless nightmares of homemade videos where, "we didn't quite get that into the picture, but it was a great scene," may I advise you not to let the emotion of your videos wipe out your judgment to the extent of showing others what belongs in the trash can.

While *National Geographic* sometimes sends out its staff photographers with 1,500 pounds of photographic gear, most travel writers settle for a good 35mm camera, perhaps an extra telephoto or wide-angle lens, a strobe light or flash gun, and a filter or two (to protect the lens as well as to make the sky bluer or the flesh fleshier). If your camera doesn't have an automatic delay feature, an extra cable release enables you to shoot smoothly on a long exposure in dim light or to set the scene, then start the release and dash over to appear in the picture.

Take plenty of film. Although within the United States it's hard to visualize an area so remote that film isn't available, it's sometimes inconvenient to track down a supplier or to wait behind twenty others who also ran out. Overseas it may also be difficult to find your particular kind of film, and it will certainly be much more expensive than at home. So start out each day with at least twice as many packages as you think you might possibly need. We did that in Aegean Turkey—and still ran out by noon. We were delighted to find a peddler who had a single package of film, and eager to pay him three times the U.S. price.

How much film is "plenty"? Eric Ergenbright, president of Thru the Lens Tours, says the average photographer on a photographic tour shoots thirty-five pictures a day. "If you habitually take more pictures than the average photographer of your acquaintance," he advises, "increase your film allowance accordingly." Whether you normally take more or fewer pictures than others gives you a clue to film needs, but you have to consider the time of year, the length of daylight, the weather, the character and interest of the sites, the number of different kinds of things you expect to see on your trip—and then double the maximum amount you think you'll want.

Sometimes it's possible to return unused film to the camera shop if it's fresh-dated, has been kept cool, and the boxes are in perfect condition. If not, put the leftovers in the refrigerator or in the freezer, carefully wrapped. Experts recommend thawing for half a day to bring the film up to room temperature before using. Several years after their expiration dates your rolls of film will be as good as new, if they have been correctly stored.

Although American airport X-rays are not considered dangerous to unprocessed film, there seems to be a cumulative fogging effect. So if you are passing through more than a couple of airports on your trip or traveling through overseas security, where they sometimes use stronger X-rays, either carry all your film in lead-laminated pouches (available at camera shops) or remove film from your carry-on bag and request a hand inspection at the airport.

Since U.S. federal agencies are said to be the major purchasers of the lead film shields, apparently they don't believe the statement that airport X-rays are harmless. Even the lead pouches cannot completely protect against the very strong X-rays used at some foreign airports, as travelog producer Earl Dibble discovered. When all his film was destroyed in the Soviet Union he complained to the company that makes the film shield. The president of the company explained that "the X-ray device employed in Moscow emits a dose of X-rays some ten thousand times greater that 90 percent of the world's airports. To protect film under these circumstances, nothing less than three inches of lead would have sufficed."

If it's necessary to leave film in your checked baggage or mail it across international borders, be sure to mark the outside of the container "Unprocessed Photographic Film. Please Do Not X-ray." (See Chapter 15 for further discussion of photography.)

Take Along a Tape Recorder

The third indispensable item in the travel writer's luggage is a small, light-weight cassette tape recorder. Before the cassette era I once met a woman who told me she prepared for her around-the-world trip by writing in a diary every night to "cultivate the habit." For most of us, who write something every day anyway, that wouldn't be necessary. But no matter how sincerely we promise ourselves to keep extensive trip diaries, to record every detail in our notebooks, to send meaningful trip letters and write descriptive postcards, our willingness to tell the microphone more than we'd ever put on paper makes the cassette recorder very handy. You're so tired when you return from a wonderful day of sight-seeing, full of the thrilling adventures you've experienced, just finding the pen and paper seems like a formidable chore. You'll do it tomorrow; tomorrow, for sure, you'll write it all down. But with the tape recorder, you'll find it easy to talk a running diary-trip letter, and you'll include details you'd never bother with on paper.

Don't forget, though, to take brief, on-scene notes so you'll remember what to tell the tape recorder. It's better yet to take the recorder along when you're sight-seeing, and develop the habit of dictating into it everything you're seeing and everything you know about it. You'll never have to wonder later: How high are the foothills? Is the church on the same street as the school, or around the corner? Why did the ship founder on the rocks? How many people can play on the golf course? When did they serve the sherbet—before or after the meat?

Always tell your tape recorder the answers to the reporter's traditional five Ws—*Who, What, When, Where, Why*—and add the *How*. You can, of course, record the sight-seeing guide's complete spiel, if you like, and if the guide has no objection. But keep in mind, voices in the open air do not carry as well as voices indoors, and voices with strong accents will reproduce with the accents exaggerated. So perhaps you'll want some written notes, too. Do take the time to label and date each side of the tape, jotting down a few words about the contents of each side.

Certainly you will use your cassette recorder to capture street sounds and native music. The yodelers, the bagpipers, the church bells, the muezzins voices calling from the minarets, all come to life again when you hear the tapes.

You'll probably also take it along to interviews you've scheduled along the way—asking for permission to tape, of course. Here, too, it will be easier to remember what the historian said, what the fisherman said, what the bank president said, what the lacemaker said, if you have it down on tape, rather than trying to unscramble it from scribbled notes.

One man used the tape recorder to great advantage when violence erupted on a Mediterranean island several years ago. He was caught in the gunfire and the bombings, which he was able to record. He also dictated a description of his plight and, later, of his dramatic rescue. Then he airmailed the cassette to a network newscaster in exchange for a substantial sum.

Even if the information on the tape itself is not salable, it may provide you with deeper insights and endless enjoyment. My husband and I laugh again each time we listen to a tape made on an overnight train when the wife of one of our host country's high government officials invited us into her VIP compartment. She and her two children were traveling to join her husband on holiday, and she apologized profusely because he had already driven ahead with the hard liquor, so she had no "spirits" to offer us. She made up for it, though, by dipping generously into a case of sherry, which she had already sampled liberally. She enthusiastically agreed to our taping the conversation, but her humorous, pungent—and slightly tipsy—comments on the inner political workings of the United States and of her own country could never be printed. The tape, however, with its background noises of children playing and train wheels going clickety-clack against the tracks, provides enrichment for other stories.

Foreign language tapes can be great for filling you in on the refresher course you've been studying. But if you're in a country where English is often garbled and directions are complex—a country like Thailand, for instance—have the hotel concierge or a knowledgeable guide dictate the directions for how to get where you're going in his own language. Then you can play the directions back for the cab driver or someone on the street who is trying to help you. Also be sure to have dictated the name of your hotel and how to find it.

Still another function of the tape recorder is to play music-cassettes of your choice that you've brought along. In addition to providing pleasant background for picnic lunches and pre-dinner relaxation, your own music can drown out crashes and bangs from the street outside or uncongenial music, television programs, or loud voices from the hotel room next door.

Although microcassette tape recorders are smaller—they even fit into a shirt pocket—the standard size give better tone quality, and it's easier to find tapes if you run out. Although various forms of Palm Pilots, DVDs and other 21st century equipment can be extremely useful, the tape recorder should not be left out of the travel writer's luggage.

Surprisingly, I once had the tape recorder, but not the cameras, confiscated for the duration of a Middle East flight during unsettled times. Generally, though, nobody has objected to the tapes or the recorder. Presumably X-rays don't hurt the cassettes, and often they're as easy to mail as trip letters. In sensitive countries, though, post office superintendents may insist on hearing what you've got on the tape before they let you mail it. Sometimes they're inquisitive about film, too. From some countries it's wiser not to mail at all—consider the political situation.

Pack a Supply of Manuscript Envelopes

Mail also plays an important part in the travel writer's fourth essential tool, a supply of large manuscript envelopes. These are especially important if you are traveling overseas by air and luggage is weighed; or squeezed into a small car, six adults with suitcases between the knees; or traveling by bus, where baggage is limited; or making many connections, where each extra ounce is a nuisance. You save weight and bulk by mailing home at the media rate (every country has a less expensive media or book rate) all the guides, maps, theater programs, museum catalogs, statistics, historical data, hotel brochures, menus, newspapers, magazines, and other printed literature you find along the way.

Make an effort to pick up as much of this material as possible. Naturally you'll take everything that's free. And don't be too frugal about buying what isn't. You'll be amazed at the way this printed material fills in the gaps when you get home and can't remember how many people can be accommodated at Tree Tops or when the first shrine was built in Cordoba.

You soon develop an inner sense about what to mail home to back up your impressions. You'll guess which materials not to bother with because they're likely to be in the vertical files of your local library, and you'll guess which ones your library would never have. Some materials you can borrow from a friend who made the same trip, or some you can easily send for later. But if in doubt, take it, and mail it in your big manuscript envelope. If your package is heavy, use two envelopes, one inside the other, to keep the corners from tearing through. If you're in a hurry, of course, you'll send your envelope airmail.

The envelopes themselves, while easy to buy in U.S. drug and variety stores as well as in stationery shops, are often hard to find overseas. I wish I had a dollar for every time someone has stopped me in a foreign hotel lobby, as I was about to take my big envelope to the post office, to ask, "Where did you find that? I've looked *everywhere* for envelopes like that!" So tuck a supply into the bottom of your suitcase before you begin to pack.

With your big envelopes, your cassette recorder, your camera, and your printed business cards, you're ready to function as a travel writer, for these are the tools the average travel writer needs most.

But some of us are special. We've spent years experimenting and adding to our lists of unique needs and take-along requirements. Obviously, different travel writers traveling by different means, with different objectives, have their own individual "musts."

Special Needs of Travel Writers

If your story is to grow out of your backpacking, mule riding, or wagon-training trip, you'll need to take along the appropriate equipment. If skateboarding, houseboating, motorcycling, or caravanning are your style, you'll need to be outfitted still differently. And if you're thinking of taking your four-wheel drive into the bush, you may want to follow the advice of Michael Bargo, Jr., who suggests in *Four Wheeler* that you carry along "all the spare parts you know how to repair." Every travel writer must take the supplies he needs for his own distinct traveling interests as well as the more general items we all find essential. Here is a checklist of things especially pertinent to the travel writer's trip:

1. *Assignment sheet.* Don't laugh! In the confusion of taking off, it's easy to forget which editors said "yes" to what, and which ones said "maybe." You probably have ideas of your own about what trip stories you'll surely write, and you'll want to keep an eye out for the stories in which editors expressed interest, but when it comes to arranging your travel time this sheet will ensure your allowing enough for the firm assignments.

2. *Itinerary.* Unless it's a real "spur-of-the-moment" excursion, have several copies of your itinerary distributed among your luggage. Put a copy in the casing of your luggage tags, including hotel names and dates—it might prevent your lost luggage from being sent home at the very beginning of your trip.

3. *Address list.* Addresses and telephone numbers of those people you plan to call or see on your trip and those you may need to call or write to at home.

4. *Tickets, vouchers, and confirmations.* Check, and check again, to be sure you have your tickets for transportation, theater, sports events, or whatever else you've arranged. Check on your vouchers for lodging, food, sightseeing tours or other items you may have prepaid, and your confirmed

reservations for everything from the boat ride at Waterton Lake to the campsite at Yosemite.

5. *Documents.* Your identification and credit cards, as well as membership cards, essential health records, letters of introduction, and whatever else you need. Notify your bank if you'll be using your ATM card overseas— a series of withdrawals from unexpected places may cause enough suspicion to have them block your account. And be sure to take along the Entertainment Card appropriate to your travel area. You've probably already used it for discounts on your hotel reservations, but you'll want it for meal discounts, too. The entertainment people are generous with press review books, so if you think you're entitled to one, call Bob McHenry at (800) 999-2234, ext. 8432.

6. *Travel literature.* Condense all pertinent information into the margins of one guidebook. Then tear out and discard any parts of the guidebook that don't apply to where you're going. There's no use carting along South America when you're only visiting Chile and Peru. Don't forget, though, to take along those city and country maps you've been studying.

7. *Postcards and snapshots.* The people you meet enjoy seeing pictures of your town, neighborhood, house, family, pets, car, and holiday celebrations. Books about your area, as well as the postcards, become treasured gifts.

8. *Hardbacked writing surface*—a lap pillow or clipboard for taking notes, expanding notes, jotting down comments, writing letters, and other scribblers' tasks while riding in a car or bus or sailing on a boat or ship. Don't forget to take plenty of notebooks, and put your name and local address on whatever one you're using.

9. *Small change.* Regardless of the financial plans you make with debit cards and traveler's checks, regardless of what country you're in, always begin each day with a pocketful of small change so you won't be paying ten times the price for a newspaper or have the cab driver tell you he can't change a twenty-dollar bill or have to choose between tipping five cents or two dollars for a five-dollar service.

10. *Alarm clock*—especially if you distrust hotels' wake-up systems or stay where they don't provide that service. One veteran travel writer recommends a pocket alarm for air travelers: "Set it for a couple of hours before landing or you'll never get to the bathroom." He blames the bathroom bottleneck on women who consider it "a private dressing room." If you set your pocket alarm far enough ahead of the face fixers, you'll be sure to get your turn.

11. *Flashlight.* This is very important if you awaken in a strange hotel room or at a strange camp ground, disoriented, in the middle of the night. It's also important when you sight-see in caves, catacombs, and other dim

areas like Egypt's Valley of the Nobles, where the illumination—sunlight ricocheting off a pocket mirror—barely permits you to see the frescoes *with* your flashlight. Take along a pen flashlight, too, so you can jot down your thoughts in a darkened theater or write up your middle-of-the-night inspiration. Traveling by car in North America? Tuck a 100-watt bulb or tensor lamp in your suitcase. Motel rooms seldom provide enough light for a travel writer.

12. *Magnifying glass*—indispensable for reading maps and essential for buying jewelry, wonderful for viewing nature's or a museum's treasures. I usually remember to take one on long trips but was furious with myself for forgetting when I traveled thirty-five miles to see a special exhibit in San Francisco.

13. *Batteries.* At least one complete set of extras for everything you're taking that requires batteries. If they are an unusual type, take two sets. Although small batteries can be found for sale nearly everywhere, they're rarely available at midnight, when you're telling the tape recorder what you saw today; or at noon, when you're shooting a flash picture inside the cavern, three miles from the souvenir shop; or at five in the morning, when you're shaving before an early flight.

14. *Glasses.* While every traveler takes care of his eyes, the travel writer needs to be especially vigilant about possible eye-related problems. If you wear glasses or contact lenses, take along an extra pair and your prescription. Take sunglasses and a sun hat to keep your vision clear on bright days.

15. *Plastic bags*, especially the zipper lock ones, are handy for carrying everything from half-a-dozen paper clips to a wet bathing suit.

16. A *first aid kit.* While every traveler has his own special "can't do without," it's generally a good idea to have such items as small bandages, mild pain relievers, and cough drops, as well as insect repellent and sunscreen.

I used to always recommend taking along a Swiss Army knife, and I still think it's a good idea. But present day inspections of passengers and carry-on luggage make it a good idea only if it is packed in your checked suitcase.

Recommended Overseas Take-Alongs

The travel writer who goes abroad should also take along:

1. *Documents.* Your passport, visas, tourist cards, International Drivers License, and whatever other foreign travel documents you need.

2. *Extra passport photographs*—for extra visas or other official documents.

3. *Currency converter* or pocket calculator, for changing dollars to guilders or pesos.

4. *Foreign language phrase book*, if appropriate. Even more appropriate might be a fairly new device, the hand-held translator that, with different cartridges, converts some fifty English phrases and fifteen hundred English words into any of thirteen languages, and vice versa. In any case, don't forget your culinary translations.

5. *A short-wave radio* is a plus under some circumstances and may be worth taking if you're heading for faraway places and need to keep up with what's going on in the rest of the world.

6. *Binoculars?* Perhaps. Animal sighting and ship identifying would be among their uses.

7. *Extra notebooks*, typing paper, colored pens, paper clips, pen refills, rubber bands, and that product of a thousand uses—cellophane tape.

It's often hard to find what you need away from home, and the search uses up lots of travel time.

Will You Actually Write on the Road?

You'll notice that I haven't said anything about a typewriter or a computer. While some writers won't stir without their laptops and others lug word processors or memory typewriters, still others rely on a tape recorder, take notes, visit cybercafes, or hire a local stenographer. If you'll be in one place long enough to really pound a keyboard, by all means take it, especially on a cruise or to a resort. If, on the other hand, you're planning a series of one- and two-night stands, you may find the lugging costs more than the productivity is worth. However, laptop computers are getting lighter and cheaper, and electronic notebooks can be useful note-takers.

Even faxing and photocopying are possible on-the-go. A fairly new three-and-a-half-pound plain paper copier fits easily into a briefcase and produces copies in 40 seconds. The price? Under $400.

If you do plan to take some electronic or electrical helper, be sure the wiring on the ship or in the hotel is compatible and will be adequate for your recharging purposes. Also be sure you won't be disturbing those in the next room or cabin.

Sometimes you can borrow equipment from the ship's purser or the hotel desk clerk, or they'll let you use what they have in the office after hours. More and more hotels, airports, and other travel facilities provide Internet access in one way or another. For a list of cybercafes near your destination, log on to Cybercafes.com (www.cybercafe.com) to locate the most convenient ones all over the world.

Some writers may feel it's more important to take along their research resources than their writing tools. With a PDA device, the personal digital assistant, able to carry programs, contacts, and notes you may need, as well as serve as a wireless connection to the Internet—in a package smaller than a paperback—it's easy to keep your data close. This can easily become the travel writer's best friend.

The Travel Writer's Wardrobe

In addition to whatever professional tools you take on your trip, you'll want to give some thought to your travel wardrobe. Insist on comfort. A travel writer's concentration should not be on his mirror. Naturally, if you're going to the Arctic, you'll pack a different outfit from one suitable for the tropics. Will you need après-ski clothes or protection from mosquitoes and sunburn? If traveling to a variety of climates, dress in layers so you can put on or take off without bother.

Unless you're going to watch the polar bears mating on the ice cap, take only a lightweight, all-weather coat or jacket. In overheated airports, stuffy bus stations, airless hotel lobbies, unventilated vehicles, and warm rooms you'll carry your jacket more than you'll wear it. Outdoors, if necessary, snuggle into a sweater beneath your coat. For every time you say to yourself, "My teeth are chattering—I wish I'd brought a heavier coat," there'll be ten times you'll say to yourself, "Why did I ever bring this coat at all—it feels like I've lugged it ten thousand miles!" The lighter the coat, the more muscle power you'll have left for other necessities.

Again—be comfortable! Don't let what you're wearing get in the way of what you're working on. Unless your trip is built around a posh event, like a coronation, a jet-set wedding, or an opera premiere, the travel writer has far less use for dress-up clothes than for casual everyday wear. So put your fanciest duds back in the closet. Even cruise ships are planning fewer formal nights, but they suggest bringing your workout clothes. Your guidebooks may tell you the kind of clothes you'll need, but the best source is somebody who has traveled to that place or in that manner.

But when you're de-selecting what to take, do not remove from your suitcase two pairs of old, comfortable, well-broken-in shoes. The travel writer with the hurting feet won't be the travel writer with the prose that dances.

The Question of Luggage

When deciding what kind of suitcase(s) will best contain your necessities, consider how you'll be getting where you're going. If it's by public transportation, check out in advance the luggage specifications of each carrier. If you're driving, test the limitations of your baggage space, and give some thought to this problem when ordering a rental car.

If you're going by air, avoid paying over-limit luggage charges. Have extra-large, extra-strong pockets sewn into your topcoat. In areas where luggage is weighed, carry all heavy items—the tape recorder, guidebook, even a pair of shoes—in your pockets. In places where luggage is counted, rather than weighed, put the *heaviest* items in your suitcases and the *lightest* ones in your pockets.

Inquire how many and what size checked and carry-on pieces are permitted for each leg of your journey. Sometimes local airlines, used for brief hops, have more stringent restrictions on the amount of luggage allowed, but will relax the rules if you have an ongoing ticket for other destinations. Airlines often make special arrangements for such special items as computers, skis, golf clubs, and fishing rods.

Even without camouflaging the weight or bulk of their possessions, women travel writers need pockets in jackets, shirts, skirts, and pants, and many men travel writers find that carrying a shoulder bag gives them a convenient container for all those extras, like maps and spare batteries and cassettes. Pockets and bags leave hands free to wield a pen, tune a recorder, or focus a camera.

On a long trip, start out with an additional small box or suitcase inside your luggage. Fill it as you go along, and send it home with everything you find you can spare. It's easier to unload a little way into your long trip as you discover what you aren't using. If you are a U.S. citizen, mark the send-home package "American Goods Returned" or "Used Clothing and Effects" for duty-free passage.

Since porters are becoming increasingly rare, be sure your luggage has wheels. Never take more pieces or bigger pieces than you can manage yourself. Above all, be sure your carry-on case has wheels or rides on a dolly. This is the case into which you're always stuffing the heaviest, bulkiest items—the telephoto lens, the hiking boots, the bronze sculpture you bought Aunt Hattie, the duty-free perfume, and Gibbons's *Decline and Fall* to read on the plane; and this is the bag you're always having to carry yourself through the labyrinth of airport corridors and the jungle of arrival and departure lounges.

Travel writing doctor Burt Kebric points proudly to his seven-week trip around the world—and many subsequent trips—with his only luggage a bowling bag that fits beneath an airplane seat. Certainly there's much in favor of an arrangement that requires no wait for the baggage to be delivered *from* the transport vehicle or to the hotel room but remains always in your possession.

In any event, always identify the *outside* of your luggage with your initials or your office business card. A home address tempts robbers, who now know you're away from home; but put full information on the inside of all baggage. For quick identification, tie two strands of colored ribbon or yarn, in identical combination, to the outside of each suitcase, carry-on bag, camera case, or coat. Keep a mental count of how many different parcels you should have with you at each stop, so a click in your brain will alert you—something's missing! Remind yourself frequently, "I should be toting four things (why do I have only three?)."

When traveling overseas, find out the luggage and customs regulations of each country on your planned itinerary. Although most countries aren't too rigid about enforcement, it's expedient to know how many cameras, rolls of film, and other special items they officially permit you to carry in. Be sure to register all foreign-made cameras, tape recorders, watches, and other valuables with your own customs before you leave so there will be no question about what you have bought abroad this trip.

The travel writer is first of all a traveler. With each trip you become more adept at planning so you don't drag along too many things you rarely use, and you can manage without the things you left behind. The comfortable, well-equipped, but unencumbered traveler is the one likely to find the story with plus value.

SEVEN

What to Look for
As You Travel

Well equipped and well prepared, here you are—on the scene at last. You look around and wonder where to begin—there's so much to see, hear, smell, taste, touch, know, and enjoy.

Sometimes you start by looking for particular information to flesh out specific ideas or to fit specific markets. Other times you approach the travel experience with an open mind, waiting for your story to find you.

In homes or palaces, temples or cemeteries, deserts or rain forests, the travel writer is always exploring, sampling the action, seeing for himself whether there's anything worth writing about.

You have to remain aware and alert, continually searching for ideas and information. Even "relaxed," on holiday, your mind is always working. One travel writer, who says 100 percent of his wanderings are related to writing and selling articles, admits that even short trips to attend weddings or visit his parents provide the basis for future travel pieces. That's because he's always on the lookout for the potential story.

When a story finds you, sometimes you immediately recognize its plus value. When we joined Japan's "Strangers into Friends" program, our visit to a Japanese home included a venerable grandmother who tore open her kimono to show us her gall bladder scar; a family argument about whether to buy a motor car, which the old lady vetoed as too dangerous; and a farewell, with us standing in the doorway struggling into our shoes while the beautiful young daughter accompanied herself on her koto as she sang, "Oh, say can you see by the dawn's early light. . . ."

Other times the story seems elusive and you have to create the plus value. On the Mediterranean island of Malta we saw what seemed like a jumble of prehistoric temples, Roman ruins, reminders of the Knights, beach resorts, British tourists, and bomb damage. It was hard to fuse them into an article. Then hospitable locals gave me a clue. Remembering that Saint Paul, shipwrecked on Malta, was also well treated by the native people, I emphasized Maltese hospitality over a period of thousands of years, which gave my story a focus.

Look for That Special Angle, Other Stories, Too

Usually the best stories cover all the ordinary things as well as some special, unique angle. Search for that special angle while you're traveling. But don't neglect the "ordinary."

Search out the details of your story, but also remain on the lookout for additional stories. Often you'll see something more interesting than you expect.

I had intended, for instance, to include a paragraph or two about the museum of San Francisco's Presidio in an article about nearby Fort Point. Exploring the museum, however, I found there was much more than military history there. The diorama of the 1806 Presidio, with a Russian ship in the background and a Russian captain in the foreground, reminds viewers that the captain fell in love with "the prettiest girl in California," who waited many years for him, only to learn that he had died on his trip home seeking permission to marry her. The diorama of the San Francisco earthquake and fire is flanked by pictures of the city before the calamity, of the city being rebuilt, of the 1915 Panama Pacific International Exposition, of the building of the bridges, and of Alcatraz and Angel Island. From an exhibit of Civil War clothing and antique medical equipment to models of the early missions and a collection of John Wayne memorabilia, here was a fascinating museum, deserving a story of its own.

"Sometimes the best story ideas come from the little happenings that fall through the cracks in the itinerary floor," says Dee Henri. She tells of traveling to Nova Scotia in a forty-six person bus which stopped unexpectedly at a tiny roadside cafe. The single young waitress-cook was overwhelmed, simply unable to serve so many cold, hungry tourists; whereupon the passengers made themselves at home in the kitchen, opening cans of soup, brewing coffee, and serving each other. "The spirit of the lunch stop was more impressive than the sights we saw," says Henri.

Orientation Comes First

A brief sight-seeing tour is the best way to orient yourself to the important landmarks and obtain an overview of the topography. Try for an aisle seat so you can see and photograph both sides and be first out when the bus stops. Sit or stand near the guide. Don't be bashful. Ask questions. If you're overflowing with questions—too many to ask—try to determine which answers you'll be able to find elsewhere—and ask the other ones. If the guide is a good one, write down his name and address in case you have a question to ask later. (If you do write later, be sure to enclose a self-addressed, stamped envelope or, if he's in another country, an International Reply Coupon, purchased at the post office.) If the guide is a *very* good one, write a complimentary letter to his boss, to encourage excellence in tour guides.

Don't rely completely, however, on everything the tour guide says—or even on the written information at the monument you are examining. James W. Loewen's *Lies Across America* explains that the log cabin where Abraham Lincoln was supposedly born was actually built 30 years after his death, and George Washington was nowhere near Valley Forge the winter he was depicted praying in the snow.

Whether or not you take subsequent tours, do rely on public transportation for much of your sight-seeing. Procure a good map of the bus or subway system. If you are in a hurry in a big city, take the subway. But if you want to see the people and the neighborhoods, the kids walking home from school, the housewives pinching the fruit at the greengrocer's, the workers relaxing on front stoops, look for surface transportation. In addition to buses, trolley cars, and trams, consider the jitney, the shared taxi so popular in many areas; horse-drawn carriages; rickshaws. Bicycles and motorcycles give you still a different view, as you actually become part of the street scene. Riding a funicular or a cable railway or even on top of a double-decker bus presents another perspective—farther removed, more telescopic.

Don't Miss the Offshore Perspective

Whenever you can, go by water. Practically all riverfront or lakefront areas offer waterborne transportation. From Westminster, for instance, you can take a water bus along the Thames, downstream as far as Greenwich, upstream as far as Hampton Court. Queen Elizabeth floated no more comfortably. The boat on Lake Geneva is a floating kaffeeklatsch. Mrs. A. embarks in Geneva, saving three seats for her friends; Mrs. B. comes aboard ten minutes later from the dock of a lakeside house; Mrs. C. boards at a small village five minutes away; then they order coffee and cakes, so they're all ready when Mrs. D. joins them at the next boat stop. The four chatter in rapid-fire French all the way to Montreux. The travel writer may not understand a word they say, but their appearance, their postures, their gestures, offer intimate insights that flesh out the story.

One of the world's biggest transportation bargains is a ride on a ferryboat. While on assignment in Turkey, we remained on deck as the ferry that leaves from Istanbul's Galata Bridge sailed past the elegant DolmaBaHce

Palace and the frowning fortifications of Rumeli Hisar and Anadolu Hisar. We zigzagged between European Turkey and Asiatic Turkey, letting off and taking on passengers and cargo at dozens of docks. Water traffic of all kinds crisscrossed the Bosporus around us. After debarking in Sariyer, where the restaurant sent a fisherman out front to catch our lunch, we took a bus back to Istanbul. The half-hour ride through fields, orchards, and peasant villages taught us much about rural Turkey. On-the-spot "research" aboard the bus and the ferry provided background for a number of stories.

It's not hard to find exotic transport. I've ridden a camel, an elephant, a mule, a donkey, and an ostrich—and I'm not a real show-off.

Nothing Beats Shoe Leather

Camel rides across the Sahara or mule rides through the Alps can make for interesting articles focused on the method of transportation, but often such episodes are just one sentence of a story. Exotic conveyances can help you get the feel of a place, but overall, the most satisfactory type of transportation for a travel writer is shoe leather. On your own two feet is the best way to catch the most intimate glimpses of everyday life, as well as close-ups of parades, fiestas, and wedding processions.

To really know what a place is like you have to see its most important landmarks several times, at different hours of the day. Some sights, like the Taj Mahal or the Pyramids, are always surrounded by rapt tourists at special times—sunrise, sunset, the light of the full moon; but even the modest plaza in a Mexican village looks different and feels different at dawn, at noon, and at twilight.

Notice what they call their plazas and squares and how they name their streets. Is the town laid out with First Street and Second Street intersecting A and B and C? Or are the streets, the squares, the gates, the areas named for famous people? What kinds of famous people? Politicians? Generals? Writers? Artists? Musicians? Entertainers? Millionaires? Sometimes it's the date that's important—Mexico City's Avenida 16 de Septiembre (named for the Mexican Independence Day) or Buenos Aires's Avenida 9 Julio (a crucial day in Argentina's struggle for liberty).

The place names give you the flavor of the community. California's San Jose and La Jolla, New Orleans's Bienville Street, Chartres Street, and Beauregard Square, evoke the areas' origins. Be sure to note interesting names to use later in stories or titles. Or write an article about the names themselves. A newspaper story, datelined Norway, Maine, explains how such a true-blue Yankee state happens to have place names ranging from Madrid, Moscow, and Mexico to Paris, Poland, and Peru. Other travel writers have studied the history or patterns of street names or town names in certain areas and have come up with salable stories.

Other clues to what the people of an area consider important can be found in their parks. Often there'll be trees planted by well-known people, noteworthy political or military figures. Prime ministers and rear admirals are invited to plant trees in parks all over the world. In whose honor were the fountains, statues, or other monuments erected? Are there more playing fields or hothouses? Has the city attempted to provide green space for its citizens?

Some museums have special information they hand out for school children's field trips. Get a copy of it if you can. Many experienced museum-goers recommend that you begin at the end—at the gift shop. They say you'll find the experience more rewarding if you first browse through the available guidebooks and check the postcard display for the showstoppers.

The travel writer needs to look for the universal as well as the specific. Never be a mere name dropper, enumerating the airports and train stations you've waited in during your trip. Instead, cultivate the essence of the place so you can interpret it for others.

What If It Rains?

A very significant question to ask your tour guide, your bus driver, or any other local expert—a question not often answered in your pre-trip research—is, "What is there to do if it rains?" If the downpour drowns out your planned activity, your travel umbrella was capsized by the wind, and your traveling companion has the sniffles, what is your fallback position?

Often there's some very interesting alternative—you just have to know about it. Then you can even write an article about what to do when fog and drizzle envelope Ayers Rock or the Adirondacks.

Tune In to Details

Improve your travel stories by *noticing*. Observe the trees and shrubs and flowers. Are the gardens well-kept or weed-filled? Are there plants in the windowboxes? Trash on the sidewalk? Animals wandering in the streets? Iron bars on downstairs windows? Are there street peddlers? Hawking what? Lots of advertising signs? Promoting what? You learn a great deal when you *notice*.

We should notice with *all* of our senses. We need to remind ourselves later how it sounded—the clear chorus of church bells, the hoarse groans of the foghorns, the echoing footsteps of a solitary walker, the cascading of stream water over rocks, the shrill sound of a single bagpipe.

Do your feet notice cobbled streets or dusty roads? Will your fingers trace the pattern of a New Orleans balcony rail or an Arizona pueblo? How do they feel, the rough, unmortared stones of the seawall?

What do we smell? Fish frying? Damp wool? Incense? Cedar trees? Hot tar? The smells are part of the place—and part of the story.

Taste is important. Does clam chowder taste different in Boston than in San Francisco? Try the reindeer steak or bird's nest soup or the borscht. Taste comingles with the sights and sounds and smells when you eat sushi at a standup counter or tamales on a street corner or drink coconut milk on a palm-shaded beach, etching the scene on your brain.

Absorbing local color is not enough. *Record* it. If you don't have your tape recorder along, jot down reminders in your field notebook and amplify them on a cassette later.

Meet the Local People

Visit a family at home if you possibly can. Practically every country has a program that encourages local families to extend hospitality to visitors with similar hobbies, professions, interests, or whatever.

Better still, take along the names of friends of friends, relatives of relatives, and even acquaintances of acquaintances. Any opportunity to see how local people live provides the travel writer with invaluable background material for stories. It's within the family circle that you really grasp the people's relationships with each other, their relationship to their government, and their relationship to the rest of the world, whether they live in august mansions crumbling in shabby gentility or in overcrowded apartments with wall-to-wall sleeping bags. The food they serve you is important in more ways than your observation of the kind of food it is. How it's served is a clue to the people's lifestyle. So is who is eating. Do the women do the serving, but don't serve themselves? Is the oldest person present served first? Are the children at the table?

Do the people speak freely about their government's shortcomings or parrot "everything's perfect" slogans? Sometimes when you dig a little deeper, long-held images are shattered. At a Moscow apartment the college professor's wife complained about the difficulty of obtaining eyeglasses in the former Soviet Union. The American visitors wondered how she had managed to procure the ones she wore. "Oh, *glasses* you can get," she said. "But it's impossible to find any designer frames."

Play where the local people play. One of my favorite memories of Venice is a vaporetto ride to the Lido, where we bounced a beachball with a group of Italian children and sipped red wine in paper cups with a visiting family from Naples. Of course, I wrote about it.

Eat where the locals eat. Sit and sip at a sidewalk cafe. Order the house specialty. Talk to the waiter. Don't rush. Observe. Eavesdrop. Stare.

Seek out old-timers to spin yarns about yesterday. You'll often find these people, who are, as John Wright says, "priceless" to the story, at the local mom-and-pop cafe. Search for a restaurant that's "a step above a greasy spoon, but a cut below fancy nonsense."

Picnic in the park. Let the sun caress your shoulders. Listen to the squeals of the children somersaulting on the grass. Watch the grandfathers pondering the next move in their eternal chess game. Taste the vanilla ice cream. Listen to the calls of the local birds. Throw back the errant ball that comes your way.

Go to the grocery store. Is it a supermarket, selling everything from laundry detergent to fresh fish, from shampoo to tennis shoes? Are the displays of canned goods veiled in layers of dust, their prices so high in relation to wages that the display is merely decorative?

Go to the outdoor markets too. You have to start before dawn at Bangkok's Floating Market, where mangoes and bananas, coconuts and papayas are bargained for and bought from boat to boat, and you, drifting through the klongs and canals, are poled right into the center of the action. Start early, too, for Curaçao's colorful Schooner Market, where dockside customers haggle with vendors in sailboats for fresh fish, exotic vegetables, and flashy fabrics. Go early, also, to Singapore's Chinatown, where customers dicker for snakes and lizards to brew into virility-producing broths; to North African suqs, where they sell spices and grape leaves and tiny cups of strong, sweet Turkish coffee; or to Pennsylvania Dutch markets selling pig stomachs, Amish pretzels, and old-fashioned sweet bologna.

Stop in at the boulangerie, which lures you with the seductive smell of crusty bread and chocolate tarts, and the charcuterie, where the aging lamb is flanked by a pair of peacocks and a selection of wild hares.

You may be surprised at some of the places where food is sold. Ferryboats which cross international boundaries may cater to long lines of people who've taken the ride for the groceries. As soon as the boat's commissary opens, the passengers crowd around, eager to buy coffee, liquor, and whatever edibles and potables are scarce or expensive in their own country.

Soak Up Local Color at Laundromats and Shops

You will also get a realistic view of the people at the laundromat. Who's there? Career singles from the roominghouses in the next block? Camping families with muddy duffle? Senior citizens? I remember a stormy day in Southern California when the first mate of a small ketch commandeered all the dryers for her life jackets, cushions, bedding, foul weather gear, and dock lines. On another day, halfway around the world, in Alice Springs, Australia, an aborigine woman lugged into the laundromat bag after bag of blankets, towels, and clothing—enough for every washing machine in the place—as five children marched behind her, licking dripping ice cream cones that were getting their shirts into condition for next month's wash. Puerto

Vallarta's main "laundromat" was on the edge of town—rocks for scrubbing, riverbank for drying. Immediately behind the washing area, at the city-built playground, the children of the laundresses sing as they scramble down the slides or swing out over the sharp stones. You can learn a lot at the laundromat. (Someday I'm going to write an article about conversations overheard in a cruise ship laundromat!)

Check out the department stores. Do they feature more dress patterns and sewing notions than ready-mades? More work shoes than ski boots? Electric orange juicers; manually operated orange juicers; or no juicers at all? What does all this tell you about the people in this community? How about the local shoppers in the department store? Are they queued up for a special bargain or because some household item, heretofore in short supply, has just been received by the store? Are people carrying string bags or elaborately decorated shopping bags? Do they look well dressed? Fashionable? Are they swathed in furs or shivering through threadbare wraps on a cold day?

Are most of the items in the store manufactured locally? If not, where are they from? What other services does the store offer? One huge Tokyo department store not only presents kimono fashion shows and demonstrates the art of flower arranging but also provides lessons in the use of knives and forks—for chopstick users who want to learn Western ways.

Don't stop with the department stores. Visit the specialty shops, the bazaars, the suqs, the flea markets. "Shopping" is more than a frivolous pastime when you're searching for your story.

Even beauty parlors and barbershops abound in clues to an area's reality. One travel writer says he's had his hair cut in countries around the world. He feels that barber shops give him insights into what the country is all about. During my own first time in Cairo, sixteen different people worked on my simple shampoo and set, from the young girl who handed me a plastic-bagged comb, brush, and towel, to the man who, two hours later, wielded the hairspray can. How to tip? Egyptian and European ladies were going around dispensing the equivalent of one cent to the teenager who brought the coffee, five cents to the shampoo girl, two cents to the young boy who removed the rollers, and ten cents to the maestro who set the hair, etc. That bit of local color found its way into one of my stories on Egypt.

Join the Congregation

While many of us are naturally reluctant to intrude upon the religious rites of others, I've often stumbled into a ceremony and been invited to stay: a prayer meeting in a Turkish mosque; a christening in a Greek church; a coming-of-age ceremony at Saint Peter's and another one, very different, at the Wailing Wall in Jerusalem; a Buddhist funeral in Japan; a Presbyterian wedding in Brisbane. Religious ceremonies always provide special insights. Be sure to look up your own religious affiliates when you travel. You'll not only meet pleasant people, but you'll probably be invited to attend a coffee hour after the service, a congregational pot-luck supper, or the annual Sunday school picnic.

Do you feel you could never bear to see a bullfight? You might find it less gory and more interesting than you expect. And the real show is the people around you and how they act and react.

Ball games bore you? Don't be too sure. Whether it's sandlot or Super Bowl, with a little pregame explanation you'll understand enough of the action to understand the other spectators' enjoyment.

Too old for circuses? No, you're not. Applaud the elephant ballet and shiver in fear for the high-wire artists along with the rest of the audience.

The successful travel writer not only attends the event, he observes the crowd. Watching the people around you often leads to a story angle. My article about the Boxing Day race meeting in Auckland, New Zealand, focused on the women spectators' hats. In an era when women everywhere practically never covered their heads, these stunningly dressed kiwis all wore their millinery proudly. I guessed there must be a reason, so I asked the woman in front of me in the buffet line. It's an annual contest, she explained, sponsored by Auckland's milliners, with a prize—a vacation in Australia for two—given for the most attractive hat at the meeting.

One of the most pleasant evenings I've ever spent was in Tampere, Finland, at the Pyynikki open-air revolving theater, where the audience is moved around to face the various changes of scene. We didn't need to understand a word of Finnish. The play was obviously the old story of the farmer's daughter and the traveling salesman. The audience laughed at all the right places. My readers enjoyed hearing about it, too.

The best part of participating in local entertainment is your opportunity to see the people of the area relaxed and having a good time. You learn from watching them, talking to them, joining them in joy, fear, amusement, grief, devotion, satisfaction, or anxiety.

Although *Sleeping Beauty* in Moscow was one of the most beautiful ballets I've ever seen, what I wrote about was the young Russian girls in front of us who insisted, with gestures, that we share their chocolates, and the coat checkers who told us, in pantomime, that there was still another act, when we thought it was over.

Your readers will want to know how many people were present at any kind of public gathering—parade, concert, ballgame, political demonstration. This figure is not only important in gauging the popularity of the concert artist or the political candidate but it lends meaning to the occasion.

Are there a hundred people waiting in line for the art show to open—or only a dozen? Are there a hundred demonstrators waving signs—or a thousand? I've never forgotten my high school journalism instructor's directions to "count the house" first thing. For a quick estimate, if the crowd is seated, count the number of seats in a row and multiply by the number of rows. If it's a restaurant, count the number of tables and the average number of seats at each table; then consider carefully the degree of fullness of the room. (If the number of seats is common knowledge, all you have to do is count those that are empty.)

Professor Herbert Jacobs of the University of California offered this formula for estimating standing crowds. First measure the length and width of the area in feet; then add the two figures together; if the people seem to be moving around fairly easily, multiply this sum by seven; if they're tightly packed, multiply by ten. Thus, an area 100 by 150 feet—a sum of 250 feet—contains approximately 1,750 freely moving people or 2,500 tightly packed people. Learn to "eyeball" an area measurement. Outdoors, is it bigger than a football field? Indoors, is it as long as three bathtubs or wider than two full-size beds?

Welcome Chance Meetings

While you're traveling, encourage chance encounters. Speak to the person sitting next to you on the plane, train, or bus. That person may turn out to be a pleasant traveling companion; and he may be the very person you need to alert you to an important story breaking along your route. Or he may be from a distant country, with ideas and insights that introduce you to that country in a way that years of reading never could.

Getting lost may be one of the very best ways to see an area. Local people love to show you the route, and the experience often leads the travel writer down interesting bypaths. While struggling with his high school French in France, John Pollack remembered Ben Franklin's advice to let others do *you* a favor if you want them to like you. He went around asking strangers to photograph him with his camera. This led to interesting conversations, vast amounts of inside information—and a huge collection of dull pictures.

While he was able to practice *his* French, in many countries people like to practice *their* English. When an English-speaking person asks for directions they're delighted to help. Never hesitate to ask questions. All over the world, people young and old like to show off their surroundings, and will often take an unbelievable amount of trouble to lead you to something they think you should see. Often the "something" is more charming, less crowded, richer in beauty and meaning than the well-known sight nearby. A stranger's description and a nudge in the right direction led us to the

Roman ruins under the city of Barcelona. Other strangers have sent us to exquisite secluded beaches, exciting but little-known galleries, and hole-in-the-wall restaurants with tasty regional menus. Always listen to local people's recommendations. Pay attention when somebody says, "Don't miss seeing . . ." or "Be sure to stop at. . . ."

Make use of every person-to-person opportunity. Sometimes you'll need special help while pursuing your on-trip research. But finding the individual who can give you the exact information you need isn't as hard as it sounds. Your at-home research provides a starting point. "Then it's easy," says Caryl Hansen. "Ask each source to suggest other sources." Jo Combs likens it to "unraveling a ball of string—find a starting person, and he will direct you to others, who will help you find still others."

While your embassy or consulate might assist in arranging interviews with people you need to see overseas, usually they won't do it until you actually arrive in the country. They've found too many people change plans at the last moment. (Remember, if you need the services of a translator, the interview will take twice as long, so budget your time accordingly.)

Naturally, you'll want to be in good shape when you get where you're going, so do everything you can to avoid jet lag. Try to pre-adapt to the anticipated schedule, and allow yourself a little time to adjust gradually. Adjust gradually, too, to a gigantic change in altitude—wait to work until you can breathe easily.

Common sense should tell us to avoid high heels when climbing the Acropolis or trekking around archaeological excavations. Common sense too, tells us to take along a sweater for evening breezes or air-conditioned restaurants, to dress as much like the locals as possible, and to wear suitable clothing if visiting religious shrines.

Mailing Precautions

In a later chapter we'll discuss photography and photo sources and how to send photographs. But let's say a word here about on-trip mailing of manuscripts, query letters, and research notes. If you're sending the original to an editor, put a copy in another envelope and mail it to yourself at a different time. Even if you're sending it all to yourself, be sure you have two copies, mailed in different envelopes at different times. If you're traveling in a country notorious for the vagaries of its mail service, you may want to keep that second copy with you.

If you're overseas, special air letters are much less expensive to send than ordinary stationery. They work well for queries and editorial and personal correspondence, as long as you don't need an enclosure. Investigate, too, the different kinds of express mail, as well as alternatives to mail service, which seem to proliferate by the week.

Regardless of what type of mailing you're doing, visit the post office or other point of departure yourself. While bellboys and concierges will offer to send your material, their estimate of the charges is not always in your favor, and sometimes, though you've paid for airmail postage, the material is accidentally sent by regular mail. And be sure not to accept an unknown item a stranger wants mailed or carried to the U.S.—it may be an illegal import.

Cultivate "People" Resources

The hotel concierge prides himself on being able to answer practically any question or solve any problem. Ask him for advice and printed information as soon as you arrive. Lois Kirchner forgot to do this at the Park Lane Hotel in London. Only as she was leaving did she discover she could have walked through nearby Green Park to Buckingham Palace and witnessed a leisurely and uncrowded Changing of the Guard.

Others can help you, too. Question the saleslady, the flower seller, the cobbler, the proverbial man in the street. The more people you talk to, the better feel you get for the place, the more you know about it, and the better story you'll write. The dining room maitre d' led one writer to a French organization that dates back to the Druids and gave her the name of a book on the legends of Brittany that was exactly what she needed for a forthcoming story.

Go to a bookstore and ask if they have anything on local history. Listen for folk tales and stories of local heroes. Jot down the names of people and places you'll be able to look up at home.

Be sure to buy local newspapers and magazines (many foreign countries publish English editions also) to find out more about the local scene, as well as events of interest. Read the want ads. Listen to local radio and television programs.

Even though you've done your library research in advance, you may want to pursue some special interest while traveling, and you'll find librarians everywhere glad to help you when you show sincere purpose.

When Winifred Johnson spent four months in Jackson, a town in California's gold country, she visited the museum so often that the curator set aside a special room for her to work in. On days when the museum and the library were closed, docents took her on tours, showing her memorabilia the more casual observer doesn't get to see, some of it from the time of the Gold Rush itself. She did her research in 1850s newspapers and in private homes, whose owners heard about her project and invited her to visit.

James Winchester also found more help than he expected. Trying to complete a *Reader's Digest* assignment about Russian trawlers off Newfoundland, he was ready to give up when he heard on his rental car radio that the Russian oceanography ship working with the trawlers had put into port with a sick seaman. He hurried to the pier, though he didn't really expect to be allowed on the ship. He was, however, welcomed aboard. Many of the crew spoke English. The captain himself took Winchester on a complete tour. Whenever they came to a locked door the captain sent a seaman for the key. While they were waiting—and there were many such waits—they had a glass of vodka, bottoms up. Winchester was happy to report that he upheld the dignity of American journalism by remaining on his feet all day.

Alcohol Can Be a Problem

While you may often deal with less glamorous opportunities for imbibing, you'll still have to work out your own rules about alcohol. Will your hosts be insulted if you refuse? Will you be too sleepy to get your story if you accept? Should you stick to Perrier? A refreshing beer? Wine with lunch? There aren't any "standard" answers.

My own most difficult experience with alcohol ended at a Turkish waterfront cafe in Izmir, where I was the only woman. It had begun several hours earlier in the hotel bar, where our host had ordered a number of American-style drinks. When we arrived at the restaurant he said magnanimously, "We'll have another round." Turning to the waiter, he pointed to me and said, in English, "A screwdriver." I expected the tumblerful of orange juice with the jiggerful of vodka, diluted by ice cubes, that they'd been serving at the hotel bar. What arrived was a ten-ounce tumbler of vodka, with an orange juice chaser. I didn't want to insult our Turkish host; yet I knew there was no way I could add ten ounces of vodka to the drinks I'd already had and still walk out of the restaurant. I remembered I had in my purse, as I often do when I'm in foreign countries, a plastic flask of pure water. I asked the waiter for an empty glass and poured the water into it. By the time I moved the glasses around, poured some of the vodka into my flask, left some in the water glass, and otherwise juggled the liquid refreshments, my host never knew I was spurning his hospitality.

Individual circumstances and your own personality will dictate your response when alcohol is served. But do take into consideration the mores of the people you're with. Strict Muslims would be deeply offended by your invitation to "stop by the Hilton Bar for a drink." But if your Viennese hosts take you out to Grinzing to a *Heuriger*, a "new-wine" garden, they'll be insulted if you don't taste the new wine.

If you, yourself, are opposed to alcohol, don't make an issue of it. If everybody else is drinking, order fruit juice or a soft drink. Toasting is a very important activity in some countries, with rigid rules, but you can participate with an empty glass.

Check into alcohol-related etiquette and establish a pattern that seems comfortable to you. In general, I remind myself that every day is a working day for the travel writer, and a professional manner is imperative.

Knowing what to look for, what to listen for, what to think about, and how to use your other senses are the travel writer's "secret weapons." Take full advantage of your on-scene position as you gather material for the stories you've already planned—and the stories you didn't plan because you didn't know ahead of time what terrific stories they could be.

EIGHT

Put Yourself in Your Reader's Place

Readers—and editors—really appreciate that special information that comes from your personal research. Put yourself in your readers' place. Remember, you are their advance man. While you're there, get all the information your readers might need or want, and record it carefully, so you can pass it on.

Tell them, "Windy San Francisco street corners make the woman with the wraparound skirt wish she'd worn something else," or "If you're going on a houseboat and you like to work crossword puzzles, don't forget to take along a pencil," or "Theater ushers and restroom attendants in many countries expect to be tipped." Explain to first-time ship cruisers that glamorous evening clothes aren't really necessary and that nobody "dresses" the first and last nights or whenever the ship's in port. Mention the fifty-six degree temperature at Carlsbad Caverns, and the fact that 11,400-foot Cuzco is apt to be cold in the evenings and early mornings, even if it's shirtsleeve weather at noon in nearby Machu Picchu.

Tell them the Portland, Oregon, Chamber of Commerce sells plastic raincoats all summer to surprised visitors unprepared for rain. Suggest they have birth certificates notarized for Mexico, observing that you had to cancel a trip when you couldn't find a notary at the airport. Give them the benefit of your experience by encouraging early reservations for camping space in California's state parks or for New Year's at the Williamsburg Inn.

Whenever possible, investigate different travel styles while you're in the area you'll be writing about. Your reader may opt for accommodations, recreation, or sight-seeing very different from what you, personally, would choose. You owe him the courtesy of checking out the entire scene. If you're staying at a youth hostel, go to the best hotel in town, stroll through the lobby, order a snack in the coffee shop, window-shop the boutiques. If you're staying at the plushiest hotel, check out the one-star around the corner, as well as the youth hostel, the YMCA, and the nearest campground.

Sample many types of transportation and travel experience. Author John Le Carre traveled through the war in Southeast Asia as he researched *The Honourable Schoolboy*. The *Washington Post* reporter who accompanied him tells of the giant bookkeeper's ledger in which he jotted every detail and anecdote as he drove to the front lines in Cambodia, flew on death-defying Cambodian planes, and "choked on the obligatory pipes of opium in one of Vientiane's more sordid dens."

Tell the "Bad" News As Well As the "Good"

Observe carefully, so you can warn your readers of the bad points, as well as extol the good ones. Is the restaurant near the dig so awful that they should return to their hotel for lunch or bring along a picnic? Is the pension around the corner the best buy in town?

The quality of service is very much the domain of a travel writer, so if your bus driver at Disney World is sour and the people in the hotel act as if they should be wearing Grumpy costumes, or if the restaurant service is "Caribbean casual" (you have to get up six times and pull your waiter out of the kitchen), let your readers in on it. If the restaurants turn out to be more expensive, the beaches more crowded, the tour operator less reliable, and the opportunities for recreation fewer than expected, take careful notes, so you can include these caveats in your story.

Today's travel writers are standing up to their obligation to tell the bad as well as the good. Some of them name names, while others make only vague references. (But you'd better *have* the names—in case your editor asks!) Write amusingly, but explicitly, about problems you've encountered.

If your own travel experience was truly terrible, can you write an expose and get it published? Maybe. But don't try to write it while you're on the trip, still seething. Wait until you cool off at home. While you're having the bad experience—the humidity; the bugs; the filth; the noise; the lack of privacy; the miserably uncomfortable beds; the long walk to meals, where they are always out of everything; the long, long walk to the beach, where tar, seaweed, and undertow make swimming impossible and boating risky; the surly service and uncongenial clientele—note everything. Be very sure of your facts and don't exaggerate or distort as you record them. Then, when you go to write the story, you can tell all, in a calm and reasonable way, providing a well-documented article that will serve as a helpful warning to others.

Never use your keyboard to settle private scores, to get even with those who gave you a bad time. Both your praise and your complaint should be tempered by the knowledge that both the restaurant, or the hotel, and *you* have had good days and bad days. Before you write too bitterly about the atrocious lunch, take into consideration the circumstances that might affect your outlook: the fact that you're suffering from a heavy cold, the airlines lost your luggage, and an unseasonable rainstorm beat against your windshield the whole twenty miles to the restaurant; the fact that it's the chef's day off and the storm prevented delivery of fresh produce. Then, if you can be humorous, rather than grim—write explicitly, but amusingly—the result is often an entertaining, informative article. Tell your readers the truth—but be sure it *is* the truth.

Praise requires its own brand of caution. The perfect set of circumstances produces an enthusiasm that lends plus value to your article. Best be careful not to make it sound better than it is.

Sometimes local citizens may want you, the travel writer, to see only certain parts of their area. They try to hide some of the less desirable aspects—the slums and shantytowns, the polluting factories, the refuse heaps, the military checkpoints. Our hosts in 1980 Johannesburg were reluctant to take us to visit Soweto, the all-black suburb of a million people, but we insisted, and we learned a great deal about South Africa as a result.

On a press junket the travel writer is usually shown only the admirable and the advertisable. However, if you ask your hosts straight questions, you'll usually get straight answers. Be prepared to look beyond the facade and get a truer picture on your own.

Check Out the Details

In addition to absorbing the *feel* of the place, you need to find and record the facts. Be sure your information is complete and accurate and current and includes all the cogent details. Keep careful track of mileage and costs. Be ready to tell your readers which landmark signals the turnoff or what track they should stand on for their train. Find out, so you can say authoritatively, the best time of year to take this trip and how long to stay at each place.

Some publications prefer what they call "mentions"—the name and address of the hotel, the restaurant, the car rental agency, the sight-seeing company. Some only want you to "mention" when you're being complimentary. And some publications would never let you "mention." The wise travel writer, though, stows away the information, regardless. Your present editor may scorn "mentions," but the next time you sell a piece on this destination, a different editor may cover your manuscript margins with questions you can't answer.

The value of this is dramatized in Eleanor Bogart's article "Oh, Yes, I Remember It Well," in which she tells of her plans to write a story describing all the streets she's loved. She has just returned from four days in St. Paul, Minnesota, and she will begin with Summit Street. Or is it Summit Avenue? Or Boulevard? Or Drive? Are the trees elms or maples? Are the houses really Victorian? Or earlier or later? Well, at least the Hill mansion she remembers. But was it brown or red? Stone or brick? It was four stories, she thinks—or at any rate, three. Surrounded by a fence. Was it wrought iron? She ends up unable to recreate Summit Street (Avenue) because she didn't take five minutes to jot down or record the details.

We all do that—think we know a place very well, until we sit down to write about it. While we're traveling it's all so *memorable*, we think we'll never forget. But we do. Make it a firm rule to scribble or record those supporting details you'll need later.

With the details firmly in mind you can go ahead and write without stopping to look things up. If you have all the facts straight you can concentrate on plus value and won't have to keep asking yourself, "Was it on the corner or in the middle of the block? Were the children wearing their school uniforms or their play clothes? Was it a canoe or a rowboat?"

A Note about Notes

Once you're home, you'll discover it's very hard to track down some small, but colorful and enriching, fact. You may find yourself spending vast amounts of time and money searching for a nebulous tidbit that you should have written down on-scene—and never uncover it.

Paul Theroux says he never scribbles in a notebook in front of the people he's talking to. He doesn't like to arouse suspicion. Instead, he absorbs the conversation for about an hour, then hurries to a private place to make his notes, and amplifies the notes that evening.

I try to organize my field notes by writing the solid information in order. The special little extras that I might want for something I either jot on a separate page or circle when they appear in the middle of more mundane information. When I tape my thoughts later I gather together all these colorful little extras and remark about them at the end of the more general information. Thus I'm reminded that the schoolgirls wore dark blue skirts with white shirts and blazers in a Black Watch plaid; and the red rowboat called *Erma* had yellow trim, a human eye carved on the bow, and shiny brass oarlocks.

It's the details that bring a place to life and make the reader eager to visit it. Robert Schiller must have been thinking of his readers when he wrote "Storybook Prague" for *Reader's Digest*. He must have marshalled all his senses and digested all the details to tell so much, so easily:

Nestled below the castle is Mala Strana, the Little Town, Prague's loveliest section. Although most of its baroque palaces are now foreign embassies and government offices, the area has changed little since the eighteenth century. You must explore its winding alleys, exquisite little squares and courtyards on foot or you will miss the charming angels, eagles, chalices, keys and fiddles carved over the doorways, which told the postmen where to deliver mail in the days before houses were numbered.

Cross the Vltava by the Charles Bridge, one of earth's most fascinating spans. Built in 1357, with elaborate Gothic guard towers at either end, it is lined with thirty sculptured groups of saints in ecstatic poses. Pious Czechs doff their hats as they pass the figure of Saint John Nepomuk, the "martyr of silence," who was tied in a sack and thrown into the river for refusing to reveal secrets of the confessional.

The eastern end of the bridge leads into the Old Town. Here is the famous Carolinum, seat of. . .

Do you, the reader, want to visit Prague?

Specifics. . . Not Adjectives

Bill Peeples, for many years one of the editors of the *Los Angeles Times* travel section, was a hard taskmaster. He always asked the writer, "How *much* was the tip you say won the guide's lifelong devotion? What do you *mean* by 'remarkably inexpensive?' How *far* is 'an easy day's drive'?" Peeples says, "It's amazing how many writers don't tell the reader what they saw. 'There was a beautiful panoramic view.' Period. Paragraph. Perhaps they never saw it because they didn't really look. But what the travel section needs are specific details, not adjectives."

Peeples, as a writer, tells about Nantucket's shops, restaurants, rental vehicles, boats, and sports, and where to get more information. He must have kept his eyes open to give his reader this vivid a picture of Nantucket:

It has been said that the shape of the island, an accumulation of debris pushed off the mainland by the last glacier, is like a sailor's hammock. A full one, with a sailor in it. If that is the case, Nantucket town is right where the sailor's hands would be if he were folding them across his stomach while he slept.

Nantucket town, safely inside the jetties at the west end of a long, narrow harbor, is a place mostly of asphalt streets although three blocks of Main Street are cobblestoned. Main Street slopes up gently toward the north, a wide avenue framed by tall trees that shade shoppers but let the sun shine through, too. . . .

Everyone watches as the moonglow becomes more golden. Then suddenly, as if someone held a ping-pong ball under the water and let it go, the moon pops up.

There's only one way you can write that way—*know* what you're talking about.

Your Reader Cares

Remember that your reader, whether armchair or active, is interested in the world as it is today. As we pass the second millennium, with Green Travel replacing the Grand Tour, it's up to us, who write about tourism, to share our insights with the reader. Who is doing what about protecting endangered wildlife? Where are the best research programs for preserving threatened ecosystems? How can 100 species of ants coexist with the lure of tourist dollars?

Not all of your readers will have the opportunity to travel to the Galapagos Islands, but they'll all appreciate careful, accurate reports of what's happening with their environment. Incidentally, e-mail is an excellent resource for conferring with others who are trying to enrich rather than destroy, so that you can write about ecology in individual terms. The hotel that donates its broken cutlery to a university art department's mosaics, the city that actively encourages carpooling and low-impact development, the steamship line that homogenizes its potato peelings and chicken bones for fish food—these are all stories waiting to be told.

How to Use Sidebars

A sidebar is a block of information that runs adjacent to an article, often set off in a box or with a different color or typeface. It can come before or after the main body of the article, or in the middle or alongside. Solid facts are needed for the sidebar, where information is expressed concisely, not necessarily in sentences, sometimes even in chart form.

If your story is interesting and moves right along, but you still need to work in more details, try using a sidebar. Magazines and newspaper travel sections regularly carry sidebars to major stories, headed "If You Go. . ." or "If You're Going. . ." The sidebars, or boxes, are filled with straightforward facts on how to get to the place in your story, how long it will take, how much it will cost, and how to get more information. Because of its conciseness and prominence, the sidebar needs to be rich in facts that matter, so collect the details carefully. Naturally you'll be guided in sidebars you plan by the layout style of your target market.

You'll want to tell your readers which airlines fly there, how they can proceed from the airport, and where to make a reservation. Additional sidebars, or perhaps additional paragraphs in the same one, will cover accommodations, restaurants, recreation, and sight-seeing. Other publications will emphasize advice on shopping—what to buy, where to find it, how much to pay for it. Still others will seek something special, such as a historical vignette or an outstanding side trip.

Brief roundups often work well for sidebars, too—assembling a group of arts and crafts or artists and craftsmen, special upcoming events or annual festivals, for instance. How something works, or how it got to be that way, or what happened when, sometimes fit a sidebar.

If there's a side trip you want your readers to know about, put it into a sidebar. Maybe the editor will like it so much, you'll have an opportunity to make the sidebar into a story of its own.

The sidebar has many advantages. It gives the editor leeway in layout, making it easier to schedule the piece. It helps the writer organize his material and tell his story in a readable manner, still confident that he's providing the necessary facts. It gives the reader in-depth information without slowing down the article itself. Many different kinds of material lend themselves to sidebars, and many pieces have more than one. To accompany a Nile cruise article for *Going Places*, a house magazine sent by travel agents to their best customers, I furnished three sidebars. One told of the many companies selling Egyptian travel, and how to get in touch; the second, of the various boats sailing up and down the Nile, their prices and accommodations, advantages and disadvantages; and the third delineated what to bring along—everything from binoculars and a strong flashlight to a warm jacket and an outfit suitable for camel riding.

The travel section in the *New York Times* and many other newspapers run similar sidebars which include this kind of information.

A story about threshing bees in *Chevron USA*, for instance, features a box explaining how a steamer thresher works and another detailing where and when western threshing bees are held.

One issue of *Travel + Leisure* featured as a cover story a one-page "Mediterranean Miscellany," with a quote from Lawrence Durrell boxed in the middle of the page, followed by two pages of consecutive sidebars, which included a map. The sidebars dealt with such subjects as "Daredevil Drivers," "Worth a Major Detour," and a chronology, showing what happened when in the Mediterranean, from the Jewish exodus from Egypt in 1400 to 1200 B.C. to the death of Francisco Franco and the crowning of Juan Carlos in A.D. 1975. The boxes also gave the names and dates of Mediterranean-born VIPs, alphabetically, from Aeschylus to Vergil; a quick rundown on art museums in Mediterranean countries; an explanation of the "ill winds" of the Mediterranean such as the mistral, which Aubrey Menen calls the "cold displeasure of God"; and a definition of such terms as "Riviera," "Costa Brava," and "Cote d'Azur." As you can see, the sidebars were even more "miscellaneous" than the article.

In another issue of *Travel + Leisure* a six-page article on Philadelphia had five sidebars, one to a page. They dealt with the Liberty Bell's new home, where to find information at the Convention and Visitors Bureau, outstanding restaurants, a brief history of the old mansions and information on touring them, and a potpourri of scheduled special events.

Alongside "Nepal, a Trekker's Paradise," in an adventure magazine, is a box written by someone other than the author of the article, which is a common device. In this case the sidebar was written by Jim Whittaker, the first American to reach the summit of Mount Everest. It describes trekking conditions in Nepal, comments philosophically on the environment and economic impact of the popularity of trekking, and advises the would-be trekker in such specifics as making arrangements through a reliable organization and planning the trek for some time other than peak season for the area.

Sometimes a travel writer asks an expert like Whittaker to write a sidebar to accompany his article; sometimes he discovers after he's interviewed an expert that the material lends itself especially well to a sidebar, and he designs one that's composed of quotes from the interview; and other times the editor makes an arrangement with the expert to write a short piece on the subject of the writer's story and uses it as a sidebar.

Consider a sidebar, even if the publication doesn't normally use them, whenever it would help you round out your material without slowing down your story. If you wonder how to write and submit it—call it a sidebar, title it if you wish, and begin it on a separate sheet following the main part of your article.

Links provide wonderful possibilities for online media. You not only find additional information—you can actually access it with a single click of the mouse. An article on finding day spas abroad, for instance, provides links to knowledge of *Health and Fitness, Family Fun, Getting Fit, Health on the Go, Family Spas, Outdoor Health, Swimming Fitness,* and other related topics.

Check and Recheck

Your reader will be quick to point out the slightest error. If you want to build a reputation as a travel writer, don't assume anything! Get the facts straight. Don't give him the chance to catch you in an error.

Once you have recorded a fact don't mindlessly use it forever without rechecking. Constantly update your knowledge so you're presenting as current a picture as you possibly can. Although I always try to do this, I still remember with embarrassment the time I, as an Enrichment Lecturer aboard a cruise ship, recommended to passengers a wonderful old hotel on the main street of Willemstad on the island of Curacao. "Sit on the veranda and sip a beer," I advised, "and watch the Queen Emma pontoon bridge open and close, as people walk over it or ships sail by." When our ship cruised into Willemstad, we discovered the old hotel had been torn down for a parking lot several months earlier.

Be sure you're recommending to your readers something that still exists. And be sure it's a travel experience the reader will be able to duplicate if he wishes.

The easiest way to write a travel article is to visualize your reader. Then say to yourself, "If I were that reader, what information would *I* want?" Your writer's eye, writer's ear, and writer's nose will uncover what you need. Your most urgent task will be selecting from this mass of material the items you want to use in your story *this time.*

NINE

Now You're Ready
to Write

You may expect your story to write itself once you get home and listen to your tapes, look at your photographs, and review the printed material you've collected. But don't count on it.

You usually need a many-pronged assault to compile the research for any story. If you're alert to the possibilities before, during, and after your trip, you can combine the various sources so they reinforce each other.

As we've said, your pre-trip research should include extensive reading—everything from brochures to the encyclopedia—and conversations with those who have been where you're going.

While traveling, you'll interview people—in person and on the telephone. You'll observe everything with your careful writer's eye, ear, nose, taste, and touch. You'll record your impressions with camera, notebook, and tape recorder. You'll collect concrete details as well as register the overall feel of the place.

You may plan your story while you're traveling (target market and capsule sentence firmly in mind), or maybe you'll even write it on the road—and find the check in your mailbox when you return. But other articles you'll wait to write until after you're home. Although I always try to gather the material I'll need on the trip itself, occasionally an editor wants a story I haven't prepared for. I wish I'd known I was going to write about sheep dogs, for instance.

The Editor Chose New Zealand Sheep Dogs

When I returned home from New Zealand I queried the *New York Times.* "I don't want a definitive piece," the travel editor replied. "Make specific proposals." A sentence in one of the eight proposals I wrote read, "You will be surprised how few commands the shepherd gives his flock-tending dog at a New Zealand sheep dog trial."

The editor chose, "New Zealand sheep dogs, provided you go into their breeding, training, relationship with their masters, etc."

My total sheep dog experience was a one-hour trial demonstration for tourists. I hadn't intended to write more than a casual paragraph or two about the New Zealand sheep dog. My notes, tapes, and big envelope materials yielded very little. My files and bookshelves seemed bare of sheep dog data.

So I headed for the public library. There, by chance, I met a friend who asked what I was working on. When I expressed disappointment at the library's lack of helpful material she suggested I call a veterinarian. Good idea! I made a dozen calls, most of them dead ends. But one call put me on the track of a veterinarian who had recently moved to Idaho. A letter to him elicited information on the breeding and training of sheep dogs and the name of a definitive book on the subject now out of print.

Meanwhile, I called the New Zealand Tourist Office in San Francisco, and wrote the people at Taniwha Springs, New Zealand, where we had seen the sheep dog trial. After I mentioned the project in my writing class, a student from New Zealand gave me the name of someone else to write to there. I had lunch with a friend whose husband knew a lot about sheep dogs, but at that point I didn't know enough to ask the right questions. Each of these sources contributed a tidbit and the names of two or three other possible sources.

At the university library I discovered a New Zealand encyclopedia and a dog encyclopedia, both with helpful bibliographies. I wrote more letters and searched for more books. Even my typist contributed an anecdote about a childhood experience with sheep dogs.

But I still hadn't found a definitive book on breeding and training, and I knew I didn't have enough knowledge yet to start writing. Then I went to a California Writer's Club meeting, where the guest speaker was the head librarian from a nearby town, whom I had interviewed several years earlier. When I went up to greet him, he said, "If there's ever anything I can do for you, just ask."

"Well," I answered, "about the New Zealand sheep dog. . ."

Next morning a member of his staff phoned. She had not only located the out-of-print book, but had also found another useful volume, and sent both of them to my local library.

I soon received information from New Zealand about dog trial rules and requirements and several booklets on the training and breeding of sheep dogs. Some of this information was so complex I went to the

Children's Library for assistance from reference books intended for third or fourth graders. It helped.

I was still sorting reference materials when I went to a dinner party and the man on my left said, "I hear you're a writer. What are you working on now?" So I told him. It turned out that he was a professor of plant ecology and had spent months on sheep ranches in New Zealand. By the time we got to dessert he was practically drawing pictures on the tablecloth to explain the finer points of sheep dog trials.

Another stroke of research luck occurred as I was beginning my final draft. When I went to the camera shop to pick up the black-and-white glossies made from my transparencies, the lady standing next to me admired my dog pictures. She raised dogs. She invited me to a local sheep dog trial and plied me with all kinds of useful information.

They all helped: the friend at the library, my student, the vet, the husband of my luncheon friend, my typist, the librarian who remembered me, the dinner partner, the lady at the camera shop—I needed them all.

That's the way it usually happens. Live research and library research; interviews and encounters; what's in the file and research by mail and computer; who you know and what you know—all combine to fill in your story.

The Chinese Opera Story

Some time after the sheep dog story, one of my favorite editors requested a piece on the Chinese Opera School at Taipei, years after I'd spent a couple of hours visiting there. I didn't know much about Chinese opera, either. But a student told me her parents lived in Taipei and would be delighted, she was sure, to send materials. Several months later eight thick books—in Mandarin Chinese—arrived.

My student had no time to translate the eight books, though she said she'd be glad to look up answers to specific questions. But I didn't know enough yet to ask questions. Back to the library!

I looked in the card catalog under "Chinese," and the cards jumped from "one-dish meals" to "Opium Wars." Under "Taiwan" the directions said "see Formosa," and under "Formosa" there were just a few books. Their indexes revealed nothing on Chinese opera. Under "Opera" there were many references—none of them any use. No help from *Reader's Guide*, either. "Maybe there's something under 'Music,'" I thought desperately. It didn't look too hopeful, but the catalog's "Music-Oriental" yielded two entries. Their indexes also didn't seem promising, but as I thumbed through *Music Cultures of the Pacific, the Near East, and Asia* I saw a photograph that looked exactly like a picture my husband had taken at the Chinese Opera School. They were, indeed, identical, and I learned a great deal about the *hu ch'in*, the bowed lute borrowed from the Mongols, and its place in Chinese opera.

Subsequent research was more informal.

A travel-writing couple I met on a press junket sent me an authoritative article on the facial expressions, makeup, and costumes of Chinese opera. Another piece of good luck followed: A newspaper story about Taiwan. When I wrote for more information, a former employer happened to see the letter, happened to be an authority on Chinese opera, and was kind enough to call me and renew our acquaintance. An actress friend lent me two books on drama that included articles on my subject, and a phone call to a nearby university for the names of several students from Taiwan resulted in a couple of helpful discussions. In time I knew the right questions to ask, and my student could find the right answers, and the article pleased my editor.

Talk About Your Subject

As you review your previous research and return to the library and expand your live investigations, don't forget to talk about your subject to anyone who will listen. You'll be surprised how many people will have something to add to your project, whether it's expertise in one facet of the subject or acquaintance with just the person you need to quote.

Notice I said *subject*—not *idea*. When people ask you what you're working on, or even if they don't ask, tell them in broad general terms about the subject you're researching. But don't go into detail about your concept and the clever words you'll use to implement it, especially if you haven't written them yet. There's danger you'll do such a good job in the telling, the freshness will be spoiled and you'll never get to the writing. So don't seek praise for your ability with words until those words are actually written and published. On the other hand, never be bashful about asking anybody— friend or stranger, face-to-face or online—"Do you know anything about Timbuktu? What have you heard about crossing Siberia by train? Do you know anybody who's had emergency surgery in Mexico? Have you heard of any families taking special vacations this year?" Keep in touch with people who helped you before and during the trip—tourist offices, travel agents, public relations people in the travel industry, superior tour guides, and interesting people you've met along the way.

In addition to consulting experts who've previously written about your area, search for experts on your own.

Finding the individual who can give you the exact information you need isn't as hard as it sounds. Newspaper and magazine bylines, library files, corporate public relations departments, and trade and professional associations often provide a starting point. Some universities publish press contact booklets, which list expert sources on the faculty. Even if your nearby university doesn't do this, it shouldn't be hard to uncover your own authority. (Why didn't I think of that when I was worrying about sheep dogs? I was lucky my faculty expert found me!)

Sometimes a quick phone call provides all the additional information necessary. For instance, a long-ago call to Pan American told me that the Around-the-World flight schedule for Istanbul had recently changed. Another time, a call to the AAA confirmed my suspicion that Highway 80 had been closed due to heavy snow. It took two calls to elicit the information that the Wasa Museum had been enlarged—one to the international Center at a nearby university for the name of a Swedish student who had recently been in Stockholm, and a second call to the student.

Sidney Sheldon says he uses the phone constantly for authenticating the backgrounds of his novels. He has obtained information ranging from the weather in New Orleans, verified by the local chamber of commerce, to the name of a train station in Milan, supplied by the Italian consulate in Los Angeles.

Sometimes a phone call will net more than your informant intends. A new clerk in an airlines office, for instance, accidentally told me an anecdote which not only revealed that the airline seemingly participated in an illegal activity, but showed some of its employees as blithering idiots. Next day her superior called to ask me not to use the information, although he never denied its accuracy. I made no promises. But because the particular anecdote added nothing to the thrust of my story, and using it would have served only one purpose—to discredit the airline—I refrained from retelling it. Had it, however, fitted in with my story, or had my purpose been an expose, I wouldn't have hesitated to include the unflattering anecdote.

Turn to Your Files

I like to edit hard copy, so I'm likely to print out anything from online research that I think may be useful. Use what's still valuable of the material in your files, but be sure to update for accuracy. When you come across an old quote from a good source, phone or write for an up-to-the-minute opinion. Reread the written materials you used in your original research, and visit libraries and bookstores to investigate new facts. If you began filling your file before you left on your trip, you'll have good resource materials to use when you return home. If you haven't done all the research you should have, now's the time to make up for it.

When you're wrapping it all up, consider the relative value of the research materials you're using. Take into consideration the author's qualifications, experience, education, and reputation, as well as the reputation of the publisher or sponsoring agency. Consider the range of the subject matter and the limitations. How up to date is the material? Does it seem accurate and unbiased? Is the book well indexed and well illustrated? Select carefully as you incorporate research material into your own story, so that you are giving your readers the most valuable information you can.

Compiling all your notes and references from before, during, and after the trip can seem like an overwhelming job. Sometimes you just don't know where to start. One way is to make a copy of everything, then put one copy away as your master file. The other copy you can cut up, moving the pieces around like blocks to judge where they best fit into your story. Or do this with your computer's "cut and paste" capabilities.

If the situation changes after you've written your piece, do your best to correct your copy before publication. If you inadvertently publish something no longer true, admit your error or defend your research.

Check and Recheck for Accuracy

As we've said, just being there is never enough—you have to flesh out your on-the-scene observations. You must check and recheck the information you've collected. For instance, a *Newsday* editor once wanted to know what I meant by "a mile-long avenue of ram's-headed sphinxes" at Luxor. "How many ram's-headed sphinxes?" he asked—a piece of information not easily uncovered.

If we want our writing to inform and assist our readers, we must guard against errors. I've had readers question a single word or name in a four- or five-thousand-word article. I casually mentioned, in an *Aramco World* piece, the names of the sculptors who contributed to the ornamentation of the Temple to Artemis/Diana, one of the World's Seven Wonders. A history professor wrote me a complimentary letter on the article, then commented cryptically, "Phidias would have been over 200 years old! Remarkable!" I found in my original notes a big red question mark after "Phidias" and then a scrawled "OK." The information came from a British Museum book written by the man who rediscovered the temple, and it obviously referred to a different Phidias from the one who ornamented Athens for Pericles. I was pleased to be able to send the history professor a photocopy of this impeccable source.

Another time a woman took exception to the hotel prices I gave in a *Los Angeles Times* travel article on Sri Lanka. She also objected to my statement that "first-class hotels there are like second-class hotels in Europe." The prices had been checked with the Sri Lanka Tourist Bureau the day I sent the article to the *Times*. The remark about the quality of the hotels was a matter of opinion. The travel writer has a right—actually a duty—to express an opinion in a bylined article. It's disconcerting, though, when you think how thoroughly your reader considers every word. A friend wrote

"Collecting from Country to Country" for an art publication, and a mutual acquaintance called with compliments on the article's accuracy. "I couldn't find a single thing wrong with it," she said. "Not a thing! I looked up everything, and the author didn't make a single mistake." While my friend and I chuckled, we both knew that she, like most readers, would have been quick to point out the smallest error.

The satisfaction of feeling you've done your best to provide accurate information for your audience cannot be matched. When a fan writes to tell you how much he or she enjoyed your travel article, you feel ten feet tall.

Asking Questions by Mail

During your post-trip research, or maybe at some earlier point, you'll often need to pursue another line of live research: Questions by long distance. Online chatrooms, forums, and other types of networking may give you the answers you need. Questionnaires are excellent for gathering a sampling from widely spread geographical areas. Usually they work best where you want brief answers to many questions but would also like the recipient to include an anecdote or two. Sometimes the very act of gathering a number of different answers to the same question—or no answers at all—forces the writer to rethink his approach, giving him a chance to refashion the story before it's written.

Questionnaires are of two types. When you want to obtain updated information or fresh quotes from the person whose initials follow the encyclopedia article or whose magazine piece interests you, you'll write a personal letter with personalized questions. Write care of the publication or get the address from a reference book or an online source. This letter is usually brief, with few questions, and geared toward encouraging the recipient to spew forth a quotable quote.

Other times you'll compose a questionnaire to be sent to many people. (Always send your questionnaire to three times as many people as you need—about one-third will reply.) Often you'll need a geographic spread for a story on primitive campgrounds or theme amusement parks or commuter airlines. On that kind of questionnaire, formulate the questions so they can be answered yes or no or with a few brief words. But leave room for lengthier, more anecdotal answers—you'll be surprised how many recipients fill up the space you've left and add a couple of pages of their own. (It's always surprising how flattered people are at being asked their opinion and how eager they are to cooperate.) Aim for about thirty questions. If the topic is controversial or touchy, you'll have to decide whether it's better to intersperse hard questions with easy ones or whether to build up to harder and harder ones. Here, as in the face-to-face interview, let the last couple of questions be the pleasant, easy-to-answer type. Make your questionnaire itself as brief as possible. One page is better than two, and don't make it longer than two. Never query in broad, general terms like "How do you feel about rental houseboating?" or "What is your position on the increase of recreational waterways?" Such questions terrify the recipient, and he's likely to throw the whole thing in the wastebasket.

With either type of questionnaire, address your letter to an individual rather than an organization. Whether you send your questions by e-mail, fax, or the U.S. Postal Service, immediately explain your topic, your publication, how you got this address, and why you think this is the only person who can give you the information you need. (It is *not* necessary to mention that you're sending the same questions to fifty others!) Subtly indicate the publicity advantages of his reply with something like, "I'm sure *Blank Blank's* million readers will be interested. . . ." Emphasize the urgency of a speedy response with reference to a "close deadline." Try to send your questionnaire at least a month before your actual deadline—further ahead if you can manage it.

Use informal language with easygoing contractions. As Max Gunther says, "Do your best to make the recipient like you." Avoid the stiff business phraseology of a bygone day: "The various endeavors of your erstwhile colleagues might seem to indicate that you would possibly be a potential candidate for assisting in achieving the objective of this communication, which is to formulate a compendium of replies to the questionnaire, so that we may ascertain. . . ." Avoid, also, the cutesy, the slangy, the ungrammatical, the marginal, like "lousy" and "hip."

One successful Western writer always asks her questions on a cassette recorder. Then she mails the cassette to the interviewee, who replies the same way. This method combines the advantages of the telephone interview (making it easy for the person to answer quickly) and the written questionnaire (giving the person an opportunity to think about the questions and come back to them). The only disadvantages to this type of research are the usual possibilities of stage fright on the part of the interviewee and mechanical problems.

Include your fax or e-mail address, and if you're addressing a private individual, be sure to enclose an SASE. If it's a big company or a government office, that's not necessary. It is necessary, though, to write a thank you note to everybody who replies.

Sometimes You'll Need a Pre-Questionnaire

Where do you find the people to tell you about houseboating all over the United States? When I returned from my first houseboat adventure and found I needed to contact sources for a national magazine story, I went to the library. The *World Wide Chamber of Commerce Directory* gave the addresses I needed for my pre-questionnaire. For other types of stories you might find the requisite addresses spread out among the *Thomas Register of American Manufacturers*; *Gale's Encyclopedia of Associations*; *Poor's Register of Corporations, Directors and Executives*; Dun and Bradstreet's *Million Dollar Directory*; the *World Travel Directory*; or in several local telephone books. Here once again, you'll find one source often leads to another. When I found the addresses of chambers of commerce in houseboating areas, I sent sixty copies of this letter:

> As a freelance writer with a *Better Homes and Gardens* assignment for a piece on rental houseboating, I would appreciate it very much if you could let me have all possible information about rental houseboating in your area. Perhaps you could include brochures and addresses of houseboat rental operators.
>
> Since my deadline is very close, I would especially appreciate it if you could let me have this information as soon as possible.
>
> Thank you in advance for your consideration.

The Questionnaire Proper

With answers to these letters (about half the recipients replied), plus addresses from ads in a houseboating magazine and other boat-related publications and information I had obtained at the boat show, I then sent several hundred copies of this letter:

> As a freelance writer with a *Better Homes and Gardens* assignment for an article on rental houseboating, I would appreciate it very much if you would send me all possible information about your houseboat rental operation. Mr. Blank Blank of the State Tourist Office recommended you as an excellent source of information.
>
> If you can take the time to reply to the following questions, I'm sure *Better Homes and Gardens* readers will be interested in your advice.

Then I wrote a dozen crucial questions: How many boats do you have for rent? How long is the average rental? How many people return to rent again the following year? etc. The next group of questions, a little more personal, but still easy to answer, inquired about clubs or families renting flotillas for a rendezvous; what special scenery or activities the area offers to houseboaters; famous people who have rented houseboats; handicapped people; people from far away; how neat the boats are left; what pets are permitted; and any unusual accidents. The third group of questions suggested the recipient might have anecdotes to add to the basic information and inquired about weddings aboard, babies born aboard, "or other human interest material." I inquired if many people bring enough gear to be marooned for years, what rental houseboaters usually run out of, and what the rental operator advises them to bring along.

I concluded with:

> I know this is your busy season, but as my deadline is very close, I do hope you'll find the time to send me as much information as you can as soon as possible. Would any photographs be available? I'd certainly appreciate having some. I'd also appreciate a copy of your brochure and current price list. I'm looking forward to hearing from you, and I thank you in advance for your consideration.

About one-third of the rental operators replied, which was enough to flesh out my story. The replies included anecdotes: about the couple who rented a "ten-sleeper" for the two of them, their Labrador retriever, their Pekingese pup, and their Siamese cat; about the British doctor, his wife, and eleven children who wanted to bring along their Saint Bernard; about the seventy-eight-year-old bridegroom and his seventy-five-year-old bride who honeymooned aboard a houseboat; about people in wheelchairs and iron lungs or accompanied by guide dogs who enjoyed houseboat holidays; about the teenage girls who dragged along their entire wardrobes, then spent the week in bikinis; and about the couple celebrating their twentieth wedding anniversary who forgot they didn't have their six children with them and brought so much food they each gained ten pounds.

With computers and word processors, it's easy to merge the message with a mailing list; a "personal" letter is no problem at all. Even with a type-writer and a copy machine, the body of the questionnaire can be photo-copied and the name filled in later on the same typewriter. Be sure to sign your letter with colored ink so the recipient knows you are making a per-sonal request.

As postage and paper costs escalate, this questionnaire-sending can be an expensive proposition. Too expensive, if you're only going to write one story from it. In the next chapter we'll discuss getting maximum mileage from your research. If you sell several articles from the same postage-paper-photocopy-and-time-for-signing costs, then it's just a matter of comparing this method of research with the price of and the time involved in tele-phone calls or transportation. A travel writer's business expenses are some-times substantial. (Remember to keep careful records for the IRS.)

Either in your original questionnaire or in your thank-you note to the source, be sure to indicate you're interested in future developments on the subject. You may find yourself on a permanent mailing list that provides a wealth of good ideas for rewriting the same story or initiating new ones.

It is certainly possible—and often desirable—to ask your questions in an e-mail. Just be sure you're asking the person you think you're asking— and write down the physical address and telephone number.

Shortcuts Spell Trouble

Whatever research methods you use, don't skimp or take shortcuts. So-called writer's block is invariably the result of too little research. If you know enough, you won't have any trouble putting it down on paper.

And never underestimate the intelligence of your reader. Don't depend on the forlorn hope that he won't know when you're bluffing. John Ball tells of a private screening of a two-million-dollar motion picture that showed a DC-8 taking off and then, a few minutes later, a shot, presumably of the same aircraft in flight, "Only this time it was a 727-200, a very different plane, with the power plants in the rear, not under the wings." When Ball mentioned this to the producer, the reply was, "Who will know the difference?" At the formal premiere of the movie, when the wrong aircraft came on the screen, the entire audience burst into laughter.

Members of your reading audience are wiser than you think. Whether or not you've done the ideal amount of pre-trip and on-trip research, be sure to do a good job on your post-trip research so you can give your readers the most accurate, up-to-date information possible.

TEN

The "How-To"
of Marketing

One of my students was vacationing on Maui, and her husband teased her about her writing class. The hotel owner, overhearing, teased her, too. "Let's see some of your writing." She showed him a photograph she'd taken of a Hawaiian sunset and a poem she'd written about it. He whipped out his checkbook and bought the photo and poem to use on his menu.

It's the unexpected sales that really spell success for the writer. You may not have many chances to sell a menu poem. But, if you're trying to sell an editor an article similar to those he's already using, STOP! Do something else! Sell him a piece he doesn't even know he wants.

When you try to sell stories on camping, national parks, or Greek Island cruises to a travel magazine; anti-burglary advice to a home and garden publication; or sunburn warnings to a health journal, your competition is keen. The secret of successful marketing is to analyze the reading audience and to try to give those readers what they don't yet know they want.

Markets Here, There, Everywhere

Travel + Leisure covers exotic destinations and exciting activities, right? Yet Max Gunther published "Foil Your Local Burglar: How to Protect Your Home While You're Away," obviously a subject of great interest to *Travel + Leisure* readers. *Better Homes and Gardens* published an article on "Station Wagon Camping," a likely subject, when you stop to think about it, for home-loving readers. *Sea*, a magazine of recreational boating, warned its seagoing readers about "Sunburn" in an issue at the beginning of boating season. *Points*, a company publication sent to General Motors truck owners that stresses family vacation and recreation activities, published "The Park of 'Gentle' Volcanoes," about Kilauea's Park of the Volcanoes on the island of Hawaii.

Again and again we see travel articles in magazines that we wouldn't normally think of as travel markets. Somebody found an angle to appeal to the readers of that publication. "Greek Island Odyssey," for instance, sold to *Cosmopolitan*, not a huge purchaser of travel material. The author explains the rationale:

> I sailed on the *Viking of Kos*. . . . There were twenty-five in my group—
> most of us young and unattached, about half men, half women. Many
> were in interesting transition—between love affairs, jobs, marriages,
> countries—and eager to talk about our personal situations as well as our
> common goal of immersing ourselves in Greece.

Would you believe it—The Land's End catalog frequently prints travel articles sandwiched between the pages of ads for warm jackets and chino pants. They pay pretty substantially for them, too.

Taking advantage of "Hot News," one astute travel writer jumped on the bandwagon when word went out about the $300 per person tax refunds. A front page story in the newspaper's Sunday travel section encapsulated the information on transportation, lodging, and food for a Northern California couple spending their $600 on cruising to Mexico, gambling in Nevada, relaxing in Calistoga, or finding recreation at Yosemite, Lake Tahoe, or Santa Cruz.

You might think regional magazines and Sunday supplements would stick to their own areas, yet *Connecticut Magazine* ran an article on Florida for residents considering retirement there. The Sunday supplement of the *San Jose Mercury News* published Sean Mitchell's "Australia, Here We Come," with the explanation that "Californians are moving to a land before the time of traffic, homelessness, and crime."

Home economists and food writers continually find good markets in boating, bicycling, outdoor, and camping publications—everybody wants to know what to take along on a picnic lunch. One writer received a check for $250 from *Field & Stream*—for a pickled fish recipe.

"A Caretaker for All Seasons," an article exploring the profession of house sitting from both sides of the "sit," is a likely enough story for an inflight magazine, but "The Tugs" at first seems a strange inflight choice. Think about it, though—air travelers are interested in sea travel, too, and it's an innocuous, time-passing kind of story, the kind the inflights want.

An article about Kyoto in an Alaska Airlines inflight magazine alerted me to markets I hadn't thought of. It's assumed that articles you send to an inflight will be about that airline's destinations. I wondered if Alaska was beginning flights to Japan. But at the bottom of the story was the answer in the sidebar "Getting There." "Kyoto is accessible via Alaska Airlines Mileage Plan partner, Northwest Airlines/KLM." So destinations of the mileage partners are welcome, too.

What the inflights do not want was described by a former editor of United's magazine, with examples that speak for themselves.

Dear Editor,

Did you know that in the past five years there have been fifty attempted skyjackings, and less than three have been successful?

Dear Editor,

My husband and I recently returned from two horrible weeks in Hawaii, complete with burgled hotel room, severe sunburn, and lost baggage. May I hear from you?

Dear Editor,

Do you think your readers would find fascinating some documented statistics on the number of plane crashes, with accompanying death and injury figures, over the past ten years?

Cybermarketing for Travel Writers

As time goes by it will become more and more evident what kind of travel writing will succeed in 21st century technology. But right now we need to be observing, testing, working, and thinking creatively about how our travel writing fits in.

Lee Foster published his travel material on CompuServe/AOL from 1983 to 2001. His income from them was based on royalty or lease agreements. He also published travel articles through lease agreements with major websites such as Travelocity and ABCNEWS.com. Currently Lee publishes a weekly travel destination article on CNN.com. At his Foster Travel Publishing website, www.fostertravel.com, he has over 200 worldwide travel destination articles with photos available for leasing by web or print publishers. He usually researches and writes a couple of new destination pieces a month. He also uses the website to promote his travel guidebooks and his travel stock photo library.

While not all travel writers are positioned to take as much advantage of the new technology as Foster does, we all need to become aware of the possibilities. We need to assess the online information available and ask ourselves, "What is missing? What could I offer to fill the gap?" When we look at various websites, again we ask ourselves, "How would my idea fit in here? How can I fine tune it for presentation to a publisher?"

Whether you're looking at a website, features for a commercial online provider, stories for an online "zine," a database, or CD-ROM, you'll need the same skills necessary for print publication, but you'll be using them in a slightly different way. Stefanie Syman, zine editor, says she has a natural bias toward people who can put together information in an interesting fashion. While she doesn't demand that the writer become a producer, she welcomes the one who has an idea for the entire feature, combining visuals and sound with the words and able to provide links for the main story.

Online magazines tend to have small staffs. In one way, this is good news for the freelancer—the editor is glad to have help with all the facets of online production. In another way, it's bad news—nobody on staff has time to massage the idea, so if it isn't "right on" in the first place, it will earn a negative response.

Online journalist Kalia Doner says you should become familiar with the tools that will manipulate your words so that you will understand that online words are only part of the package. Web zine editor Rachel Hager agrees but encourages writers to make proposals of all kinds, which her staff at *Parents* will "hammer into desirable form."

Each of the online zines has its own format, its own goals, and its own needs, but in planning original work for online publication there are several caveats to remember. One is brevity. Since it's harder to read a computer screen than a magazine page, the travel articles are usually shorter, more focused, more specific, yet often lighthearted. On the other hand, much of the material accepted for cyber publication is more service oriented than we find in print travel magazines and newspapers.

Links to Links

Many online articles have links to other information. As we have said, links are something like sidebars—suggesting additional stories related to the main story—and these may be provided by the same author at the same site, or they may be provided by an entirely different author on an entirely different segment of the Internet. And since the reader can begin at any one of these links, each has to be autonomous. A Thailand Web page, for instance, links to a Lonely Planet book, which links to a story and pictures about an elephant and its *mahout*.

The possibilities for pictures, animation, sound, and audience interaction are unique to the Internet, and as a prospective author, you have to consider them. However illustrations take longer to download, and surfers become impatient, so you need also to consider the time necessary for the graphics and hope the site gives the viewer a choice to express the selection (without graphics) if desired.

A slightly different audience reads travel material in cyberspace—a younger, more technically savvy group. And while more women buy books and magazines, more men surf the Internet. Naturally, the advertisers are aware of this, and this awareness dictates the focus of the editorial material. It also means that those members of the publishing community who make their way into cyberspace to complement their printing presses are not always successful at directly translating printed material there.

Electronic Media: New Opportunities Abound

Another characteristic of online writing is individual response. It's easy to tell if anybody is reading the travel material you are writing, because the new technology tells how many "hits" each piece in an online zine receives. You can also evaluate your effectiveness by noting the response on message boards and other interactive media. Then, too, material remains at the online site for a long period of time and is not always replaced weekly or monthly.

A substantial amount of travel material, in addition to the pedestrian publication of airline schedules, prices for cruise packages, and ads for car rentals, makes its way to the Internet. *Fine Travel* magazine, for instance, offers an eclectic mix of cover stories, with directions to the viewer to "Beat the Snow with Baja California Golf," "Charter a Virgin Island Yacht," "Ride a Museum Rail Train in Holland," and "Visit Park City, Wisconsin." Other stories feature "Phoenix, America's Great Desert City," and "Clint Eastwood's Hometown, Carmel, California." Certain departments are covered regularly, such as Backpacking, Camping, Cruises, Eco Adventures, Skiing, and Great Escapes.

Editor and publisher Lou Bignami and his wife Annette, who also publish the online magazine *Fine Fishing*, say, "*Fine Travel* aims at the traveler, not the tourist, and is updated frequently." Could your travel articles belong here?

Trip magazine says it's "for people who would rather spend a month in Peru than a night at the Four Seasons Hotel for the same price," and its approach bears out this declaration.

December issues of e-zines predictably feature articles advising how to avoid the crush at the airport, the untold (?) story of the "Nutcracker," reminiscing about favorite holiday destinations of the past, and telling readers "How to Survive Holiday Visits from Relatives."

At the *New York Times* website the Travel Section says it's "designed as a resource for business and vacation travelers alike," and it regularly offers five collections of features selected from its regular weekly travel pages: What's Doing ("In Sydney Celebrating as Summer Arrives"); Frugal Traveler; Practical Traveler ("Learning About the Art of the Concierge"); Business

Traveler ("International Gift-Giving Can Be Worthwhile"); and Q-and-A, with a variety of tips and trends.

Online newsletters and columns are another way of entering cyberspace with travel material. K. L. Smith's "Cruise Letter," for instance, is essentially a promotion for the various cruise lines, but it encourages readers to send in reviews, trip reports, and other articles. For this sort of thing, there's no pay for the writer, but it's a start! And you may manage to arrange a contract for producing a travel newsletter of your own.

Online writers can download samples of their material into library files, and again and again we hear of writers who receive wonderful assignments from "writer wanted" ads on message boards or from chatting with others on writing forums. Lisa Iannucci, who has profited greatly from logging on, makes several suggestions for gaining recognition in this area. She urges you to visit many forums, introducing yourself with such words as "travel writer" or "author of," to read all messages, to reply to possible writing assignments in whatever manner is suggested, and to keep in touch with editors who post online requests, reminding them again of what you can do for them. There can be many advantages to lurking online.

Many websites welcome proposals for forums, with you as online moderator. Who would you interview in your forum? What would your theme and your goal be? Make a proposal, after you think through what you could offer that is presently missing. Because there are no rules yet, you can be as creative as you wish.

Lee Foster optimistically belives that "the Internet presents the purest vehicle ever in the history of publishing." He says it's the first time that independent content providers have been able to attract a worldwide audience without the burden of heavy capital costs. If you decide to establish a website, it's wise to employ a knowledgeable webmaster to get started. For example, the webmaster will help you put certain key words, called "metatags," at the first page of your website so that the search engines will find your page when people are looking for your travel subjects.

You can generate revenue from your website in several ways, such as selling space to advertisers or sponsors, as Foster has done with the banner ad at the top of his site. He says his largest income is through leasing his writing/photo content to web or print publishers. He also receives a small sum from "affiliate" relationships with commercial sites such as Lodging.com and Amazon.com.

A website can also sell your services as a speaker, teacher, or travel consultant. Perhaps you'll choose some combination of all these possibilities.

How about book publishing online? If this possibility interests you, you can easily explore its potential for the travel book you have in mind. Your computer will lead you to many of the entrepreneurs who are establishing some form of "print on demand." The author pays either a modest up-front fee or a percentage of the sale price for each book sold.

One of the advantages of online publishing is the possibility of developing both print and electronic versions of the book, and marketing both, as Foster has done with "Northern California History Weekends."

What They Pay for Cyberwriting

Pay for writing online content varies considerably—from nothing-at-all to more-than-fair. In general, at the better paying e-zines, it compares to medium-market print magazines, about a dollar a word, sometimes quite a bit more. On the other hand, *Travel Watch* expects a writer to submit four unpaid articles which are accepted, and then they will decide whether you should be on the paid or unpaid staff. You might invent a travel quiz that would be a link to your story that would pay much more than that per word. Or you might be so eager to promote your skills as a presenter of travel lecture programs that you would be glad to write a related piece with no remuneration expected.

Foster feels that he has been fairly paid for his online work. The clue, he says, is thinking in terms of leasing, rather than selling, your writing and photographs, preferably on a non-exclusive basis. He suggests selecting websites where there is a definite revenue source, such as substantial ad revenue or major travel purchases.

Whatever you do, though, it is very important to have a clear understanding with the editor, the publisher, the website provider, or the person with whom you are dealing. In cyberspace there are many opportunities for misunderstanding. If all your correspondence is via e-mail and the company you're working with goes out of business, what then? Be sure to get everything on paper, including the physical address and phone number of the people who are going to pay you. Get it written down—exactly what is expected of you and exactly what is expected of them.

We're talking here about a whole new world, in which the writing industry is changing dramatically, and it is up to travel writers to protect themselves against print publications that insist on electronic rights also, for no added remuneration. Writers don't know yet what the future holds, but when their contracts talk about relinquishing their rights for all media, known as well as yet unknown, they are being cheated.

Of course you'll hope to combine all facets of your online and print publishing as Lee Foster has. This may take a while, but if you look at your travel writing seriously, it can happen.

The Nuts and Bolts of Marketing

Whether it's online or in print, selling the stories of your travels is still a matter of finding the right audience for your ideas. Pore over marketing information with the unexpected in mind. Don't try to compete with the hundreds of travel writers who are trying to sell typical destination pieces to *Travel Holiday*. Think, instead, of an offbeat feature that would appeal to *Travel Holiday's* readers. A tennis vacation to *Glamour*? Maybe. A cruise article to *House Beautiful*? Perhaps. But if you have any unusual game recipes, try an outdoor magazine!

You'll find, as you become more familiar with the field, that market research will occupy a large part of your time. Try to do it as efficiently as possible. Although I sometimes search out one market for one story, I generally prefer to make marketing a huge, once-in-a-while project for 40-odd ideas. Perhaps for two or three of these ideas I have only the vaguest glimmer of a thought. Then there are four or five where I've focused the idea but I'm not ready to research and write it yet; and a dozen full-blown ideas are waiting to be written. There are probably two or three articles already written—and rejected—and perhaps twenty recently published articles, for three-fourths of which I own the residual rights so they can be resold for additional mileage.

That word "mileage" is a very important one, and often in online publications gives us the best opportunity for re-sales or for publishing rewritten rejected material. The five or six pieces to which I've sold all rights still offer the possibility of being rewritten, using the leftover research, and submitted to some other publication.

With an itinerary sheet for each of these possibilities and marketing materials within easy reach, I go to work. When I speak of marketing materials I mean, of course, the marketing manuals; the torn out suggestions from writers' magazines; samples of the publications themselves, with paper clips alerting me to special approaches; online information and lists of online editors; twenty or thirty letters from editors encouraging further discussion; and what seems like half a ream of disorganized notes to myself: "Try H. B. on Corms. in 6 mos." or "New ed at P. G. Try Bar RF?"

On yellow legal sheets I write all the working titles, alphabetically by country, five to the page, with a hunk of space between each one. At the tops of two white legal sheets I write "query," for those publications that prefer it, and "send" for those that want to see the complete manuscript right away.

Then I go through the editorial correspondence, noting on each article's itinerary which ideas or finished pieces have attracted an editor enough for her to say "We're overstocked now, but try us again on this in six months," or "Have you anything else on Indonesia? We're running a Bali piece this month, but we could use another Indonesia story in February," or "We're holding your Denmark article and the three transparencies. Do you have any black and whites?" If I have the black and whites or another Indonesia story or the six months is up, I find the items and place them in a "send immediately" pile.

Next come the scribbled notes to myself. Sometimes I've commanded myself so firmly to "send" something that it, too, goes in the "immediately" pile. Other times, I transfer my directions to the itinerary sheet, or, if it's about something that hasn't yet materialized, like a rumor about a new online travel publication whose premier issue hasn't yet launched, I consolidate those notes on a new sheet of "futures."

Some of the markets on the old "futures" list are viable now. My latest marketing list says *Big Brass*, publishing its third edition, is looking for Caribbean cruise stories, and they prefer queries. So I write "*Big Brass*" at the top of the long white query sheet, "Carib. Cr." in parentheses. On the long yellow sheet of working titles I jot under "Caribbean Cruise," "*Big Brass* (query)." If *Big Brass* is not listed in a marketing manual, I circle its address in red for easy recognition later.

Naturally, I give strong marketing preference to publications and sites where I've sold previously, and even to those where I've had a near-miss.

Then I study the marketing lists and marketing manuals, juggling my forty ideas around in my mind and wiggling my cramped toes from time to time. When I come to a market I think suitable for one of my ideas, I write the name of the market under the working title on a yellow sheet, and the title of the idea under the name of the market on either the white "query" sheet or the white "send" sheet. Between times, I check against the itinerary sheets for markets already approached and make sure I have the latest address for any I plan to try.

The Crossfile is Ready

Two days later I have a crossfile of markets for each idea and ideas for each market. Now comes the careful scrutiny. Here are twenty ideas suitable for *Paradise Magazine*—which three or four shall I select for the query? And here is that Caribbean cruise idea with twenty possible markets for it— where shall I send it or query on it first? I begin with the idea for which there are fewest possible markets and the market for which there are fewest ideas and continue matching and cross-matching from there. Taking into consideration pay, prestige, and likelihood in an indefinable combination, I end up, the following day, with orderly itineraries for each of my forty ideas. Any articles that have already been written I send immediately to the first market on the itinerary if that is suitable, or I query on it, if that's what the magazine requests. On the still-to-be written articles I send queries, marking on the itineraries and in my "out" book (which tells what has gone where and when) what I'm doing.

Does this sound like a lot of trouble? It is at the time. But the information acquired on "Marketing Days" lasts many months. If the big envelope comes back, I know immediately where to send it next. If a query letter results in a negative response, I query the next market on the itinerary. Replies to all these queries usually result in enough go-aheads and assignments to keep me working full speed until next Marketing Day, which may be anywhere from six months to three years later, depending on how much traveling I do, how many other projects I have, and the usual variables of writing and marketing.

Of course, I'm constantly updating, as I read marketing information and listen to the experiences of other writers, and adding to or subtracting from my idea list. All of this material could, indeed, be entered in a personal computerized database, also used for tracking what has been sent where, and response time, payment time and other information, or it could be added to a purchased database designed for writers that has been adapted to your particular needs. But, mechanical or electronic, assembly-line market research is a lot easier than looking up markets for each of forty ideas individually.

Sell Your Story Again and Again

Now that you've figured out where to sell your story, it's time to think of where to sell it *next*.

No travel writer can afford to take a trip and write only one story from it. If you do the research you should, you have made too great a time investment for a single story to suffice. So before you even leave on the trip, begin to think of what you will write and how you will get additional mileage from it. While you're traveling you'll see more mileage possibilities, and you'll find still more as you do your post-trip market research.

How can you sell your story more than once? There are a number of ways. Sometimes you'll use a combination of them and find that one article becomes almost an annuity for you as you go on selling the material again and again. The most familiar method of collecting several checks for the same research is to sell only **one-time rights** to each story buyer. I haven't room here to go into a full discussion of copyright, but it's well to remember that the 1978 copyright law favors the author, making him the recognized copyright holder. (However, some publications today insist that the writer sign a "work for hire" agreement, thereby making the publisher the copyright owner, which is contrary to the spirit of the law.)

Resales are available with the many publications that have no objection to simultaneous submissions or the submission of previously published material. Usually these are religious magazines (the Methodists don't care if the Catholics are reading the identical article in their publication), regional periodicals (Texans might be interested in taking a trip on the Great Lakes and so might Floridians, and neither one cares what the other one is reading), trade journals, company publications, and association magazines (where no individual is likely to encounter the same article twice, since he's not likely to be a hairstylist and also a fireman).

But if there's any doubt in your mind that simultaneous submission might give less than full value to your editors or your readers, be sure to check it out with your buyer ahead of time. Newspaper and Sunday supplement editors usually don't care if you submit to their colleagues in other parts of the country. When you send something to them, mark it "Exclusive Your Area," and don't send it to a competing newspaper. Nino La Bello, based in Europe, sometimes manages to sell the same story to three hundred newspapers around the globe. Even if you sell first rights to the first buyer, you'll still make money on additional sales of one-time rights.

Subsequent publication is another way to get greater mileage out of a single article. When *Reader's Digest* condenses an article from another periodical, it pays the periodical and the author. Sometimes the *Digest* will help you place the article in another magazine so that they can later excerpt it, if they feel the story you originally submitted to them isn't strong enough for a *Digest* original. Other magazines also sometimes excerpt from each other, books are condensed or excerpted or serialized in periodicals, articles are collected in anthologies. International reprints and translations are an excellent mileage-maker for the author. One of my students published an article in a U.S. magazine, and within a week an Australian magazine had contacted her for reprint rights. Another student's article in a U.S. magazine was reprinted by *Reader's Digest*, and immediately a Canadian firm requested the right to reprint it in pamphlet form. Subsequent publication is not always author-instigated, but when the opportunity presents itself, seize it.

Syndication is a good answer to multiple sales, if you can interest a syndicate in your material. Sometimes sibling publications, especially trade journals put out by one publisher, will share some of their non-technical copy.

Payment Without Publishing

Can a negative editorial decision extend your mileage? A publication may offer a "kill fee" if the finished article does not turn out to be what they need. The kill fee is usually about one-fourth to one-third of the agreed upon price, and the article, of course, then belongs to the writer and can be resold.

If an editor takes your story and pays for it on acceptance, and then many months go by and it isn't published, chances are there's been a change of editors and/or a change in editorial policy, and your piece will probably never run. If you ask if you can have it back the answer is usually yes, and then you're welcome to sell it again.

If editors keep your article and/or photographs for an unreasonably long time without making a decision, they sometimes pay a "holding fee" if they decide in the end they can't use them. Sometimes the holding fee is substantial, as it was at the *Smithsonian* magazine.

Another mileage-maker is an outline. Some publications, as we've said, prefer an outline to a query. And sometimes they'll buy the outline—leaving the writer free to sell the actual story elsewhere, with the outline money as a bonus. When I sent an outline on Malta to *Aramco World*, the editor wrote that he was planning to travel to Malta himself and would write his own story. However, he said, he liked my outline so much he wanted to buy it. Then I was free to sell the story elsewhere—the outline money was pure bonus.

Get the Most Mileage from Your Research

So far all the mileage-makers we've discussed are at least partially outside the writer's control. But how can you, alone, within the framework of integrity, get maximum mileage from your work?

Charlotte MacDonald begins her itinerary with a single subject, which she fragments into all the possible ways she can treat it for different markets. If the subject has several angles, it's easy to change the emphasis. Sigiriya, that gigantic rock rising from the plains of Sri Lanka, inspired me to write an article about the aerie-fortress occupied by a wicked king. So far it's been published by half-a-dozen newspapers and non-exclusive magazine markets. That article mentioned in a sentence or two the picture gallery that's situated two-thirds of the way up, where soldiers on guard duty painted murals of beautiful ladies in diaphanous dresses, their colors still glowing today. An entirely different article, "The Painted Ladies of Sigiriya," concentrating on "the world's most unusual picture gallery" and barely mentioning the fortress, sold to an art magazine. If Sri Lanka again becomes a popular tourist destination, perhaps I'll work out another angle on the Painted Ladies or some other facet of the Sri Lanka travel experience. Would Discovery.com be a good possibility?

Often world events change the salability of the travel articles we've written. I once prepared an article on Aegean Turkey in response to a go-ahead from a military magazine. It was rejected. Why? Because while I was writing it, the U.S. government looked at Turkey with unfriendly eyes, and the Army began discouraging our troops in Europe from visiting Turkey while on leave. I re-cast the story, sold it elsewhere, and forgot about the whole thing. Seven years later, and about four editors down the road, the military magazine wrote me a letter: "We're planning to use your article on

Aegean Turkey in a spring issue. Please update the sidebar and send photographs as soon as possible."

I've written so many articles about Turkey I can hardly count them. The emphases have been recreational (Aegean Turkey is a beautiful area, with many inexpensive resorts); religious (Saint Paul and Saint John stayed at Ephesus and so, perhaps, did the Virgin Mary); ecological (environmental disasters occurred long before humans coined the term ecology, such as silting by the Maeander River); strictly travel (whether your cruise ship puts in at Izmir or Kusadasi, be sure to visit Ephesus); and historical or archaeological or political. Each time some of the same basic facts, like location, are introduced somewhere in the story, but the various factors weigh differently, according to the emphasis.

Hal Schell did a piece on hot-air ballooning and then ballooned his research into the following sales: to *Motorhome*, a story of how a group of North Carolina balloonists use Winnebago motor homes for promotions; to a woman's fitness magazine, a story about prominent lady balloonist Andrea Floden and how the sport keeps her fit; to *LP-Gas*, two stories on the LP gas in balloons; to *PV4*, a story on how drivers of pickups can retrieve hot-air balloons in their vehicles; to a medical magazine, a story about Dr. William Grabb, president of the Ballooning Federation of America; to *Four Seasons Trails*, a story about the fun recreational vehicle owners can have at ballooning events; to *California AAA*, a story on Brent Stockwell, a well-known California aeronaut; to *Highlights for Children*, a history of hot-air ballooning.

What Do You Do with Overflow Material? Sell It!

Sometimes you have a lot more material than you can possibly use in one article—unless your editor's willing to let you make the article 10,000 words long. Actually, if you have enough solid material for 10,000 words, you should be able to write at least five or six articles on that subject without plagiarizing yourself. Some of the basic facts you'll have to repeat in each one, of course, but if you make the beginnings and the endings all different, vary the emphasis and the anecdotes, and tack on new titles, you'll have five or six distinctly different articles. I've found this superfluity of material to occur especially in subjects involving lots of live research, where I have an unlimited source of anecdotal material from interviewing a variety of people.

Using the overflow is a good way to gain mileage. After you write the first article, gather up the bits and pieces you have left and concoct another story from them. Juvenile writer Mabel Watts says to be careful about doing this, though. After a trip to the British Isles, she sold one story with a Scottish background; then she used her leftover research for another story.

But the editor to whom she submitted it said, "You sound like the old Scottish lady who threw all the leftovers into the haggis!"

Often, though, you can get another story out of the overflow of material or a spinoff from the one you're working on. Many of the spinoffs I've sold have been fillers or featurettes, such as the one to *Ladies' Home Journal* about how to avoid coming home from vacation to a houseful of dirty laundry, and the one to the *Denver Post* supplement on the origin of the English word "meander." When research for an assignment on Spain and Portugal led me to the many Iberian areas connected with Christopher Columbus, a Columbus Day story fell easily into place. And further research produced additional Columbus stories connected with the 500th anniversary of the New World discovery.

New Life for Old Themes

Sometimes you'll expand your horizons years later, when you update and change a travel article written long ago.

Remember when John Fairfax and Sylvia Cook crossed the Pacific Ocean in a rowboat and landed at Hayman Island on Australia's Great Barrier Reef? Well, that was just about the time I was finishing my Barrier Reef story for the *San Francisco Examiner* travel section. So I wrote a new lead:

> John Fairfax and Sylvia Cook arrived at Hayman Island in a rowboat one year, six thousand miles, and four cyclones after their departure from San Francisco.
>
> Most visitors arrive at Hayman via helicopter or motor launch. Unlike John and Sylvia, who rushed right off to publicize their Pacific rowboat safari, you'll probably want to relax at Hayman for days or weeks.

and a new ending:

> You can count on good weather any time of the year. And it's not absolutely necessary to row across the Pacific to land on Hayman. . .

before I sent it off. Through an incredible comedy of errors, that article was accidentally "killed" in the composing room several months later. The *Examiner* paid me for it, but by then it was too late in the year for an article on Australia, where the seasons are reversed. A few months later, by the time I had queried *Relax* and had a go-ahead on the article, the world had long since forgotten John Fairfax and Sylvia Cook, so I snipped them out of the story and wrote a new beginning and ending. Another visit to Hayman Island expanded my information, and when airfares to Australia were sharply reduced, I used that as a peg for a newly expanded Barrier Reef story. Still later, when Qantus began direct flights from California to

Brisbane and Cairns, giving Barrier Reef visitors the option of bypassing Sydney, the news gave me another updated lead.

Often your mileage expands with the years. As you grow and change and become a better writer, you're inspired to re-treat ideas you now feel you didn't do justice by, and through your growing expertise an entirely new story emerges.

In your zealous quest for mileage, be careful, though, not to violate anybody else's rights. Sherman Grant says it's difficult to sell a story to an additional publication when the people you interviewed agreed to talk to you as the representative of the specific magazine that assigned you the story.

Other Ways to Increase Mileage

Other ways you can make mileage from your research are: rewriting an adult article as a juvenile, or vice versa; by using your travel background for a short story, a juvenile story, or a play, or taking the background from one of them for a travel article; by expanding a local story (usually by working out a "geographic spread" through additional research) into a national article; or by converting a national article, such as my *Weight Watcher's* piece on travel charm bracelets, to a local one, using local people and local anecdotes for an additional sale to a Sunday supplement.

Larry Holden speaks of seasonal articles that can be used year after year, when that season rolls around again. He refers not only to holidays but also to special times, like tornado season, about which he frequently writes. Fanny-Maude Evans has done that with her research on lightning, which also has a "season."

Holden speaks of "blending" and "paring" for increased sales, too. Blending means taking bits and pieces from several stories you've previously written to make a new story. I snipped tidbits from several advice articles on how to save money and how to have a good time on your trip and added new material for an article on "How to Get the Most Pleasure from Your Travel Dollar." Paring is the opposite of blending. If you've written a definitive article, you can often slice out a specific section and sell it as a short separate article, once you've changed it around a little.

As you think about it you'll probably come up with additional ways for stretching mileage from your research. There simply aren't enough hours in the day for a travel writer to be continually researching new articles, and it's not necessary. Research thoroughly in the first place. Then write your story as well as you can each time. Willa Cather advised long ago, "Give your best every single time. Don't hold back and save anything out for 'next time.' 'Next time' will take care of itself."

If you put the best of everything you can think of into the story you're writing now, more good ideas will appear, ready for use in the next story.

One of the strongest examples of making one trip pay off is A.R. Roalman's three-week visit to Japan. He started off with assignments (resulting from queries) from *National Wildlife Magazine* for a story on Japan's loss of natural resources, from the *Chicago American* for an article on Japanese baseball, from the *National Observer* for a feature on the Mickey Mantle of Japanese baseball, from the *Lion* for a profile of an important Japanese who is a member of Lions International, from *Car Life* for a major story on the Japanese auto industry, from *Progress* for an article on cormorant fishing, and those two assignments from *American Forest* and *Popular Mechanics* for the oldest wooden building. His chance meetings with a Japanese garden expert and an American who was studying reading habits resulted in profitable stories. The Lion he interviewed told him about the Small Kindness Movement, which turned into another good assignment; his interviews for the auto industry uncovered a remarkable outboard motorboat, which led to still another assignment; and his baseball stories sold to about a dozen other publications.

Selling the International Market

Sometimes you can spread your message internationally—and increase your profit, too—by selling to English-language publications in foreign countries. When you're overseas you'll naturally survey the kiosk displays of newspapers and magazines and select a few to send home in your big envelopes, along with the foreign inflights and in-rooms you pick up. This is the best way to obtain foreign publications to analyze as possible markets; but you can also send for sample copies or buy an issue or two at a large bookstore or newsstand at home. Airports can be good sources.

In *Writer's Market* you'll find an occasional foreign periodical, but the two major sources listing foreign periodicals are the *International Literary Marketplace* and *Ulrich's* multi-volume *International Periodicals Directory*, both published by Bowker. The *International Literary Marketplace* is divided by countries, with information on periodicals, publishers, and related matters listed under each country. *Ulrich's* begins its Travel and Tourism pages with *AAA Chicago Motor Club Home & Away*, but continues with *AIM* (Adventures in Mexico Newsletter), *Angling Holidays in Ireland*, the *Asia Magazine*, published in Thailand, and *Auberge de la Jeunesse* in French. It goes on through the alphabet to *Xiandi Funu* in Chinese and *Zeina* in Saudi Arabia, giving editors' names, addresses, and circulation figures.

Whether your special interest is jungle animals, international business, Catholic shrines, scuba diving, black travelers, or oriental art, you'll find an international magazine in the market for your work.

The *Australian Women's Weekly* buys material similar to that which appears in U.S. and Canadian women's magazines and often runs articles on international, as well as Australian, destinations. Other foreign publications that might make good markets for you are not only in the South Pacific, the British Isles, and South Africa but include countries around the world that publish in English or translate from it.

Although payment from these periodicals is practically never as high as in the United States, they usually have no objection to previously published material. (The pay may be lower because the country—and therefore the circulation—is smaller than a North American magazine.) If you can sell the same piece over and over, that's mileage and worth doing. Don't use up all the profits in the postage, though.

When James Joseph gives seminars, sharing his expertise in the global marketing of articles, he explains his system of sending return postage with articles to foreign markets. Instead of using expensive International Reply Coupons, he has a special checking account and writes checks for the return postage, which are seldom cashed. Joseph feels that many subjects intrigue people all over the world, and with proper marketing skills the same story can be sold again and again. He suggests "de-Americanizing" the language in articles for foreign consumption—getting rid of familiar slang and local idioms—but reminds us that people in other areas are greatly interested in all facets of American life.

How To Market Overseas

Usually it's best to first send a query or an outline to a foreign market. (e-mail and fax are perfect for this purpose.) Then, if the editor wants to see the article, perhaps accompanied by photographs, find out from a courier service or the post office the safest, cheapest, and fastest way to send the material. If you want the article and/or illustrations returned if unused, enclose a self-addressed envelope and an International Reply Coupon or some other kind of return postage. It costs less, though, to send a photocopy of the article and tell the editor to destroy it if he can't use it.

What kinds of travel stories are likely to sell to foreign markets? Both foreign stories *and* North American stories. If you have something on the area the publication covers, wonderful. Many foreign editors would also welcome pieces about areas you know well.

Michael Sedge, well-known Italy-based writer and photographer, emphasizes the importance of researching, in print or online, the culture of the country whose publication you're planning to approach. Do Muslim periodicals prohibit reference to alcohol, dogs, pigs, and body parts? Are European shoppers, accustomed to visiting a different store for each purchase, unaware of Wal-Mart and Target? Do the Japanese cringe in embarrassment when an author carelessly mentions shoe-shod walking indoors, soaping up in a public bath, or backslapping greetings among friends?

However, most subjects that sell well in North America sell well in other countries, too. Sedge likens his global successes to cutting a pie into many slices and often sells the same story many, many times, in different countries. He does recommend eliminating colloquial expressions—and converting inches and feet to metric measurement. Most foreign publications tend toward British usage and spelling rather than American. Although they probably won't reject your excellent article just because you've called them trucks and elevators instead of lorries and lifts, or spelled what you expect them to send you as check instead of cheque, make it as easy for the foreign editor as you can.

Countries likely to have English-language publications include:

Australia	India	Pakistan
The Bahamas	Indonesia	Panama
Bangladesh	Ireland	The Philippines
Bermuda	Israel	Republic of South Africa
Denmark	Japan	Singapore
Egypt	Kenya	Sri Lanka
Fiji	Korea (South)	Sweden
Finland	Malaysia	United Kingdom
Gibraltar	Malta	Western Samoa
Greece	The Netherlands	Zimbabwe
Hong Kong	New Zealand	
Iceland	Norway	

Explore the foreign markets as you plan your strategy for getting the most mileage out of your research.

The "Back-of-the-Book" Market—A Great Place to Begin

Now let's look at a few market possibilities perhaps you haven't thought of. Some of them can be mileage markets, too. Have you wondered about those oddly numbered pages in many magazines—P1, PS4, G9, C12, or W31? And have you wondered why the stories on those pages never appear in the table of contents? Those are "back-of-the-book" stories. They may be located in the front of the book or the middle of the book, but they're still back-of-the-book stories. And that is a good market for the travel writer.

This market exists because nearly all national magazines accept regional advertising. That's the advertising on pages P1 and G9 and C12. Sometimes the letters have special meaning only for the publication, but at

Travel + Leisure you don't have to be Sherlock Holmes to figure out that "C" stands for California and "W" stands for West, and both sections appear in the magazine sometimes. Because the ads don't entirely fill these pages, editorial material is required, and it's an entry-level opportunity.

Travel + Leisure Puts It Tactfully:

> You might break in with a short piece for the front or back of the book. The regional pages don't pay as much as our national articles, but it's a good way to start.

Now this doesn't come right out and say, "Our regional editions are open to amateurs," but it does get across the point that slightly less polish is required. In other words, it's a good place for the less-experienced writer to begin.

Back-of-the-book stories don't have to be geographically related to the region represented; a New York edition had a feature on San Francisco's Carousel Museum while a California edition devoted a number of pages to "Getting to the Core of the Big Apple."

Ladies' Home Journal's back-of-the-book section appears often and carries such features as "Family Fun at Deer Valley." One recent issue has back-of-the-book stories on "Travel Scam Alert," "Sun and Fun in San Diego," "The Art of Packing Light," and "Prospecting Montana's Gold West Country"—all of them very simple and straightforward, between 500 and 1,000 words. *Better Homes & Gardens, Good Housekeeping,* and many other general magazines have similar back-of-the-book sections specializing in travel briefs.

How do you tell the editor you're sure your article isn't good enough for the national section so you're only asking him to consider it for the back of the book? Obviously, you don't. If the *Writer's Market* listing suggests you send regional material to a regional editor, then you'll do so. If the publication masthead lists a regional editor, you'll act accordingly. Otherwise, let the travel editor or the articles editor, or whomever is in charge of that kind of material, decide where your piece should go. (You'll follow instructions in the listing, of course, as to length, photographs, and whether or not to query.)

Other special magazine and newspaper sections may be better markets than you'd think for different types of travel material. *Good Housekeeping's* "The Better Way," for instance, often features such subjects as trip and vacation insurance, better gas mileage, tips on packing a car for travel, and other loosely travel-related subjects. They want "just the facts, please," for this section—*they* adapt it to their format. Reading-rack books sometimes use similar material in advising their audiences.

Look for special departments in all publications, and try to bend your ideas to fit into some of them. Remember that short pieces give you clips and credits, too. While advertorials, those special advertising sections with considerable editorial material, are not for amateur travel writers, here, too, opportunity may beckon. Usually the writer's fee jumps higher for an advertorial.

What Are Your Other Markets?

Let's look at some different types of publications that use travel-related material of one sort or another.

Have you noticed the recent proliferation of travel newsletters? Mailed to subscribers, whether singles, seniors, or families, these purport to give the traveler the inside dope about hotels, transportation, restaurants, etc. A large percentage of this information is supplied by other travelers, who get paid for it. *Travel Smart*, for instance, says it's 60 percent freelance-written and pays for candid advice on good travel values. There are several others of this type. They want the information to come from personal experience, but not always written in the first person. They need "mentions." If you've had a really good or really bad experience, you could detail it briefly, and consider one of these newsletters. Most of them prefer queries. They'll send report forms, if you like.

If you want to keep busy while traveling, but don't want to embark on a full-scale career as a travel writer, or you want something to supplement your career as a travel writer, consider providing hotel reports and/or ship inspections for travel agents' reference books. The pay is infinitesimal, and the editors are sometimes difficult to work with, but it's a handy plus if you're in the right place at the right time.

Many magazines and newspapers run regular sections covering lifestyles and cultural situations in other areas of the world. While these are not really travel-oriented, they provide the travel writer with an opportunity to use some of the material observed.

Some kind of "trip sharing" column is often a feature of both print and electronic publications. You tell about your trip in an informal manner and perhaps send a photograph. Some of them pay and some don't, so inquire first. Both newspapers and magazines occasionally run special contests for travel articles or photographs, and sometimes the prizes are substantial. Keep on the lookout for these. They often add mileage.

We've spoken of *Guest Informant*, which is one of the hardcover, four-color books placed in hotel rooms around the United States. Hotel rooms in foreign countries often have books of this type, too, in English. They use travel information only on the city in which they appear, and since it's such detailed information, you could work on one only for a city you're very familiar with. But they do use freelance material, so look into it further if you're interested.

Writing for *Guest Informant* is something you could do without leaving home. Let's look at a few other stay-at-home travel possibilities.

Stay-at-Home Travel Writing

A magazine like *American Demographics* is interested only in statistics on where Americans take their vacations and what kinds of trends are evident. One like *Incentive Magazine* takes material on travel that firms use as a reward in motivational promotion.

You can interview travel agents for travel trade journals. There are a number of travel trade journals, some monthly, some weekly, and they do use freelance material on various phases of the travel industry.

A Sacramento, California, woman, lamenting the fact that she doesn't get to travel much, contacts the Sacramento Convention Center to find out which groups, such as Rotarians, Presbyterians, etc., will be meeting there soon. Then she writes the editors of their publications with suggestions for travel stories on Sacramento.

Another possibility is writing brochure material advertising travel lecturers. The last brochure writer who interviewed me was producing such purple prose I asked him what qualifications a brochure writer needed. "Oh," he said, "you have to know how to exaggerate a little."

Opportunities for writing publicity and advertising copy in travel-related fields increase every day. Whether you're writing about the objective of the travel—the restaurant, hotel, whatever—or the person who is going to tell others about those objectives, try not to exaggerate more than "a little"!

Writing guidebooks, on your own area or elsewhere, perhaps something like "State Parks of New England," often provides good income for the travel writer. Travel puzzles and quizzes, as well as cookbooks, can be devised by the stay-at-home, too. Manuscripts for computer libraries are another way to go.

Travel lectures and radio and television programs, on the other hand, are the province of the active traveler. Juvenile and young adult audiovisual materials are another market for the returned traveler. In addition to the magazine and newspaper articles and adult and young people's books on travel, we mustn't overlook the value of the travel background for other types of fiction and nonfiction for all ages.

You can see the tremendous importance of market research and what a variety of possible markets are available. But we keep coming back to the same precept: "There is no such thing as writing *generally*." Everything you write must be slanted to the reader for whom it's intended.

The same week as the Hawaiian poem-picture sale for the menu, another of my students made an unexpected "sale." An elderly gentleman, he was traveling on the highway when a Highway Patrol officer stopped him and fined him, although he felt he wasn't guilty of the infraction charged. His letter to the officer's superior stated his case so clearly and was so well designed to appeal to the person who would be reading it, that he immediately received a refund of the fine.

Whether online or in print, look for the unexpected sale, but be sure you're approaching the right audience.

PART TWO

ELEVEN

Sell Your Story
Before You Write It

In Jaipur our Indian guide proudly mentioned his publications in *National Geographic* and *Vogue*. *National Geographic* I could understand—but *Vogue*?

"How did you happen to publish a travel article in *Vogue*?"

"Oh, I sent them a query letter," he replied. "They liked my idea and told me to send it along."

This man had guided a group of American travel writers working on a Jaipur story, and they advised him about his own writing: "Always query first."

Your Most Important Sales Tool: The Query

Good advice. Those travel writers believed—and I believe, too—that the query letter is the most important sales tool in the travel writer's repertoire. Although it looks like an extra step in the writing process, it's usually the quickest path to publication.

What is this magic tool, the query letter? It is, as it sounds, a letter of inquiry; a letter inviting the editor of a publication to express interest in your idea *before* you proceed to research and write the article.

Sometimes your query will sell your story before you write it; sometimes it will elicit the encouragement that indicates you're on the right track; and sometimes it will help you see that this particular idea isn't worth pursuing.

In this chapter we'll consider why the query is such an important tool, what elements it should contain, and what it can do for you. In Chapter 12 we'll take up the where and the when (and the when-not-to) of query letters, as well as different types of queries and possible editorial responses.

Why is the query such an important tool—what can it do for *you*?

First, it saves you time. It saves you the time spent researching and writing an article that is never going to sell. Although presumably you will study such compendiums as the *Reader's Guide to Periodical Literature*—either printed or electronic—and the publications themselves to see what has been written on your subject lately, you have no way of knowing whether your target market is currently considering or has recently purchased an article on the same subject. While you're riding your mule to the bottom of the Grand Canyon, your editor may be buying a Grand Canyon piece from somebody else.

The query saves time, too, because it is read by a more important editor than the first reader, who plucks unsolicited manuscripts from the slush pile. Even if the first reader likes your complete story, it still must be approved by several others before reaching the decision-making editor, who is usually the one to consider your query immediately. And what busy editor wouldn't be tempted to rest his eyes on a short letter, as he postpones his attack on a long manuscript?

You can generally expect a reply to your query within a couple of weeks, except during the summer, when all editorial responses take longer. If your answer is delayed, after five or six weeks inquire if the staff will be considering your idea at the next editorial conference. You'll find that any time of year a "no" answer arrives sooner than a "yes" or a "maybe." When you see a "no," quickly query the next periodical on your marketing itinerary.

Preliminary inquiry may save you money, too. While e-mail queries can be accompanied by clips and/or photographs, sent as an attachment, in regular mail they go along in the envelope. That envelope will still require far less postage than one containing the completed manuscript.

Another important reason for query writing is the chance it gives you to avoid the editor's taboos and to find his or her main interest. An objection to your subject matter or stance might make it pointless to send the completed article. But an editor may let you know that while he's not interested in the religious history of Aegean Turkey and won't permit you even to mention Saint Paul, Saint John, or the Virgin Mary, he's fascinated by the sixteenth-century Barbarossa brothers, pirates who pillaged Turkish beaches. He wants you to include every possible kernel of information about that era. Could you research and write your story in the direction he prefers? You'll never know *what* he prefers unless you send a query.

Come Up with Ideas

Too many writers, however, attempt to rely entirely on editorial preference, without making concrete suggestions of their own. I'm afraid I was much that way some years ago when I began writing about travel. I called or wrote every editor I knew with a "Guess what! We're spending the summer in Europe! What can I do for you over there?" While their answers were polite, they added up to, "If you don't know what you can do for me, how am I supposed to know? Give me some definite ideas, and I'll tell you what I like."

Recently visiting an editor's office while he fielded a phone call of a similar type from a writer spending the winter in Mexico, I heard him mutter "What does he want—a nursemaid?" I cringed.

If your plans are firm enough to solicit sales several months before your trip, you increase your chances of traveling with go-aheads and assignments. As soon as your pre-trip research reveals writing possibilities, suggest one or several ideas to your target market. Sometimes your insight will catalyze the editor into suggesting ideas of his own—assigning you to research them. This query, for instance, produced a favorable result:

> When we revisit Australia this winter we plan to see a part of the country we missed on our last trip (Perth and Western Australia), stay longer in a city we enjoyed but didn't allow enough time for (Canberra), and repeat our wonderful experience at a favorite resort (Hayman Island on the Great Barrier Reef). Any of these destinations—or all of them— would make a good story for your readers.
>
> Americans remember Perth as the City of Lights, its buildings illuminated for our space travelers. The gold-rush ghost towns and the working outback are very close. So are the beaches. Where else do residents rush to spend their leisure at a nearby island called "Rottnest"?
>
> Canberra, Australia's capital, is so interesting it's too bad many Americans allow too little time for it. In addition to taking the launch ride around American Walter Burley Griffin's planned lakeside community, we'll visit the unique embassy buildings and the spectacular War Memorial Museum. We'll travel to the nearby Tidbinbilla Deep-Space Tracking Station, as well as Mount Stromlo Observatory and the Cotter River Recreation Area. We've been invited to visit the Snowy Mountains— both the complex engineering development and the excellent ski areas. We've also been invited to spend some time at Tralee Sheep Station, where we'll watch working dogs and sheepshearers, boomerang throwers, and native fauna.
>
> Hayman Island on Australia's Barrier Reef has always seemed like a dream come true, and I can hardly wait to return there. The hotel grounds and superb beach are so spacious, most of the time it's as though you, alone, have discovered paradise. Yet only a few yards away there is activity, conviviality, or any luxury you've a whim for. Fishing, snorkeling, fossicking on the reef, boat trips to Hook Island's underwater observatory, sailing, water skiing, and just plain dozing in the sun

are some of the activities Hayman offers. You can enjoy tennis and bad-minton, lawn bowls, and the biweekly Chinese New Year, where every-body eats with chopsticks.

May I write one of these stories for you while I'm in Australia or immediately after my return?

The editor replied:

Not the Barrier Reef. We already have too much Reef material on hand. But how about combining the other two? Would something like "Two Australian cities seldom visited by Americans—you'll learn to love them both" sound like a good theme for the combination? Compare and contrast the two cities. Better tell how to get from Canberra to Perth and how long it takes and what's to see en route. Why don't more Americans visit Canberra or stay there longer? (I can see why they don't visit Perth!)

Is it better to see Australia via package tour or on your own? Be sure to include something about the cultural life of each city, as well as sports and recreation. How about prices? Everybody seems to be interested these days in just how much a U.S. dollar buys. If the details get in your way, develop a sidebar and spell it out there.

You say you're going this winter, but I'm not sure when you'll be back from Australia. I wouldn't want to run the story much past May 1. (Doesn't it get too cold for tourists after that?) So let me know when you could have it ready. About 2,000 words. Ten or twelve black and white photos. Have a good trip!

An even more important plus value of the query is the way it makes a reservation for your story. If your subject intrigues the editor and he asks to take a look, he won't buy that subject from another writer, or encourage another proposer to work up a similar piece, until he at least sees what you produce, providing you do it within a reasonable length of time. While you're watching the icebergs "calve" at Alaska's Glacier Bay, your pre-trip query protects your story.

A Good Query Elicits Feedback

If the editor is in a hurry for your article, he'll tell you. He may suggest an approach, form, length, additional research sources, or other aids to enrich your piece. If you follow the suggestions, your manuscript will have a head-start toward publication. Not only will you be able to mail it directly to the editor who encouraged you, but when he sees it he will recognize the idea as one he liked. If you've used your story lead in the query, he'll also rec-ognize the words. Having encouraged you to send it, he's ready to praise your piece at the editorial conference. He has a stake in your success. To ensure this recognition, many writers enclose a copy of the go-ahead or assignment when following a query with a manuscript.

The most important plus of the query letter is the opportunity it gives you to get organized. Obviously you can't write an appealing letter until you've thought through what your article will cover. Many times I've started to write a query and found I didn't know enough yet to make a strong presentation. Several times I've discovered that what I had at first thought so fascinating didn't really make a story after all. On other occasions, trying to formulate the query proposal helped me find the focus for the finished piece.

While the focus should be clear in the query, it should be stated briefly. Without brevity, you lose your advantage. One page always attracts more favorable attention than many pages, so if necessary decrease your margins to avoid spilling over onto another sheet. In no case, write a query longer than two pages.

We've all heard writers say, "My idea is so wonderful, so unique, so exciting, so stupendous, there's no possible way I could confine its description to two pages." We've even heard writers say, "My idea is so wonderful, so unique, etc., there's no possible way I could describe it in writing—I have to *see* the editor and *tell* him about it."

Ridiculous! A writer is supposed to be able to write. If you can't describe your idea by putting words on a piece of paper or you can't describe it briefly enough to appear appetizing to an editor, you should enter some other profession.

Your Letter Is Your Showcase

The query letter is your showcase. To function as a sales tool it needs the aura of unmistakable excellence. It should sparkle with well-selected words and significant statements. The editor assumes that your finished work will be no better than your proposal. He takes it for granted that muddy thinking goes with mixed metaphors, and supposes that the person who wrote the following query would, if encouraged to send a complete article, turn in something unreadable:

> Two women and three small children on a rainy day in Tahiti! We had
> excitedly, unbelievably figured for years on the freighter that took us
> across the Pacific along with five others only there were supposed to be
> 7 but one couldn't make it at the last minute because of I don't know
> what and the other said she was canceling reluctantly the captain said.
> Our freighter schedule was a delay in arrival necessitating an unplanned
> overnight as it seemed we would miss the boat when it left without us
> before breakfast.

Sad spirits were soon turned around by the warm and spontaneous generosity of a woman shopkeeper, Sue. After shutting up shop in case of burglars for 2 hours because she came from N.Y.—originally—though she's lived lots of places like Frisco, Alaska & Mexico, etc. In her car she drove us around Papeete, showing us houses, boats, plantations, answering our many questions of the businesses, imports that include oil and coffee, proposals for growing pineapple and Captain Bligh.

In 3500 words may I give your readers a fascinating and unplanned for travel account of four stranded lambs and how we conquered obstacles through circumstances and friendly feelings in "SEE THE PACIFIC BEFORE YOU DIE"?

May I also interest you in other articles in my "Travels Around the World?" Which have spurred me to dream of writing especially as a career if I could be a travel writer which I do as good as some.

The professional travel writer plans and polishes the sales tool until he is proud to send it forth. Sometimes it's a good idea to begin the query with the hook you've devised for the finished piece. Designed to attract readers, it's also likely to attract an editor. Wouldn't the editor who received a letter like this want to read further?

When the tour bus stopped near the Acropolis, the tour leader pointed across the road. "Climb up and take a look," he commanded, mopping his brow. "But be back in ten minutes. We're leaving for Delphi." A middle-aged woman in sagging seersucker turned to her companion. "I've always dreamed of seeing the Acropolis," she said. "But how can I climb that hill in this heat and make it back before the bus leaves—even if I don't stop to look around?"

Another lifelong dream punctured because of selecting the wrong sightseeing plan.

Types of Query Letters

Sometimes it seems more appropriate to encapsulate your idea in the first paragraph of your query, briefly summarizing what your proposed article is all about. This opening paragraph in a successful query was used by one writer to woo the editor, although these exact words never appeared in the finished piece:

Malta, one of the world's newest independent nations, encompasses one of the world's oldest civilizations. A dazzling gem to fifty centuries of would-be conquerors, this Mediterranean paradise today offers excellent climate, unspoiled beaches, and interesting landmarks.

Another type of query can begin with a startling statement:

> One out of every ten Americans will die in a transportation accident. An article I have in mind would help your readers protect themselves and their families against transportation accidents on their vacations.

There are many ways to launch your query, but be sure you begin with a grabber that induces the editor to read on. As you concentrate on keeping the "you" big and the "I" small, remember the editor isn't interested in what he can do for you—only in what you can do for him. Your success may depend on how well you can identify with his outlook.

Whichever way you begin, somewhere in your query, in one concise sentence, indicate the thrust of your message. Indicate also what your viewpoint will be. Are you writing a first-person experience, a second-person how-to, a concealed viewpoint destination piece? Are you the "devil's advocate" in a travel expose or a researcher/reporter gathering facts that a staff writer will use in his roundup article?

Give hints about how you will develop your story. If your message is, "South Carolina is the cheapest vacation spot in the United States today," show the editor how much it costs for a superior hotel room and a good dinner, and how much you tip the cab driver. If you say it's good, as well as cheap, show why.

Toot Your Own Horn

Use examples that bolster the importance of your story and convince the editor that you are the only one to write it. Have you published in this periodical previously? In a sibling publication? In one or several big-name publications? Say so. Whether or not to include copies of published articles with the query is an individual decision—you're balancing between showing off your best and burdening the editor with additional reading. If the editor asks for tear sheets, a resume, or a credit list, of course you will comply if you can. Otherwise, the decision often depends on how appropriate the tear sheet or the credit list is to your present query, in terms of subject matter, style, and market.

What in your educational, vocational, or avocational background fits you to write this particular story? It may sound immodest to say:

> Several recent trips to Turkey and extensive library research make me well qualified to write this article for you. I have a master's degree in communication from Stanford, and my historically oriented travel articles have appeared in *House Beautiful*, *Modern Maturity*, *Bride's Magazine*, and many other publications of national circulation.

But this is no time to be modest. The editor is probably also interested in knowing if you are just leaving for the site of your story or just returning from there. Have you been there often? A long time ago, as well as recently? Do you have relatives there? Friends? Special connections?

If you have access to unusual research sources or unique skills as a researcher, mention them. Queen Elizabeth invited you to Buckingham Palace to see her favorite flower arrangements? Cairo University's dean of archaeology guided you through the Valley of the Nobles? You have an extensive bibliography of original sources? Don't keep these facts a secret.

While you're trying to think of everything you can in your favor, it's not necessary—or desirable—to include a five-page *curriculum vita*. And don't include anything unrelated to the subject of the query. The editor is interested in you as a writer for this particular story. He's not interested in the fact that you are a widow with grandchildren or a divorced man with a girlfriend. He is not interested in honors and achievements unrelated to the present business. Sending a list of your military decorations, details of your golf handicap, or recommendations from your mother-in-law will sway his decision in only one direction—a negative one.

The editor is also uninterested in your previous literary achievements if all they add up to is the assistant editorship of your high school yearbook or a sonnet published in a literary magazine long ago. On the other hand, it's foolish to confess in your query letter, "I have never written anything before," or "I have no tear sheets to send." If you have nothing significant to say, say nothing.

Query Do's and Don'ts

Your relationship by marriage to the publisher's second cousin probably doesn't matter either, although I must admit that my own first job on a magazine, as a first reader, materialized because the publisher owed money to one of my relatives. (I highly recommend this type of summer vacation job if you are nineteen and as ignorant as I was.) The editor usually is not interested in your financial situation. Telling him how badly you need the money for the article is more likely to elicit antipathy than sympathy; and describing in your query the reasons you need the money is like talking yourself out of the assignment.

Attempting to ooze affluence, on the other hand, or embracing a "what's the difference?" attitude about finances, does nothing to gain editorial favor either. Never offer to work at a cut-rate price because you're "so anxious to break into print, I'll do anything—even give it to you for nothing." This not only indicates that you may have a low opinion of your own individual worth or value, it exposes your amateur standing. The time to discuss money is after the editor says he wants your story. That's also the time to discuss editorial changes. Do not, as so many amateurs do, tell the editor in the query, "Feel free to change anything you want to." She already feels free.

Be truthful and don't exaggerate, but don't be falsely humble. If you start your query with something like:

> You probably won't be interested in my idea, but I just thought I'd ask you anyway, because now that I'm retired from my job as a bookkeeper I have lots of free time, and I used to think when I was a little boy I'd like to be a writer when I grew up. I just took a trip to Catalina Island, but lots of people have been to Catalina Island, so you probably won't want my story. My sixth-grade teacher used to say I was very clever at telling little stories, but you probably won't think my writing's good enough.

The editor wonders why you bothered.

If you're not a regular reader of the target publication, don't say so. It's amazing how many would-be writers begin a query with "I never read your magazine, but. . . ." If, on the other hand, you've subscribed for thirty years, it's less important than a concrete demonstration of your familiarity with the magazine's contents.

If your selected market or a competitor has recently published something even slightly related to what you have in mind, it's wise to defend your originality and show how your approach, your idea, your information would be different—and therefore desirable. This letter addressed to the editor of *Better Homes and Gardens* begins with mention of similar material:

> Although you published a houseboat piece last year, I would like to suggest a more practical, definitive article on rental houseboating vacations. My article would be addressed to the hesitant—to those who would like a houseboat holiday, but are afraid they can't afford it or that they don't have the necessary skills to run the boat.
>
> While your previous article was helpful to the houseboater searching for destinations and activities, I had in mind something with more emphasis on life aboard the boat. Those who don't know much about outdoor recreation in general often wonder if they'll find comfort and enjoyment with a rented houseboat, and I would be prepared to answer their unasked questions with specific information.

A query addressed to the editor of American Airlines' inflight magazine begins:

> Although you naturally encourage your readers to travel to Cairo by air, once they get to Egypt they can have a wonderful time cruising the Nile by boat or traveling alongside it by train.

If your material is controversial, tell how you will show the other side, also. If you foresee objections to your idea, try to answer the objections before they arise. Be wary of sweeping generalizations and unverified facts—the editor may know more about your story than you do. Although it's all right to say, "I have never seen another article on this subject," do not say didactically, "Nothing has ever been published on this subject," or "Not much has been published about this subject recently."

If you have a catchy title for your article it helps the query (see Chapter 13 for discussion of titles). If your actual title, which you refer to in the body of the query, is "Go Where the Goodies Are," you might create a favorable impression by typing a banner across the top of your page: Proposed article on "How to Get the Best Possible Vacation Free." The words *new* and *free* are always attention getters. So is the word *you*. Remember, however, that the editor to whom you are sending the query is not the "you" to whom your article will be addressed. If you start your letter to the editor with "Are you hesitant about renting a houseboat or afraid you can't afford to?" you will give the wrong impression entirely. Editors say they are often offended by this type of query beginning.

Although a good writer should be able to shorten or lengthen any story according to directions, if your information is so limited or so extensive that the length of your manuscript is necessarily predetermined, suggest your projected length.

If you expect the publication to pay part of the expenses involved in obtaining your story, you'd better mention that in the query, too. If you're a newcomer to travel writing, the chances for expense money are slim. If you're an oldtimer, they're not much better. Sometimes, however, you can persuade an editor that although he cannot afford to send his personal representative halfway around the world on a story, he's getting a great bargain in providing you with a modest expense account. Explain that you'll also be using a combination of other expense accounts, travel perks, and your own vacation funds. Be sure all arrangements are spelled out on paper before you leave home.

Photos Help You Sell

If you have illustrations or you can secure illustrations, say so. And help the editor to visualize them. Bert Goldrath thinks the key to his hundreds of magazine sales is the camera that is part of his *modus operandi.* "I research the picture possibilities first," he says, "Then in the query I always include details about the photographs I'm prepared to supply."

Some publications like you to include a couple of sample photographs with the query, and they so indicate in their market listings. An editor of a military-oriented magazine sends out frequent letters reminding his contributors that "the cupboard is getting bare again." He asks for pictures plus a few sentences describing the story line. If he likes your photographs, he invites you to send your manuscript. Many other editors reply to preliminary suggestions with, "That might make a good story for us. Let me see your pictures and I'll let you know whether or not to go ahead with writing the piece."

Do try to offer the kind of illustrations your target market desires: color transparencies, black-and-white glossies, digital images, line drawings (see Chapter 15 for tips on taking salable pictures, advice on securing illustrations from other sources, and information on how to send photographs).

The Book Proposal

If you're seeking an assignment to produce a travel guidebook, your preliminary queries to book publishers or e-book producers will be similar to article queries. When your introductory letter of inquiry elicits interest, you will probably need to develop a full-scale book proposal.

Presumably you'll select a likely publisher for the kind of book you'll have in mind, and you'll plan your approach to reflect a similarity to that publisher's existing list. If you propose something very different, it may or may not be appealing.

In any case, most successful book proposals include certain basic information, such as the proposed title and subtitle, probable length, and promising readership. Of course, you will include your own qualifications for writing the book and a description of what you can do to help promote it.

The necessary "selling handle" is a brief, enticing sentence or two that will make the buyer want to buy and the reader want to read. As Michael Larsen says in his excellent book, *How to Write a Book Proposal*, "The selling handle should broadcast the benefit readers will gain from your book." Larsen also recommends including a substantial chapter-by-chapter outline and one or more sample chapters as part of the proposal.

While the objective of your inquiry is always to arouse the editor's interest and cause him to ask for your book or article, don't oversell. Again and again my students have said, "You taught me to write such a good query letter, I keep receiving go-aheads. But I can't write well enough yet to come through with what I've promised in the query. So when I send the finished article, I get it right back."

In your query or proposal don't promise more than you can deliver. But *reach* in your query. *Reach* for an anticipation of excellence in your article. And within the article, *reach* for the best writing that's in you—and a little beyond.

TWELVE

Make Your Query
Work for You

Reach for a better market than you think you'll hit. You have your marketing itinerary—compiled according to considerations of pay, prestige, and
likelihood—so send your query first to the target market at the top of
your list.

Address Your Correspondents by Name

Once you've decided on the publication, how do you know which editor
to address? The most important rule is to address somebody. A query directed to somebody by name and title, even if it's the wrong name or wrong
title, has a better chance of landing on the right desk than the letter simply
addressed to "Editor." If it's a query for an online assignment, find out
whether the editor, producer, content director, or someone else, should be
addressed.

Your marketing book gives you the first clue as to who gets the query
letter. You will find there the names of the editor, articles editor, features
editor, travel editor, or someone especially assigned to deal with your type
of material. Throughout the year, writers' magazines and yearbooks help
you keep your marketing book up to date as they announce editorial
changes. Another clue comes from the publication itself. Which staff member listed on its masthead is the one most likely to be concerned with your
idea?

Don't be too timid in your selection of a staff member. When a student
sought my opinion of his query letter I asked why he had addressed it to
Maribelle Simpson, first reader of *XYZ Magazine*.

"Well," he replied, "you said to address somebody on the staff. And I
figured I'm such a new writer there was no use bothering the editor, the

assistant editor, or even the editorial assistant. So I found out the name of the first reader."

While Ms. Simpson may be flattered by a query addressed to her, usually your query works harder for you if you aim higher.

But if you've had previous correspondence with anyone on the staff, you'll address your letter to that person. If you've had a recent nice rejection letter (we'll examine "nice" rejection letters in a minute), you may even want to refer to your previous idea in your present query.

This, for instance, went to an editor who had rejected three recent suggestions as sounding too "pedestrian"—an editor who had published many of the writer's articles, including one the previous month:

Dear Tim,

Thank you for your note full of no's. I see what you mean about "pedestrian."

The Travel Dollars piece looked great last month. As a matter of fact, that whole issue looked especially sharp.

Three other ideas I'd like to work out for you soon are:

1. Rental campers, from the angle of how to do it. Having just returned from a week's safari to the seashore, I'm compiling a list of things we should have taken, should have left at home, should have done differently, etc., to make this very pleasant excursion still more pleasant. I have rental information for nearby areas, and I had in mind a composite of where, when, how, and what, rather than a mere personal experience.

2. Travel charms. Did you know that. . . .

Queries Range from Formal to Personal

How well you know the editor and your previous relationship always determine the tone of your inquiry. A query to a stranger who has complied with the writer's request for sample copies and guidelines might read:

Dear Mr. Adams:

Thank you for your June 15 letter and the sample copies.

Your rural mailbox story made me feel you would be interested in a photo feature on laundry lines around the world. I have always felt nothing so unites the peoples of the world as the necessity for getting out the wash; so in all my travels I collect photographs of people washing, as well as mute testimonials to the fact that they have washed. Sometimes photographing the wash imperils the photographer. At a Spanish inn, for instance, where Cervantes is said to have written Don

Quixote, when the innkeeper's wife saw me taking a picture of her laundry line she pinned up a soaking wet sheet and positioned it to drench me.

Even to a stranger, let your personality shine through. The editor is, after all, a human being. Be warm and friendly, rather than cold and impersonal. Don't be cutesy, though—that kind of personality is better concealed. To an editor you know through previous letters you'll be even more informal and friendly. This query followed much cordial correspondence and several sales, although the writer had not yet met the editor, whose assistant had reported him ill:

Dear Jack Smith,

By now I hope you're up and feeling better. About all you can say to a rough break like that is, "Well, that's it for this year!" Soon, I'm sure, you'll be good as new and will settle back into your regular routine.

When you are up to considering material for future issues, I hope you'll look favorably on an article about that marvelous engineering triumph, the Corinth Canal. During the half hour you're traveling through the canal you can almost reach out and touch the ice-smooth sides, while. . .

This is a query to a longtime friend who has published many of the writer's stories:

Dear Frank,

Your trip to "The Top of the World" sounds fabulous. When I read your story about Iceland I could hardly restrain myself from calling a travel agent to make reservations.

As your travel pages grow more numerous you seem to be adding departments, and when I saw your "Destination for a Day" label on that Mendocino Skunk Train story last week I wondered if that is the beginning of a new department. Will you be running Destination for a Day pieces regularly? If so, I hope you'll consider an article on Buena Park, where there are activities to please every interest and every age group.

Within five minutes you can ride. . .

The late Mort Weisinger spoke of his "outrageous good luck" with much briefer queries to friendly editors during the years he was a regular contributor to the then-weekly *Saturday Evening Post*. When a picture on the *New York Times* financial page gave a tiny credit line, "Courtesy Chase National Bank's Collection on Moneys of the World," he sent the clipping with this sentence attached: "This collection contains over 75,000 specimens, representing every known medium of exchange. How about a story on its curator?"

A few months later, on a trip with his children to the Bronx Zoo, Weisinger was prompted by a couple of guidebook photographs showing keepers feeding fresh oxen blood to the vampire bats and ground-up bamboo shoots to the pandas to send the *Post* a one-line query: "How about a piece on the problems of feeding everything that walks, flies, swims, or crawls at the Bronx Zoo?"

You have to be a very regular contributor to make such a capsule query work for you.

Should I Send a Query or the Manuscript?

When do you send a query and when do you just go ahead and send the whole piece? In general, you send a query whenever the research is more important than the style. Although the query letter is an excellent tool that can provide a strong plus value for the travel writer, there are times when it cannot be used.

Some publications prefer to see finished manuscripts, and if you try to send them a query letter they may send it back unread. At *Trip and Tour*, for instance, the editor says firmly:

> We receive manuscripts on speculation only, so there is no need to query first.

Magazines from *International Living* to *Catholic Digest* say: "No queries. Send complete manuscript."

There are times, too, when the material is so dependent upon the author's style, rather than upon the subject matter, that a query would be pointless. This is especially true of humorous, nostalgic, and personal-experience stories. Sometimes, too, the story is very short, especially if it's intended for a newspaper travel section or as a magazine back-of-the-book piece. If the finished story is shorter than the query, or only a little longer, send the story.

Also, if the time element is so limited that a query would jeopardize the sale, go ahead and send the story itself. I happened to be in London, for instance, one January when national strikes and fuel shortages were causing travelers to avoid London. I was surprised to find the situation less uncomfortable than anticipated. Although theater coatcheck girls looked forlorn when muffled members of the audience refused to surrender outdoor gear, the hotels and restaurants were warm enough. Lights, food, and transportation were available, if sparse; and Londoners made cheerful jokes about fewer calories and more walking helping them slim down. It was a good thing I sent my "It's really not so bad" story off quickly, because within a few weeks the strikes ended, the fuel situation stabilized, and the weather turned warmer.

As a general rule, send a query first whenever the subject matter's significance eclipses the style, unless the editor says he doesn't want one, or the length or timeliness of the story indicates otherwise.

If the publisher asks for the query (or, indeed, the manuscript, itself) on disk, on tape, or online, of course you will try to comply. Many publishers say, "Don't fax," and even more say, "Don't phone."

When you query an online zine or attempt to become part of an online production, you first need to decide whether you are offering content, concept, or both. (When somebody else has the concept, the producer will often hire writers to fill in the content.) Your query will be similar to one for a print publication, but you will send it by e-mail. E-mail queries have one tremendous advantage—the subject line. Be sure to begin the subject line with the word "query," and then add the sharpest banner you can think of. But don't forget that e-mail only provides your e-mail address. In case the editor wants to phone you, fax you, or write you about the project, be sure to include in your letter other ways she can contact you.

E-mail queries are usually a bit more formal and should come right to the point. Don't send photos or writing samples until requested, and don't load up your queries with attachments. An e-mail query to an online publication goes like this:

(Subject line) Query on Mexico Cruise

COMEDY OF ERRORS IN MEXICO

Ms. Laura Miller, Editorial Director
www.salon.com

Although a comedy of errors, including late planes, lurid cruise ship, and lost documents, launched my Mexican Riviera cruise, it all worked out just fine. Watching the divers in Acapulco was a spectacular experience. Getting arrested in Mazatlan was less delightful.

For Salon I have in mind a short piece similar to "One Fateful Day in Istanbul" in a recent issue. Although Salon has suspended the full "Travel and Food" section, I see that you are publishing travel articles, and this one would be perfect for your readers.

Excellent photographs, both black and white and color, would accompany the article, in any format you prefer.

As a well-published travel writer, I would be happy to send you credits and clips, also in the format of your choice.

I look forward to hearing from you soon.

Cordially,

Name
Address
Telephone number
Fax number

When to Send Your Query

When do you send the query? You send it as soon as you've done enough research to make an attractive sales presentation. "Enough" is hard to pinpoint. It might take one writer on one subject a couple of hours to research enough material for the query, while another writer, working on another subject, might spend six months gathering enough solid facts to put together a salable story idea.

An anticipated opportunity to sail through the soon-to-be-reopened Suez Canal sent one California writer to the history books for a pre-trip query that began:

> We will be on one of the first ships to sail through the Suez Canal when it reopens later this month, and I'm planning to compare and contrast the reopening with the 1869 opening extravaganza. Then, as you know, fifty vessels bearing many of Europe's crowned heads sailed from Port Said to Suez, accompanied by blaring bands and fireworks. The celebration was climaxed by a $7 million banquet and a special performance of *Rigoletto* at Cairo's new opera house. (Giuseppe Verdi had been commissioned to write *Aida* for the occasion, but scenery and costumes were held up in Paris by the Franco-Prussian War.) This time *Aida* will be performed, all right, but it will have to be outdoors, since Cairo's Opera House burned down a few years ago. Doubtless, the spectators' heads—both crowned and uncrowned—will be different, but I understand that fireworks and brass bands will proliferate once again.

A restaurant reviewer, on the other hand, says, "What research do I need before I send a query? Either the editor is interested in *poulet en croûte* at Four Seasons, or he isn't. And whether the *poulet en croûte* is outstanding or merely adequate—that I can't know till I get there."

But a career army officer, who's sent three children through graduate school on editors' checks, says, "I've traveled so much—I have an instinct about where to look for the salable story. As soon as I smell it, I start researching. It takes me about half a day to get together enough for the query."

His wife interrupted to observe that he always seems to "smell" the story—and start researching it—the week they move to a new post, when there's the most to be done in the way of unpacking and getting organized.

Your Query Must Instill Confidence

In any case, you want to be sure to always do enough research so the editor knows you know what you're talking about. You have to have enough facts to instill a feeling of confidence, because every editor is haunted by the fear that he will accept a story by an inexperienced writer that later proves to be untrue or inaccurate.

It isn't only the inexperienced writer he worries about. Some publications now insist on written verification of facts and sources from everybody. One editor explains, "We've seen too many freelance stories reporting on interviews that never actually took place."

For another publication, an imaginative travel writer even described an island that never existed. The editor especially liked his story of a small Caribbean island that supposedly never appeared on charts because it had been a secret U.S. Navy installation during World War II, and the Pentagon deleted it from all maps. The author described the island—discovered by him—as an Eden with a "happy native population virtually untouched by civilization."

Letters and phone calls from readers begged for directions to the island paradise. Only one protesting voice spoiled the climate of bliss. "It was Ernest Hemingway's brother," says the editor. "And he knew the Caribbean like the back of his hand. According to him, no such island existed or ever did exist."

When questioned about his sources, the writer, unabashed, replied, "I've always wanted to do a story about a mysterious, undiscovered island. But since there weren't any that I knew of, I just made the whole thing up."

Can you blame editors for being wary?

So in your query, allay the editor's fears with what is clearly well-researched information. If there's material you expect to use but haven't yet verified, call it unverified, so the editor knows you know the difference. A query like one of these works for you by building a feeling of confidence:

> All over the world parents, relatives, and friends spend millions of dollars (exact amount to be determined—maybe it's billions!) to. . .

or

> Mr. Alex Chambers, Director of the Western Division of World Wide Travel, says tourism will increase by 27 percent this year, with 50 percent of that increase representing families who have never before traveled farther than fifty miles from home. (Mr. Chambers has promised me an interview next week, and he has indicated he will say something like this, since these are the approximate statistics, but I will quote him precisely in the article itself.)

Do Your Homework Before You Query

Never take shortcuts with your research. But don't fall into the trap of endlessly researching something that may never sell. Many writers do this. The research itself becomes so attractive they postpone writing even the query until they spend "just another couple of days" and then "just a few more days" researching, and they somehow never get around to writing.

"That's my trouble," says an archaeologist-writer. "Although I've managed to sell two popular articles on Pompeii, I have a dozen more archaeologically oriented travel stories written in my head. But before I send the query I always check and recheck—and then check again—every single word. Did the original source find exactly the same thing I did? Perhaps I should look for just one more original source? Eventually the whole thing seems sort of stale. I begin to wonder whether anybody else would be interested, so I don't bother the editor by inquiring."

This writer is losing one of the great advantages of the query. A query works best if you do only enough research to write the letter. Then if no one thinks your idea is as good as you do, you haven't wasted much time on something nobody's going to buy.

You will, of course, send some queries before you start on your trip. Others you may send while you're traveling. ("I often take *Writer's Market* along when I travel," reports Mary Jane Beck. "When I stumble over a story unexpectedly, I want to be sure to interest an editor immediately.") Still other queries you'll send upon your return home, and some you'll send long after your return.

The Travel Writer Thinks Ahead

The travel writer learns to think far ahead. Some writers use special calendars to remind them to plan the "Old-fashioned New England Christmas" story in March, to get ready for "Easter Week in Spain" the beginning of June, and to start querying in December on "Give the Kids a Treat at Disneyland Before They Go Back to School." If your target market says it needs material six months in advance, add to that how long it will take you to write the finished piece, plus a couple of weeks for response to your query, and a couple of weeks in the mail. Then add a couple of weeks for unexpected delays. Do you have enough time? If it's already August and you don't have the story written, there's no point in sending a query about New England this Christmas. Begin, instead, to plan for next year.

If you have a travel story that's really *hot* news—something like a confirmed seat on the first space shuttle to the moon—you may want to telephone the editor for an early okay. Since telephone calls are seldom popular in editorial offices, try to find out when deadline times are, so you won't be calling at the worst possible moment, and always ask, "Is this a convenient time for you to talk to me?"

If the editor answers "yes" to your proposal, firm it up with a supporting letter, to protect yourself. Make it a pleasant, friendly letter, thanking him for the consideration and outlining your understanding of the arrangements.

Sometimes even a negative telephone call has value. As one prolific writer, who often telephones proposals, points out, "If the editor tells you 'no,' he'll probably tell you *why*—which is important information for you to have."

If you are at the stage where you're making appointments with editors, make those appointments productive. Plan ahead. Prepare to discuss your specific ideas with the same care you'd put into a query letter. If you don't have enough facts yet to show the editor what you mean, do more research before you meet him. A social occasion, where you vaguely inquire, "Is there anything I can do for you," may be personally pleasant, but professionally it's a waste of his time and yours.

Field & Stream editor Jack Samson says an oral query shouldn't be "so aggressive as to be obnoxious, but don't hesitate to ask." He reminds travel outdoor writers that once the editor has given the affirmative nod to an oral query, you're obligated to show the finished article to him first. He tells about a writer who discussed with him at great length a story about some lakes near his home. "The idea sounded good," he explains, "and I told him to send the article to me when it was done. I finally saw the story but it was in another magazine."

Don't play games with the editor. If he seems interested in your proposal, let him see the finished product before offering it to somebody else. Otherwise, don't expect him to even appear interested in your *next* proposal.

Give the Editor Choices

Face to face, you'll probably discuss a number of different ideas with your editor. But most inquiries will still be by letter. How many ideas should you propose in a single query letter? Many professional writers oppose presenting more than one idea at a time. "You only compete against yourself," they warn. "Send one idea, and if the editor likes it, then send another. If he doesn't like it, still send another. But send them separately, one idea at a time."

I disagree. If you have—as most of us do—more ideas than you'll ever use up in a lifetime, what difference does it make if you compete against yourself? I see no problem in proposing three ideas, and next time proposing three different ones. I often receive encouragement on the second or third idea, rather than the first one. Although I have occasionally proposed four or five stories in a single query, I usually find two or three make a more manageable letter and an e-mail query usually supports only one.

I have several opening gambits for tying the ideas together:

Several articles I feel would interest your readers include: . . .

Two articles I have in mind for your readers are at opposite ends of the world. . . .

Three diverse articles I'd like to write for you emphasize unusual facets of the travel experience.

Now that some of your readers will be traveling to more remote parts of the world, I have in mind a couple of travel pieces on areas far from the tourist circuit. . . .

Two very economical—but exciting—areas I'm sure would interest your readers are. . . .

I compose two hopefully irresistible paragraphs about each idea and link them with transitional phrases like, "Another article that would interest your readers," and "Still another idea for your publication." I add a paragraph about photographs, a paragraph encapsulating my qualifications if this is a new market for me, and end by promising prompt action in response to editorial encouragement. I try never to suggest that the editor has a choice of *either* this idea or that one, but to indicate I hope he likes *all* my proposals. Sometimes an editor will ask to see two or three of the articles I've suggested, and will occasionally buy more than one at a time.

I've even sold *postscripts* to query letters. The first one accompanied a suggested article on Bangkok for *Coronet*, then a general magazine. After I finished extolling the beauties of Bangkok's rainbow world of rivers and klongs I discovered, in that pre-computer day, that I hadn't spaced the letter very well on the page. There was too much white space beneath the signature. Should I retype the whole thing? No. I'd add a postscript. What could I propose in a postscript? I thought of the *Wasa*, that seventeenth-century Swedish battleship that sank before she'd sailed a mile, and was brought up in mint condition after three centuries of immersion at the bottom of Stockholm harbor. I really wasn't ready to write about the *Wasa* yet, but I hastily researched enough to add a postscript that said:

Another article I'd like to write for you is about a ship that never went to sea—the *Wasa*. A seventeenth-century battleship intended for service in the Thirty Years' War, it sank in Stockholm harbor on its maiden voyage. Only recently recovered from the harbor, it was found with food still spread in the galley, carpenters' tools safe in their box, and coins jingling in the skeleton sailors' pockets. A museum has literally been built around the ship, and the *Wasa* story is one of the most fascinating in sea lore.

Coronet's editor replied, "We already have in inventory an article about Bangkok, but the *Wasa* sounds interesting. Could you send us 2,500 words?" I could and did. And they published it.

A postscript also triggered my first sale to *Off Duty*. After signing the query containing three of my current ideas, I remembered a story on taking our four teenagers to Russia that I'd sold to another magazine. Although I'd been paid, I was disappointed at not seeing the story in print. Recent inquiry had revealed a new editor making a clean sweep, willing to return my rights. Would that story interest *Off Duty*? I inquired in the postscript. The editor's response included his reasons for rejecting my first three proposals. Then he said:

> I like your fourth idea, the reaction of your four teenagers to a trip to Russia. . . This will not be an easy article to do. . . . If the reactions are of interest in themselves—not because "it's just what we in the family expected Janet or Frank to do"—the article will be of interest.

He didn't know, of course, that the article was already written.

When I sent it, he wrote, "Just what I needed! What else do you have for me?"

Pre-trip query letters often evoke interest from editors. Then you can concentrate on the facets of your trip experience that interest your prospective publishers.

Sending Out Checklists

The late Louise Boggess, whose travel writing was largely concerned with antiques, usually sent out a checklist of ideas before she started on her trips. After her initial research, she composed three or four one-sentence ideas and sent the list to an editor on a page with extra-wide margins. On another page she outlined her travel itinerary, noting nearby antiques subjects. The editor usually commented in the margin, suggesting an approach to one or more of her ideas, or presented ideas of his own. As each editor made selections, she substituted other proposals before sending the checklist to the next publication on her preliminary marketing list. She continued doing this until she was ready to leave—with a dozen firm assignments in her attache case.

Other writers save the checklist approach until they return from their travels. Then they compose a couple of fascinating paragraphs about each facet of the trip. They juggle them back and forth in the word processor using "paste" and "copy" to endlessly add, subtract, or rearrange.

Still others feel idea sheets of that type work best for previously sold stories on which they own residual rights (see Chapter 10 for discussion of mileage). A friendly personal letter accompanies the list, which they offer to print or online markets that accept previously published material.

Sometimes an editor will prefer one idea at a time, and will tell you so, either in his market listing or in mailed guidelines or in a personal letter responding to your multi-subject query. Of course you will accede to his wishes. Usually, though, try to make your query cover more than one idea.

With technical improvements in word processing and computerization, the writer is offered various shortcuts to sending query letters. Donna Dowdney plans her query letters to go out in batches—duplicating the paragraphs about her qualifications, her photographs, her recent trip, and changing only the addressee and the paragraph about her specific idea. She then uses word processing equipment and turns out many query letters in a single afternoon. With the help of technology—and boilerplate—the writer's sales job becomes easier.

There are several types of commercially produced quick-query forms, where you merely indicate with a check mark whether your proposal is fiction or nonfiction, whether or not photographs are available, and how soon you can have it completed. The form gives the editor a chance to check anything from "Not interested" to "Send complete outline" to "Yes, let's have a look." I think these forms are much too cold and impersonal to nurture the kind of editor-writer relationships that lead to repeated sales and assignments. Even the few seconds to make a check mark is a waste of editorial time, since these quick forms tell absolutely nothing about the questioner's writing ability or his integrity and very little about his idea or how he would handle it.

Different writers use different formulas for presenting their queries. Anne Holmes makes hers look like a press release. "It has to begin with a grabber that's every bit as enticing as direct mail advertising," she says. "I want to lure the editor into reading on. So I type a banner headline across the top of the page and begin my letter with an aggressive '5 Ws' lead. This type of query seems to work best for me."

The Outline-Style Query
Other writers use other favorite forms. Hayes Jacobs believes in the outline query, beginning with the double-spaced lead of your article, then single-spacing the essential elements of the entire article in informal memo style.

Some editors say they prefer an outline, so that is what you give them. But it doesn't have to be the topic-sentenced, Roman-numeraled, lettered-subhead type.

The outline could follow a chronological pattern, recounting events in historical order, or a geographical pattern, taking the reader on an orderly journey, or it could follow some other logical sequence, according to the material covered. For a sight-seeing story on San Francisco (this was not a definitive destination piece, so I included no restaurants, shops, or entertainment) I tried to select the most important things to see according to the time available, keeping in mind the interests of the particular reader for whom this article was intended:

> When you have only one day in San Francisco, climb to the top of Telegraph Hill, see Golden Gate Park and its museums, Japanese Tea Garden, etc., include Fisherman's Wharf and Chinatown. . . .
>
> If you have two days, go out to the Cliff House, see the Japanese Cultural Center, the Opera House, the Cannery. . .
>
> Four days is twice as good as two. Take a trip across the Golden Gate Bridge to Sausalito, Muir Woods, etc., visit the Palace of the Legion of Honor, the Museum of Modern Art. . . .
>
> With six days, ride BART or take a trip across the Bay Bridge to the University of California at Berkeley, the Oakland Museum, Lake Merritt; travel down the Peninsula, see Stanford University, Great America. . . .
>
> If you're staying eight days, include Alcatraz, Aquatic Park, ethnic museums. . . .

I could as easily have chosen an historical or geographical pattern for this outline, but this one, based on the length of time the visitor might have available, seemed best for its purpose.

As you can see, there are many ways to make an outline. On subjects where you have access to unlimited information, offering a huge variety of approaches, the need to unscramble and classify this material for a query outline makes it ultimately easier to write the travel article. It also makes it possible to write a stronger, more interesting, better organized, and more accurate travel article.

I have from time to time sold the outline. Sometimes an editor will be about to take off for the destination I've suggested, planning to write his own story. He thinks my outline will save him time in getting all the elements together, and he's glad to pay me for it. Although I couldn't then send that identical outline to another editor, I'd be free to use the information in it.

Query Mechanics

Regardless of the form you use, put your best foot forward in the query. Neatness and care will never sell a poor idea; but smudges and typos will eclipse a good one. To make your query work for you, make sure its mechanics meet the highest standards of excellence—including the correct spelling of the editor's name. Remember, you have only one, thirty-second chance to make a good first impression. The editor suspects your manuscript will be no better than your query.

Is a letterhead important? I think it is. It makes you look—and feel—professional. In the beginning you probably won't invest in four or five different sizes of stationery for different lengths of letters, so stick to business size (8½ x 11) with matching envelopes. I have always felt black type on white bond paper was the only way to go. And I'm still convinced that red script on neon yellow or kelly green on sheets of hot pink will attract *un*favorable attention. But when one student showed me his letterhead—black ink on off-white paper—I liked the back of it as much as the front. He had arranged an attractive montage of the beginnings of sixteen of his published travel articles, some with photos, all with byline prominently displayed, then had it reduced to 8½ x 11 size for the back of his letterhead. It's eye-catching and interesting, without being intrusive.

With desktop publishing facilities, it's easy to create your own special letterheads, complete with logo. Some travel writers even make up different letterheads for different publications or types of stories. If you have congenial software, you can personalize fax or e-mail queries, too.

Whether or not to follow the old rule of enclosing a stamped, self-addressed envelope for the editor's reply to a query is something you'll have to decide for yourself. Sometimes it works—it makes it easy for a busy editor to say "Yes." And sometimes it makes it easier for her to say "No." Often the "yes" involves a phone call, anyway, and sometimes the "no" never arrives—your letter just falls through the cracks. All too often the publishing office doesn't have enough help, and fitting replies into your SASE is not a high priority.

In today's world the whole subject of envelopes is controversial. Would an anthrax threat prevent an editor from opening the envelope? Would it prevent you from opening the return envelope? The entire question about mailed queries and manuscripts, with or without the SASE, is in a state of flux. You, naturally, will send your query in whatever form the editor requests. But remember that e-mail and fax queries demand the same kind of neatness, courtesy, and common sense as a letter sent by regular mail.

Turning Rejections into Acceptances

Once you have gotten your query together, agonized over each word, typed it neatly, enclosed the SASE, and sent it on its way, what kind of reply is it likely to elicit?

Unfortunately, the most common type in the beginning may be a small printed slip with a message something like this:

Thank you for your proposal, which has received careful consideration. We regret that this material does not meet our needs at the present time, but we appreciate your interest.

There's not much encouragement either in the printed form whose only personal touch is the X marked beside one of these negative possibilities:

( ) Subject matter not in line with our present needs

( ) Similar material on hand

( ) Idea too vague or too general for readership

( ) Similar material recently published

( ) Overstocked at present

Still worse is your own letter returned with something like "No thanks" scrawled across it.

Disheartening as these rejections are, overcome the temptation to throw them in the trash or burn them in the fireplace immediately. Save them. If later you take off some writer's expenses on your income tax (see Chapter 17 for discussion of tax deductions), rejection letters are good evidence for the IRS that you're at least trying to be a writer. Eventually you'll have enough rejection letters to paper a wall. But as one writer says, "By the time I had enough rejection letters to paper the living room, I was also getting enough assignments so I could afford real wallpaper."

Learn to read between the lines of a rejection letter. The printed slip or checked form with somebody's indecipherable initials scrawled at the bottom or "sorry" scribbled across the top are a step above the lowest form of rejection. Across the miles you can picture the editor regretting, just a trifle wistfully, that he must turn down your masterpiece of an idea in so casual a manner. If "Try us again" is inked in the margin, that's definite encouragement.

A photocopied form letter may have the same message as the small printed slip. If your name is typed in and the title or capsule sentence of your idea is mentioned, it's a good sign. If there's a signature, a date, or any written message, you're moving up. The next step is also a form letter, but it's individually typed, addressed to you personally, with the name of your idea in the body of the letter and a signature at the bottom. A scribbled postscript explaining the rejection, such as, "We've already planned a Niagara Falls feature for next month," shows a definite glimmer of interest in you as a potential contributor.

A still better rejection letter is the one written especially to you by a specific editor detailing the reasons your idea(s) won't work for him right now.

Often you can turn a "nice" rejection letter into an acceptance by simply reading between the lines. Does the editor say your idea is too complex and would make too long an article for him to use? Amputate and requery. Does he say he has too much material on hand now, but "try again in six months"? Mark it on your calendar. Does he like the subject area but not your approach? Suggest a different one. Does he name another publication that he thinks would provide a better home for your idea? Try it. Does he say "no" because he feels your idea wouldn't suit his readers, while you know it would be perfect for them? Convince him.

Several years ago, when Hal Schell queried a major magazine on a European article, the editor didn't think most of his readers were affluent enough for European travel. Schell thought, "Well, I'm not very affluent, and I've traveled in Europe." He rose to the challenge with a more convincing query: "How to see Europe without bending the budget." His article, "It's *In* to Camp Out in Europe," appeared as a beautiful center spread with four-color photographs.

Sometimes the editor explains why he doesn't like your proposal, but encourages you to try him with something else. Use care in selecting another subject—either a similar one or one quite different, depending on what the letter said—and submit another query to that editor immediately.

Keep good records of where and when you've queried on what, and don't accept a "no" as final. Often a new publication, a new editor at the same publication, or the same editor in a new mood, months or even years later, will transform a *no* into a *yes*.

Suppose you don't have any response to your query? How long should you wait to inquire? That depends on how urgent the time element is, but in general six or eight weeks. Then write a nice letter of inquiry, enclosing the original query, or, if you're on good terms with that editor, call or e-mail to ask for a decision. Often the response will be something like, "I'm so glad you called. I was interested in your idea, but somehow your letter seems to have gotten buried somewhere. Let's see what you can do with the article."

Dealing with the "Go-Ahead"

Not all answers to query letters are "yes" or "no." A great many of them are "maybe." That's what a go-ahead is—a "maybe." That's what the editor is saying when he indicates, "We'd like to see it on *speculation*." This is not an assignment. It makes no guarantee. All it promises is a careful reading. When you do send your manuscript, addressed to the editor who gave you the go-ahead, it won't land at the bottom of the slush pile of unsolicited manuscripts but will be carefully read by someone who at least liked the idea in the first place.

Professionals are divided as to whether or not to send a photocopy of the go-ahead along with the completed article. Is it a handy reminder, or is it an insult to the editor to remind him? If you don't send the photocopy, you should at least mention the go-ahead in your letter accompanying the article.

> Here, in response to your May 14 go-ahead, is the article on Mount Rushmore you asked to see. I hope you'll like "Four Faces for the Future" for your readers, and I look forward to hearing from you.

A go-ahead does give you the advantage of being able to say to an information source, "*XYZ Magazine* is interested in having me write an article on Mount Rushmore. Can you help me with my research?"

How long dare you wait to send your manuscript after the editor's expression of interest? That depends. It depends on the timeliness, both seasonal and topical, of the material. It depends, if you've queried before your trip, on how long you'll be away. It depends on the difficulty of the research. And it depends on the enthusiasm of the editor, which may or may not be related to a particular hole he has to fill, a special edition he plans, or the possibility of securing an accompanying advertisement.

What if the article is already written, having been rejected by somebody else? Should you send it as soon as you receive the go-ahead, thereby alerting the editor to his second-choice status? Or should you wait four or five weeks and pretend you're writing it just for him? A variety of circumstances will dictate your decision in this situation. Is the subject matter so timely it will soon be obsolete? Are there enough other possible markets for you to adopt a casual attitude toward rejection? Is the research so complex and time-consuming that this sale is all-important? There's no single "right" answer.

Always, though, reply to a go-ahead with a thank-you for the invitation to send your article. Indicate how long it will take you to complete the manuscript. In your estimate allow for all possible detours and distractions, and if in doubt, say, "I'll send it soon." Consider six months an outside limit, and aim for four to eight weeks.

If the writing takes longer than you anticipate, send progress reports, so the editor doesn't lose interest or assign the idea to somebody else.

The late Dr. William Rivers, professor of communications at Stanford University, felt the writer puts himself at a disadvantage by sending only the query and then the manuscript. "There is reason to believe," he said, "that a freelancer should undertake much more correspondence." He went on to tell of writers who greatly improved their percentage of sales after sending subsequent letters indicating progress of their research and asking for the editor's reaction to the shape the article was beginning to take, which was sometimes quite different from the shape originally suggested. Dr. Rivers concluded:

> The value of this process should be apparent. Correspondence helped the writer involve the editor. . . . After two or three letters, the editor had a stake in the writer's success. Sometimes the idea became more editor's than the writer's; [it]. . . evolved into an even better idea—at least from the editor's point of view.

Once your article is accepted, or even if it is rejected, but the editor sends an encouraging note, follow up quickly with a new query for a different idea.

What Are Your Query's Chances?

How likely is the beginner to receive any kind of positive response to his query? The statistics on receiving a go-ahead are one in ten when you're just starting out. And then you may consider the article half-sold. That doesn't mean some other editor won't encourage your idea or buy your piece eventually—the statistics only mean it may take twenty queries to sell an article.

More than twenty queries and no bites? Perhaps it wasn't such a good idea after all. Or perhaps your query isn't enticing enough, or your marketing itinerary was not astutely selected. Five go-aheads in a row—followed by prompt rejections? Either you haven't lived up to what you promised in the query or the five editors who gave you go-aheads have all died, retired, resigned, or been fired.

But don't be discouraged. As you learn to write better query letters, as you study markets and read between the lines of your rejections so that you're matching ideas and target markets more accurately, the statistics improve. An experienced freelancer expects a go-ahead or an assignment to result from one query letter in three. And then the statistics zoom. Instead of selling five out of every ten articles the first time out, you'll be selling nine out of ten or better.

Add the skills of a salesman to your skills as a writer for an unbeatable combination. You'll sell your travel stories as fast as you write them when you learn to make your queries work for you.

THIRTEEN

Writing for Others to Read

Writing, it is said, cannot be taught—it can only be learned. "But what about talent?" is a question potential travel writers frequently ask. "How can I tell if I have what it takes?" If you like to write and you like to travel, you can learn to write well enough to succeed. If you are writing for others rather than merely to please yourself, you'll want to follow the principles of effective travel writing, so let's pinpoint some of the fundamentals.

One basic precept we encounter again and again—and travel writers need to be reminded of it again and again—is that there's no such thing as "writing generally." Writing has to be *for* somebody—a particular publication, a particular reader. Remember, on paper or in cyberspace, that reader is always asking, "Why are you telling me this now?"

"Slant" Your Story

Study your target markets carefully, as we've said before. Then slant accordingly. "Slant" is not a dirty word. Slant is a means of ensuring that your material is read by those for whom it is intended. If you're writing for the *New York Times*, slant it for *Times* readers. The well-written travel article is filled with general information and enough slanted specifics to appeal to a particular reader.

In "Favorite Fly-Outs: To Penn's Cave and the Luray Caverns," Jack Elliott tells readers of an aviation magazine published for owners of small, private planes about interesting journeys they can take. In addition to describing the great natural wonders of the sites and the pleasures of spelunking, he inserts such flier-oriented specifics as:

> Caves are wonderful places for one-day flying trips. Luray Caverns
> Airport has a beautiful, 3500-foot paved strip with runway lights and

193

VASI on both ends. The field is about a mile away from the caverns and there is a courtesy car. . . .

Online readers, too, generally read what's slanted for their individual concerns—in shorter versions. To capture and maintain their interest, the content needs to be directed to a global audience, average age 32, mostly college educated, tech-oriented, with substantial income. And that content is usually presented in short chunks, with many subheads, sometimes bulletted, and often linked to other articles on related subjects.

Write a "Capsule Sentence"

Intrinsic to the travel article is the *message*. You must be able to express the idea behind your article—your message—in a single pithy capsule sentence. The capsule sentence should appear early on, and it should remain in your mind (and your reader's mind) from the first word to the final period.

What is your message? What are you trying to say?

The Kona Coast is a beautiful place to vacation.

Take your children to the Circus World Museum in Baraboo, Wisconsin—you'll enjoy it, too.

New York in summer is very different from New York in winter.

At Club Med the young at heart welcome new adventures.

Once you've settled on a clear-cut capsule sentence, tack it above your keyboard or write it on each page of first-draft paper as an ongoing reminder. Then everything in your article will relate to or confirm or amplify the message you've selected. Don't make that message too broad and general: "Wisconsin"; "New York." And don't make it too narrow: "My little boy liked the unloading of the circus wagons at the Circus World Museum in Baraboo, Wisconsin," or "Take the Staten Island Ferry on July 14 at two p.m." Once you've decided what you want to convey in the completed article, it's easy to fit the pieces of information into the mosaic of the whole.

The length of your article can be controlled by manipulating the capsule sentence. If you need a longer article, broaden its scope: "Hawaii has many beautiful spots," or "Investigate the Club Med." If you need a shorter article, narrow the scope. Because computer screens are harder on the reader's eyes and often download slowly, the finished piece may need to be built around "The fishing's good at Kona," or "I learned to snorkel at Tahiti's Club Med."

Unless all segments of your story relate to the capsule sentence they form what editors call "a string of pearls"—a series of unrelated incidents. No matter how interesting the individual anecdotes, unless they're skillfully slanted and connected to each other and to the capsule sentence, they will not hold the reader's interest. I've had students write of fascinating experiences in Chile, Portugal, Tahiti, and Ethiopia, with no commonality, no single thread or theme that united them. Until we could agree on a capsule sentence that expressed the student's reason for writing about these particular experiences, and could tie each incident to that sentence, there was no story.

What Is Your "Viewpoint"?

Another fundamental is viewpoint: the identity from which you're telling the story. Every piece of writing is told from some point of view, so decide in the beginning which you will use. You have several choices. First-person travel articles (I, or we, saw this and did that) of all types are becoming increasingly popular. And they are particularly popular in cyberspace, perhaps because the diary style seems to bring the writer and the reader closer to each other, whether the first person is a major or a minor character.

> My favorite experience in Japan was watching the cormorant fishing and seeing the merrymaking aboard adjacent boats.

Although most personal-experience stories are written in *first person major character*, don't feel this is the only possible viewpoint for travel articles. *First person minor character*, while less common, sometimes works out best:

> On the boat next to ours they were setting off firecrackers. "Soon the cormorant fishermen will come," said the geisha girl. "I hope they never come!" I heard the man beside her say. "Or at least not for a long time. After the fishing boats have come and gone, then I'll have to go home to my wife." He spoke in English, which surprised me. . . .

Will Stanton frequently presents himself as the minor-character observer when he travels with his children. He tells the story through the major characters, the children, giving their reactions to New York or Disneyland.

Third-person viewpoint, either major or minor, is used less often in travel articles, since it lacks the warmth and on-the-scene feeling of the more personal "I" or "you." *Third person minor character* is like this:

> Yoshi watched the geisha girl. She looked like she was getting tired, but she was still smiling. "The fishermen will be here soon," she said. He wondered if she. . .

Third person major character is like this:

> The Japanese worker looks forward to cormorant season, not only for the spectacle itself, but also for the fun aboard the chartered boat.

195

Sometimes a third-person travel article is unavoidable, as I discovered when I wrote about the travels of my daughter's Girl Scout troop. Since I did not accompany the girls on their trip, I tried to make up for the once removed viewpoint with quotes from the girls, substantial amounts of dialogue, and liberal use of anecdotes that showed the Brownies and the Girl Scouts during the nine years they prepared for the trip as well as while they were traveling.

Second-person viewpoint is popular in travel articles, usually used in combination with first person or third person:

> I enjoyed the train trip.
> You'll find the trains comfortable. . . .
>
> Their room overlooked the river.
> If you ask for a riverfront room. . . .

When second-person articles are structured like recipes or how-to-do-its, commanding peremptorily, "Take the nine o'clock ferry" or "Buy the tickets in advance," it's still obvious that I, the writer, am telling you, the reader, what to do, even if neither the "I" nor the "you" is mentioned. For example:

> In Japan be sure to take the excursion to see the cormorant fishing.

Another viewpoint without personal pronouns is the *implied.* Although the person telling the story is not identified, the reader is aware of someone providing the information. Through word pictures, active verbs, and strong emotional responses, the writer projects a "you are there" feeling. Implied viewpoint usually requires greater skill and more writing experience, so it often develops a stronger story.

> Acting much like a Big Game busload of convivial old grads, a boatload of Japanese co-workers makes merry while waiting for the cormorants. Men and women, comfortable in kimonos, sing and dance as they cook supper over hibachis, pass the sake bottle, and shoot off sky-brightening fireworks.

The *objective* viewpoint appears only in such straightforward travel writing as the encyclopedia:

> Cormorants can stay underwater a long time when they dive for fish.
> They swim with their webbed feet.

The *omniscient* viewpoint, where the author enters the minds of all the characters—the Japanese worker, the geisha girl, the fisherman (and possibly the cormorant) —is presently eschewed by most writers since it produces a weak and wordy article.

Switching Viewpoints

Must the entire article remain in one viewpoint? Generally, yes. Since the reader identifies with the viewpoint, switching complicates the story and requires extra wordage to prevent confusion. However, many travel articles do switch viewpoints—the only popular feature articles to do so. The piece might begin in first person:

> "Can it get much better than this?" A fellow passenger from St. Paul leaned back in his deck chair and sipped from his champagne flute as he asked the question. We were finishing our lunch of fresh salmon mousse, accompanied by three kinds of wine, a sunny autumn day, and a languorous desire to watch the scenery glide by at four miles an hour as we floated through France's champagne country aboard the barge Linquenda.

Then the article continues in second person:

> If you want to really see a country's hinterland, without the strain of driving, a week's barge trip on its waterways can be the most relaxing journey imaginable. You can stand at the rail and wave to the field hands harvesting the grapes or chat with the lock-keepers as they open or close the gates that move you from one water level to the next. Or you can. . .

Next, an implied viewpoint:

> The *Linquenda*, which carries a maximum of 14 passengers, has a pleasant sundeck, lounge-dining room with books, cards, music, and a well-stocked bar that's open all the time.

Back to "you" again:

> From the fresh-baked croissants in the morning to the chocolate on the pillow at night, you'll enjoy the five-star cuisine that includes. . .

And back to "us":

> We toured the cellars at several champagne houses, including Pomeroy and Moet Chandon, and, of course, tasted as we went.

And implied:

> This chalky, hilly countryside is ideal for the growing of champagne grapes, and it was here that Dom Perignon discovered. . .

First person again:

> An especially meaningful sight-seeing tour to those of us who had heard our parents or grandparents talk about Chateau Thierry and Belleau Woods, was the trip to. . .

The transitions must be accomplished smoothly, and you have to make sure that every time you switch viewpoints, you gain more than you lose.

The "Hook" Must Catch Your Reader

Your narrator won't operate in a vacuum. A good travel piece has a beginning, a middle, and an end. Unlike the traditional inverted pyramid of a newspaper story, where the most important facts are told in the first paragraph, with decreasingly important facts spelled out in succeeding paragraphs to allow for hasty cutting from the end, the travel feature story is a unified entity, and can only be shortened through paragraph-by-paragraph or sentence-by-sentence or word-by-word deletions.

A travel article's beginning should be sparkling, exciting, compelling: a *hook* that induces the reader—and the editor—to *read on*. Considering you have only a few seconds to nab a busy editor, page-flipping reader, or online surfer and involve him in your story, the importance of your opening cannot be overemphasized. Some writers say they spend half their writing time on the hook. Yet it's hard to describe what makes a good hook, although many writing teachers have tried.

I group travel article hooks into these three categories:

The **you** approach tells the reader why the information in this article will be especially valuable for him.

The **compare-and-contrast** hook builds tensions, arouses the reader's curiosity, and stimulates him to learn more.

The **scene-setting** hook hints, in an almost fictional manner, about a fascinating story to come.

The following "**you**" examples plunge right in and tell the reader how he will benefit from this article. Notice how many of the benefits concern money, such as:

> If you want a vacation spot where your dollars buy full measure of sunshine and sport, culture and cuisine, history and hospitality, head for southern Spain.

or

> If you bemoan the fact that your travel dollars never seem to take you where you want to go, if you return from vacation feeling frustrated because you spent more money for less fun than anticipated, it's time to analyze exactly what you want your vacation dollars to buy.

And notice how many of them are concerned with providing pleasure or alleviating discomfort, such as:

> For vacation activities to please every member of your family, try Buena Park in Southern California. There, you can ride an Old West stagecoach, inspect a $250,000 Rolls-Royce, or pet a lion cub. . . .

or

> If winter rains and post-holiday letdown are sending your thoughts toward a warm-weather vacation, remember it's summer in Lima and Buenos Aires.

In the "**compare-and-contrast**" type of hook, sometimes the tension that forces the reader to continue is provided by a surprise element.

> Thanks to Prohibition, juvenile delinquency, a crippling accident, drunken brawlers, and Johnnie Holzwarth, Rocky Mountain National Park opened its first living-history exhibit.

This hook compares and contrasts us and them:

> Ask a Texan his nationality, and he'll tell you he's American. Ask a citizen of Germany's southernmost state the same question, and chances are he'll answer, "I'm a Bavarian."

Sometimes hooks compare and contrast now and then:

> The fastest transportation available to man in the year 2000 B.C. was the camel caravan, which averaged approximately 3.5 miles an hour. Invention of the horse-drawn chariot raised the maximum speed for short distances to roughly 20 miles per hour. Little over a century ago this was still a record. It took 3500 years to get man's travel speed up to 100 miles an hour. Yet in the past century it soared from the railroad's 100 miles to the Concorde's designed speed of 1350 miles per hour.

Some hooks compare and contrast here and there:

> How does it feel to suddenly find yourself hospitalized six thousand miles from home in a strange land, worse yet in a Communist country with whom your own America had severed all ties more than a generation ago?

Comparing and contrasting seasons leads to a good hook:

> It's summer. All the skis, toboggans, boots, sweaters, mittens, and snow shovels are gladly packed away. It's time to load up the kids and the dog, the golf clubs, tennis rackets, swimsuits, sunglasses, sunburn ointment, and picnic basket and head for the nearest ski resort.

> That's right. Ski resorts are fast becoming the hottest summer vacation spots in New England. . . .

A "**scene-setting**" hook lures the reader into the story. Conflict provides a big part of the enticement. All three kinds of conflict—man against nature, man against man, and man against himself—can be used to good advantage.

Man against nature:

> He stands an instant, poised at the cliff's edge, then springs. His flying body plunges through the air, hurtling down more than 130 feet toward a narrow chasm of churning tidewater. . . .

Man against man:

> Anyone who has traveled abroad without knowing the local language has worried about being able to communicate. I thought I'd learned enough French in high school to get me from Paris to Marseilles, but a waiter in Lyons taught me differently. He not only brought me cream of watercress soup instead of crème caramel, he overcharged me ten francs.

Man against himself:

> After practicing six months in preparation for the canoe trip, I didn't believe the doctor when he said I wasn't strong enough to go. "I intend to go anyway," I told him. "Even if I have another heart attack, it's worth it."

"Key West Isn't a City, It's a State of Mind," at Lodging.com, begins with a wonderful scene-setting hook.

> Being a "Conch" is a state of mind, a condition of the heart and a fore-closure of the soul. Many Key Westers wear that epitaph proudly.
>
> This is a city that three times has threatened to secede from the Union and establish its own republic. It's a city whose former mayor water-skied all the way to Cuba to emphasize the importance of the U.S. Navy's presence. (And whose current one faces a federal charge of corruption.) It's a city whose melting-pot character permits a large, liberal body to mingle with Miami wheeler-dealers, out-of-work smugglers and other scallywags.

Begin at the Mattering Moment

We can't help observing how many of these hooks don't begin at the beginning—just as Homer didn't start with the day Helen of Troy was born. Like Homer, learn to begin in the middle of the action, then occasionally flash back to those parts of the beginning the reader needs to know. Whether it's an adventure tale or a nuts-and-bolts travel article, begin at the "mattering moment." That's the moment immediately preceding the action. Although the story may flash back and tell us about his first heart attack and his canoe trip preparations, the moment he decides to defy the doctor is, for this story, the mattering moment. We may later learn about the

Acapulco diver's training and practice and even something of the history of diving, but the story begins with the diver poised at the cliff's edge, about to start the action. Draw the reader into your story with something exciting, then, later, give him, as briefly and unobtrusively as possible, the background he needs.

As far as tenses go, more zine stories use present tense than we find in print media. Perhaps this, too, is an effort to be close to the reader.

W. Ruth Kozak's "Reaching for Heaven: Meteora, Greece," in *Travelwise Online*, begins:

> On a bright May afternoon I travel by train across the lush Thessaly Plain in central Greece, through the valley of the Pinios River.

Then come three paragraphs describing the landscape in an implied viewpoint. Going back to first person, present tense, she says

> Here I find reasonable accommodation and set off to explore the hills behind the town, following a goat trail. . .

Salon's Mark Hunter begins "France's Hidden Treasure" with

> So when I walk across Mischa's acre, which hasn't been grazed in years and is now overrun by neck-high nettles, I look first and test the grass with a beech stick I cut in the woods.

Hunter, actually in the I/you viewpoint, keeps switching tense, too. Usually simple immediate past tense is easiest for both writer and reader.

Travel Stories Need Plots, Too

The travel article, like its cousin the short story, is plotted. Although you should never distort the facts to improve the story, you can, by careful selection and arrangement, through screening and emphasis, create a plot.

Theodore Vogel begins at the mattering moment in his *Realities* story "Where It's Still Fair Whaling." While the subject matter is controversial, and the actions very graphic, it's a good piece for analyzing the use of flashbacks and flash-forwards.

> A harpooned sperm whale had turned and was coming back toward us with monstrous ease. Twenty-five tons of fat and muscle, and a tail four yards wide capable of disintegrating our frail boat with a single blow. . . .

> The gigantic snout rose slightly, then slipped below the boat.

> There are about thirty teeth in a sperm whale's mouth. A tooth can weigh ten pounds. No one had expected those teeth to surge from the water and clamp onto the *Claudina's* rim—but there they were, just a yard away. . . .

Then Vogel flashes back two centuries:

> Azorians hunt whales the way it was done two hundred years ago, when
> American companies recruited oarsmen in the islands and introduced
> the whaler's ways. . .

Back to the present:

> Today Azorians still hunt whales better than anyone else. . .

A brief flashback:

> Four years ago the *Maria da Conceicdo*. . . harpooned an enormous sperm
> whale which turned and attacked the boat. . . the whale boat. . . smashed
> in three places. . . two men. . . dead.

He then flashes to his own pre-trip agreement to "accept all the responsibilities that would result from my death. I signed quickly," he says, "and
handed it to the captain. . . ." He explains that lookouts in a whale-hunting
village fire flares and radio the tugs when they see a white spout. Then he
takes us back to his own whale hunt:

> The sperm whales seemed monstrous to me in their surges and dives. . .
> At a yard's distance, Almerindo flung his harpoon, hitting the whale just
> below the hump of its back. Everything happened so fast that I had
> trouble registering it.

Vogel discusses the danger and tells of whalers who have been hurt.
Then he flashes to the present, where their boat is being towed by the
whale. They move in for the kill, hunters and whale fighting, the water
growing red. An hour and a half and twelve spears later, the whale is finally dead.

Vogel introduces philosophical remarks about the whaling industry,
international protection of whales, and the future of whaling. Then back to
the present:

> It was two p.m. I felt as if years had passed.

A storm comes up and the eight men huddle together in the stern, but they
are in good spirits:

> And for a moment, I really understood what it was. . . that had sent men
> out to sea in ships, for centuries, to hunt.

Had Vogel begun with the history of whaling, mentioned his own
adventure in the middle, where it comes chronologically, then ended with
the outlook for whaling in the future, the story would have lacked the
drama, excitement, and emotional impact it imparts. When you write for
others you soon learn to seduce your reader by presenting the most spec-

tacular item in the beginning and adapting the chronology to your own plotting purposes.

The Anatomy of a Travel Story

My *Wasa* article in *Coronet* involved an additional problem, since the here-and-now aspects—the discovery and recovery of the ship—were already some ten to fifteen years in the past, too long ago for a news peg. So I started with an earlier *mattering moment*, the day the *Wasa* sank:

> As the seventeenth-century battleship *Wasa* raised sail to begin her maiden voyage, holiday crowds lining Stockholm's Royal Quay waved cheerfully and shouted good wishes. Sweden's naval pride moved majestically into midchannel. . . .
>
> And then the *Wasa*, sails billowing and flags flying, heeled over and vanished without making even the harbor exit.
>
> Three centuries later the ship returned from her eighteen-fathom grave. . . her figurehead still glittering with gilt and her captain's tankard still filled with schnapps.

Then the capsule sentence, appropriate for *Coronet's* general readership:

> The story of the *Wasa's* downfall, her subsequent resistance to decay during three centuries of submersion, and her ultimate recovery is, indeed, stranger than fiction.

Next I tell about present efforts to preserve the *Wasa*, flash back to events leading up to the mattering moment of the hook, then explain subsequent attempts to raise the ship, extending over several hundred years. Then:

> In a way, the teredo, or shipworm, led to eventual rediscovery of the *Wasa*, after three centuries.

Anders Franzen, as I explain, thought a ship sunk in the teredo-free waters of the Baltic would be well preserved. The flashback takes place in his mind:

> Surely, he reasoned, someone must have notified the king.
>
> After months of searching he found the message. . . . "Off Beckholmen."

Back to the immediate past, with divers discovering an old ship with two rows of gunports:

> . . . Franzen was sure. It had to be the *Wasa*! But. . . What does one do with 1400 tons of seventeenth-century warship anchored in mud, 110 feet beneath a busy harbor?

I continue with the salvaging and recovery of the ship and its contents. This leads to a discussion of seventeenth-century shipboard life. Then back to the present with a description of the museum where the *Wasa* and the finds are housed. Then more about seventeenth-century life aboard ship, tied in with the present museum exhibits. I next cover the steps being taken for the *Wasa's* preservation and her probable future. Then:

> Visitors can stand on the museum's catwalks and look down through the chemical fog to the heart of the ship. . . They can, with a little imagination, see the *Wasa* as she looked on the day of her debut, sails billowing and flags flying . . . sailed less than a mile in her lifetime . . . reincarnated to live forever.

Ten years later, when I wrote a completely different *Wasa* story for *Off Duty*, I was able to tie the hook to the 350th anniversary observance of the ship's sailing (and sinking). Because *Off Duty's* European edition was published for U.S. servicemen who might go to Stockholm on leave, the capsule sentence of that story is:

> Today the *Wasa* occupies a museum, complete with skeleton sailors, seventeenth-century schnapps, and slightly rancid butter.

After mentioning the guns being fired with a false charge for the anniversary celebration, I go back to the sailing day disaster, then return to what you can see today, interspersed with explanations of why everything is in such good condition. Then a chronological report of salvage efforts, the recovery of the *Wasa*, the building of the museum, and a forecast for the future, ending with:

> . . . this ship now lives to carry tourists and scientists . . . back into history.

A sidebar tells when the museum is open, how much it costs, etc.

It's easier to write a story like this when you have an anniversary peg to tie it to, but a heavily historical article written for a popular audience always requires many flashbacks and flash-forwards.

"Show, Don't Tell"

What else goes into your travel article? Ideally your content will sing with active verbs and precise nouns that appeal to the reader's five senses. Salt sparsely with adjectives and adverbs; avoid cliches, today's slang expressions, and anything that dates the piece or sounds "cutesy." On the other hand, utilize all the tricks of the fiction writer's craft. Anecdotes, scenes, dialogue, characterization, and dramatic action belong in the travel story. Write with the breathless excitement of the best travel brochures—but only within the framework of truth and accuracy.

A *New York Times* travel editor summarizes the *Times* formula for good travel writing:

> You must use all the devices of the writer's skill to keep readers interested—a hook beginning; a "billboard" to tell them what the article is about near the beginning; word pictures, which is what travel writing is all about; what it looks, smells, tastes like. Amateurs use adjectives instead of word pictures. They write, "It was a lovely scene," instead of telling us what kind of scene it was. Was the sun slanting in from the west? Was there ice on the ground? Were there leaves on the trees? What kind of scene was it? Show, don't tell.

When you hear a writer or an editor say "show, don't tell," it means you should sharpen it up by getting rid of all the nonworking words, all the dead weight, and, at the same time, flesh it out with details that count. For instance:

> **Telling**: Many medieval people were convinced that the dust from the tomb of Saint John held extra special curative powers, and many ailing pilgrims climbed up Ayasuluk Hill.

> **Showing**: Medieval Christians on three continents whispered to each other that dust from Saint John's tomb held special curative qualities. Thousands of them plodded up Ayasuluk Hill carrying blind babies or lugging lame relatives on donkey-drawn stretchers.

Or

> **Telling**: One night during the cruise there is a passenger costume competition where everybody dresses up like a sheik or a dancing girl or a mummy. Then passengers adjourn to the dining room for a spectacular Mideast buffet—from sculptured lamb to baklava and grape pudding.

> **Showing**: When the pseudo-sheik with the bath towel turban beckoned to the black-veiled harem "girls" they thrust out their stomachs and bellydanced around the passenger salon. . . . They adjourned to the dining room. Earlier that day our guide had gathered us together and spelled out procedure. "Use your elbows and your shoulders," he advised. "This buffet is really something—and everyone rushes to be first in the dining room line. Don't stand back politely—push like everybody else!" Actually, there was plenty to eat, even for latecomers. But at first sight, that buffet table was worth a little elbowing. The artists of the galley had even sculptured the meat into the shape of a lamb, kneeling on a bed of rice that had been browned to simulate the desert. Roasted pheasants and game hens climbed an ornamental superstructure and a half-dozen varieties of fresh fish surrounded the "desert." Purple half shells of savory eggplant alternated with stuffed green peppers and tomato-topped Oriental salads. Dishes of black olives and plates of yellow cheeses

adjoined the platters of grape leaves rolled into dolmas, which encircled a huge bowl of yogurt. Steam rose from the couscous and the kabobs. Melons, grapes, oranges, and a dozen unfamiliar but delicious fruits and a garden of miniature decorated cakes accompanied the baklava and grape pudding, and were followed by demitasses of strong, sweet coffee.

Obviously, "showing" can take up a lot of space. It presents a challenge when writing for online markets or when your print editor is rigid about the number of words you're entitled to.

Good Writing Is Always Good Rewriting

When you feel your article is finished, put it away for at least a week and try not to think about it. You'll return to it with fresh insights and a renewed ability to recognize its faults and to set about correcting them. Many times you'll find ways to cut constructively. Practically all writing is improved by careful cutting. Consider:

> If you are a passenger on board a cruise ship, you will know whether or not to buy the ship's shore excursions. (22 words)

> Aboard ship, you'll know whether or not to buy the shore excursions. (12 words)

> Houseboat operators usually require a $50 to $100 deposit when you make your reservation. This becomes your damage deposit, which is refunded when you return the boat intact. (28 words)

> The $50 to $100 that accompanies your reservation becomes your damage deposit—refunded when you return the boat intact. (19 words)

You'll find the more times you go over your finished piece, the more words you'll discover you can cut. Don't skimp on rewriting time. In college I asked a favorite professor who had published many books and articles if he thought there was something wrong with me because it always took me five or six drafts to write an article. "If there is," he replied, "there must be something wrong with *me*, too, because it always takes me five or six drafts."

Read your article aloud when you're working on it. A word of caution, though: if you put enough vigor into your voice and your posture and your facial expression, anything sounds good; the editor, unable to see or hear your performance will be limited to the words on the paper. So read it in a monotone, to recognize words carelessly repeated, "fat" that could be cut, inactive verbs that need active substitutes, abrupt transitions that should be smoothed, and complex, dense, or convoluted sentences that need recasting.

Try to eliminate slang and jargon and any language that dates a piece you hope will live forever. Reach for unusual figures of speech as well as descriptive ones. Rolf Potts in *Salon.com's* "One Fateful Day in Istanbul" uses a number of figures of speech that pull the reader right into the scene:

I fell over. . . . like a wind-up toy on a rumpled bedsheet.

. . . the gypsy girl in the oversize Metallica T-shirt

. . . from the lavish Ottoman halls of Topaki Palace to the crowded dagger-and-houka pipe stands of the Grand Bazaar

A transition is like a road sign that points your reader toward the next paragraph. We're all familiar with the standard "ongoing" words and phrases, such as *and; furthermore; similarly;* and the "backup" transitions: *however; on the contrary; despite.* We know, too, the cause and-effect relationships: *as a result; because; consequently.* These are often overworked, though, so look for additional types of transitions to guide your reader to the next phase of your story. Time is a good transition: *the next morning; the following year; by six o'clock.* More subtle time transitions might be: *my coffee grew cold; the daffodils were blooming; when our ship sailed in.* Repeating a word from the previous paragraph, repeating the rhythm of the last sentence, comparing and contrasting—are all good transitional devices. You'll find ways to smooth out your forward motion as you revise.

Leave Your Reader Satisfied

Your reader will consider your ending almost as important as your beginning. An article's ending should grow out of the article itself, to provide a finale that seems logical and inescapable, leaving the reader satisfied. Many travel writers write the end at the same time as the hook. This not only brings you full circle, with beginning and ending written in the same mood, but defines the boundaries of where you're going. It's easier to stay on the track when you know where you will finish. The ending should usually not be a summary of what you've said in the article, nor should it be what Professor Rivers called "a crashing conclusion"—an ending with more force than the story itself, an ending that "tells all" and then tells it again. Instead, it should be a convincing culmination that leaves your reader either smiling or frowning, but definitely thinking about what you have just said. Notice how these endings grow inevitably out of the article beginnings:

Beginning: Sigiriya bursts upon you. As you round the bend of a jungle road in central Sri Lanka, the gigantic red rock "fortress in the sky" looms six hundred feet above its surrounding pleasure gardens. Visiting this preserve of a fifth-century royal murderer is a memorable experience. . . .

Ending: When you leave Sigiriya the red rock disappears as suddenly as it appeared. Then you see only the lime-green plain where Kassapa met Moggallana, and the ever-encroaching jungle.

Beginning: The wonderful thing about oysters is that they taste the way the ocean looks and smells.

After describing a day's boating on Tomales Bay, which included fresh oysters for lunch, author Robertson Pease concludes:

Ending: The wonderful thing about Tomales Bay is that it looks and smells just the way oysters taste.

Margaret Bennett's very good article "A Japanese Orientation to Travel" extols the excellence of the Japan Travel Bureau and the arrangements it made for her and her friend. She begins with a compare-and-contrast question.

When is a tour more of a tour by being less of a tour? Although this question may seem to resemble one of those unanswerable Zen problems, like "What is the sound of one hand clapping?" it can be easily answered by anyone who has taken an "independent tour" of Japan arranged by JTB, the Japan Travel Bureau.

The story continues in first person, then switches to second in the last paragraph:

So if you're considering a trip to Japan, you should also consider that considerate organization, JTB. If you do travel with them, when you get back home, although you still may not know the answer to the eternal Zen question "What is the sound of one hand clapping?" there will be no doubt in your mind as to what the sound of two hands clapping is— it will be you applauding the services and the personnel of the Japan Travel Bureau.

Oh, Yes, Your Story Needs a Title

You wonder perhaps how I've brought you to the end of this chapter without saying anything yet about titles. There are two reasons: First, the best titles often grow out of the article itself—sometimes I don't decide on the final title until I'm putting the manuscript in the envelope—and second, the title should be influenced by the kind your target market routinely uses. Are they usually mere labels (The Alcan Highway) or questions (Where Can You Find the Cheapest Airfare?) or direct orders (See Europe This Winter!) or how-tos (How to Travel with Teenagers) or cutesy (Portuguese Climate, Customs and Madeira, M'Dear)?

If a wonderful title occurs to you early on, of course you'll use it, regardless. If you can't think of a thing, try some of these possibilities: Everybody likes a title that talks about saving money or time; a title that promises improvement in health, creativity, or prestige; a title that hints of the newest, the latest, the most up to date; a title that tells you the article will tell you how to do something. *You*—either spelled out or implied—is a very important word. The title should be intriguing, startling, or thought-provoking and usually no longer than six words. Its sales pitch becomes increasingly important in magazines that depend more on newsstand sales than mailed subscriptions. Today, more titles are used on the cover, to lure the potential buyer, and the titles themselves have more punch.

Even if the editor changes your title, and he often does, its value as a sales tool cannot be overestimated. Some of the best titles combine the familiar with the unfamiliar. "Lewis and Clark Were Name Droppers" tells of their mapmaking activities; "Rooting Around in the Gambia" discusses the *Roots*-inspired desire of black Americans to find their own roots in Africa.

Alliteration in the title is a plus: "Shannon is Super for Shoppers" or "Patriots in Petticoats." Hyphenation can be used to advantage: "Charm-ed, I'm Sure" (about travel charm bracelets) or "Turkish Delight-ful."

Some of the best titles use reversal: "All Is Good in the Badlands" or "Wild Horses Could Drag You There" (about untamed stallions in Wyoming) or "Don't Come In Out of the Rain" (about taking travel photos in bad weather).

A play on words is always welcome: "How to Operate a Den of Antiquity" (about flea markets), "Virginia City's Silver Lining" (silver mining in the Old West), "They're Forever Blowing Bubbles" (a tour of champagne wineries), or "The Last Resort" (Canada's northernmost fishing lodge) are all alluring. Another Canadian-inspired title about the Rockies in winter appeared in a February *Travel Holiday*—"Canada: To Brrr is Human."

Online titles are similar to print titles—just a bit briefer and more blatant. Would "I Fell in Love in a Korean Bathhouse" or "Scuba Mom's Gateway to Caribbean Dive and Vacation Information" tempt you to scroll in that direction at *About.com*?

Most cyberspace publications mention the destination's name in the title. *Travelwise Online* (www.travel-wise.com), for instance, offers "Walking Santo Domingo," "Bermuda—Love and Onions," "Touring Gaudi's Bracelona," "Carlsbad Caverns—Time Tunnels," "Rio—Brazil's Marvelous City," and similar pointers to their travel articles.

The title should always, of course, give honest hints about what's in the story. Don't mislead your reader. Have you heard the legend of the old *Liberty* magazine's cover story from 1940, "My Sex Life" by Mahatma Gandhi? Well, the story begins, "In 1906 I took the vow of celibacy." And that's the end of the story. Don't try to fool your reader that way.

Do remember your reader as you're writing your travel article. Give that reader the best, most interesting copy you can write. Remember, a dull story from Istanbul or Bombay is just as boring as a dull story from Podunk.

FOURTEEN

Asking Questions–
The Interview

"Where were you?" my daughter asked as I slipped into a seat beside her in the ship's lounge. "Where did you disappear to after dessert?"

Dessert had been flaming baked Alaska carried around the darkened dining room by a platoon of waiters and kitchen helpers. The baked Alaskas not only looked spectacular, they tasted delicious. As soon as we finished eating, I went to interview the chef.

When you have an assignment to write a cruise article, the chef is one of the principal characters. Other principal characters—such as the purser or the deck steward—may have something to say for your story, too.

When you need information, what do you do? You interview the people who can supply it. How many dozen eggs are whipped to froth in the ship's galley each day? What is the ratio of crew members to passengers? Do many people get seasick or need treatment for other ailments? How many hundreds of sheets, towels, etc., are washed in the ship's laundry every week? When celebrities sail aboard this ship do they sit on deck with the hoi polloi? Or do they relax in the solitary splendor of their veranda suites? What percentage turn out for the various shipboard activities?

If it's statistics you want, ask the head man, the purser. The deck steward is more likely to tell you an anecdote about the famous actress whose string of oriental pearls broke while she was swimming in the pool. He might even whisper the name of the aging politician whose tinted hair turned green in the sunlight. And don't forget the ship's doctor, the head housekeeper, and the cruise director.

Keep Your Interview in Focus

The face-to-face interview is one of the travel writer's most important tools. Interviews translate abstract ideas into human terms, and they're indispensable for many types of stories. You, the interviewer, are not only asking questions you expect the subject to answer, you're acting as a sounding board, listening to the subject's message and interpreting his stance.

Your purpose in interviewing may be to know more about an individual for a profile, but in travel writing it's more likely to be the topic that interests you. You're trying to draw out the person's expertise so you can write an authoritative story for your readers. It's very important to know your objectives. What are you searching for? Insights into personality, basic background, oral history, personal anecdotes, enriching secondary facts, pithy quotes—or do you have a variety of objectives?

You should, before you even arrange an interview, have in mind the *focus* of the piece you intend to write, or, in some cases, several different thrusts for several different pieces. Then you can successfully steer the interview toward the specific information you need.

People Like to Be Interviewed

Don't ever hesitate to ask for an interview. Most people *like* to be sought out. As a noted interviewer says, "No one objects to questions about the measure of his or her own accomplishment." You are not imposing or invading privacy. If face-to-face won't work, try e-mail or voice to voice—preferably with instant messaging.

Even though original travel articles designed for online reading are usually shorter than those designed for print, the basic research of the interview remains just as necessary.

Sometimes beginning travel writers are timid about requesting interview time. "I don't represent anybody," one complained. "I'm a nobody, myself, and I can't even say I'm writing the article for a particular publication. How do I know if I can ever sell it?"

This is a problem. If you have an assignment, of course you'll mention it when you ask for the interview. But even if you have just a go-ahead answer to a query, you can say, *"Blank Blank* magazine has expressed an interest in this story." Or you can say, "I'm writing this for *Blank Blank* magazine," as long as you're careful not to imply an assignment that doesn't exist. Surely you'll have in mind the publication you'd *like* to be writing it for before you begin interviewing.

Generally even the busiest, most prominent people are cordial and cooperative to an interviewer. But even such experienced reporters as Joan Didion speak of experiencing "sweaty palms" and "knocking knees" when trying to make the arrangements.

If you can, telephone or write for an appointment, indicating the length of time you'll need—usually an hour—and whether or not you'll be photographing at the same time. If, however, an interview becomes important during your travels, and you've had no opportunity to plan it in advance, try to get it anyway. You'd be surprised how often such spur-of-the-moment attempts succeed.

Find Out What You Can in Advance

Do as much homework as you can before the interview. If you're at home, search the library for general background about the person and the subject, and seek online information. If an opportunity presents itself while you're traveling, perhaps the local library can provide clues, or the secretary or assistant to the person you're interviewing can give you some information before the interview itself. Aboard ship, reread the biographical material in the brochure and the ship's newspaper. If you can, ask in advance for printed materials, scrapbooks, excerpts from speeches or other interviews—anything to help you get acquainted beforehand and prevent you from wasting your time and the interviewee's with "Where did you go to school?" or "How long have you been with the company?" Already knowing the answers to questions like these saves time, and you get off to a good start when you can say, "How do you like it here in Texas? I understand you grew up in Wisconsin and went to college in Minnesota—this must seem quite different to you."

Some interviewers like to send the interviewee an advance list of possible questions or outline of areas they want to discuss. This gives the subject an opportunity to think about the focus before the interview and perhaps collect enriching information. These questions should be broad and open-ended, not the kind that can be answered yes or no.

Aim for Specific Answers

You may not want to ask these specific questions when the time comes, but you'll want to at least jot down a few starter questions that will move the interviewee in the right direction. An interview should not be an exercise in "Q-and-A" but should give the subject an opportunity to speak freely about the topic, with the interviewer only occasionally inserting another question or deftly moving him back onto the track. Starter questions should be designed to encourage colorful, anecdotal, quotable answers. Again you'll want to avoid questions that can be answered with yes or no or a date or statistic. The open-ended question is fine for stirring up the interviewee ahead of time, but when you're actually talking to him, avoid this kind of question. Where there's no precise answer, sometimes the subject just talks on and on, without saying anything quotable. Try to get specific answers. From the specific you can generalize, but not the other way around.

The ability to frame effective interview questions is the mark of the professional.

Jessica Mitford said she prepared for an interview by asking an expert in the field what questions to ask. "If I were going to interview a prosecuting attorney I'd . . . ask [a defense lawyer] if he were a reporter what would he ask the prosecutor."

This is good advice when the subject matter is controversial. However, you're not always meeting your subject in an adversary relationship. When you ask the chef to identify the most difficult, or the most popular, dish he prepares for the passengers, there's no need to be aggressive in your questioning.

The main thing to remember is: Put yourself in the place of your reader. What questions would *he* like answered? What part of your proposed article could be better explained through a quote from the interviewee? Often you, the travel writer, are merely the middleman interpreting your subject for your reader. Again the framing of the questions ensures the accuracy and completeness of that information.

Framing the Questions

Sometimes your editor, wanting the interview to follow a particular format, will suggest the questions. When I wrote up a series of interviews with travel agents for the trade journal *Travel Age West*, the stories were for a regular feature called "Counter Intelligence." The directions were to "focus on the travel agency's staff, rather than the manager, and make it light and gossipy. We want to hear about unusual travel experiences, difficult or funny clients, worst or best travel experiences, interesting or strange hobbies," the directions continued, then went on with what not to do. The editor suggested that a question about how long the travel agent had been in his position or where he had worked before was okay to start him talking but "it does not make very interesting reading. Neither does how much they like the travel business. . . ." Instead, she suggested, "Be warm and light and, if possible, be funny. What we are after is the personality of the agent, not the stuffy professional image that some may wish to give."

Following directions, I made up a list of warm-up questions about the person's hobbies and interests, family, unusual trips, difficult customers, etc. I also designed a few broad questions to lead into what I hoped would be quotable material, such as "What special service do you feel you and your agency have to offer? Are most of your customers realizing a lifelong dream or are they traveling because they think it's the thing to do? What changes do you think should be made in the travel industry?" As soon as the travel agents began talking, I listened for opportunities to elicit "light and gossipy" material. That's how I found out about the travel agent whose attempt to bring back swords from Taiwan as gifts for her husband and son resulted in a confrontation with the Taiwanese authorities who refused to let her board the plane, shouting "No! No! Weapons!" while she shouted back "Yes! Yes! Souvenirs!" And about the client who put his traveler's checks in the pocket of a shirt left on the beach while he went for a swim—forgetting that the tide was coming in. Others mentioned complex itineraries that eventually "jelled," unusual services performed for unusual clients, and personal hobbies that led them to far-out places.

Whatever your list of questions, be sure to number them so you can refer to those numbers as the questions are answered. How will you record the replies? Will you use a tape recorder or a keyboard, write notes, or rely on memory? Perhaps all four.

Recording the Information

You must ask permission to use a tape recorder. This permission will usually be granted by people who are accustomed to being interviewed and who feel comfortable with mechanical devices. Sometimes they prefer it: They're sure of being quoted correctly. The tape, of course, gives *you* a perfect record of the conversation, and on sensitive subjects might provide a valuable reference for direct quotes. Try to use a tape recorder with a built-in microphone, as small and inconspicuous as possible. Be sure it's working properly, has fresh batteries, and that the "record" button is depressed if necessary. Watch for the end of the tape, and change it unobtrusively. Remember, also, that music or loud background noise of any kind, such as the clatter of dishes in a restaurant, may prevent a clear reproduction.

Even if you use a tape recorder, take careful notes anyway. There are two reasons for this: first, the danger of mechanical failure. I never completely trust a tape recorder—I've seen too many chagrined expressions after interviews, as the interviewer unwinds a twisted mass of tape or plays what turns out to be a blank cassette. The second reason for taking notes is the way it makes you focus on what the person is saying. Too often the interviewer relies on the tape and doesn't listen attentively because he thinks, "It's all there—I can replay it any time," thereby losing the essence of the interrelationship with the subject.

Getting it Down

"What do you use for taking notes?" is a question students frequently ask. I, as well as most interviewers, use a stenographer's notebook—the kind issued to newspaper reporters. It's not only a good size—large enough to get lots of thoughts down, but small enough to handle comfortably—it also features easy-to-turn pages and a firm cover. It has an additional advantage, too: Many interviewees, accustomed to dictating to secretaries, are psychologically receptive to the steno pad. Today, most are receptive, also, to the interviewer's laptop or handheld, both of which become lighter, smaller, and less obtrusive every day.

Two note-taking rules every interviewer should commit to heart:

1. It *is* possible to take notes without looking down at them (thus losing eye contact with your subject). Practice. Keep your eyes on a person or a TV screen as you write what is being said.

2. Transcribe all notes before you go to bed that night. Regardless of what kind of personal shorthand you use, regardless of how well you think you'll remember every word that was said, "cold" notes lose about half their value in forty-eight hours and three-fourths of it within the week. A month later your notes, unless you've immediately clarified and amplified them, are practically worthless.

Some interviewers, of whom Truman Capote was perhaps the most notable example, spurn the tape-recording, note-taking process, claiming total recall without memory aids. That may be. But if you don't take any notes it makes the interviewee nervous.

I recently spent an evening with a friend who had been interviewed at noon by a writer who took no notes. "How can she possibly remember what I said?" my friend muttered. "There she was, eating her shrimp salad and acting like it was just an ordinary conversation—and all the time asking me questions that could get me fired if she misquotes me." He was very apprehensive until the interview—which did not misquote him—appeared in print. It's usually reassuring to the subject when the interviewer jots down answers—especially to critical questions or those involving facts and figures.

Gay Talese says he gets information by "just hanging around." But every once in a while he takes out his notebook and asks a question like, "What year did you say your uncle was born?" just to remind subjects that he is, after all, a reporter and is not trying to conceal that fact.

Sometimes Your Memory Is All You Have

Sometimes, though, tape recorders, computers, and even notebooks are prohibited, and the travel writer *must* rely entirely on memory. Such was the case in Cairo when we attended a briefing at the U.S. Embassy during a critical period in Middle East affairs. Although questions were permitted, writing and recording the answers was not, and the material discussed was to be used for background only.

While we're all familiar with movies where the cub reporter violates a confidence to scoop his competitor, and everybody cheers his ingenuity, real life is different. The travel writer who accepts an invitation to a briefing at the embassy with the understanding that no direct or indirect quotes will result from it had better not violate that confidence—if he expects his sources to continue to help him.

The *Washington Post's* Sally Quinn feels it's very important to wear the same kind of clothes and behave in the same manner as your interview subject. "Create an atmosphere of sympathy. Don't scream, 'I am different from you!' as soon as you enter the room," she says. She relates it to method acting—actually becoming the person you're interviewing.

Ways to Warm Up Your Subject

Every interviewer has a special way of warming up the subject with preliminary small talk. I once heard Alice Phillips say, after doing hundreds of interviews, that she always asks a male subject who gave him his necktie, and this usually produces a good anecdote and leads into questions she wants to ask. I thought of her technique when I interviewed the manager of Waikiki's military hotel, the Hale Koa, about changes Congress was imposing that affected the administration of the hotel and admission of retired military personnel. Because the entire operation was in the midst of a congressional investigation, the manager asked the colonel who was deputy chief of staff for the U.S. Army's Western Command to sit in on the interview. But I was unable to follow Phillips's advice. Both men wore open-necked Aloha shirts.

Usually the interviewer begins with a simple question like, "Have you enjoyed your tour of duty here?" This is to get the subject in the habit of responding. Be sure to keep the focus on him. Do not permit him to turn the conversation to you for any length of time. If he asks how you became a travel writer, say something like, "I've always liked to write and I've always liked to travel." Then turn it back to him with, "I know you've done a lot of traveling, too. What's your favorite part of the world?"

Keep in mind why you're there, and don't let the conversation ramble off in all directions. If the subject expounds on a technical matter in technical phrases, ask, "How shall I explain that to my readers in layman's language?" If he makes a controversial statement, don't pounce gleefully and hurry to scribble it down. Be casual. Ask another question while you're writing the controversial answer. Don't bulldoze your way into the conversation: Use gentle tactics, beginning your controversial questions with "I imagine that. . ." or "It appears that. . . ." If you can't seem to pin the interviewee down to specifics, give him a misquote, like, "Others are saying the airline is losing two million dollars a year." This encourages him to reply indignantly, "That's not true. It's less than a million! Only about $875,000!"

Some travel writers believe in interspersing the "hard" questions with the "easy" questions, while others favor an easy beginning, getting progressively harder and more controversial. With either method, make your last two questions soft and innocuous, to end the interview with pleasant feelings on both sides.

Keep 'em Talking

If you want a reluctant subject to explain something, say, "Nobody seems to understand about this situation," implying that the interviewee is the only one who might be able to set your readers straight.

Silence is sometimes an excellent interview technique. Don't rush in to fill the void as soon as the conversation flags. Observe a moment of silence, and let the interviewee be the one to break it.

When you don't know anything about the topic under discussion, try to relate it to something you do know. When I was freelancing for my local newspaper, the city editor sent me, on ten minutes notice, to interview a missionary visiting from her post in Korea. I had never been to Korea and didn't know much about missionaries in general or her denomination in particular. But I soon discovered she was an English teacher at a college. That I knew about—English and colleges. We progressed from discussing the architecture of the college to the architecture of the surrounding city of Seoul, from the teaching of English to Koreans to Korea's place in the world today, from a woman's adventures teaching in a faraway land to her travel adventures and experiences in other places.

If your subject doesn't say what you want him to, sometimes you can persuade him by putting phrases in his mouth. Begin, "In other words. . ." and then frame the sentence you want, asking only for an affirmative nod.

Expert interviewer John Brady admits that you may not get results by saying to your subject, "Tell me an anecdote." He suggests using the phrase, "What can you tell me about your experiences in the field?" Sometimes, too, you can elicit an anecdote by telling a related one to the interviewee. If you tell him about the Greek Island jeweler who almost managed to get you arrested, he may respond with his story of a weekend in Guatemala under "house arrest" at his hotel. One mistaken identity story leads to another mistaken identity story. But don't get more involved in the telling than you do in the listening.

Physical Details Add an Extra Dimension

Give the reader the feeling he's met the person you're interviewing. Provide insight into character through selected details. Don't just note, "He's a big man," but be prepared to write, "He gingerly lowered his muscular six-foot frame." Don't be satisfied with, "He's fair," but fill your tape recorder or notes with details: "afternoon sunlight reveals sprinkling of freckles," "blond hair appears almost white."

When you see an office with a picture window, a rosewood desk, an oriental rug, you're seeing a man of substance. Observe how he sits at his desk—ramrod straight, leaning back with feet on the desk top, or simply relaxed? Is music playing? What kind of music? Is the desk cluttered or bare? What books are in evidence? Family photos? What is the subject wearing? A necktie? Desert boots? A gold bracelet? If you're interviewing a woman, did she have her hair styled for the occasion? Is she wearing jogging shoes? A diamond wristwatch? Are her fingernails short or long? Be a sponge. Absorb everything.

When Alex Haley was still traveling around collecting material for *Roots*, I heard him say at a writers' conference, "When you interview a man, if his wife is present, watch the expression on her face. It can tell you a lot." That evening, as I listened to another big-name writer present a rather boring speech, I glanced back a couple of rows to check out his wife. She was sound asleep.

"On" and "Off" the Record

Some interviewers have trouble with "off the record" and it's very important to clearly settle that matter at the start. Always set guidelines: Anything that is said will be on the record unless agreed to be off at the time it's said. This prevents the interviewee from remarking at the end of the interview, "Oh, you know, that whole bit I told you about the State Department investigation of the travel industry—that was off the record, of course." Whether or not to listen to off-the-record material depends on how badly you need it for background and whether or not you'll be able to get it on the record from somebody else. Once having promised it's "off," you must keep your promise. Then it's awkward if the same information comes to you on the record in another manner, so consider the overall situation and the various people involved before you decide yes or no.

When your subject says, "Not for attribution," you can use the content but must not name your informant. You must attribute the statement to some shadowy source, such as "a West Coast travel agent" or "an American traveling in Italy." While it's all right to use such quotes occasionally, too many of them destroy the writer's credibility. Be sure your article has fewer "blind" quotes than direct ones.

You may want to ask your subject's permission to refine the quotes since spoken language, full of extraneous sounds and words, often looks silly in print. It's usually all right, though, to go ahead and edit clumsy or unclear words if you're careful not to change the sense or the color of the statement.

At the interview, don't overstay your allotted time unless it's apparent that the subject wants you to. If you notice him glancing at a clock or an engagement calendar or if he says something like, "Well, I guess that's about all I have to say," it's time for you to leave. On the other hand, your interviewee will sometimes tell you more than you really care to know. One of the traits of a good interviewer is the ability to keep the subject on the desired track and not let the interview take up more time than is productive for the writer. In any case, at the end be sure to say, "Is there anything I should have asked you about that I've overlooked?" Request permission to call back for any additions or clarifications you might need. Then listen carefully for the casual remark, the gem of an anecdote, the perfect quote that is nearly always uttered as you stand with your hand on the doorknob, glasses off, notebook put away.

Never Relinquish Editorial Control

Do be aware of libel laws and write your article accordingly. But never promise you'll submit the finished article for the interviewee's approval. You are under no obligation to do so. You may, as a favor to him and as an insurance policy for yourself, submit facts and figures or direct quotes to verify their accuracy. But under no circumstances permit the subject to delete something he told you "for the record" or to alter in any way the thrust of the article.

As the instructions to writers from the *St. Petersburg Times* say, "We like to think that editors are editors and writers are writers, and the subject of the interview cannot assume those responsibilities."

Do follow up the interview with a thank-you note on your letterhead. This is not only common courtesy, but it also reminds the subject of where he can reach you should he think of any additions or corrections, and it paves the way for you to go back if you need to. If you promise to send a photograph, or copies of the published article, be sure to do so. Taking good care of your sources is future-story insurance.

The Telephone Interview

If a face-to-face interview is impossible, try for a telephone interview. For this, too, make an appointment and indicate how much time you'll need. You might want to suggest, "Call me collect Tuesday at two, or let me know if there's a more convenient time." Some writers find it best to conduct telephone interviews in the evening. The subject is more relaxed at home than at the office. Again you may want to presubmit a list of questions, giving the person a chance to prepare the answers before the interview. If the subject is willing, you might be able to tape record your telephone interview. Sometimes a telephone interview turns out to be more chatty and unstructured than a face-to-face situation; other times, it's more formal and punctilious.

One East Coast writer attributes his successful telephone interviews to his habit of calling long distance from a pay telephone. "When the person you're interviewing hears the clink-clank of all those quarters," he says, "he knows it's your own money you're using, not a publisher's expense account credit card. So he's especially helpful and informative."

The proliferation of cell phones frees the writer from the constraints of time and place. But don't let your interview fall apart because you and your cell phone have too many distractions.

E-mail Interviews

E-mail interviews can work out very well for the travel writer. You want to find an expert on how the current influx of cruise line port calls is affecting a tiny island in the Pacific. Through clever use of a search engine, up come the names and online addresses of members of the island's local government, a representative of the major retail establishment, a longtime island resident, two local pastors, and the public relations director of one of the cruise lines.

Sounds promising, doesn't it? It probably is. But be sure to verify any information you receive by e-mail—including the physical addresses and telephone numbers of your informants. You may discover that both pastors left last month, the retail "representative" is only a "go-for," the cruise line fired that employee, and the longtime resident is a bum. Worse yet, the information you receive from the online sources may be partially or completely untrue. So, convenient as e-mail is, it requires more checking.

Five Major Kinds of Interviews

What kind of interviews do you need? That depends on the story.

A **here and now** story about a new tour being featured at San Simeon might materialize from the tour itself, some PR handouts, a few questions to the tour guide, and a phone call to the state official in charge of San Simeon tours.

A **definitive destination** piece would include interviews with a city official, with somebody from the chamber of commerce or tourist bureau, with a spokesman for each or several attractions, and probably with a hotel executive and several restaurant owners.

An **in-depth analysis** of a foreign country's new approach to tourism would probably require interviews with the director of tourism, someone in the public relations department of the country's chief airline, and the manager of the leading hotel. It should include scattered quotes from restaurateurs, on-the-spot tourists, spokesmen for car rental agencies, and other hotel managers. Several owners of sight-seeing companies and tourist attractions, the mayors of principal cities, a museum director, and a representative of a wholesale tour that includes the country would make good additions.

When a travel story requires interviews with more than one person, it's especially important to remember your theme, and base all the interviews around it. That's what makes the piece hold together.

In covering an **event** you'll usually have several people to interview: the fans, who are participating in the activity; the sponsors, who make the time and space available to enhance their public image; the experts, who excel at this particular talent; the public relations people, who are eager to catch your ear and often come laden with handout sheets; and the spokesman—usually the master of ceremonies or guest of honor.

Introduce yourself to the spokesman first, presenting your business card, of course. Ask about taking photographs. (See Chapter 15 for more on photography.) Discuss the problems involved in this particular field. Then, later, when you interview the expert, you'll impress him with your knowledge of his problems at the same time you're getting information from his viewpoint.

A good example of **roundup** interviewing is "Living with Others in a Small Boat" by Patience B. Wales in *Sail*. Telling of a four-year world cruise she and her husband and another couple took in a forty-two-foot ketch, she says the number-one question people always asked was, "How did you all stand each other for so long in such close quarters?" That's probably what gave her the idea for this article because she not only analyzes some of the factors that made this relationship possible but tells of other people she's interviewed whose relationships foundered in close quarters at sea. She did much of her interviewing in Tahiti, where, she says, "the waterfront seethes with the remains of friendships."

In researching *my* roundup story about what causes traveling couples to argue, many of those I interviewed protested at first that they had nothing to say. "We *never* argue when we're traveling," both Sally and John assured me. Then she remembered: "Of course, there was the time John got us lost looking for that old country inn in the Berkshires, and it got to be midnight and we hadn't had dinner and. . . ."

"*I* got us lost!" John interrupted. "*You* were the one that looked at the directions and told me to go north when you meant south!"

"What's there to argue about?" asked Tim and Ellen. "When we're on vacation we always have a great time."

"There's just one thing," Tim said hesitantly. I wish Ellen wouldn't always take so long getting ready. When you're trying to make a plane—gee, I hate trying to get through security as they're calling our flight."

"*Tim!*" Ellen almost shouted. "How can you talk that way! You're the one who always leaves everything scattered all over the place. If you'd be neater it wouldn't take me so long to get ready. And besides, if you'd. . . ."

The face-to-face interview can be revealing. It can also be amusing, informative, and controversial. It's one of the travel writer's most valuable tools, and using it with professional skill can make the difference between a good, publishable travel article and a batch of meaningless, indecipherable notations.

FIFTEEN

Bring Back Your Story
in Pictures

The traveling photographer on San Francisco's Chinese Heritage Walk stopped to take a picture.

Half a roll of film later he looked around for his twenty-odd tour companions. They had disappeared. He walked up to the Alley of the Balconies. Down to Grant Avenue. Back to the Chinese Cultural Center. No, nobody knew where the tour was. The Chinese Heritage Walk he'd reserved and paid for ended, for him, in the first ten minutes. He hadn't realized he was taking such a long time with lens switching, light meter reading, and picture taking.

Another eager picture taker took a step backward to get a better view of his wife walking down the steps to the Dreaming Room at the Aesklepeion in Pergamum. He tumbled into the Sacred Spring.

Other traveling photographers have become so engrossed they've fallen into the Grand Canal in Venice while trying to frame the pigeons of Saint Mark's Square, plunged over a cliff while getting a light reading on Lincoln's nose at Mount Rushmore, and been arrested taking pictures of Iranian pilgrims on their way to Mecca. Many have missed seeing or hearing or understanding some significant facet of the travel experience because they've been concentrating on taking pictures of some other facet.

While photography is important, don't let it become the only significant activity of your trip. Instead, use all your senses and expose yourself to a variety of travel impressions.

It's exciting, though, to feel you can capture a memorable moment and recreate it for your readers. And whether they're active or armchair travelers, you move them on-scene and add to their knowledge and enjoyment through a combination of your words and your pictures.

The successful travel writer knows illustrations in print or online help sell his story, because they enhance and enrich his words, giving the editor—and subsequently the reader—the entire picture. He understands how more and more publications break up their blocks of type with photographs; and more and more editors prefer to receive manuscript and illustrations in one package, rather than having to make separate arrangements for photographs.

As noted earlier, even an inexperienced photographer can take pictures useful for recreating the travel experience, and a travel writer with modest shutter talents can illustrate his own stories. While it's impossible to "cover" photography in these few pages, we'll discuss different types of cameras, their advantages and disadvantages, and what editors say they want. We'll also mention photo genres and photo mechanics, shooting on the move, and selling what you have, sending pictures, avoiding legal problems, writing captions, and how to find illustrations if you don't have any.

Digital vs. Film 35mm Cameras

The digital camera has many advantages. It is usually lighter and easier to handle than a 35mm camera. It whips through airport security, as experts believe its memory is not affected by X-rays. You can immediately see your shot in its LCD screen or its viewfinder and quickly re-shoot if it doesn't quite fit your desire. You can transfer it to the computer, where you can crop, size, lighten, darken, adjust contrast, alter the background, and even ease an ex-spouse from the photo of family festivity. You can print the picture at home, or upload to one of several websites for a printed version. Prints from a digital camera are less prone to fading or damage when displayed over a long period of time if higher quality paper and ink are used.

On the downside, the digital camera usually doesn't give the photographer quite as good a grip as a 35mm single-lens reflex. It can gobble batteries like a hungry teenager gobbles food, so it's wise to use only longer-lasting lithium batteries or look for a camera with a rechargeable battery option. Always carry spare batteries, as well. To store the images you'll need to lug along your laptop and a cable for the camera and possibly floppy disks or CDs, or buy extra memory cards. A battery-operated "digital wallet" has more storage, but you'll need extra batteries, a battery charger, and, if traveling in a foreign country, an adapter. All this equipment can be a nuisance. But one travel writer sold an article and photo to a motorcycle magazine on how to pack all this auxiliary paraphernalia so as to offset the damaging vibrations of the motorcycle.

It is possible to rent a digital camera to see how you get along with it, and this may make sense.

We don't hear much about cameras that accept Advanced Photo Systems film, which are usually smaller and lighter than 35mm cameras. You can load APS film in its cartridge, and swap film in mid-roll without losing any frames. However, the 35mm camera usually has better flash and other features and options.

Terry Shuchat, expert photographer and camera store owner, believes that digital and 35mm will co-exist "for years." He says that even a $500 digital camera has a high enough pixel count to get good prints with a photo quality printer and paper. While he indicates that a digital camera costing two or three times as much as a film camera will get the same results, he reminds customers of the economy of never having to buy film.

What about publishing and selling your photos? A photo taken with what kind of camera is most likely to entice the editor? Opinions range all over the place. As I asked various knowledgeable colleagues about their preferences, some said they have moved away from 35mm, but most said they wouldn't think of changing at this time.

Then I asked the real experts—a couple of dozen magazine and newspaper travel editors. The response was ambivalent:

We review only slides, prints, negatives, and proof sheets.

We are an electronic magazine, and we expect electronic images.

Digital photos never have good enough resolution for a cover or even quarter-page picture. But we can sometimes use them for "mug shots" or two-inch photos.

Send digital photos for Mac or PC.

We prefer color transparencies but will review small-size digital pictures or color prints.

Although digital photos at present are usually less desirable than 35mm, they are getting better all the time. Who knows what next year will bring.

Send color transparencies or color prints from film.

We are a trade publication, and digital pictures suit us very well.

Digital photos are only usable if taken with a "top of the line" digital camera—the kind that costs at least $3,000.

We don't bother with digital. The resolution isn't good enough.

Film will soon be as useless as carbon paper.

However, a few months from now these replies might be quite different. As more and more sophisticated digital cameras become less and less expensive, and are used by an ever-increasing number of photographers, an ever increasing number of editors are likely to prefer them.

Video cameras, as we've said, can provide both meaningful memories for amateur photographers and professional programs for the more experienced. While audiences are still interested in travel slide talks, the number of excellent professional travel videos increases daily, and both active and armchair travelers applaud them. A first-class script and excellent narration are important components of the travel video, as well as the travel audio, which sometimes accompanies photographic presentations. Although much of the information about still pictures applies also to images that move, your expertise with the video camera will evolve from reading the directions and practicing religiously.

Again and again we are reminded that the mechanical equipment is not the most important element of photography. What counts is the eye behind the camera and the brain that tells the eye what it all means.

What Equipment Do You Really Need?

With over a dozen major manufacturers, each producing several camera types, the range of sizes, prices, advantages, and disadvantages is too great to discuss here. The main thing to remember is: If you're buying a new camera, get as much information as you can before deciding, and select a model that's best for the kind of work you'll be doing—action shots, portraits, heavy-duty work, wilderness photography, whatever. Be sure to get a camera that feels comfortable to your hands and to your eyes. (To your glasses, too, if you wear them.)

Ideally, you'd travel with three identical camera bodies, plus three interchangeable lenses of different focal lengths, with black-and-white film in one camera, and both daylight and faster film for transparencies and/or color negatives in the others. Add to this a video camera and an instant-processing camera for friend-making pictures to give away, and you'd be well prepared. But for most of us, all this would be too costly and too cumbersome, so you'll have to decide for yourself what's an acceptable compromise. If you're traveling alone, a 35mm camera with a zoom lens, plus an extra camera body as a backup, might be all you can comfortably manage.

As you probably know, the "normal" 50mm or 55mm lens sees everything approximately the way the human eye does. To produce more interesting pictures you need a wide-angle lens (which lets you take a picture of the whole room after you can't back up any farther) and a telephoto lens (which moves you right up to your subject). A zoom lens offers many different focal lengths, and it's convenient to carry one lens instead of several.

If you're thinking of buying a camera or other equipment overseas, check out the exact model you want and jot down the hometown price, so you can see if you're really getting a bargain. Even if you are, remember, you'll be losing your chance to try out the new equipment at home and to shoot a couple of rolls of film. If you buy a new camera *before* you leave home, be sure you're throroughly familiar with it before you start on your trip. New camera or old, check all the batteries and replace them if there's any doubt about their lifespan. A pencil eraser cleans batteries and terminals, or you can clean the batteries and battery compartment with a cotton swab dampened with alcohol. Clean the other parts of the camera with lens tissue and a camel's-hair brush.

If you buy an electronic flash to light your indoor shots and possibly provide additional light for outdoor pictures, be sure to get one large enough for your purposes, and be careful not to burn it out while recharging on uncongenial current. However, in situations where flash is not permitted or you have to pay extra to use it, you can usually take a time exposure with available light.

A time exposure requires a firm resting place for the camera—a table, a balcony rail, a windowsill. If no steady surface is available, you'll wish you'd brought your tripod. But large, sturdy tripods are a nuisance to carry, and small ones are often rickety and unreliable. There are several substitutes such as: a shirt-pocket-size platform with an elevating screw; a vise that threads into the camera and clamps to a firm surface; and a cloth bag filled with beans or Styrofoam that can be placed on a fence post or in a tree crotch, and the camera then placed on it. My husband even developed a method of taking time exposures without auxiliary equipment. He braced the camera on my shoulder, its strap around his neck. He adjusted and focused, holding the camera with both hands. As he pulled the cable release we each took a deep breath and held perfectly still until the exposure was completed. It took a little practice for us to perfect this maneuver. All these methods, of course, work best when you use the camera's automatic timer or a cable release to prevent jarring the shutter.

One of the most important pieces of photographic equipment you'll carry is your notebook. You'll write down not only the opening and closing scene of each roll, and identification for any other sites you may have trouble remembering, but you'll also mark the exposure, time, light, distance, what the light meter said, what you actually did, and any other mechanical factors involved in taking the picture. That's the best way to learn what to do next time.

Whatever photographic gear you decide on, don't pack it in a fancy camera bag. That advertises the fact that you're carrying expensive equipment. Since at some point it'll probably be left in a car trunk or hotel room, vulnerable to theft, most professional photographers choose something as unlike a camera bag as possible—an airlines bag or a shabby tote with several zipper pockets—anything that holds gear safely and blends inconspicuously.

Keep careful records on whatever equipment and supplies you buy, and follow professional advice when it comes to deducting or depreciating it. Such photographic expenses as film, developing, darkroom supplies, reference books, photography-related phone calls, and materials for filing and sending pictures are probably deductible. More substantial equipment must usually be depreciated. For darkroom deductions or conventional expense deductions you need professional advice. Be sure to keep all records that show you're attempting to market photographs. (See Chapter 17 for more on tax deductions.)

Your homeowner's insurance policy or your travel baggage insurance policy may or may not protect such items as cameras and tape recorders. Check it out, and if necessary consider a "floater" policy.

What About Film?

As we've said, take along enough. Color or black and white? That depends. While only a few publications, like *National Geographic*, reproduce nothing but color, many use color *and* black and white, and quite a few restrict their coverage to black and white. Most of the latter, however, still use color on the cover, and more and more newspaper travel sections are turning to color, at least for the lead story.

When working in color, *take slides, not prints.* Why? Because publications nearly always use slides, not prints, for color reproduction. Slides (call them transparencies when you're writing to an editor) cost about a third less and can be duplicated or copied in color or black-and-white prints.

While color photographs are more desirable when the hues of the landscape, the clothing, the marketplace dominate the picture, black and white is best where contrast, texture, and tone are important, such as a flight of birds against a winter sky, or the silhouette of a snow-laden evergreen.

Try not to take too many different kinds of film. Keep each type in a different-color plastic bag, exposed film in a bag of still another color. Before going through airport security, either encase all film in protective lead foil or put your plastic bags on the counter and ask for inspection by hand.

As airport security becomes increasingly strict, it may be more and more difficult to get that hand inspection. Yes, the lead foil bags are a help, but they are not absolutely fool-proof. Running your film through many airport inspections is said to have a cumulative effect, and some countries use X-rays strong enough to penetrate just about anything. However, never send your film in your checked luggage—that gets a stronger dose of radiation.

Will most of your travel shots be indoors, at churches and museums, or outdoors, at horse races and regattas? Will more of them be at midnight or at noon? It's impossible to take along the ideal film for each situation, so you have to make compromises, sometimes by adding filters. Kodachrome gives rich color to daylight slides, and Ektachrome 400 does well with less light. When there's barely *any* light, change the ASA to 800, then buy a special processing envelope ESP and the Ektachrome will be "push" processed, giving you the same amount of additional light as an extra f-stop on your camera.

For black-and-white pictures, Plus-X or faster Tri-X are good all-around films. In some cameras you can change film type in mid-roll, sometimes losing a frame or two, sometimes not. Use a changing bag, or follow the manufacturer's directions very carefully, and gently roll the film backward and, later, forward on the spool. Whatever kind of film you use, you'll doubtless want thirty-six-exposure rolls for traveling. But take along a twenty-exposure to use the last day. Then shoot it and have it developed right away—don't leave it sitting in the camera, where it deteriorates if you don't take pictures for awhile.

When you're buying film, be sure the date on the box gives you enough time to use it. Whether you have film processed while you're traveling, send it home, send it to a processing lab at home, or keep it with you throughout the trip depends on climatic conditions, reliability of mail service, how long you'll be gone, and a number of other factors. Remember that the price of film bought overseas usually includes processing, which may be done at any U.S. processing plant, but the mailer can be used only for the film with which it was packed.

Some travel writer-photographers are still following George Zimbel's recipe for "Cooked Film." Be sure you aren't one of them!

> Take one roll of color film, place in camera, expose in bright summer sun. After exposure, place film and camera in automobile glove compartment, and heat for three hours. (If you don't have an automobile, try putting camera on blanket in sun, or on top shelf of hot closet.)
>
> After film is thoroughly heated, take it to your film processor and have it developed. If you follow this recipe, your finished photographs should have an overall hue called *ghastly green*. Sometimes, if you are lucky, you may even get *brackish brown*, accompanied by disintegration of the image. This recipe is used by thousands of photographers and the results are guaranteed.

Photo Mechanics for Travel Writers

Don't forget to bracket your exposures. Take one picture at the shutter speed and lens opening you think correct. Then take one an f-stop smaller and one an f-stop larger. One of them will be perfect.

Shoot both horizontals and verticals of each scene. You change the feeling of the picture when you turn the camera, and this gives the editor a choice. If you're hoping for a magazine cover, of course you'll shoot verticals, keeping in mind the need for a "loose" area where the logo will be.

Compose all your pictures on the loose side, giving the editor opportunity for creative cropping.

Vary the distance shots and the close-ups. Get the overall scene and then the particulars. Be sure to make those close-ups close enough to capture the emotion and detail you need. The best photographers remember this rule: Move in until you think you're close enough–then step three feet closer. Try unusual angles on cliche scenes. Kneel down and shoot up or climb on something and shoot down.

Try not to date your picture by its background. Sometimes the people's clothing and hairstyles, cars, and advertisements for trendy items spell out the year the picture was taken. Clothing styles change less often for men, middle-aged women, and small children, so use them as models when possible. And perhaps you can block out parked cars and advertising. Make your picture usable for years to come.

If the person is the most important part of the picture, try to also include a recognizable landmark. A beach is a beach is a beach; but if Diamond Head is seen in the top corner, we know where we are. Titles and road signs are useful, too, when selected thoughtfully, so that they aren't distracting. Take pictures of the Continental Divide, the state line, the Mexican border, the highest point in the Sierras. If the sign says, "Elephants have the right-of-way" or "Golf balls in hippo footprints may be lifted without penalty," think how to pose somebody looking at the sign. Even if you don't have anybody to pose, you can take poignant pictures, as Tom Biema did for *Rider* magazine. His photographs of the Australian outback include one of a road sign depicting a black wombat on a yellow background and the legend "Wombats next 26 km." His riderless bike stands beside it, a white helmet decorated with an American flag resting on the seat. Another picture shows the motorcycle in the foreground, the emptiness of the outback stretching in front and on both sides, the mirrors reflecting the emptiness behind.

Sometimes, when you don't have any particular illustrations in mind, you'll be taking travel pictures as you see them.

Henri Cartier-Bresson, one of the most respected photographers of all time, tells us what to look for.

> To me, photography is the simultaneous recognition, in a fraction of a second, of the significance of an event as well as of a precise organization of forms which give that event its proper expression.

Cartier-Bresson speaks often of the "decisive moment," that instant when it's about to happen: the hiker finding himself at the edge of the crevasse;

the child about to begin dancing; the young man ready to take off on his motorbike; the tourist deciding which necklace she's going to buy. That "decisive moment" is the instant we try to capture.

Beating the Weather

Need I say it? *Always* keep your camera and film out of the sun! In hot weather keep the film wrapped in foil or store it in an insulated bag. If mailing a roll of film, never deposit it in an outside mailbox.

Avoid shooting in the middle of the day in warm climates. You'll get better pictures before ten or after three. When changing film, if you don't have a changing bag, try to find a shady spot to avoid sunstreaks on the film. You can even use your own body to shade the changing operation.

If you'll be a long time in the tropics, you'll need to take special precautions against moisture. Buy silica gel. Read Kodak's booklets for expert advice on handling photography under extreme weather conditions.

In cold weather moisture is a worry, too. Keep the camera under your coat as much as possible, pamper it with sportsmen's hand warmers, and protect it inside a plastic zip locked bag. This way, whatever condensation forms after you bring the cold camera into a warm room will form on the outside of the bag, not the camera. Protect all your equipment from snow. Cold always makes film more brittle, so be especially careful in advancing or rewinding. If you're going to a below-zero climate have your camera professionally winterized first.

Rainy climates shouldn't deter you from picture taking. If you don't want to invest in an underwater camera or underwater housing for your camera, buy inexpensive special umbrellas and raincoats for the camera, as well as the photographer.

Sometimes the rainy-day, foggy-day, misty-day pictures are the best ones.

Should You Process Your Own Film?

Before deciding to undertake your own processing, consider carefully the cost of equipment and materials and the amount of time you'll be spending in the darkroom. At least wait to set up your darkroom until you're thoroughly familiar with *taking* pictures so you won't be wondering whether any errors you see are from the photographing or the processing.

Developing and printing color pictures requires significantly greater skill and a significantly greater outlay for darkroom equipment than developing and printing black and whites, so many photographers end up with a darkroom for black-and-white work and send their color work out.

If you decide not to do your own darkroom work, do give some thought to patronizing a custom lab. Somewhat more expensive, but often worth it, the custom lab follows your processing specifications, and treats each picture individually. It can correct under- or overexposed film, right a crooked horizon, and perform other miracles.

Worried about the lab losing your exposed film? Make the first shot on each roll a sheet of paper with your name and address so there's no way it can be misplaced. I have never done this, however, and of the thousands of rolls of film I've had processed, not a single one has ever gone astray. Do, though, be sure to write the roll number on your receipt or on the address label the processor will use. When you arrive home with a hundred-odd rolls of film, it's difficult to try to determine, "Is that Lake Michigan or Lake Superior?" And a year later, if you haven't labeled the pictures, you may wonder if it's Tahoe.

If you're planning a home page on the Internet but feel insecure with the new technology, you can hire a professional webmaster to help you with the text and the photography.

How to Send Your Pictures

How do you send your photographs to the editor? Safely, but as inexpensively as possible.

The scanning process, of course, enables you to store your travel photographs and text in your computer, edit both, and then send the package electronically. But this is not for everybody. However, cost of the equipment is being reduced and quality of the image is being improved, so it may soon be quite practical.

While the many facets of electronic media represent an entirely new market, don't get carried away. We should remember the length of time it takes a photographic image to download to a not-very-fast computer. Web watchers and zine readers grow impatient if the picture is so elaborate that it takes extra time to download, and they are likely to surf on to something else.

With digital or print images be sure to have your name, identifying number, and copyright notice on each frame.

For print publications there are several schools of thought about sending proof sheets of black and white. After the film is developed, you can have a contact sheet, or proof sheet, made that will show on an 8½ by 11-inch page a roll of prints the same size as your negatives. Some editors prefer this submission, giving them the chance to choose which images they want to see full size. Others can't be bothered and want you to choose the photos that best illustrate your article. Some travel writers cut out the best pictures from several proof sheets and paste them onto a single sheet of paper, unwilling to have the editor see the two or three disasters they've managed on a 36-print roll.

Whether or not you send a contact sheet, do blow up a few of the most irresistibly appealing photos. Most publications specify 8 x 10 black and whites, although often they'll also consider 5 x 7s, which cost less. Usually editors prefer glossy finish. Double-weight paper withstands more mailings and presents itself more assertively. Be sure your prints are clean and don't have previous editorial crop marks in the margin.

Remember that photographic paper is a fragile item, the image upon it even more fragile. Do not write on the back of prints with sharp pens or pencils; do not fasten them with paper clips; protect them from sharp objects.

Usually you'll keep the negative and you'll notch the ones from which salable pictures have been printed, perhaps double-notching when it's sold and triple-notching when it's published. You'll handle them carefully, and store them carefully. If you must send both negatives and prints, never send them in the same envelope or even from the same mailbox on the same day.

With transparencies, the publication will indicate the smallest acceptable size, usually 35mm. If you've taken several pictures of the same scene, you won't need duplicates. If not, perhaps you'll want to send duplicates instead of originals if it's on speculation. I usually send a large selection of duplicates and extra shots for the editor to choose among—similar to sending a proof sheet. Or you can have a fairly expensive color proof sheet made, and then send color photocopies, which are cheaper.

I group the pictures and caption them and send only those that are of good quality and related to the text. Editors are not enamored of travel writers who send along boxes of uncaptioned, unsorted transparencies with a note saying "take what you want." Editors expect you to have some idea of what illustrations would be suitable.

On the other hand, they don't like to have the writer-photographer plan the layout for them, so I only gently suggest possible photo spreads. After the editor has made a decision about which pictures he wants, I send the originals for color separation.

Transparencies can be sent in several ways. If you use the box in which they came from the processor, check with the post office to see if it's large enough for their regulations. If not, put it in a larger box or big envelope. For a large number, especially on assignment, check with the editor how to submit. I feel the best method of sending between twelve and a hundred transparencies is in slotted archival plastic sleeves, available at camera shops. They hold twenty transparencies safely and can be placed over a light table for scrutiny.

Clean your transparencies before sending them—buy a can of air to blow away the dust—and take every precaution to protect them from fingerprints, scratches, ink, glue, dust, etc. Never send glass-mounted slides—

the risk of breakage is too great. If it's a very special transparency, have an internegative made. This is an expensive proposition, but it ensures the possibility of making new transparencies (not duplicates) forever, with no impairment of color.

Send your photographs, either color or black-and-white, like a sandwich filling, between two layers of corrugated cardboard, which you can either buy at a stationery store or cut from grocery cartons. Or you can buy a regular photo mailer—a kraft envelope with two boards—at a camera shop. Ribs of one of the sheets of cardboard should be vertical, the other horizontal for greatest protection. A few transparencies in plastic sleeves or black-and-white prints can be set into corners cut from old envelopes, attached to the cardboard. Secure the sandwich with rubber bands. For a large number of photographs, use a box or a fiberboard mailing case.

If you value your photographs—and you should—you'll take great care to pack and send them safely and speedily. Stamp the outer envelope *Photos—Do Not Bend*, and discuss with your postman the place he will leave returned envelopes, so he won't try to squeeze them into the mail slot or leave them in the hot sun. You will, of course, include an SASE with your photographs. For best results, send both manuscript and illustrations first class. If there's need for special speed, consider express mail or one of the many alternatives to the Postal Service. When sending negatives or original transparencies, be sure to register, certify, or insure them, preferably with return receipt requested.

James Joseph, a very successful freelance travel writer, says he uses e-mail and fax a great deal for sending correspondence and text, both in the U.S. and abroad. But photos to accompany his travel articles he usually wraps and addresses in the old-fashioned ways, using mail or overnight carrier.

When sending photographs overseas, mark them *Press Photos—No Value*. Otherwise, your editor at the other end will have to pay duty on them—and he may not wish to. (If he refuses, the pictures will be returned to you by surface mail, which takes months.) Sometimes, when air mailing overseas, it's cheaper to separate the manuscript from the photographs. Always inquire about up-to-the-minute mailing rates and regulations.

As digital images become more and more popular, any problems involved in sending photographs will disappear due to the ever-present ability to dispatch them electronically.

Can You Shoot Both the Planned and the Unplanned?

In taking travel pictures, sometimes you plan in advance the pictures you want, something to illustrate a story already designed or already written. Other times the photography is spontaneous—you see something interesting and you shoot it.

To portray a geographic area so your reader can really know it, you'll want pictures of people of all ages and occupations in all types if situations, wildlife and domestic animals, landscapes and gardens. You'll also want food markets and restaurants, hotels and historical sites, clothing and costumes, handcrafts and souvenirs, art and architecture, signs and flags.

What will you do with all these pictures after they're processed? Some you'll send along with the first article you write about the area—color or black and white, as the editor has indicated. Send more than you think he'll need—to give him a choice and perhaps to persuade him to use more photographs (and send you a larger check) than he had originally intended. Even in situations where the photos are part of the article "package," for which there's no extra payment, I've often found editors send a bonus for a large selection of good pictures. File your leftovers carefully, to use with future articles. Some of them might prove useful for roundup stories or roundup photo essays, where you have around-the-world variations on a single theme.

Just as some people collect rare gems or antique scimitars, I collect laundry lines. For years I've collected photographs of people washing, along with the lines of clothes they have washed. I also collect pictures of schools and colleges, uniformed schoolchildren, shoeshine boys, and several other universal themes. These make great international roundups—"Wash and Wear Around the World"; "School Days from Country to Country"—as well as illustrating individual aspects of a specific area.

Shoot lots of pictures. Whether or not you're using film, the price of the picture is cheap compared with the cost of getting there. And it's always more desirable and less expensive to take several pictures of the same scene instead of duplicating later.

How Will Your Pictures Be Used?

Certainly shoot whatever appeals to you. But if you're thinking primarily in terms of illustrations, it helps to think of how the photographs will be used. In a *picture story*, the photos do most of the telling, and need little, if any, explanatory caption material. For instance, in Christchurch, New Zealand, where they have big red city buses with hooks on the front for carrying strollers and prams, my husband shot a picture story from our hotel room on the main square. The big red bus is loading: a distraught mother, carrying a young baby in her arms and wheeling a toddler in a perambulator, looks around helplessly, obviously wondering how she will board the bus; a well-dressed businessman comes up to her and says a few words; she smiles; he lifts the toddler out of the perambulator and sets him on the bus step; then the man hooks the pram to the front of the bus; everyone climbs aboard and the bus roars off. All this with the very British-looking background of Christchurch Cathedral, vehicles moving to the left, and uniformed schoolboys in straw hats guiding their cycles through the park.

A bridge overlooking Istanbul's Golden Horn harbor was the vantage point for another picture story. An old man in a rowboat that's tied to the bridge is frying fish over a charcoal brazier. As soon as the fish is browned a blue-smocked helper puts it on a piece of bread and passes it to an eager bystander, who hands his money over the bridge rail, then moves on. The next customer pushes himself into position, the helper puts another fish on bread, and the old man continues to turn the browning fish in his pan.

Whenever you see action that's a story in itself, hasten to focus. Keep on the lookout for those picture stories—many publications use them. Some are always open to picture stories, while others consider only those that are outstanding in both interest and technical quality. There's usually no set number of pictures required—however many it takes to tell the story.

Photo Genres

A **sequence** uses several pictures, too. It can feature something occurring in stages, but is accompanied by explanatory copy; the pictures themselves do not have to carry the entire story. For instance: When you're packing for your trip, first you place the shoes and the toiletries bag in the suitcase; then you put in the underwear and nightclothes; on top you lay the dress clothes, spread out over the suitcase; then you fold them so they fit in; then you shut the lid and, *voila*, the next scene shows you carrying the case to the airport. Or a *sequence* might be an evening at a nightclub. First scene shows the headwaiter escorting your party to the table; next picture shows you ordering dinner; then comes the nightclub act; you and your friends applaud; then you lean back smiling; then reach forward to toast with your brandy snifters.

If you witness something like the divers at La Quebrada in Acapulco, try to take the full sequence—the diver blessing himself at the shrine; descending the steps that have been cut into the cliff, mounting the starter platform; making the starter dive; scrambling up the steep cliff to the top of La Quebrada; and then the flaming torches illuminating his arc through the air; his sixty-mile-an-hour splashdown into the rock-girded cove; and finally his head emerging from the churning water, his arm upraised in a victory gesture.

A **juxtaposition** usually consists of two contrasting scenes. A picture of a Europe-bound Girl Scout troop as high school seniors and a picture of the same girls as second-grade Brownies beginning their plans for the trip would be a juxtaposition. So would a photo showing a scene in Chicago today placed next to one of the same area immediately after the 1871 fire.

For these juxtapositions you and your camera would have to have been present after the 1871 fire and when the Girl Scouts were in second grade, or know someplace to obtain a picture taken at the time. To present a juxtaposition of a rural Finnish lake in summer and in winter, you'd have to make two trips there or work in tandem with a friend. Such a juxtaposition would be easy to do, though, illustrating some of the features of your home area. But the shot of the Acapulco diver standing on the cliff, juxtaposed with one of him in the water, raising his arm in the victory salute, would *not* make a good twosome—the action in between, the *real* story, would be lacking. Captions for juxtapositions are especially important. Be sure to make the meaning of the two pictures clear to your reader.

The **stopper** is a one-shot situation. This picture is used to draw the reader's attention to the story, so it needs to be vivid and dramatic: the mountain fortress of Sigifiya rising from the plains; the parachute ride at Knott's Berry Farm; tourists viewing Montreal's Old Town from a horse-drawn carriage; the dramatic architecture of Funchal's new casino on the island of Madeira, framed by mountains and sea; two canoeists exploring a river that's flecked with ice floes and bounded by snow-covered banks; a dramatic silhouette of Rio's seven-hundred-ton statue, Christ the Redeemer, atop Corcovado mountain—all are *stoppers*. But the parachute ride is taken from an unusual angle, the canoe appears against an extraordinary background, the wheels of the horse-drawn carriage are distorted to emphasize a focal point of the picture—otherwise these situations would surely be cliches. Once the reader's attention has been captured he'll learn from the writer's copy what the stopper is all about, so it doesn't have to tell a story all by itself—just hint strongly that an interesting story accompanies it. If you examine the pictures in print advertising, you'll find they're usually stoppers.

Drop-ins can consist of any number of shots, or possibly just one. They are what we often think of as illustrations—something strongly tied to the text, used by the editor to emphasize a certain aspect of the article, as well as to break up large blocks of type and create an attractive layout. Usually they are captioned with explanatory material.

Almost anything can be a drop-in. For instance, to accompany an article on Australia's Barrier Reef I sent six photographs: only two people in sight on the vast beach of Hayman Island, with the hotel and mountains in background; adults and children beachcombing on the reef at low tide; the launch, with people aboard, leaving for the outer reef; the underwater observatory, with its huge viewing windows, on Hook Island; Hayman's gaily painted train that transports guests on this island where no cars are allowed; and the Hayman Island airport, with a helicopter about to land.

The magazine used the beach scene as a stopper (at the top of the center-spread story) and the launch ride and the underwater observatory pictures as drop-ins.

With one of my stories about the *Wasa* I sent eight photographs: the ship as it looks today; the ship inside the museum building; the ship in a cradle of cables on its concrete pontoon in 1961; the ship during salvage operations; the museum building from the outside; the Swedish coat of arms from the sterncastle; the gigantic lion figurehead; and the brazier that once graced the captain's table. The editor selected the ship today, the ship in cables, the coat of arms, the museum building, and the brazier as drop-ins.

Occasionally I have only one photograph to illustrate a story—so I send it. The most important thing to remember is, if the picture intrigues you, it will probably intrigue somebody else. Film is comparatively cheap, so if in doubt, shoot.

Can You Make It Look Real?

When you know ahead of time what you want, make a storyboard or a shooting script. Use an index card for each picture you intend to take, rough-sketching on it what you want the picture to show. For a "set piece," jot down all pertinent data: time of day, models, location, camera angle, clothes, props, etc.

Don't hesitate to use props that will enhance the meaning of your picture. Whether it's a parasol for a Japanese girl walking beneath the blossoming cherry trees or an ornamental lifebuoy chaperoning a shipboard buffet, if that's the prop that makes the picture, get it. I once illustrated a California garden article on a tight deadline; as a set piece, the only possible illustrations were of the garden. But nothing was blooming at that time of year. Even citrus was out of season. I had no choice: I scooted to the grocery store and bought a couple of dozen oranges, which we tied to the orange trees. I'm not in favor of faking as a general rule, but in this case it was necessary and the scene came out looking more like California than California, itself.

What if the prop is there, but you can't get it in your viewfinder? Sometimes both the subject and the background are important. Yet if you picture a man against twenty feet of metal, who's to know that's an airplane behind him? Or is it the Empire State Building, or the Eiffel Tower? On the other hand, if you shoot him in front of a recognizable airplane half a football field away, he'll be a skinny black stick. The solution is to back off until the background object exactly fills the viewfinder. Then bring the subject forward until his head and shoulders fill about one-third of the frame. Focus on him, letting the background fall slightly out of focus, and you'll have your picture.

Can You Compose in the Viewfinder?

Although this chapter is not intended as a course in elementary photography, you'll find reminders of some basics we should keep in mind. If you have a single-lens reflex camera, your finished print will reflect exactly what your eye sees in the viewfinder. Too many photographers don't really see what's in that viewfinder. Is your finger or camera strap in the way? Is a telephone pole growing out of somebody's head? Is your horizon line in the dead center of the picture, thereby ruining it? Are there a dozen distracting centers of interest?

If you were to draw a ticktacktoe grid on your viewing screen you'd find your best pictures would have the center of the interest at one of the four points where those imaginary lines cross—either one-third down from the top or one-third up from the bottom and either one-third in from the left or one-third in from the right. Many pictures are confusing because the viewer's eye doesn't know what to center on. Of course, the less irrelevant material in your photograph, the more the focal point stands out.

Try framing your subject with a tree branch, an arch, a wall, to give it depth, keeping the frame at least five feet from the camera. Consciously look for a natural frame, such as the man playing bongo drums between the upraised arms of his fellow musicians, or the little girl's smiling face framed by the two dogs she's roughhousing with, or the woman walking between two tall buildings.

Experiment with silhouettes, especially those instantly recognizable, like the man with the sombrero or the woman with the baby in the backpack. To take a silhouette you need heavy shadows on the camera side of the subject, against a bright background. A figure standing in a doorway against the sunny outdoors or in the open, outlined against the sky, makes a good silhouette. Adjust the exposure for the bright-light area of the picture, and print (or have printed) for the lighter areas, too, so the main subject remains poorly lighted and underexposed.

Learn to *see* what makes a picture. A natural line should lead into it— a pathway, a freeway cloverleaf, the movement of the waves, the placement of the objects. The viewer's eye moves, naturally, toward the center of interest, so any action shown should lead *into* the picture, not out of it. The repetition of forms gives unity; so learn to use the lines you see through your viewfinder to express your sense of significance. Look for rhythms—patterns of shape, length, angle, curve, direction, or interval that strengthen your composition and tie the elements together to present a unified picture for your reader. If what you see isn't exactly what you want to convey, move a few steps in one direction or another, shoot from lower down or higher up, adjust the scene until it is the one you want.

Learn which camera techniques enable you to concentrate on the center of interest and blur the background, and learn which filters will help you differentiate, on your print, the dirty white sails from the pale blue sky. Use reflections whenever you can—the snow-capped mountain in the outside rearview mirror of the camper, your houseboat in the unrippled lake, the kids jumping into the puddle that reflects them.

And one last "should": If you see some dramatic episode about to unfold, and you have only two frames left on your 35mm roll, you should— you *must*—change your film now. Film, as we've said, is comparatively cheap. Don't waste an opportunity to take an outstanding picture by changing rolls in the middle of the action.

By "dramatic episode" I mean something you're able to foresee and that you're sure is worth more than the two frames: the herd of elephants lumbering across the horizon out of camera range, as your safari bus approaches them; the opening set of the Davis Cup; the Israeli kindergartners about to present a biblical vignette for the visitors.

Can You Shoot on the Move?

Yes, it is possible to shoot a usable picture from a moving vehicle. We sold and published a picture taken through a fast-moving car's dirty window of a boy on a fast-moving bicycle in the midst of heavy traffic just at dusk. Technically the picture leaves much to be desired. But the subject matter redeems it. (The boy had draped over his shoulder a live lamb he was taking home for his family's celebration of a Muslim holiday.) So don't think "why bother," just because there's motion or there's traffic or it's getting dark. If the subject matter is interesting, take the picture anyway, on the move or not.

Your best on-the-move photographs will result when you're sitting in the front seat taking pictures through the windshield of a car or bus but you can shoot through the side window, too. Try to sit on the shady side of the car, bus, or plane, to avoid reflections on the glass, and don't use a polarizing filter, which reacts poorly with Plexiglas windows and creates a bizarre effect. Take scenes in the middle distance, preferably those you're moving toward or away from, and pan to hold the object in position if necessary. Hold the camera close to the window, but make sure that neither it nor any part of your body is touching the vehicle frame—the vibration will blur your picture. On a heeling sailboat, however, you'll have to brace yourself.

Protect your equipment as much as possible to lengthen its troublefree life and ensure high-quality pictures. To minimize the effects of vibration on your camera in a plane, train, or bus, put it on the seat, if possible, preferably secured with a seat belt. In a car, place it on the floor behind the front seat, on the side opposite from the exhaust. Avoid, as much as you can, the ravages of dust, sand, and sea spray.

If your camera jams or something else seems wrong, don't force it—you may do irreparable damage. Instead, find the nearest expert and let *him* take it apart. However, telling the difference between an *expert* and an "expert" is not always easy. Two unhappy experiences, one mine, one a friend's, resulted from trying to sneak a thirty-eighth picture out of a thirty-six exposure roll (you can practically always sneak thirty-seven) in a foreign country. When I took the jammed camera into a nearby camera shop, the "expert" opened it in the darkroom, removed the film, and handed the camera back to me. I didn't discover until several hours and two hundred miles later that he had neglected to put back a small but important part, without which the camera would not work. It took three days to find a replacement. My friend's "expert" also opened the jammed camera and removed the film in the darkroom. He ran to the front of the shop triumphantly clutching the thirty-seven (thirty-eight?) exposed negatives, crying, "See! I got them out!"

Anyway, try to find an expert. And don't push for thirty-eight!

Can You Picture the People?

Most good pictures are better pictures with people in them. Sometimes the people are mainly there to show scale—how infinitesimal is the human being looking up at the enormous statues of Ramses II at Abu Simbel, or the gigantic Daibutsu (each of Buddha's eyes is three feet long) in Kamakura.

When we say there should be people in the picture, we mean local people—not tourists. A photograph of the Plaka, with a dozen Athenians sipping ouzo at a tavern, is charming. A photograph of the Acropolis, with a dozen gaping American tourists, is not. If you want to shoot the Acropolis try to wait until the tourists leave.

How the people in your pictures look, how they're dressed and coiffed, can be very important in relation to the markets you're aiming for. Would you use the same models to illustrate an article for *Car and Driver* as you'd use for *Town and Country*? If the photo's okay for *Cosmopolitan*, does that mean it'll work for *Business Week*?

When a single human being is the focal point of the picture, ideally he or she will look at ease, will not be staring into the camera, and will be actively engaged in some pursuit typical of the locale and his lifestyle.

Group shots are trickier. The more people there are, the more difficult it is to photograph everybody in an unselfconscious and flattering pose and retain the picture's interest. When my oldest daughter's Girl Scout troop left for Europe, the local newspaper sent a photographer to the leader's home. We set up some attractive photos, the girls all clustered around a globe or a map, looking at it and laughing and talking in a natural way. At the airport the airline photographer also took their picture. He lined them up in front of an Exit sign that had a No Smoking sign beneath it. The twelve girls and their two leaders are pictured in a stiff double row, twenty-eight black-shod feet, twenty-eight white-gloved hands, and fourteen mouths saying "cheese." (I was never able to use *that* picture!)

Watch out for distractions in the background. Don't frame your picture with a No Smoking sign. If a boy in a red jacket is flying a kite behind the statue you must shoot, wait until he leaves. Otherwise, nobody will look at your statue.

You may want to ask permission to take the picture. For a human close-up, that's only good manners. And people will usually welcome the photographer who wants to take home an image of them if you establish rapport, making them feel you're a friend who wants to share their activity rather than a foreigner who's ridiculing them.

Except at the farthest travel frontiers, people are accustomed to photographers and tolerate them, at least. We've always been amused by a friend who bought a miniature camera for his trip because he "didn't want to look like a tourist." This friend is six feet four, blond and blue-eyed, and the country he visited was Japan. In addition to the fact that he could hardly conceal his foreignness, no people in the world are more camera-happy than the Japanese. Everywhere you go in Japan, there are dozens of tourists *and* dozens of Japanese, snapping away.

We've felt welcome as photographers in most countries. On many occasions we've taken a picture of a person or a landmark, only to have other people rush up, begging to be photographed also.

Sometimes locals expect you to pay them for posing. It's rumored that the old man and woman in coolie outfits who position themselves at a popular tourist stop near Hong Kong's Chinese border have earned enough to send three sons through college in England. If the deal is made ahead of time, that's fine, but sometimes you'll snap the picture and *then* discover a row of outstretched palms. You'll want to be prepared at least with small change, chewing gum, instant photos, or other modest gifts. Sometimes, though, the gift for posing is refused. A group of us recently photographed some charming little Greek boys dressed in their national holiday costumes of the Evzone Guards. We had asked their mothers if we might take pictures, and then we asked their permission to give the children a few coins. They politely but firmly indicated "absolutely not."

When you take pictures for publication, do you need model releases? Let's take that up in the next section, as we discuss:

How to Avoid Legal Problems

Most of the legal problems surrounding photography can be solved with common sense. There seem to be two major areas involving the law. One is your pictures, the kind of rights you are selling, and who is entitled to reproduce them. The other is the people in your pictures, and their rights.

Try, if at all possible, to get a model release. Sometimes you don't need one for a picture used for editorial purposes, but some publications, both print and online, demand one, anyway. If that picture is used for advertising, a release is imperative. And "advertising" may refer to more situations than you'd expect. For instance, a magazine's cover is considered to be advertising, since it attempts to sell the publication. The entire magazine is advertising if it's a house organ or company publication, since its purpose is to promote.

Sometimes you can take a picture in such a way that a person's identity is not apparent. Journalist Sherman Grant says he does this whenever possible, and when it is not, he insists on a release.

If, however, you have good travel pictures, with recognizable people in them, for which you have no releases, look for markets that don't require them. (Usually that information is included in the *Writer's Market* or *Photographer's Market* listing.) A Sunday supplement editor told me once that he never bothers with releases, except for the cover. "I've never had any trouble," he said. "Or at least only once." It seems he ran some freelance photographs of the Hell's Angels on the beach at Santa Cruz; one of them showed a Hell's Angel eating a popsicle. Monday morning the cyclist—and his attorney—were in the publisher's office, protesting that the picture destroyed his image, that the photographer had had no right to take it nor the editor to publish it.

The photographer did have the right to take the picture, and the editor did have the right to publish it because it was taken in a public place. The courts have held that it is not an invasion of privacy to take pictures in a public place since the photographer is a stand-in for the public—photographing something any member of the public could see if he happened to be there at the time. If, however, you go to somebody's house under false pretenses and with a hidden camera take pictures of him eating leopard's paw soup with snail darter dumplings—that's an invasion of privacy. He'll probably sue you and he'll probably win.

The courts have also ruled that the subject cannot recover damages from the photographer or the publication for taking and using his picture without permission if the picture was newsworthy and was published in the spirit of communicating the news, or if the person is a public personality, who has thus renounced the right to privacy.

Suppose, for instance, you're the survivor of a plane crash. You take pictures of the dead and injured, and a picture is published in the local newspaper and in a weekly news magazine. That's all right, but publishing that picture two years later, simply for its sensationalism, is all wrong, and the people pictured might have grounds for court action. Publishing the picture on the anniversary of the crash or as part of an air safety campaign might be debatable. It would be wise to check with your attorney before submitting.

Surely you will want to restrict your photographs to those that don't violate privacy or good taste. But in case you want to protect yourself with a model release, here's an example of one:

> In consideration of value received, receipt whereof is acknowledged, I hereby give (*name of photographer or publication*) the absolute right and permission to copyright and/or publish, and/or resell photographic portraits or pictures of me, or in which I may be included, in whole or in part, for art, advertising, trade, or any other lawful purpose whatsoever.
>
> I hereby waive any right that I may have to inspect and/or approve the finished product of the advertising copy that may be used in connection therewith, or the use to which it may be applied.
>
> I hereby release, discharge, and agree to save (*name of photographer or publication*) from any liability by virtue of any distortion, alteration, optical illusion or use in composite form, whether intentional or otherwise, that may occur or be produced in the taking of said pictures, or in any processing tending toward the completion of the finished product.
>
> Date   Model
>
> Witness   Address

This is an example of the "ultimate" model release, and simpler wording might be equally satisfactory, and less intimidating, when you're trying to get a layman to sign. The main thing is to have the subject indicate he knows you're taking his picture, and he's willing for you to use it any way you want without any (further) compensation to him. If the subject is a minor, be sure the release is signed by a parent.

Some countries prohibit the photographing of military installations, airports, harbors, or other strategic or sensitive areas, and it's not only good manners but solid common sense to observe the restrictions they outline.

You Can Copyright Your Shots

Now let's talk about *your* rights, as a photographer. While we haven't room to discuss the subject of copyright, for either photography or writing, in any detail, keep in mind that the writer and the photographer do have rights, and should protect them. Putting the copyright symbol and the year next to your name on the photograph and on the caption sheet protects you to some extent. For absolute protection of your photographic rights register your pictures with the copyright office in Washington, DC. Since the per-picture fee soon adds up, either register a number of photos as a collection, or group a number of them together and take a picture of the group, copy-righting that single photo. If your pictures are published in an uncopy-righted medium (e.g., most newspapers) before you register them with the copyright office, be sure the medium prints the copyright notice alongside the picture.

For up-to-date information on the copyright law, visit the Library of Congress online at www.loc.gov/copyright or write:

Copyright Office
Library of Congress
Washington, DC 20559

Request special circulars relating to photography, as well as a copy of the revised statutes. Ask to be put on their mailing list—you'll receive a steady stream of material about every nuance of copyright.

New material appears on a regular basis on the Library of Congress website. Check back often since many facets of copyright and payment for online photographs and online text are still in limbo, as yet unsettled.

Your Rights Are Valuable

Usually you'll sell "one-time rights," which means the publication is enti-tled to use the picture only once, and you may sell it again and again. Definitively state what you're offering: Stamp your picture or caption sheet with "One-time editorial use in one issue only." As a general rule, with black and whites you keep the negative, and the print may or may not be returned after use; with color transparencies, if you send the original for one-time use, it should be returned. If you sell "all rights" or "exclusive rights" you should be paid several times the amount of "one-time rights," since you're relinquishing the picture's future value to you.

Whether you sell your photographs on assignment or on a freelance basis, be sure you and the buyer are in complete agreement, in advance, as to the rights offered, the price to be paid, the expenses covered, and any other possible sources of misunderstanding. Generally, I've found media people fair and decent, but it's always wise to have the terms spelled out. Occasionally a photographer will complain that a newspaper has run a pic-ture of his without paying him. Newspapers receive so many free publicity shots that you have to make it very clear that what you're sending is for sale, not a giveaway. In addition to indicating on the pictures and captions what rights you're offering, attach a note that says something like, "I'll call you in a few days to see if you'll be using the pictures or will be returning them, so I can submit them elsewhere."

Standard prices suggested for pictures used in various situations have been compiled by the American Society of Media Photographers, 150 North Second Street, Philadelphia, PA 19106; www.asmp.org. Check *Pricing Photography* by Michal Heron, *Writer's Market*, or *Photographer's Market* for current prices paid by individual photography buyers.

Selling Your Photographs

Often you'll sell the photographs you send to accompany your article. But sometimes the pictures will be so outstanding you'll want to think first in terms of selling them, accompanied by subsidiary written material. Naturally you'll check *Writer's Market* and *Photographer's Market* for likely targets.

Many other company publications, trade journals, inflights, newspapers, travel magazines, and so on, sponsor photography contests, either regularly or sporadically. And many publications, from *Modern Maturity* to *Diversion*, showcase their readers' photographs under a general theme, such as "Night Portraits" or "Pets from All Over."

As you become more and more expert, a new marketing possibility opens up. Practically every magazine occasionally runs some kind of feature on how to take good travel pictures. You can be the one to sell them that feature.

All About Captions

It is not enough to send a picture to an editor—that picture has to be carefully captioned. (You may sometimes hear it called a "legend" or a "cutline.")

The most important part of the caption is your name and address, which should be on every picture you send, whether it's your own or bought or borrowed from someone else. The credit line—the name of the person to be credited for taking the picture—and the copyright notice should be included in each caption, too. For transparencies, the easiest way to do this is to write the name and copyright symbol on some small stickers and affix one to each cardboard plastic mount. Write a number on the mount also. This can be your regular file number or a special sequence for this submission only. In either case, each number corresponds to one on the accompanying caption sheet, also identified by your name and address, which tells what is in each picture.

For black and whites or color prints there are several ways of identifying with captions, but your name and address should be on the back of each picture, written very, very gently in light-colored felt pen or rubberstamped or stickered. The prints can be numbered, with the caption appearing on an accompanying caption sheet, as with transparencies, or the caption can be attached to the print itself. There are three schools of thought about how to attach them. Some photographers like to type the caption on a small piece of thin paper and rubber-cement or tape it to the back of the picture itself. Both other methods involve typing the caption on a full-size sheet of paper and attaching it so it folds over the print, thus protecting the front of it. Some photographers like the type facing the image, readable when pulled down, while others prefer the type facing out, immediately readable. Either way, put your name on the caption sheet as well as on the picture. Any of these methods is acceptable unless an editor expresses a preference.

It's also important to identify any people recognizable in your picture. Of course, you will have taken down their names, *spelled correctly*, at the time of the photographing, and this identification must be included as well as the name of the place where the picture was taken.

What should the caption say about the picture? The first thing to do is study the captions in the publication you're dealing with. Do they use bare-bones identification, or is the caption a direct quotation from the text? Do they introduce subject matter that is not covered in the text, or do they use mere labels? Do they include lengthy chunks of information, or is the photograph integrated into the text in such a manner that it has no caption at all? In some cases you merely need to provide the reporter's who, what, when, where, why, and how to identify the picture.

Some publications, on the other hand, prefer rather literary captions with supplementary material. For such captions, don't say, "These are sheep." Instead, pick something that is not obvious to the observer and is not covered in the text. Something like:

> A flock of fat-tailed sheep, especially prized in the Middle East, graze on the slopes of Mount Atzmon, near the northern Israeli village of Tarshiha. The fat around the sheep's tails is used in baking special delicacies. The tail can weigh as much as thirty to thirty-five pounds; the shepherd must attach a special cart to the sheep's body to support the tail, which would otherwise impede the animal's mobility so severely that it couldn't graze.

It needn't be a literary masterpiece, but give the editor all the information he might possibly need. If you think of an especially charming line, send it along. But send the Five Ws information, too—in case the editor wants it.

Picture Sources for Non-Photographers

Photographs, of course, are not the only possible illustrations for either print or online articles. Maps, charts, and other types of graphics work well to break up the copy and create satisfaction for the reader. Artists usually travel with their sketch pads and return with drawings they can polish for publication.

But if photographs are needed to accompany your article, and you don't have any, don't give up—use somebody else's. There are hundreds of sources of travel photographs. Some sources will supply them free, others will impose a small charge. When the photograph is reproduced for an educational purpose, the reproduction fee is often reduced or waived. Promise the source that you'll ask for photo credit, which is about all you can promise.

These few pages only touch the tip of the iceberg as far as photo sources go. They include sample suggestions, but you'll find additional listings in *Photographer's Market* and *Writer's Market*, published by Writer's Digest Books, *Literary Market Place*, published by R.R. Bowker, and on dozens of government and commercial lists. Most of these sources can be accessed online.

One writer, working on an article advising travelers not to forget their medical kits, garnered six outstanding photographs from six different pharmaceutical houses; another, writing about a visit to Stockholm when it rained every day, received a dozen sunny-day pictures from the Scandinavian Tourist Office; still another writer, preparing a nostalgic travel piece on passenger ships, was able to use three photos from the San Francisco Maritime Museum.

Contact the Superintendent of Documents, U.S. Government Printing Office, Washington, DC 20540, for catalogs and information on availability. The National Archives houses vast collections of pictures, with entries from Mathew Brady's Civil War coverage to the present, while the Geological Survey has photographs of earthquakes and volcanoes, historical mining operations, Lake Baikal in Siberia, Comanche Conyon Lands, and a lot of etceteras. All government departments have photo libraries. These are just a few of the agencies housing usable pictures: the United States Armed Forces, the U.S. Forest Service, the National Parks Service, the U.S. Fish and Wildlife Service, the U.S. Children's Bureau, the Center for Atmospheric Research.

Foreign sources. The United Nations, as well as foreign government bureaus, has an extensive file of photographs. Travel agencies, hotels, and sight-seeing attractions, as well as airlines and railroads, are glad to have you use their pictures.

Tourist bureaus never charge for photographs—they want you to call attention to their attractions—so you're likely to get good results if you ask them for pictures.

State and city archives. State historical archives, charitable organizations, public libraries, museums, zoos, and church headquarters often have fine collections of photographs. They'll sell you a print for a small sum. Local chambers of commerce are good sources, too.

A random sampling includes the American Friends Service Committee, the Bancroft Library at the University of California, Chicago's Field Museum of Natural History, the National Recreation Association, the Red Cross, the Southern California Visitors Bureau, and Philadelphia's Office of the City Representative.

Commercial archives. The Bettman Archive, Brown Brothers, and Culver Pictures, all in New York City, have huge photo collections, with subject indexes available. You can buy practically anything from them.

News sources. Sources for news pictures, both historical and current, include:

Associated Press Pictures	Keystone Press Agency
50 Rockefeller Plaza	202 E. 42nd St.
New York, NY 10020	New York, NY 10017
The New York Times	Fotos International
229 W. 43rd St.	4230 Ben Ave.
New York, NY 10018	Studio City, CA 91604

Also, check your local newspaper morgue, which may have pictures for sale.

Industry. The Corning Museum of Glass, in Corning, New York, has the most comprehensive photo library in the world on the subject of glass.

In New York City, AT&T lists, in a free catalog, pictures that show aspects of telephonic communication. Shell Oil can supply photographs of camping, fishing, vacations, and outdoor recreation. Westinghouse Electric in Pittsburgh has a photo library related to science and industry, and Wells Fargo Bank in San Francisco offers illustrations for many areas of the Pacific Coast.

If any of these sources are near you, it's best, of course, to visit in person and inspect the collection. Call first for an appointment. If you have to inquire by mail, allow plenty of time. Identify what you want as specifically as you can, and ask for a photocopy of the picture if in doubt.

Photo Sources Abound

Keep in mind several other sources of photographs, too. If your subject appears in a recent *Readers Guide to Periodical Literature* or other magazine directory in print or online, see if the listings says "il.," indicating illustrations. If so, try either the magazine itself or the photographer for outtakes— pictures taken at the same time which weren't used. Newspapers and book publishers are often sources for outtakes, also.

Public relations agencies and PR representatives for practically all organizations are always ready to help you with pictures, and a note in Betty Yarmon's *Party Line* (Chapter 2) is sure to bring results.

Be selective, though. Free or cheap isn't necessarily good. When choosing photographs to accompany your travel articles, apply the same standards of selection as you would to your own work.

Other possible sources of illustrations are picture-taking friends, if you can manage to neither sever the friendly relationship nor settle for artistic duds. But if you have a friend who takes good travel pictures, you may find exactly what you need—and start your friend off on a new career.

If the story is a local one, where the newspaper sends a photographer, see if you can arrange with him for extra prints. Consider, also, the possibility of having a high school or college photography student work with you on local stories. Clarify the financial arrangements in advance, and hand him a shooting script.

The most expensive way to find photographs, but still a satisfactory one in certain situations, is through photo agencies. Some agencies deal with clients (you) and photographers (maybe you some other time) on an assignment basis; you tell them what you want and they find somebody to get it for you—at a price. Other agencies keep huge files of stock photos, paying the photographer when the picture is sold. Tell them what you want and they'll try to find the picture for you in their stock. Some of them have catalogs and websites, and there are various "on approval" arrangements. There are hundreds of photo agencies, some specializing in black and white, some in color, some oriented to special subject matter or certain types of pictures, others more general. Study their listings in *Photographer's Market* if you think this might be the answer to your present needs.

The most satisfactory solution, of course, is to learn to take your own photographs—to learn to say with pictures, as well as with words, exactly what you have in mind. But if this isn't possible, don't give up—you can still accompany your article with photographs provided by others.

Photography is increasingly important to the travel writer, so don't forget the vitality of visualization. Explore the medium of photography. Experiment. Experience. Enrich your travels and your life.

12 Sure-Fire Patterns for Travel Articles

Most popular travel articles follow one or another of 12 patterns. Falling into 4 general categories, the patterns interlock and overlap, and often more than one pattern is discernible in a published piece. Sometimes, on the other hand, it seems as though no definite pattern can be distinguished. But that doesn't mean the writer didn't have a pattern in mind—the bones of the structure may be camouflaged, but they provide a helpful framework. So it's a good idea to start with a popular pattern when you're planning or looking for a travel story.

Category 1: Travel Articles from Your Own Experiences

These are the travel articles that only you can write. They are born of your own experiences, either mundane or unique, and they fall into three types: the *personal experience* article, the *advice* article, and the *humor* article.

The *Personal Experience* Travel Article

It seems, doesn't it, as though the easiest travel story to write would be your own? Isn't it always easy to write about your own experiences—the things that actually happened to you? And isn't that the best kind of story?

It is easy to write about your own experiences. But the very ease with which we write about the familiar causes us to lose our perspective, so it sometimes makes the good personal experience article especially hard to construct.

When we start a travel experience piece, it seems as though we could go on writing forever about our own adventures, with no time lost for research and no time spent searching for plot or focus. Sometimes that's part of the problem—we can't resist the temptation to tell all. Each of us, of course, feels that any happening we experience is spellbinding. So, confident that the rest of the world will be fascinated, we tell the reader more than he cares to know:

> Today Maggie and I got up and brushed our teeth. We called room service for our breakfast. The waiter was late bringing it. He said he was sorry. The orange juice was in a tiny glass—only half the size of the glass we get at home.
>
> We went downstairs in the elevator and waited for Nick, our guide.

The reader doesn't want a blow-by-blow account of your trip. What he wants is to see your trip through his eyes, enjoying the highlights and putting himself in the hero's role. While the blow-by-blow may be all right for a trip diary, it will have a limited audience. In published pieces, the old-fashioned devices of diary style and letter style were originally intended to make the reader feel as though he were looking through the keyhole, getting exciting insights into esoteric goings-on. But the goings-on most people report are neither esoteric nor exciting.

Far better than an hour-by-hour, day-by-day account of a trip is a highlighted account, showing some of the good, some of the bad, some of the commonplace, some of the unusual, in an order other than chronological. Charles and Renee Overholser begin somewhere past the middle of their "First Camping Trip" in *Family Circle*. After introducing us to their three children and discussing a fairly common experience, family travels by car, they describe one moment of the journey:

> The children had suffered six days of torture from poison oak. . . . The bait of Disneyland had been expended, and we still had 4,000 miles to go. We felt travel weary and glum. Then, a few hours later, in one of those switches so characteristic of a long trip like this, our mood changed! We stood on the rim of the Grand Canyon of the Colorado, breathless at the spectacular expanse that lay open before our eyes. Our spirits were suddenly refreshed and our enthusiasm rekindled.

After describing some of the most memorable sights of the trip, they go back to its original planning. Discussion of the mechanics of itinerary, food, campsites, etc., follows, interspersed with anecdotes about individual days, both good and bad, such as:

> . . . we nursed Charlie, temperature 102°, in the heat and dirt of a Cheyenne parking lot . . . while all around us, like a nightmare, swirled the noise and excitement of Frontier Days.

or

> . . . the night near Yosemite when we counted 17 twinkling campfires strung along the shore of Tioga Lake like Christmas lights.

One of the differences between a publishable personal experience piece and a "Me and Joe," which all editors say they *don't* want, is in the choice of details. A publishable piece includes many details, but they are all relevant, all connected to the main theme, all interesting. A "Me and Joe" is a personal experience story in which the details are profuse but irrelevant and uninteresting to the reader.

Again, we must overcome the inclination to tell everything exactly the way it happened. One of my students wrote a charming story about her adventures as a guest at various Japanese inns. She couldn't sell it. Her shots were too scattered: there were too many names and places—too many hot baths and low-table meals; too many helpful, giggling maids at too many delightful inns. "But," she insisted, "that's the way it really *happened!*" I finally persuaded her to have all the anecdotes and experiences occur at one mythical inn with one composite maid, with the time-and-place framework holding the story together. She sold the revised piece immediately.

I never recommend the slightest deviation from the truth where the details are important. If the hotel charges $149.95, don't round it off to $150.00. If the service is terrible, don't dignify it as "mediocre." But where precise details are of no consequence, the travel writer must learn to use the fiction writer's techniques in moving the facts around to express the truth more clearly and more interestingly.

The fiction writer creates plot through a combination of personal experience and applied imagination. The travel writer creates plot largely from personal experience; but the selection of material used, its *arrangement*, the *order* in which it is presented, and the *emphasis* accorded each facet— *that's* what makes the story.

Victoria Brooks leans heavily on an important current event in "Paranoia on the Spanish Steps," for GreatestEscapes.com. As she tells about her visit to Rome she describes some of the monuments and interjects a few words about Romulus and Remus, the legend of Trevi Fountain, and the fact that John Keats died young in a house at the bottom of the Steps.

Then she sees it on the Steps—an empty cigarette package beside a small heap of white powder! Anthrax!

CIA warnings about chemical and biological contamination frantically flash through her mind. Should she begin taking antiobiotic Cipro now? Then, en route to their hotel they glimpse exquisite fountains and statuary that cause her to think about the angels guarding Rome. Feeling more relaxed, they return to the Trevi Fountain with a pocketful of change.

While print media use all of these 12 article patterns, in cyberspace, stories written in the first person from personal experience predominate. Donald George, former travel editor of the *San Francisco Examiner* and now an online editor, has published many personal experience pieces. He says,

"The best journeys illuminate not only pieces of the planet but also pieces of the person—and in so doing reaffirm the sacred connection between the traveler and the world."

People often reveal more than they mean to in writing their travel experiences, and sometimes the personality they reveal is unattractive. The whiners complain, "Why wasn't I told that it would turn cool," or "Everybody's always trying to cheat me—the sight-seeing tour was interesting but it wasn't worth the price." Their personal experience stories seem to be litanies of personal grievances. Everybody, it seems, is out to trick them, insult them, and lead them astray. By all means, tell it like it is. Warn readers to bring jackets or eschew the sight-seeing tour. But don't *whine* about it.

Some personal experiences are very personal. For instance, there currently seems to be an epidemic of women-traveling-alone stories that are more a guide to the mind and personality of the traveler than to the geographic area covered. Sometimes the tour is interesting; sometimes not so very.

Don't Be Grim

Don't be too grim when relating your experiences. The most mind-boggling catastrophe often seems humorous when the dust has settled. So try to inject some fun for your reader into dead ends and disasters. And don't tell too much. Stop when you come to the end. If you don't have a long story, tell a short one.

In all successful personal experience stories, even when written in first person viewpoint, the main focus is not on the author but somewhere else. Among the most successful personal experience stories are those that tell the reader how he, too, can savor this experience. In these stories the "you" is strongly implied and the "I" small—so the writer is never the star.

Often it's this universality and familiarity that makes the personal experience worth writing. The experience was the author's, but it could be anybody's. The once-in-a-lifetime personal experience story, on the other hand, gives an enticing glimpse of faraway places and a taste of adventure that the armchair traveler can identify with in a roundabout way. The unique experience—mountain climbing in Nepal, sailing solo across the Atlantic, even being at the critical place at the critical time as a war explodes into reality—doesn't necessarily invite the audience to participate by following the writer's example. But when deftly done, this most fiction-like personal experience technique draws the reader into the story and keeps him breathlessly awaiting development.

One of the masters of the once-in-a-lifetime personal experience story is Thor Heyerdahl, whose lifetime encompassed many. As Heyerdahl sailed across the Pacific on the raft *Kon-Tiki*, he wrote:

Sometimes . . . we went out in the rubber boat to look at ourselves by night. Coal-black seas towered up on all sides and a glittering myriad of tropical stars drew a faint reflection from plankton in the water. The world was simple-stars in the darkness. Whether the time was B.C. or A.D. suddenly became of no significance. We lived, and that we felt with alert intensity. . . . Time and evolution somehow ceased to exist; all that was real and that mattered were the same today as they had always been and would always be.

and aboard the *Ra*:

. . . Once again the masts were jumping in their flat wooden shoes, while *Ra* writhed about in the wildest gymnastics to follow the chaotic dance of the waves. She was making a new, hoarse sound we had not heard before. It sounded like a mighty wind roaring to and fro as our ten thousand bundled reeds bent in the water.

Although Heyerdahl's experiences are unique, the emotions he depicts are universal. The strong, precise language puts the reader aboard the rubber boat or the pile of balsa logs or the 10,000 bundled reeds. When you read Heyerdahl, creating an exciting story from true personal experience seems compellingly possible, doesn't it? The plus value of his writing lies in his ability to show, so that one man's personal experience becomes an adventure for all of us.

Although the personal experience story is harder to write than it seems, it is an excellent article framework for describing travel experiences from the mundane to the unique.

The *Advice* Travel Article

Some of the most popular articles you can shape from personal experiences are those that offer advice. I have advised, both humorously and seriously, how to get the most mileage from your travel dollar and the most pleasure from your vacation, how to select a sight-seeing program and a traveling companion, and many other travel-related "how-tos." Most of the themes have sprung from those notebook entries headed "Things I've Done Wrong."

At the Mount Kenya Safari Club, for instance, when I offered my husband a taste of my fish appetizer, he said, "Just cut me a tiny corner."

I started to cut the square in half.

"No," he said sharply. "I *told* you—only a small corner."

I pushed the plate toward him. "Here—take what you want."

He shoved it back. "Just cut me a corner!"

I burst into tears.

Did you ever hear of such a ridiculous quarrel? Back in our room, seething in silence, I began to write an article. I thought of other spats we'd had while traveling and of friends' arguments with spouses—in the Paris taxicab over who took too long in the bathroom and that's why we're late; in the New England rental car over who misread the map and that's why we're lost; in the Cairo airport over who wanted to buy that camel saddle in the first place and that's why we're paying all this overweight. What is it that makes ordinarily congenial couples so touchy when they travel, I wondered. The article answers that question and suggests various ways couples can foresee friction and either avoid it or cope with it constructively. At the end, I explain about the eye infection, the jammed camera, the shortchanging, the springless safari bus, the lack of sleep, the paucity of game—it wasn't the fish appetizer, it was everything!

Often an unpleasant travel experience turns out to be not so unpleasant after all, once enough time has passed so you can laugh about the experience—and convert it into helpful advice for others.

Evelyn Preston did just that after a disastrous auto trip to Yosemite. She warns that mountain vacationers are often so enthralled by woods and waterfalls that they forget the possibility of being stranded with "a volcanic radiator, stripped gears, or fading brakes." Her own experience with brakes giving out as she careened to a stop at the valley junction, smoke streaming from the front wheels, points up the importance of having your car thoroughly checked before you start off.

A "Things I've Done Wrong" notebook is an invaluable source of ideas for advice articles. Be sure to log all the information that you'll need to write your article.

"Things I've Done Right" can expand into advice articles, too, so jot down the details for future use.

When you think in terms of advice articles, be sure to select a relevant theme, and then show the reader how that theme applies to him.

Some themes are repeated again and again. Money—the saving of it or the spending of it—is always popular. Even articles with themes not explicitly connected to dollars and cents advise readers to consider in advance the amount of vacation money they'll have to spend, or remind them that car trouble at a resort can lead to expensive extended reservations or a rental car to transport them home.

Implicit in most money articles is the thought that the reader not only wants to save money while traveling, he wants to spend the money he has to buy the things that mean most to him. But when you're talking about money, know your readers; the words "expensive" and "inexpensive" are subject to a whole range of interpretation.

A travel advice article could take a hard look at the romantic prose of travel brochures or could deal with finding travel situations with the best of something—whether it's weather, food, accommodations, friendliness of the locals, nightclub acts, or ruins.

Comfort and Safety

On a more downbeat note, but still much needed and extremely useful, are the many advice articles that concentrate on the reader's comfort and safety: the least tiring arrangements; the best ways to protect yourself from injury while traveling; the steps to take if you are injured or ill. Health advice runs the full gamut, from learning CPR to staying alert with in-car exercises to snacking on grow-as-you-go alfalfa sprouts.

Mary Reeves Mahoney begins her "Injury Abroad" article dramatically:

... As two of last year's "statistics," my husband and I were typical.

One moment of a spring afternoon we were motoring across the wild-flowered hills and pastures of desolate Thrace; the next found us at the bottom of a fifteen-foot ravine, our car overturned and crushed, no exit except the rear window which we were to beat out with bloody fists. A curtain of gasoline streamed from the ruptured tank above us, and some-where among the jumbled upholstery was the burning cigarette our now unconscious driver had been holding at the instant of lost control.

She goes on to tell of the additional preparations she would make for any future trip, such as pre-trip tetanus shots, extra eyeglass prescriptions, and critical examination of the touring car and its insurance coverage. You can help your readers prepare for their trips with wise words on the selection of luggage; guides to unraveling the mysteries of airfares; suggestions for the care of elderly relatives left behind. You can advise them on such post-trip matters as what to take off on their income tax and how to present an interesting slide show.

Travel advice can be general, or it can be directed to a special group: how retired couples can find quiet motel rooms; how to pack for a convention; how to stock a boat with a month's equipment and supplies; "Ideas for Easy Trailering"; "How to Care for Your Camera While Traveling"; "How to Protect Your Oil Pan in Baja."

Slant for your specific audience. The readers of *College Bound* won't look for the same advice as the readers of *Modern Maturity*. "What to Do with the Children on the Rainiest Day of Your Vacation" won't appeal to the same audience as "Ordering Wine with Assurance at a Three-Star Restaurant."

Naturally, the travel advice article sometimes grades into the how-to-do-it or the self-help article, which is fine. What it should not become is a sermon. Take great care not to sound preachy to your readers. Be gentle and tactful; never make your reader feel foolish for not already knowing what you're telling him.

Present your information in a friendly, straightforward manner, and talk *with* the reader, not *at* him. Make sure he understands that you, too, are stupid sometimes and often share his shortcomings. On the other hand, don't make yourself seem like such a bungler that he loses confidence in your advice. A sort of "before and after" technique ("I used to do this wrong because I didn't know any better, but since I learned the right way I want to share it with you") is best.

The responsibility of the advice-giver is tremendous. Remember, people are going to act on what you're telling them. That's why it's important to ask yourself whether your problem was a typical one or a fluke. Will what you're advising work in the demographic group you're advising it for? It's always good to incorporate the experiences of others with your own. Quoting others gives your advice substance and credibility. Some subjects, such as income tax or health care, *demand* quotes from an expert. And if you, as a result of personal experiences, are yourself an expert, be sure to make it clear to the reader why you are qualified to give this advice.

Update Your Information

I cannot emphasize enough the importance of updating your information before passing it along to others. One of my favorite travel tips was: Two people traveling together by air should occupy an aisle seat and a window seat, in hopes that, if the plane isn't completely full, nobody will sit between them. That's still good advice, *except*—most planes today have few three-abreast rows, most seats are preassigned, and few planes fly with empty seats. Another piece of outmoded advice: Check in early for best plane seat selection. Today, if seats are not preassigned the early arrivals in the discount section will be seated from back to front, leaving the choice forward seats to those who check in at the last minute. By the time you read this, the seating situation on airplanes may have undergone some revolutionary change that makes this whole paragraph obsolete. The travel writer must check and recheck to stay on top of the situation.

The travel advice article can be tightly structured: "Ten Do's and Dont's for Winter Travel"; "The Pros and Cons of the Organized Cruise." Or it can employ a one-two-three format, where I, the writer, am telling you, the reader, to first visit your library, then your travel agent, etc. At other times it's more general or more subtle—the reader is being counseled, but gently.

The advice article may be in the first person or it may be in the typical "how-to" pattern of the "I-You" viewpoint. Sometimes it's written in an implied viewpoint, without personal pronouns, that takes the reader on-scene and into the story through active verbs and picture nouns, authoritative approach, and emotion-tinged information.

Although the theme of your travel advice article should be one that's of consuming interest to your readers, it need not be—it probably cannot be—a *new* theme. The same good ideas sell over and over again. "I was amazed," a librarian told me, "at not only selling a story of my first trip to

Europe but at the amount of favorable response it received. All I said were things like 'Wear comfortable shoes' and 'Take along a sweater'—things I thought everybody already knew."

Some advice is timeless.

The *Humor* Travel Article

The *travel humor* piece is usually forged from your own experiences, also. It amusingly relates something you've done or seen or heard or felt.

Ask any editor what he wants and he'll say more humor. Why then is humor so hard to sell? It's hard to sell because it's iffy—humorous *if* the editor thinks it's humorous. And often the editor doesn't know if what he thinks is humorous will be humorous to his readers. Because he doesn't trust his own judgment about what will make his readers laugh, he tends to decide conservatively.

Still, today's travel writer can sell amusing experiences if he takes the trouble to analyze the ingredients of a good travel humor piece. He may find himself writing the kind of humor that leaves the reader with a wry smile rather than a belly laugh.

That wry smile comes forth in response to tales of human foibles, where the reader can easily identify with the blundering traveler who's forever making wrong moves. Usually the joke's on you, the writer. (One travel writer, however, says she stopped writing humor—she got tired of making herself out to be such a *jerk* all the time.)

Patricia Brooks is a "jerk" we feel a chuckle of sympathy for, especially when she talks about some of the "bargains" she's bought while traveling. She purchased a pair of huge, low-fired clay pots in Haiti for four dollars apiece. First, each pot required a custom-built mahogany case to ensure its safe shipment; then there were the handling charges; then she found it necessary to hire a customs broker to retrieve her treasures from the jaws of the government. As she says, "At $4 the pots were a steal, at $14 a good buy, but at $40.50 apiece, they were a luxury I could have skipped."

An inside look at the writer's ineptitudes makes the reader feel superior.

However, hyperbole is often an element of humor. But, the exaggeration must be told within the bounds of logic. The reader should be able to say, even while he's laughing, "I know somebody like that," or "That sounds exactly like me." Gerald Nachman pokes fun at himself in "The Obsessive Sightseer":

> It doesn't seem enough, somehow, just to go someplace, or even take a snapshot of it. If you don't go all the way to the top (or, in certain cases, the bottom or the end or the edge) and collapse, you think you haven't properly "done" it.

There is the equally silly experience of going somewhere famous and not quite knowing what to do once you've arrived . . . . It took all day to get to Carthage and only about ten seconds to see it . . . . I felt very dumb walking around the ruins looking for more ruins to look at and trying to think of more telling comments to make than, "Well, well, so this is Carthage, eh?"

Humorous Protest

While travel humor is often born of an unpleasant personal experience, it doesn't usually spring directly from raw, unleashed fury or righteous indignation. You have to wait until you've calmed down a little before you're capable of making it humorous social commentary.

Bill Farmer writes amusingly of shipboard accommodations so terrible the passengers can say:

> Poor Aristotle Onassis. He probably had to walk to the steam bath and massage parlor on his yacht. Both were combined in my cabin. The air-conditioning had failed, bringing the temperature to an equatorial 100 degrees. Luckily, too, the drive shaft or a faulty piston rod the size of a telephone pole ran between my mattress and bedsprings to massage my travel-wearied spine all night. After four hours of wrestling with the washcloth someone had mistakenly used as a sheet. . . .

He's making a humorous protest over a serious complaint, and through humor drawing attention to the problem.

Art Buchwald deals in human conflict, a favorite form of travel humor. He's subtle, and yet not so subtle that any of his readers could miss the point. He attributes his knowledge of "Gamesmanship Aloft" to his friend Oscar Nimbleby, who taught him to always let women with children board the aircraft first so they would select their seats and there would be no possibility of them sitting near him. Nimbleby has also solved the problem of walking miles to and from the departure gate. By assuming a limp and then requesting a skycap with a wheelchair, Nimbleby hasn't walked ten steps in any airport for four years. Is Buchwald exaggerating? Of course he is. Isn't that what humor's all about?

Nobody who travels with a family ever runs out of humorous incidents to relate. Take care, though—before you set up members of your family as laughingstocks or embarrass them, be sure they'll perceive the experience in the same spirit as you do.

Excellent travel advice camouflaged by humor is often the best vehicle for reaching your readers. Gerald Nachman makes the reader wonder, "How does he know me!" His "Fear of Packing" begins:

After 25 years I still make the same mistakes in packing, only today I'm a lot faster at it. . . ."You never know" are the three most lethal words in a traveler's lexicon. . . . Maybe you'll spill shoe polish on your socks in Madrid and the stores will be shut for a big Spanish holiday. Suppose they don't sell Crest in Tokyo? . . . What if you meet a wealthy couple in London who invite you back to their castle in Scotland for a fancy dress ball? Better bring that black bow tie and dark shoes after all.

And then he gives you the kernel that counts:

. . . It is only in the quiet of your bedroom at home that all of these silly exotic notions occur. On the trip itself, it never matters what you have on.

The rigors of dealing with the complexities of modern life are intensified when you're traveling, and the humor inherent in the problem intensifies, too. Erma Bombeck was prepared to deal with the complexities in the best possible way—humorously.

It has always been a mystery, she said, how the Fates know which gate to send me to. When I am carrying a newspaper and my handbag and have two hours and a half to change planes, I am at Gate 2.

However, when I am carrying my own luggage, a three-pound novel, hot rollers, an extra coat and live cactus for my hostess, and have 12 minutes to make a connection, my gate is still being built.

Often it's best to select a small but universal subject, rather than write superficially about a vast one. As Richard Armour says, "In humor, part of the fun is seeing something inconsequential developed by the ingenuity and imagination of the author. The very overdeveloped may lead to the absurdity which, properly handled, is basic in a great deal of humor."

One "inconsequential" subject for travel humor is the universal misunderstanding of language. "Inglish Spocken Here," for example, compiles signs from all over the world, like the one from the cathedral in Seville, where "It is forbidden to enter a woman, even a foreigner if dressed as a man"; or the Hong Kong dentist's sign, "Teeth extracted by latest Methodist"; or this one on a ship's cabin door regarding the "Helpsavering apparata in emergings behold many whistles! Associate the stringing aparata about the bosoms and meet behind, flee then to the indifferent lifesaveringshippen obediencing the instructs of the vessel." Why not become a collector of such gems?

Other humorists translate from English to English, as in "How to Savvy a Sign," which explains that

A sign will inform you the next place down the road has a "Rustic Setting." This means the mosquitos are terrific and the parking lot is a morass of mud. Or the sign might say "Leisurely Dining." This does not mean your leisure but rather that of the cook, who has a hot cribbage game going with a salesman.

As Dorothy Parker said, everything is stacked against the humorist from the start because anybody feels free to object: "I don't think that's funny." Still, with ingenuity and an indulgent attitude toward the frailties of human nature, the travel writer can make important points while entertaining his readers.

Art Buchwald does this and more in "The Tourist's Prayer."

Heavenly Father, look down on us your humble, obedient tourist servants who are doomed to travel this earth, taking photographs, mailing postcards, buying souvenirs and walking around in drip-dry underwear. We beseech you, O Lord, to see that our plane is not hijacked, our luggage is not lost and our overweight baggage goes unnoticed.

Give us this day divine guidance in our selection of hotels. We pray that the phones work, and that the operators speak our tongue, that there is no mail waiting from our children which would force us to cancel the rest of our trip.

Lead us to good, inexpensive restaurants where the wine is included in the price of the meal. Give us the wisdom to tip correctly in currencies we do not understand. Make the natives love us for what we are and not for what we can contribute to their worldly goods.

Grant us the strength to visit the museums, the cathedrals, the palaces, and if, perchance, we skip an historic monument to take a nap after lunch, have mercy on us for our flesh is weak.

Dear God, protect our wives from "bargains" they don't need or can't afford. Lead them not into temptation for they know not what they do.

Almighty Father, keep our husbands from looking at foreign women and comparing them to us. Save them from making fools of themselves in nightclubs. Above all, please do not forgive them their trespasses for they know exactly what they do.

And when our voyage is over, grant us the favor of finding someone who will look at our photos and listen to our stories, so our lives as tourists will not have been in vain. This we ask you in the name of Conrad Hilton, Thomas Cook, and American Express. Amen.

Category 2: Travel Articles for Special Audiences

Travel articles for special audiences include the *who*, the *how*, and the *what*. They are aimed at the reader who is interested in a particular kind of traveler, a particular kind of travel, or a particular kind of activity at the destination.

While it isn't absolutely necessary to be one of those people you're writing about, you do need to identify with them as well as with the people you're writing for.

The *Who* Travel Article

The *who* travel article is a people-oriented piece, told in a straightforward manner. You can tell a travel article is a *who* when the reason for the article's existence is that it centers around parents with school-age children or mothers traveling with young babies; penny-pinching students or retirees with more time than money; swinging singles or lonely widows; teenagers on initial solo trips or servicemen on leave, starry-eyed honeymooners or couples celebrating their golden anniversary.

Most readers have many identities—a man may be a golfer and also a father, a homeowner, a gardener, an employee, a stamp collector, an accountant, a Nebraskan, a son, a Methodist, a Rotarian, and a winner of the lottery. But if you're talking to him about the links at St. Andrew's, you're addressing him in his role as a golfer, and that becomes the organizing principle of your story.

When the people in your article share one of your reader's roles, that reader will care about their travels. So you have to ask yourself, "*Who* is doing the traveling?" and then, "*Who* is the interested reader?"

Bridal Guide and *Modern Bride* emphasize, predictably, honeymoon locales. Is Virginia what the newlywed couple has in mind?

> There is no better place to start a new life together than on a mountain. Looking down from your aerie over the landscape spread below, you can examine the life you've lived up to now, and the vastly different life you've just begun.
>
> There are no lovelier mountains for such beginnings than the Blue Ridge Mountains of Virginia.

While Virginia is a pleasant destination for non-honeymooners as well, and many aspects of trips there could be emphasized, this particular story is written about and for people *who* are going on a honeymoon.

Young Children

Chronologically speaking, the next traveler after the honeymooner may be the young parent, describing a trip with a young baby. While predominantly a *who*, because the who is the most important feature, an article on baby taking a trip could also be a personal experience or an advice article, with overtones of humor. If baby's going in a backpack, it's also a *how*. If you interview other parents on their best ideas for traveling with babies, your story could become a *roundup*; or you could relate it to a *here and now* or focus on a special *gimmick*.

But if we stick to the parents of the baby as the *who*, we'll find that such publications as *American Baby*, *Expecting*, and *Parents* magazine occasionally publish "Baby Takes a Trip" articles, especially in late spring. One successful story about seven-month-old Susan is a highly structured piece, with sub-heads pointing the way to "The Five Minute Preparation Bonanza," "The Right Kind of Car Bed," "Setting Up Happy Naptimes," "Keeping Baby Happy and Quiet in a Restaurant," and other essential information. Remember, the *who* is not Susan but her parents.

"Camping with Your Toddler" is highly structured, too, with instructions for "Packing," "Meal Planning," and "Setting Up Camp."

Any parent should be able to write a *who*. Whether your travel experiences with children involve an hour's trip to the beach or a year's sabbatical around the world, whether you camped or cruised or visited relatives, your adventures with your children can be made into something other parents would like to read. Remember, though, to focus on only what will interest *others*.

A *Parenting* story on teenage travel abroad describes in detail the various opportunities, but the article is not really addressed to teenagers—it's addressed to their parents, who will be selecting and paying for the arrangements.

You don't *have* to be a member of the *who* group you're writing for, but sometimes it helps. The seventy-four-year-old grandmother who writes in *Modern Maturity* about her "Adventure in the Galapagos" uses her kinship with *Modern Maturity's* readers to good advantage in communicating her excitement to them. It's not just a trip to the Galapagos, it's one grandmother's dream come true by dint of moonlight jobs and help from her children.

Vocation or Avocation

Often the *who* is related to the reader's vocation, for vocation often influences vacation. A story about a jeweler studying the Crown Jewels at the Tower of London or a tennis player studying the prospective opposition from the stands at Wimbledon has vocation as the focal point. If you're an architect, like Bruce Beebe, you also might want to visit, as he did, Stonehenge; the Masjid-i-Jarm in Isfahan, Iran; Katsura Palace in Kyoto, Japan; Angkor Wat, Cambodia; and Chandigarh, India. What ties together these diverse destinations is the *who*—the architect who selected them as the world's most interesting architectural sites.

Trends naturally affect the *who* of travel—whether it's the promoter drumming up trade in China or the woman who wants to stay fit. Keeping abreast of trends is part of the travel writer's responsibility.

Sometimes it's the avocation that determines the *who*. When *Flower and Garden* published an article about Yorktown, Pennsylvania, it was, understandably, "Yorktown—a Gardener's View." This article appeals to anyone knowledgeable about gardens and/or about history; the way the two are woven together makes it doubly interesting.

Do you have a hobby that you travel with? Could you become the *who* and write about it? Or can you visualize a reader whose hobby makes him the *who* of your story?

Sometimes special circumstances determine the *who's* identity. For example the *who* should be black in a story for *Ebony*, which publishes "achievement and human interest stories about, or of concern to, black readers."

Other special circumstances make the experiences of a particular who especially interesting to a particular reader. *Travel + Leisure's* article "The Bespectacled Voyager" was written by an optometrist. Using a question-and-answer format, he supplies information on such queries as "How can I make on-the-spot repairs?" "Is it safe to have contacts duplicated in other countries?"

A more seriously handicapped traveler is featured in *Light Magazine*, published by the Braille Institute of America. Stories of special trips made by Institute members are often published in the magazine. A group of teens and young adults found the textures aboard the *Queen Mary*—wood, bronze, and cast iron—different from those they were more familiar with in today's world.

John Collins in *Arthritis Today* advises readers how to "Rent the Right Car," with a checklist of features to ask for. Other handicapped travelers often write their stories as personal experiences. While the *who* is the handicapped person, whose impairment makes special arrangements necessary, the story, if written well enough, will appeal to many readers.

Ralph Schoenstein does a wonderful spoof on a strange bunch of *who's*—nail biters, bed wetters, thumb suckers, transvestites, masochists, nymphomaniacs, and a man who nuzzled a blanket. He says, "as the S. S. Menninger sliced through the beer cans of New York Bay," he went to the starboard bow with the other nail biters where:

> A splendidly manicured young intern named Roger Roth . . . began our
> therapy by having us sit on our hands. . . . "The first thing I want you to
> know," Dr. Roth merrily said, "is that ocean therapy works. I've already
> been cruising with the fatties and the smokers, and next month I'm
> going out with a really great group of drunks. In fact, if any of you are

dypsos, too—or if you think you might like to become one—you can sign on with me right now at a special Nautical Neurotics Club rate."

Then:

The deck suddenly tilted so sharply that I tobogganed away from the nailbiters and into the lower back of a lady in the masochists' group.

"Wonderful!" she cried. "Do it again! Harder!"

"You're supposed to be kicking your habit," I told her.

"I'm failing," she said. "Oh, how I long for a good dose of pain! If I could just go through customs at Rio or try to get a cab at Kennedy or see a shrine with some Germans again!"

You won't always travel under special circumstances, but you can find a *who* if you look for one.

The *How* Travel Article

In *how* stories, the method of transportation is the most important feature. The function of the story is to outline the conveyance's distinctive features and add helpful ancillary information. Whether it's water, wings, or wheels, you, the writer, must communicate to your readers the excitement of that particular means of "getting there." After all, as they say, that's half the fun. Water, the primal element, is enjoying a resurgence of popularity as a medium for getting from here to there, and travelers' choices of waterborne vehicles grow ever more varied.

Jean Kerr prefers an ocean liner. "Being on a ship," she says, "is something like being pregnant. You can sit there and do absolutely nothing . . . and have the nicest sense that you are accomplishing something. I mean, you're getting there."

A "Mini-Cruise Guide" in a trailer magazine begins:

Nestled in the rolling Illinois farmland, less than an hour to the northwest of Chicago, lies the picturesque Chain o'Lakes. This chain, made up of ten interconnecting takes, has the Fox River flowing right through it and offers boaters more than one hundred miles of boating pleasure.

The story continues:

Launch facilities are far too numerous to list, so let's just say that no matter where you are on the Chain, a ramp is nearby.

Fishing just below the dam is excellent, as it is at many spots along the way. Now and then a tiny riverfront bar pops into view, cradled softly in its picnic grove of oaks.

Canoe and Kayak Magazine assumes, not surprisingly, that its readers are already interested in getting wherever they're going in a canoe or kayak. Its articles tell of good rivers for paddling, good equipment to consider, good strokes for getting there. One of the best articles I've ever read is Marilyn Doan's "Kids 'n' Canoes," which gives the reader everything he ever wanted to know about safety measures, traveling with children, and "the acid test of any trip—the kind of memories brought home."

David and Lyn Hancock profiled an offbeat style of water travel for the readers of a boating magazine in "Adventure by Inflatable." *Adventure*, singular, may be the wrong term, since the Hancocks not only live for months at a time in a thirteen-foot inflatable dinghy "packed to the pontoon with all our requirements for living and working," but cruise in their rubber inflatable along the rugged Alaska-British Columbia shoreline. As David is a wildlife biologist, the Hancocks often carry as passengers a mountain lion, a seal, or a raccoon; eagles, falcons, or sea birds. While much of the article deals with the Hancocks' adventures in camping with this arkful, the inflatable boat remains their constant (and often their only) link with the outside world, and its importance as a *how*-to-get-there figures prominently in the story.

If wings are your *how*, you'll find plenty of opportunities to tell readers all about it. We all know how many stories there are these days of new airline routes and old airline bankruptcies, of new kinds of service and old strategies that are changing. New fares, old fares, high fares, low fares—there's a how article in every one.

Wingless, but still airborne, and the epitome of adventure, is the ten-story-high hot-air balloon that takes you on an African safari, as described by Bert Keating. Lions, giraffes, warthogs, dik-diks, elephants, buffaloes, ostriches, rhinoceroses—"all the drama of an East African sunrise passed 500 feet below our feet. . ."

Traveling on Wheels

When it comes to wheels, the standard passenger car isn't the only *how* on the road. Roberta McDow's "Van-Touring Central America" is the tale of a nine-month trip she and her husband took in a Dodge Maxivan. Any kind of a recreational vehicle is a good bet. Jack Seville remembers a corny couplet,

> The only difference between men and boys
> Is the price they pay for their toys,

as he heads for an RV rally, which he described for *Saturday Evening Post* readers in "Wagonmasters of the 20th Century."

Wheel stories abound. An airline inflight featured "Provence à la Cart," about gypsy carts and horses that can be rented to tour some of the most spectacular scenery in France while "Covered Wagon Adventure" showed modern-day travelers, aged six to eighty-four, romping through Kansas in Stetsons and calico sunbonnets aboard authentic prairie schooners.

A bike story can be even more ambitious in scope. In "Across Canada on Two Wheels," Mandy Joslin says each of her knees had to flex 4,250,000 times to get her and her bicycle from Vancouver to Newfoundland on the Trans-Canada Highway. Her many adventures during her three-month journey are vividly rendered, with her *how* providing the focus.

In Lloyd Sumner's "How To Bike Around the World for Less Than $50 a Week" the focus is not really on the *how*. Instead, the bike is merely a means for conducting the four-year adventure, and the focus is on his destination—the world. Along the way, Sumner combines his how with good advice. He admits that he:

> was probably the least prepared adventurer to ever leave home. I was out of shape, had never taken an overnight bicycle trip, didn't know how to repair a bike, and had only $200 in my pocket. What I learned along the way could help anyone who thinks life is worth more than a two-week vacation once a year.

He advises:

> When you are planning a major adventure, the most important preparation is psychological . . . unless you reorient your priorities, your beautiful dream will dissolve with the rising sun. Forget the pursuit of comfort, because one rarely learns anything valuable while comfortable.

Another wheeled adventure was undertaken by a 14-year-old boy, who navigated the Great Wall of China—by skateboard! In an interview with a reporter, he called it "a bumpy experience."

Riding the rails is a big *how*. A newspaper travel story about Scandinavian trains begins:

> Americans who remember train travel might agree that the clicketyclack of the wheel on the rail is a pleasant inducement to sleep.

> But for passengers riding the rails in Denmark, Norway, or Sweden, each click is an invitation to see another distinctive view of fairytale villages, Arctic tundra, awesome fjords, towering mountains, great forests, glittering lakes.

The *how* is what's holding together the scenic diversity of the story.

For some travelers the only way to go is by animal-back. An article in *Aramco World* deals with Jordan's Camel Caravans, an organization that specializes in introducing Western visitors to a camel-back view of Lawrence of Arabia's desert. William Tracey, author of the article, describes the second day with the Caravan:

> The next morning saw us "making friends with our camels" as the brochure explains it, a process that involves adjusting the foam rubber cushions beneath the woven saddle bags, stretching one leg across the kneeling camel's back and hanging on frantically as the mount lurches to its feet grumbling and protesting. Once up, however, riding a walking camel is as easy as sitting in a rocking chair. Unfortunately the chair keeps rocking and rocking and rocking.

When you begin to think *how-to-get-there*, dozens of ways present themselves. Some are exotic, some not so. But the best, most universal means of transportation, always available, always useful, is on your own two feet. "A Walking Tour of Honolulu," "A Walking Tour of Philadelphia," "A Walking Tour of Denver"—such articles are appearing with increasing frequency. They're designed for the normally sedentary traveler who wants to explore the sights in a good-sized city. Current interest in fitness and ecology add to the popularity of walking tours.

Perhaps, though, you'd like to write an article addressed to more serious hikers, describing wilderness areas that can only be reached afoot. Maybe you have in mind something like the *Sunset* article about Olympic National Park, titled "Walking—the Only Way to Go." Wonderful! Many readers would welcome your description of an off-the beaten-track hike.

Whether it's on your own two feet or via pogo stick, cable car, or magic carpet, your transportation introduces your reader to a vital element of any trip—the *how*.

The *What* Travel Article

Active travelers are interested in *what* they'll be doing, and they like to read about the variety of activities at their destinations. Whatever type travel activity you, yourself, prefer, you'll find readers interested in it.

Practically every traveler cares about the *what* of accommodations—eating and sleeping. Regular readers of such food and drink publications as *Bon Appetit* and *Gourmet* naturally expect to have their taste buds titillated, whether or not they're planning to visit the Hôtel de France in Auch or Ernie's in San Francisco; but even "meat and potatoes" people are lured by references to sophisticated dining when the locale is on their itinerary.

Most regional and city magazines carry special restaurant sections covering their areas. A health magazine, like *Bestways*, will review a restaurant that prepares its food "in the health tradition." Even the newspaper travel sections will sometimes run roundup restaurant reviews under such titles as "Dining Out in Milan." So if you think of eating as your reader's *what*, consider the target market first, before planning your story. But while you're on your trip be sure to jot down the details of memorable experiences.

Sleeping is a little different. Often the story deals with the ambience of a particular establishment, such as Frank Taylor's *Off Duty* article about the old Hotel del Coronado, which has been declared a national landmark. He not only describes the eight-foot chandelier and the brass elevator, but also reminds readers that it may have been here that Edward, Prince of Wales, first met Mrs. Simpson.

Sometimes sleeping and eating go together, as in a *House and Gardens* travel feature on finding cozy places for bed and breakfast in the English countryside.

Camping can be the *what*, as well as the roof over the head, the dining site, and possibly the means of transportation. Camping abroad stories proliferate—so much so that it's hard to sell one without a special angle. So create a special angle! Bill Thomas authored an article on "Theme Camping" that tells about camps with special facilities for farming, cowpunching, exploring history, picking fruit, digging for artifacts, or panning for gold.

Often your readers will have a favorite activity they plan to pursue during their trips—the *what* they want to read about. Is it golf, tennis, skiing, fishing, or surfing? You can tell them where to find these activities and describe special festivities that may be connected.

For some travelers, the real *what* is in the shops. Information on what's available to buy is always popular, as is a recommendation of the best stores. Some notable shopping areas, such as the Virgin Islands, appear again and again in travel-oriented publications, with the writer telling the reader why the shopping is a bargain, what to look for, and what to do if you buy more than your customs quota. Even if your readers aren't shoppers, they'll be interested in features about offbeat purchasing such as Madrid's El Rastro. Madeline Dane Ross calls it "Madrid's Bargain Basement," and describes the setting:

> Sunday is the day for the pushcarts, canvas-covered stalls, and the largest display of wares of the whole week, placed right on the ground. . . . You can find anything from camping equipment and plastic furniture to rosaries and even secondhand tombstones. Along with the vendors hawking, people arguing or laughing, and children yelling in their street games, you'll hear the guitars of gypsies and popular. . . tunes from the secondhand records and players. On the breezes, too, you'll scent the sharp and tantalizing aromas of roasting chestnuts.

Enriching Activities

For some readers the *what* will involve animals—San Diego's Wild Animal Suburb, a dude ranch in Arizona, or the Kissimmee, Florida, rodeo. Perhaps they know about these attractions already and just seek specific details before planning a trip. Or they may be grateful to you for introducing them to a new vacation destination.

Part of the travel writer's function should be to introduce readers to enriching activities. For instance, Dorothy Loa McFadden says, "Nothing can hold your attention like watching something being made." She suggests that seeking out craftsmen—to watch, to photograph, to buy from—can lead to many happy traveling hours. "When you go to Europe," she says, "look for the places where you can see things made, of native materials and with designs which have often been handed down for generations." She goes on to describe some of the craft work that can be seen, telling her readers where to find it and how to arrange to watch the artisan at work.

Today many readers seek meaningful vacations. Would they be interested in your adventures tagging birds, counting coral, or digging into history as a contribution to the total body of human knowledge? Or are they seeking personal enrichment through learning to sail, scuba dive, photograph, or fly a helicopter? Do you have a *what* story to tell?

Perhaps you'll introduce your readers to a hobby like gravestone rubbing, which was the subject of an excellent article in a travel magazine. The article gives a little of the art, poetry, and history of gravestones, lists the equipment and supplies needed for rubbing, and explains the details of the technique.

If your readers have a long-treasured hobby, you can help them to enrich it through their travels. Julia Child's *Travel + Leisure* article on "Mastering the Art of Choosing a French Cooking School" gives food for thought to those who are considering spending hundreds of dollars to watch the master chef in action. Her advice is helpful for those who intend to select a French cooking school and interesting even to those who do not.

Joyce Winslow's *what* is one that's becoming increasingly popular; as our civilization becomes more overpopulated, harried, and complex—what she seeks is *solitude*. She speaks in *Redbook* to readers who may be similarly attuned:

> Solitude is becoming almost impossible to find. Even our national parks, which once were havens of tranquility, are more popular—and more crowded—than ever before. Last year 3 million visitors thronged Yosemite, elbowed for room around Old Faithful, and bumped into fellow hikers on Glacier National Park's most remote back-country trails.

But if you're planning a trip to a national park this year, take heart. Here is a list of serene, beautiful spots, many of which have not suffered exposure.

A bit off the beaten path but not inconvenient, these special places include homey motels that are clean and inexpensive, family restaurants that pack homemade muffins and preserves into your lunch bag, and trails that range from sandy tracks that take you to secluded coves to hiking paths with vistas so magnificent that you feel you can walk right into the sky.

Although the listing of the offbeat places might become a *roundup*, the article's search for solitude is so overwhelming that it becomes the basis for the *what*.

Look for the *what* when you're traveling. Think about which ones would interest which readers. Whether it's an old reliable, like playing ping-pong, or a new skill, like racing down a cresta run, do think about *what* your reader, the active traveler, will do at his destination. Once you've defined him and transported him, write about activities he's likely to enjoy.

Category 3: Travel Articles That Take Readers on a Journey

So far we have talked of travel articles for the active traveler—the reader who is thinking of following in the footsteps you are delineating. But many readers are armchair travelers, and this group of articles appeals to the armchair as well as the active traveler. The *flavor* article, the *definitive destination* piece, and the *gimmick* story are for everybody.

The Travel *Flavor* Article

Whether your reader is looking forward to a trip or reminiscing about one traveled only in his daydreams, a *flavor* piece will take him on a journey. When done well, it makes him feel he's right there with you, experiencing the car-shattering sounds and shoulder-shoving crowds of the bazaar; or the quiet and tranquility of watching, just the two of you, the sun setting beyond the gentle breakers.

The flavor piece is really a literary exercise; to write a good one you must be a good writer. Also, you have to feel strongly about the travel experience and be prepared to recreate that experience for your reader through emotion-evoking details.

Can you make your reader see the flavorful details? Bill Thomas, in the *Elks Magazine*, shows his readers the Suwannee River:

> The Suwannee runs slowly and meanders, its black water feeling its way between soft white sand banks and rocky shores, choosing an uncertain path at times in the low cypress swamps that crowd close to each side.

And along its path are great blue-water springs that emerge from the forest to flow sweet, cold and fresh. . . . The sandy bottoms of the springs, some of them 40 feet deep, are carpeted with watercress and other edible aquaplants. You can glide above them in water so crystal clear it's almost like flying.

He reproduces the *sounds* of the river, too:

The rustle and swish of the lazy water is remindful of the pace of life here. . . . Feel the earthshaking rumble of logs drifting down to the mills and the chop and slap of the paddle wheel ghost boats. . . .

John Updike's *New Yorker* article on Ethiopia takes us to the Addis Ababa Hilton, where you can see the cruciform swimming pool and the long white facade of the palace from upper-floor balconies. "In the other direction," says Updike, "there are acres of tin shacks, and a church on a hill like the nipple on a breast of dust."

He tells the reader what Ethiopia *feels* like, too:

Emerging from the pool, which feels like layers of rapidly tearing silk, one shivers uncontrollably until dry, although the sun is brilliant and the sky diamond-pure. The land is high, and the air is not humid. One dries quickly.

And toward the end he tells us that the young American taking a picture sees through his viewfinder a scene "exactly like the sepia illustrations in his Sunday-school Bible."

Paul Theroux writes of a train trip in India:

At Sirpur, just over the border of Andhra Pradesh, the train ground to a halt. Twenty minutes later we were still there. Sirpur is insignificant: The platform is uncovered, the station has two rooms, and there are cows on the veranda. Grass tufts grow out of the ledge of the booking-office window. It smelled of rain and wood smoke and cow dung; it was little more than a hut, dignified with the usual railway signs, of which the most hopeful was "Trains Running Late Are Likely To Make Up Time." Passengers on the grand Trunk Express began to get out. They promenaded, belching in little groups, grateful for the exercise.

Joan Didion imparts the flavor of Bogota to her readers. After viewing a mine that produces enough salt for all of South America and a cathedral carved into the mountain 450 feet below the surface, where 10,000 people can hear Mass at the same time, she had lunch in a chilly dining room on the side of the salt mountain.

There were heavy draperies that gave off a faint muskiness when touched. There were white brocade tablecloths, carefully darned. For every stalk of blanched asparagus served, there appeared another battery of silverplated flatware and platters and *vinaigrette* sauceboats, and also another battery of "waiters"—little boys, 12 or 13 years old, dressed in tailcoats and white gloves and taught to serve as if this small inn on an Andean precipice were Vienna under the Hapsburgs.

I sat there for a long time. All around us the wind was sweeping the clouds off the Andes and across the savanna. Four hundred and fifty feet beneath us was the cathedral built of salt in the year 1954. One of the little boys in white gloves picked up an empty wine bottle from the table, fitted it precisely into a wine holder, and marched toward the kitchen holding it stiffly before him, glancing covertly at the maitre d'hotel for approval. It seemed to me later that I had never before seen and would perhaps never again see the residuum of European custom so movingly and pointlessly observed.

As we can see, each of these *flavor* articles introduces the reader not only to the geographic area but also to the personality of the place and of the writer.

The *Definitive Destination* Travel Article

The *definitive destination* article also takes your reader on a journey. For that kind of comprehensive article you have to know *everything*. You have to anticipate the questions your reader is likely to whisper and answer them before they occur. Some destinations are easier to define than others, and some destinations demand a longer article than others. In any case, the article has to be information-packed and tightly structured, with sure transitions holding it together. And even though you're trying to tell everything, you'll still need to decide what to emphasize and what to skip over. You need a strong capsule sentence to define your message.

Trailer Life's article on Washington, DC, is a *destination* article. It begins:

If you're an American, no matter where you live—Dubuque, Dallas, Minneapolis or Muleshoe—you have a second hometown. All of us do. That other repository for our loyalty and allegiance is our splendid national capital city, Washington, DC.

And it ends:

. . . only Washington is every American's second hometown, and every visit is a happy homecoming.

And everything in between is related to that framework. The article tells the history of the building of Washington and describes the sights in considerable detail. It goes into the geography of the city and the attractions on its outskirts, like Mount Vernon; discusses musical and theatrical events; and tells the reader how to see the government in action. But because of the readership of this publication, the article says nothing about hotels or restaurants. It does mention that there are no campgrounds or RV parks within the city limits but tells where they can be found outside the city.

Of course a *destination* piece for a different type of publication includes more on where to sleep and eat.

Bon Appetit's destination piece on Rio de Janeiro focuses, quite naturally, on food and drink.

> Brazilian wine is poor. If you must drink wine in Brazil ask for Chilean or Argentine, but here in the Alba-Mar and along the bayfront nearly everyone drinks *chopp*.

Extensive research is needed to produce this kind of article. While some of it can be, and should be, started in the library at home, it's still vitally important to set up interviews with key people at the destination. Often a *definitive destination* piece results from an assignment, or at least a pre-trip discussion with the editor, and this opens the door to the key people.

National Geographic stories often cover the destination completely. While the *flavor* piece is nearly always written in first person viewpoint, the *definitive destination* story can be in any viewpoint, and often shifts from one to another.

If it defines a large area, the *definitive destination* article is enhanced by subheads and sidebars—it's easier for the reader to get the whole picture if it's divided up into specific segments. The well-structured *destination* piece, "Auckland," in *Pacific Travel News* tells about the geography of the city, its population, surrounding areas, volcanoes, water on all sides, shopping areas, climate, and transportation. And then come the subheads—"Hotels & Dining," "The Overview," "Museums," "Sightseeing by Car and Boat," "Sports & Events," "Shopping," and where to send for more information.

Still different, and more comprehensive in some ways, is Herbert Gold's *definitive destination* piece on Los Angeles. This is a type of piece that goes beyond mere detail in an attempt to actually grasp the *meaning* of a place. It expresses its theme by telling the reader the *city's* theme:

> Mobility is the theme of Los Angeles, not status, monuments, concern for the past. It is called a city: it is, in fact, an immense post-urban process, the tentative validation of a concept New York only hints at and neither Cleveland nor Des Moines dares to express. But L.A. is settled by refugees from New York, Cleveland, and Des Moines, from the Dust Bowl and the South, from Heartland America. They are here for this. It is the first American experimental space colony on earth.

And analyzing the ethnic components:

> That there are large black, Japanese, Chicano, Chinese, and Russian communities that guard their ethnic purity is well-known. There are

277

also extended families of those faithful to UFOs and Scientology, and you can listen to soft Scientological rock on an L. Ron Hubbard radio station. There are those who converse in tongues and those awaiting a call from mail-order prophets who bless cripples and change the tires on their wheelchairs.

Not exactly a travel piece perhaps, but definitely a destination piece. The author ends by urging the reader to laugh along with him at a city with signs such as this:

L.A. MINI SUPERETTE
Gas, Food, Tums
OPEN 24 HOURS A DAY
(Closed Midnight to 7 a.m.)

The *Gimmick* Travel Article

When you want to take your reader on a journey, consider the *gimmick*, too. The *gimmick* is a very narrow subject or a specific facet of a larger topic or a small topic treated in a special or unusual format. The *gimmick* is often a good travel story pattern, and an easy one to write because it focuses so sharply. When you don't have enough space to tell everything, as in a *definitive destination* piece, or you don't have enough material to write an in-depth overview, or for some reason you can't or don't want to cover that much, write a *gimmick*.

The capsule sentence for the *gimmick* type of article usually falls into place easily. If you're taking your reader on a journey to the Kentucky Derby, the Grand Rapids Furniture Museum, or Seattle's Space Needle, your capsule sentence is limited by the objective of the story, so there are fewer choices and fewer bypaths down which the writer can accidentally wander.

Individual sights and events often make good *gimmicks* when you're traveling, so learn to look for them, recognize them, and create them.

Very small segments of the traveler's world can be turned into profitable gimmicks. For example, "Our New Sign Language"—a description of the then upcoming new highway symbols—appeared in *Motorland*; "Senet"—an ancient Egyptian game shown in the tomb paintings and billed as "King Tut's Favorite Game"—appeared in *Games*; and "Topkapi's Turkish Timepieces"—an outstanding collection of clocks and watches in Istanbul's Topkapi Palace—appeared in *Aramco World*. These are all fragments of a subject. They are definitely limited in scope.

Equally limited, although covering a bigger area, are subjects like "Wyatt Earp's Kind of Town" (the ghost town of Bodie); "Placer County's Big Tree Grove" (a special race of giant sequoias); "Day Outside Amsterdam" (getting out in the country to Vreeland); and "The Little Volcano that Couldn't" (a resort hotel in El Salvador that was built so guests would have a good view of the volcano erupting, which hasn't happened since the hotel was built and thus the hotel has had no guests).

"The New Face of Yellowstone Park" sticks to the changes that have occurred in the park since the 1988 forest fires and explains why the park looks better—and worse—than visitors might expect.

Keep your eyes and ears open—and your field notebook handy—to record the significant fragments of your trip that will make good *gimmick* stories. Often the *gimmick* is a single event, perhaps taking up only a brief amount of time during the trip. My sheep dog trial was like that. (Incidentally, by the time I completed all the research, the *New York Times* had a new travel editor who thought sheep dogs "not compelling enough.")

The most "gimmicky" kind of *gimmick* is the puzzle or quiz. You often see this sort of thing in inflight magazines. There's the crossword puzzle with gems like "What to eat in Honolulu, 26 across" and "What to call your friend's father in Spain, 39 down." Sometimes you'll see a map of a confusing area like the Caribbean, with all the islands numbered, and the reader is supposed to guess which islands the numbers indicate. Or there'll be a questionnaire with a heading like "Are You a Graduate Globetrotter?" and questions like "Where would you be calculating coinage if this is what you had in your pocket: drachma, yen, bolivar, schilling, or guilder?" or "Which country's airline would you be flying if you go: Aer Lingus, Sabena, Lufthansa, El-Al, or KLM?"

You've probably seen some gimmicky things like this, too—"Bermuda: From A to Z," with "A" for ale (they tell you which pubs to patronize) and "Z" for Zebra Crossing (the black and white striped pedestrian crosswalk). If you're clever at making up games and puzzles of this sort, don't hesitate to work out a travel theme and send it off.

As you cultivate the habit of selecting travel *gimmicks* to write about, you'll wish the days had more than 24 hours.

Category 4: Travel Articles with Easy Pegs

Stories with natural pegs are easy travel stories. You can train yourself to find them anywhere. The *roundup*, *history*, and *here-and-now* travel articles practically write themselves.

The *Roundup* Travel Article

The easiest peg to use, as well as the most familiar, is the roundup. You've seen these in many magazines, and the possibilities are endless. It's often easy to ask twenty celebrities, say, about their favorite vacations. You probably don't even need twenty: five or six might do. It's even easier to interview one celebrity and ask him to name his favorite places for something or other, such as Lee Tyler did with Mike Roseto.

She asked him to name his favorite golf courses, in terms of character, nearby accommodations, and surroundings, and a *roundup* of eight golfing areas resulted.

For a *roundup* the travel writer can take a group of whatever and convert it to a salable story—"The Covered Bridges of Indiana," "The Paradores of Spain," or "Burma Shave Signs I Have Loved."

Some publications seem to savor the *roundup*, even to seek it out. *Accent*, for instance, usually runs at least one *roundup* in each issue, and they range from "Guarded Manners" (guards on duty at the Vatican, Prince Rainier's palace in Monaco, Buckingham Palace, and elsewhere) to "Odd Customs and Beliefs" (unusual religious ceremonies around the world).

Travel/Holiday uses a *roundup* in nearly every issue, and here the variety is astonishing. "Swiss Ski Resorts," "Britain's Stately Homes," and "Spain's Royal Palaces" may not seem so unusual, but how about "Aerospace Museums"—the many museums throughout the United States that document each step, from Kittyhawk to the moon, during the past eighty-odd years; or "The World in Mosaics"—from the floor of Diocletian's Bath in Rome to the steps of a Jain temple in Calcutta.

Better Homes and Gardens runs frequent travel *roundups*, too. Is the reader interested in "America's Zingiest Zoos"—from Cincinnati to the Bronx, from St. Louis to San Diego? In "Indian Country Vacations" accommodations "from the super deluxe to the primitive" are mentioned, and the reader is told where to get additional information. Another issue features "'Foreign' Vacations in the U.S.A.," rambling from Little Tokyo in Los Angeles to Holland, Michigan's Tulip Time Festival and San Antonio's Paseo del Rio.

Roundups of cruises, train trips, car rental agencies, even articles about the best buy in cell phones, frequently appear online, as well as in print. *Gorp.com* recently carried a very good *roundup* of "Best Parks for Biking," including 10 national parks.

Numbers lend themselves to *roundups*—"Seven Places You Won't See the Joneses This Summer" in *Metropolitan Home*; "Five Great Places to Get Away from It All" in *Medical Economics*; "Three RV Tours That Are High Roads to Adventure" in *Minnesota Motorist*; and "Seven Great Tennis Vacations" in *Glamour*. Be sure you use the numbers instead of letting them use you. If there are only nine really outstanding nudist camps where your reader can reserve a holiday, don't round the number off to ten.

Roundups, like other travel articles, especially appeal to readers when they emphasize how to save money. Add the words "you" and "secret," and it's hard for the reader to resist looking to see what's offered. *Family Circle's*

"Super Sunbelt Vacations Your Family Can Afford" is a case in point. Throughout this entire article, the themes of "super" and "sun" and "saving money" promised in the title are emphasized.

Roundups sometimes introduce the reader to things he can do himself. "Games Europeans Play" was a roundup of interesting keep-fit exercises; and *Gambling Times* tells "Where to Take a Gamble on Your Next Vacation," evaluating foreign casinos.

The items being rounded up are not many, perhaps only two. A *Redbook* article on "Two Seductive Cities" links Santa Fe and San Francisco by more than their initials. If this is the year for your second honeymoon, says the author, you can find elegant hideaways, extraordinary scenery, sumptuous but inexpensive dining in both of these cities, and there are so many things to do you may even want to take the children along.

Sometimes you can create a *roundup* from parts of several previous travel articles by finding a common peg to tie the information together. And sometimes, if you don't create the *roundup*, the editor does. When I sent an article on Buena Park to *Off Duty* without querying because I felt the article was perfect for the market, the editor informed me that another writer was already researching California's theme parks, but he had requested him to exclude Buena Park. When the article appeared in print, it included all that I had written plus material on Disneyland and other theme parks by Hal Schell. The editor ran it all together as a *roundup* and gave us a joint byline, although Schell and I have never met.

Practically any segment of the travel experience works well with this easy peg, and you'll find yourself using it again and again. Either first person or implied viewpoint suits the *roundup*.

The *Historical* Travel Article

When you're writing an *historical* travel article, it's your job to bring the reader right to the scene of the action, so you must make it read like fiction. Usually this is best done in an implied viewpoint, with many active verbs. You have to be sure, however, that your *facts* are not fictional but are absolutely accurate. Your target audience determines how many of these facts will be introduced and how scholarly your presentation will be.

Another factor, of course, is how much space you have. While an historical travel article on Peru in *Americas* would not be as scholarly nor as finely tuned as one in *Archaeology*, if it's the lead article it must be significant and in-depth.

Let's examine a 23-page, well-illustrated article on "Mexico: A Story of Three Cultures." It covers the geography and the cities and landscapes in considerable detail, dividing the country into northern, southern, and central sections. After explaining the constitution and government, the article moves on to culture and customs, folk arts, and literature. Under economic and social development it discusses labor, communities, housing, health, education, agriculture, gas, minerals, industry, electric power, banking and finance, foreign trade, communication, transportation, and tourism; thus the article becomes a comprehensive overview. Its major focus, though, is Mexico's history, from Pre-Columbian to the present. It discusses Mayan and Olmec civilizations, Zapotec and Mixtec, Toltec and Aztec and explains the present archaeological zones. Then it details the wars and revolutions, the backward steps, and the forward steps from Cortez to the present. Although factual and accurate, the article's style is readable:

> Father Miguel Hidalgo y Costilla issued the now famous *grito de Dolores*: "Long live our lady of Guadalupe, down with bad government, death to the Spaniards!" His followers, an "army" of perhaps fifty thousand ill-clad men armed with bows and arrows, clubs, machetes, and a few guns, seized Guanajuato and nearby towns and marched on Mexico City.

As is often the case in historical articles, the writer assumes a certain knowledge on the part of the reader, as, for instance, when he speaks of "now famous." Online historical articles assume this knowledge, too, but perhaps in a different way since brevity is so important.

There are two frequent reasons for writing the historical travel article: to remind your reader and help him review the facts of history, and to shed new light on an old story. "The City That Died to Live," a *Reader's Digest* piece on Pompeii, does both. Although written long ago, its authors, Donald and Louise Peattie, did such an excellent job of bringing Pompeii to life, within the framework of historical accuracy, the article could serve as a model for all travel writers who try similar pieces. Notice the devices that bring the reader on-scene although more than 1,900 years have elapsed between the time Mt. Vesuvius erupted so disastrously and the time the story was written:

> The city of Pompeii basked among its silvery olive groves and dark umbrella pines. The marble on suburban villas and on the temples in the heart of town glittered sumptuously as the sundial shadow crept toward the fated figure I *post meridiem*. The shopkeepers were closing their wooden shutters for the long Latin lunch hour. A baker shoved 81 loaves into his oven and closed the iron door. In a wineshop a customer laid his money on the counter. Suddenly an earthquake convulsed the city. The barmaid never picked up the money. The baker's loaves were burned to a crisp.
>
> Thousands fled at once. These were the wise—and the wisest kept on traveling all that afternoon and night. Nothing else could have put them outside the circle of death that Vesuvius was inscribing around itself.

Some publications lean especially toward historical travel articles, so we expect to see in the *Iron Worker* an article on the restoration of Colonial Williamsburg, in *Early American Life* an article about "Savannah, a City Reclaimed," and in *National Motorist* an article about the copper mines of Jerome, Arizona. All of these stories combine history with the present, telling the reader what he can see if he goes there today and what it all means.

Instead of an entire community, sometimes the historical travel article deals with a more specific theme, such as the restoration of a 19th-century sugar plantation, in *Historic Preservation*, or the transporting of Cleopatra's Needle from Alexandria, Egypt, to New York City, in the *Saturday Evening Post*.

As with all kinds of writing, the easiest way to make history come alive is to tie it in with people who lived it. When Fanny-Maude Evans wrote "Take Along a Hero or Heroine" for *Redbook*, she emphasized to her readers the value of doing their homework before they traveled in order to know the people who made the places memorable. She tells about Harriet Tubman silently leading 300 slaves to freedom along Maryland's Eastern Shore; Sybil Ludington, a "teen-aged Paul Revere," who summoned New Yorkers to rebel against the British; and Sam Houston, who hated violence yet "won one of the world's most decisive battles." She concludes:

> By reading about the men and women who helped to carve the nation's history, not only will you be giving your children inspiring models to follow but also you can make your travels more interesting.

Nostalgia, too, enters into the *historical* travel article. One writer who "first met Bill and Anna Wilkins at a flea market on Maryland's Eastern Shore when they had been dead for several years" took their scrapbook, stuffed with postcards and trip mementoes, and followed in the footsteps of the trip to Florida they had taken 40-odd years before. He compares and contrasts the train ride, dinner in the diner, and the hotel. And then he *flies* home!

Whether you're introducing a bit of personal nostalgia or sticking to the strictly historical, you'll find that this pattern, with its easy peg, is often a good one to use.

The *Here-and-Now* Travel Article

In some ways the easiest travel article of all to write is the *here-and-now*. It takes advantage of the fact that a locale—or a topic—is already in the forefront of readers' and editors' attention for some reason. Sometimes you can hang a basic story on a *here-and-now* peg by merely adding a sentence or two at the beginning and another sentence or two at the end. For example, a magazine article about Evora in the *Retired Officer Magazine* begins:

> Now that the political upsets in Portugal seem over, the country as a whole and the Algarve and Lisbon in particular are going to be prime tourist targets.

The article continues with the charms of Evora.

Other times, you'll be inspired by the event itself to write the *here-and-now* so the peg will be integral. Look for news events, like improved relations with a foreign country such as Cuba or China; the opening of an entire new tourist area, such as Vietnam; or major political changes like the increased accessibility of Eastern Europe. A new kind of plane or ship being launched, wars, riots, strikes, adventurers taking off from or landing at a particular place—all these provide us with the nucleus of reader interest and the framework for a *here-and-now* story. But be sure to hurry when you're writing a story like this. A magazine's long lead time sometimes makes a newspaper travel section or an online zine a better market for a current event.

A major happening, such as the 9-11 disaster, spawns travel stories for a long time—what tours, cruises, and other trips have been cancelled, and which ones then reappear; what new security measures are being observed, and how difficult do they make transportation; how many people decided not to go to faraway places; and, most of all, reports from the people who did go—what was it like?

Before the Winter Olympics opened in Salt Lake City all media outlets searched for something new to say. In addition to stories about the upcoming games themselves, transportation to Utah, sleeping and eating upon arrival, and the landmarks of Salt Lake, there were many articles about what to see in the surrounding area. There were even stories like "A Primer on Tippling in Utah," telling how and where to find alcoholic beverages in this anti-alcohol state.

The end of an era can be *here-and-now*, too. When our famous regional train whistled at its last grade crossing I wrote (and sold) a reminiscence involving my two-hundred pound father and four quart jars of dill pickles squeezed into an upper berth of that train.

Look for regional events to write about for local newspapers and regional publications: the county fair; the marble-shooting championship in the state capital; new attractions at the nearby theme park.

Can you make a *here-and-now* out of an anniversary? While the Pompeii story as history needed no other peg, a more recent *Reader's Digest* article was tied to the traveling exhibition, "Pompeii A.D. 79," which was drawing "record crowds" to view the three hundred artifacts recovered from the excavations; both the exhibit and the article were tied to the anniversary of the Vesuvius eruption.

Anniversaries of cityhood, statehood, or nationhood and upcoming commemorations of other civic occasions give you more time to plan ahead if you're familiar with or going there. The Golden Gate Bridge, the Statue of Liberty, the Empire State Building, and dozens of other landmarks have important birthdays. Zeke Wigglesworth, former travel editor of the *San Jose Mercury News*, began planning in early 1991 for coverage of the 50th anniversary of the attack at Pearl Harbor, to be commemorated on December 7, 1991; the Olympics in Barcelona, to be held in summer, 1992; and the celebrations and activities surrounding the 500th anniversary of Columbus' discovery of the New World, in October, 1992. Then editors planned again for the commemorations in 2001, 2002, and onward.

Many publications, both print and online, had before, during, and after stories about London, and the British Isles in general, in recognition of Queen Elizabeth's 50 years on the throne.

General trends, while not as mercurial as isolated news events, sometimes do change suddenly, so when you're writing about a trend, act quickly if you think a change is likely. Broad general trends are, however, likely to continue, such as younger teenagers traveling farther, "new" gold hunters becoming hobby prospectors, and people saving money by traveling close to home, which may give you a little more working time. Health and fitness will probably be with us forever.

As we've said, adventure travel these days is the province not only of the very young and unusually hardy; it is catching on with mainstream vacationers and senior citizens, tired of the three-day, four-night deal to Disney World with the complimentary rum swizzle or the week's Caribbean cruise on a ship that looks and acts more like a resort hotel than a ship. And the trend toward ecotourism, with care given to protect the environment, is even more all-encompassing.

Watch the Calendar

Learn to watch the calendar and allow enough time (usually six to nine months, but check the publication) to fit your story into seasons of the year and special holidays only salable to a certain periodical or online zine. Create "seasons" if you can, with phrases like, "Now that the kids are back in school" or "Now that the wildflowers are in bloom."

Be aware of annual events such as: the International Balloon Festival in Albuquerque each October; the Calgary Stampede in the late summer; Aloha Week; Tulip Time in Holland, Michigan; fall colors; whale watching; the Great Raft Race, which is the Labor Day blowout in Tulsa, Oklahoma, and other repetitive occasions.

Seasons of the year make great travel stories. Spring brings "New Season Show in the Smokies" and "Great Springtime Vacations Along the Gulf of Mexico." In the fall it's "Share the Excitement of a Football Saturday" and "A Rainbow of Fall Foliage Awaits the Camper Who Follows a Back Country Trail." In winter there's advice to "Go Winter RVing" and "Get Away for a Winter Weekend."

The holidays are a gift to the travel writer. *Travel Life* had a wonderful three-way Christmas travel piece—all personal experiences: a caravan Christmas in Mexico; "Head Home for Christmas"; and "Camp the Holy Land at Christmas." "Christmas in Europe" and "Christmas Around the World" are perennial favorites, supplemented by stories that tell how Christmas is celebrated in individual countries. If you have any new ideas on Christmas travel, editors will welcome you.

Washington's Birthday, Valentine's Day, Halloween—all make good stories. Look for obscure holidays, too. Groundhog Day? Flag Day? Benjamin Franklin's birthday?

Another *here-and-now* can have what is termed a "this reader" peg. "This reader" will read your story because it's in a particular publication. Therefore, it's often a story with a limited market—only salable to a certain periodical. Usually, the story will concern travel connected to an association, an industry, a profession, a religious group, or an area of the world. Fishermen want to know where they're biting, and cyclists will read stories about the roads and trails. If you're writing for *Sea Kayaker* or *Trailer Life* or *Motorcycle Tour & Cruiser*, you have a built-in audience.

If you know of a Rotary International project, a shrine-hopping trip planned by a denominational organization, a "Sister City" or "Neighbors Abroad" event, your chances of selling an article escalate.

As we have said, many travel articles combine the elements of several of the dozen patterns described in this chapter, and the structure of the finished piece is sometimes blurred. But beginning with a definite framework will give you a head start, and you'll be able to decide on combinations of your own. You'll also find that you can apply several different patterns to the information gathered from a single trip, thus netting several different stories from your experiences and research.

SEVENTEEN

Freebies and Tax Deductions– Yes or No?

When people hear I'm a travel writer, they always ask two questions. The first is, "How about the freebies? You say freelance travel writers get to see the interesting and the offbeat. Do they get to see it free?"

Then comes the second question—"How about your income tax? Can you take all those trips as tax deductions?"

The only possible answer to both questions is, "It depends." Circumstances vary from trip to trip, from year to year, from day to day. Yes, being a travel writer generates some trip advantages and some tax advantages. No, it doesn't create a payless paradise of pure pleasure.

With freebies, it depends on *who* is offering *what* and *why*, as well as *where* and *when*. And, most of all, it depends on how *obligated* you become.

As your name gets known in travel circles, offers of hospitality may come your way—from the Christmas cocktail party to the all-expense world tour. We all know, though, that hospitality often carries at least an implied obligation. Since my opinion is not for sale, I never want to feel committed to praise something that might turn out to be unpraiseworthy.

We've spoken before of the travel writer's great responsibility—how readers count on finding a destination as you describe it. Sometimes readers pay out thousands of dollars and weeks of time to take a trip on your say-so. Sometimes it's the adventure of a lifetime for them—a honeymoon, a retirement celebration, a return to the roots of their ancestors, or a place they've always longed to see. Are you going to advise Hotel A instead of Hotel B because you sincerely believe A is in a more convenient location, gives faster service, has more cheerful employees, and provides a better value for the money? Or are you going to advise A because the manager invited you to spend a weekend as his guest? If the weekend was super, was it because your registration card was marked "VIP," or is Hotel A a regular provider of super weekends? It's your duty to find that out. And it's your duty to make it clear that you, as a person of integrity, will seek the truth to relay to your readers.

Travel Freebies

There are several kinds of freebies available to the bona fide travel writer, on a sometime basis. If, for instance, the country or the region invites you, or you and your spouse, specifically to cover a recent change in government, an important anniversary, or a newly enthusiastic attitude toward tourism, it's likely the proverbial red carpet will be rolled out. You will be escorted to the airport, or at least met at the departure lounge, where you will be directed to a first-class seat aboard the country's chief air carrier. You will stay at the most luxurious hotels, eat and drink the most exotic offerings, and receive gifts that range from press kits and promotional gimmicks to flowers, fruit, champagne, and anything the public relations people think you might like. As for sight-seeing—you'll be taken to see everything of possible interest. Your hosts will probably provide lists of story angles, research sources, and potential markets.

There is a downside to this, though. To protect your reader, you must never let yourself, as a communicator, be used. In sensitive countries my husband and I have sometimes had the feeling that our popularity as guests was due to our host government's desire to present a favorable image to our North American audience. If you mix politics with travel writing, listen carefully to all sides, then evaluate the facts; but don't become a mouthpiece for any self-serving faction.

Hotel chains such as Hyatt, Westin, or Sheraton sometimes invite individuals or groups to tour several of their hotels that are new, remodeled, or especially newsworthy for some reason. They provide first-class transportation, meals, entertainment, sight-seeing guides, and recreational opportunities.

Press Junkets

The press junket that includes representatives of various media from various parts of the U.S. —usually about 10 to 20 participants—is often sponsored by hotels, transportation companies, or recreational attractions. Sometimes it's a special public relations event, like a Chinese banquet in San Francisco to promote travel to Hong Kong or a gathering at Hawaii's Mauna Lani Bay to watch chefs and winemakers prepare "Cuisines of the Sun."

Sometimes the press junket is sponsored by the country or region, and often several travel-oriented entities get together to arrange a gathering of travel writers. I will never forget an invitation my husband and I accepted that combined the efforts and resources of an airline, a city, and a cruise ship.

The week's trip turned out very well, and we enjoyed it and wrote about some of its facets. But its beginning, at a major airport at 7 a.m., did give me pause for thought. We had left our suburban home at 5:30, without even time for coffee, in order to arrive promptly for the junket. Our hostess rushed up, shoved envelopes into our hands, and hurried us onto the plane. What was in the envelopes? Coupons for eight free drinks apiece! I don't know how you feel at 7 a.m. when you haven't even had a cup of coffee, but the mere idea of consuming eight drinks—free or otherwise—during the 55-minute plane ride did make me wonder what lay ahead.

Cruise lines sometimes invite well-known travel writers to cover special stories, such as Radisson Diamond's re-creation (in modern style) of the voyage of Columbus on that event's quincentenary, or American Hawaii's nostalgic cruises commemorating the 50th anniversary of Pearl Harbor.

Professional travel writers' organizations, such as the Travel Journalists Guild or the International Food, Wine & Travel Writers Association, often arrange special familiarization trips for their members—from the Arctic Ice Cap to the romantic Del Coronado. It's always a pleasure to "talk shop" with other travel writers, and that is a significant reward of such junkets. Networking is always valuable.

Freebies Have Advantages, Too

One of the most important pluses of the freebie is the opportunity to get behind the scenes and see and experience facets of the travel experience that the ordinary traveler seldom knows about. Whether it's viewing an unreleased program at the Kennedy Space Center, riding in a balloon over the hidden vineyards of Provence, or walking through the alleys of San Francisco's Japantown, you'll find the special angle for your story in the unusual and the memorable.

Sometimes your freebie is the result of an assignment. An editor will call and say, "XYZ Airline is opening a new route, and they invited me to cover the inaugural flight and be their guest for a few days, but I can't make it. Would you like to go?"

More often, the writer has to secure the assignment before the freebie becomes a reality. The public relations people handing out the hospitality want to be sure they're handing it to "writers on assignment."

If the story that results from the hospitality is not an assignment, what will you do with it when you get it researched and written? Will it be acceptable to your target market? This whole business of freebies and how they might or might not influence the journalist's conclusions, and whether a periodical should publish the resultant stories, has been extensively debated in the *Conde Nast Traveler*. And this is a subject often discussed among travel writers and editors.

Policies on Freebies

Several publications, of which the "New York Times Travel Section" heads the list, feel that the travel writer cannot serve more than one master at the same time, and therefore they will not publish an article that grows out of a trip paid for by airlines, hotels, or any other organizations with an interest, direct or indirect, in the subject being written about. Other publications don't preclude the use of stories resulting from sponsored trips, but they want to know just how much hospitality the writer has accepted. Then they read the article with particular precision, searching for any possible bias.

Still other periodicals will not permit their staff or freelancers to accept freebies but are willing for them to travel at a deep, deep discount. Others pick up the travel tab themselves and pay the going rate for their writers to travel. Because travel, especially to faraway places, is such an expensive activity, it would be impossible for many travel writers to take the trips they write about without financial help of some kind.

Many jobs related to travel writing, such as teaching resort writing classes or editing a resort newspaper, are not exactly freebies, since you're expected to work in payment for your vacation, but they provide interesting interludes in a travel writer's life. Port lecturers, enrichment lecturers, or tour leaders work hard, but sometimes find their jobs seem more like play than work. At home or abroad, there are more travel-writing-related positions than you may think.

Freebies May Exact a Price

Because my husband and I often collaborate in writing, photographing, and lecturing, we often accept—or decline—freebies together.

Sometimes we've regretted accepting hospitality because the thing our hosts wanted us to do was less interesting than what we had planned.

In one place, which I'm purposely leaving vague, we were invited to tour a cultural center, watch the entertainment, then stay for dinner and the evening show. It was a three-hour drive from our hotel. Since the invitation said noon, I thought it began with lunch. My mistake. But there was no mistake about it being noon. The midday sun fried us during the two hours we sat on bleachers in the open, watching some worse than mediocre folk dancing.

We spent another two hours listening to the church that owns the cultural center patting itself on the back. Everyone assured us that the dinner would be lovely and the evening show outstanding, but we never stayed to find out. When we left at four, mumbling hurriedly invented excuses, handing back to the PR people the expensive, unused dinner and show tickets, we were hungry, thirsty, hot, tired, bored, and disgusted. Mainly I was disgusted with myself for not finding out more about the program in advance.

If the dinner and the evening show were the big thing, why didn't we spend the morning and early afternoon in beachfront research, departing for the cultural center around three? We didn't because our hosts insisted on showing us *everything*.

Sometimes it wasn't the host's fault that we wasted our time. For instance, a famous resort, where the hotels, restaurants, and sight-seeing attractions all belong to a tourist organization, invited us to visit. Unfortunately, the only time we could work it in was the two days that the officers of the association were out of town, at a national tourism meeting. They assigned their "best guide" to take us around in her car and show us everything. However, when the "best guide" came to pick us up, she said her car wasn't working well, and she would sit in the back seat of *our* rental car and direct us. For some reason, perhaps because she was accustomed to driving herself or guiding on a bus, she kept getting us lost, and we drove up and down, back and forth, over the bumpiest back roads imaginable. We saw nothing very interesting, and most of what we heard was the story of her life, also not very interesting.

You soon learn to regard freebies in the same light as entertainment you're paying for. Ask yourself, "Is this going to be worth the time I'll have to spend on it?" Sometimes it isn't.

We were in Cairo, for instance, with an alumni group tour for which we'd paid full price. We'd been told before leaving California that an international airline would take care of our transportation to complete an assignment at our next destination. The airline's Cairo representative would firm up the plans. Unfortunately, the appointment with the Cairo representative was at the time our group was scheduled to see the Papyrus Museum, one of the most interesting sight-seeing opportunities in Egypt.

But our sacrifice of the museum visit was useless. The representative explained that during the weeks since we'd left California the airline had decided to discontinue its service between Cairo and our next destination, and the last plane had flown there yesterday.

We've discovered that it never pays to adjust your plans in hopes of securing something for nothing. As one experienced travel writer says, "Nothing is ever *really* free."

Freebie Philosophies

City guidebook writer Martin Fischhoff feels differently, however. He says bluntly that he lives on free meals. He defends this practice by assuming there's no way the restaurant can change its menu or do anything unusual to impress the guidebook or travel writer, even after he has identified himself. Therefore, according to Fischhoff, the reviewer's critical judgment cannot be impaired. He has found free meals easy to come by—except for one restaurant where the manager told him frankly that he had masqueraded as a guidebook writer for a year in New York to feed himself.

Tom Gannon, another tour-book author, takes a contrary view, pointing out that the writer's function is to encounter the travel experience exactly as a reader would, without preferential treatment of any kind. He feels that the acceptance of free meals makes a difference. It is an untypical, and therefore unreliable, experience.

My own philosophy follows a line somewhere between these two. I feel it absolutely essential for the travel writer to keep in mind, "For whom am I working?" The freelance writer's obligation is to the reader. And while it is possible to do a terrific public relations job of glorifying a travel attraction, and also possible to perform an excellent journalism job of evaluating it from the reader's viewpoint, you can never do both jobs on the same story at the same time. Presumably, even your public relations job would be based on truth, but it would concentrate on presenting the most attractive side of your client's business. As a journalist, you compare this client against that client (mentally, at least) to give your reader the best possible advice. You are always representing *somebody*, and you must be clear yourself, and clarify for your readers, which *somebody* you represent on a particular story.

While the freelance travel writer has some responsibility to the attraction—to not, for instance, spew out a careless and undeserved witticism about a restaurant serving barbecued horsemeat or sauteed kitten that harms the restaurant's business—his real responsibility is to his reader.

One of my favorite types of hospitality occurs when somebody invites me to be a guest *after* I've written enthusiastically about a place I've paid to get to and simply loved. Then I already know what it's like, and I have an idea of the angles that might make good stories. The public relations people for the chamber of commerce, hotel, attraction, or whatever already know the way I write and apparently like it. But if I encounter something unpraiseworthy on the second trip, I don't hesitate to point it out to my readers.

Freebie Ethics

Most national and international writers' organizations espouse specific rules and guidelines about freebies. For example, the Society of American Travel Writers feels that its purpose is to serve the traveling public by providing "complete, accurate, and interesting information on travel destinations, facilities, and services." The Society believes that "travel is a bridge between peoples," and its earnest desire is "to make and keep travel a quality experience for everyone."

Concerned with possible abuses, the Society "supports the limited and intelligent use of assistance from government travel departments, carriers, and others involved in the travel field. Reduced fares and trade discounts should be approved for bona fide travel writers to make such travel practical." The Society capitalizes the following guideline for its members:

> Free or reduced-rate transportation and other travel expenses must be offered and accepted only with the mutual understanding that reportorial research is involved and any resultant story will be reported with the same standards of journalistic accuracy as that of comparable reportage and criticism in theater, business and finance, music, sports, and other news sections that provide the public with helpful information.

P.E.N., an international association of poets, playwrights, essayists, editors, and novelists, stresses the need for freedom of expression throughout the world, but points out that:

> . . . since freedom implies voluntary restraint, members pledge themselves to oppose such evils of a free press as mendacious publication, deliberate falsehood, and distortion of facts for political and personal ends.

The Outdoor Writers Association of America is especially concerned about members accepting courtesy discounts on manufactured goods, and indicates that while discounts are common, ethical conduct precludes any stipulation that a favorable review be given in return.

The Society of Professional Journalists, Sigma Delta Chi, spells out its code of ethics still more firmly:

> Journalists must be free of obligation to any interest other than the public's right to know the truth.

The Travel Journalists Guild, the International Food, Wine & Travel Writers Association, the American Society of Journalists and Authors, and other professional groups have similar guidelines.

As you become more professional in your writing and selling, you will probably want to join an appropriate writers' organization. Membership can be helpful, and you'll abide by the codes and guidelines of your organization. Even more important, you'll want to abide by your own code of ethics. Surely you have enough common sense to know the difference between right and wrong, and enough gumption to proceed accordingly. Accept free hospitality? Perhaps—if you're positive your host isn't attaching any strings to it, and you're convinced that you, yourself, would never be influenced to favor the most hospitable attractions in the travel industry.

Be Your Own Person

Usually when you're invited on some kind of press junket there's no mention of the story you might write when you return. And, of course, you may, for one reason or another, write nothing at all. Or you may write it but not sell it. Or you may sell it, but it falls through the cracks and never gets published. But even if there's no expressed expectation of publication, everybody knows what you're there for. Your hosts want you to have a good time, and they want you to report favorably on their facilities. However, more and more travel writers are speaking out candidly, regardless of who picks up the tab for the trip.

One travel journalist returned from a junket and began his story:

> If this is England at its best, I'd hate to see it at its worst.

He writes about British Airways inaugurating daily nonstop service, San Francisco to London, and inviting a dozen journalists as guests. He goes on to say that the first month found planes less than half full, then adds, tongue in cheek, "Business must be booming this month. Two prospective travelers . . . tried unsuccessfully for two days to call BA on its toll-free number."

He continues disparaging his hosts and their country, detailing Britain's "inflated prices" on hotels, gasoline, restaurant meals, and even June cherries at $5.40 a pound. He calls crossing a London street "an adventure" since "the American pedestrian invariably looks the wrong way for approaching traffic." Although more charitable toward the hospitality of the English countryside, he concludes that "London can be fun if you don't mind crowds, high prices, usually poor weather, and don't tire easily."

This sounds like he had an unfortunate trip, doesn't it? But many travel writers, in fact, have returned from junkets and written about food that was "more homestyle cooking than international gourmet," a sight-seeing tour that gave "intimate glimpses of several souvenir shops," or "a hotel room that hasn't been cleaned since Pericles stopped by on his way to the Peloponnesian Wars."

On the other hand, some of the best travel stories I've ever written leaned heavily on the particular insights and experiences that resulted from travel hospitality. I've learned a great deal from hosted trips and press junkets and have cherished the opportunity to see offbeat places and meet special people. I enjoy the hospitality I accept. But I've learned to accept only if the arrangements fit in with my own writing plans and I'm satisfied that the invitation is not a compromising one.

Tax Deductions

You can see that the answer to questions about what the travel writer enjoys free is, "It depends." That's also the answer to the often-asked questions about what kinds of tax deductions the travel writer can take.

The best advice I can give you is—go to an expert and follow his or her advice. Have your financial books set up properly in the first place, then follow through according to the plan.

An East Coast tax attorney says a travel writer can save himself a lot of money and aggravation at examination time if he keeps an accurate diary of expenditures, accompanied by receipts, with a description of the purpose for which the expenditure was made, speedometer readings before and after auto trips, and other pertinent information.

"But most of those who come to me have *already* made a mess," he laments. "Please remind your readers that the IRS requires a receipt for any large deducted expense. In order to tie down travel and entertainment deductions, the taxpayer must substantiate the amount, the time and place, the business purpose, and the business relationship to any person or persons being entertained. So tell travel writers to keep good expense records."

Minding Her Own Business

One business book writer says she always keeps the receipts for anything possibly tax deductible because, she says, "Since you have to be in a position to provide the information, anyway, it's easier to keep the original receipt, and identify it carefully."

The book *Minding Her Own Business: The Self-Employed Woman's Guide to Taxes and Recordkeeping* reminds taxpayers to "hold on to all records (receipts, canceled checks, IRS correspondence, etc.) connected with your tax return until the statute of limitations runs out for all applicable taxing agencies." State and local laws may differ from federal.

While the IRS will usually permit you to deduct all reasonable costs, backed up by receipted bills, for a trip you clearly took to obtain a story, provided you sold the story and the sale price was greater than the expenses involved, most tax problems don't fit into such neat categories.

Can you take off the price of the trip if you've written the story but haven't sold it yet?

Can you take off any part of a four-thousand-dollar, twenty-two-day trip during which you did research for travel writing, and now you've sold $50 worth of content to a website that took you two hours of those twenty-two days to research?

What about the story you've just sold from the trip you took three years ago?

Can both spouses deduct an eight-thousand-dollar trip because one of them writes the story and the other takes the photos for the package that produces five hundred dollars in income?

Can both spouses take off the trip if one writes and photographs and the other provides secretarial assistance? Or can the one who is doing the writing deduct normal secretarial expenses paid to the other one, and the secretary then deduct the trip as a necessary expense to earn the secretarial money?

Can you take off food expenses on a weekend camping trip that results in a sale, even though you would have eaten that same food at home? How about restaurant meals? Do you deduct or depreciate your new computer? Your filing cabinet? Your telephoto lens? Your postal scale?

Can you take off on your income tax for all the books you buy, regardless of subject? All your film and developing costs? How about your car? A room in your house? Somebody to clean that room? Your basic telephone bill? Membership in writers' organizations? Membership in travel organizations? Membership in the country club, where you meet a lot of people in the travel industry?

These are some of the questions you'll have to ask your expert.

A senior tax consultant for a large accounting firm says that deductibility of travel and entertainment expenses requires that the expenditure be ordinary and necessary in the operation of the taxpayer's business and directly related to or associated with the business, as well as properly documented. He explains that in order to satisfy the "directly related to" test, the taxpayer must expect to derive income or some other specific business benefit (other than goodwill) and demonstrate that active conduct of business was the primary purpose of the activity.

While indicating that expenditures for entertainment at theaters, nightclubs, or sporting events generally will not satisfy the "directly related to" test (unless the writer specializes in reviewing theater, nightclubs, or sports), he admonishes travel writers to remember that "it is extremely difficult to justify a business discussion taking place in a distracting surrounding such as a nightclub." However, "the taxpayer may still be able to claim a deduction if he can prove the event was associated with his business, since business-related activity took place immediately before or after the nightclub rendezvous."

A Florida tax consultant also reminds travel writers that good records will help segregate travel expenses, which may be 100 percent deductible, from meal and entertainment expenses, which, even if directly related to business, are only partially deductible.

This talk of tax deductions may trigger other questions in your mind. Now perhaps you're wondering whether you can take a deduction for travel expenses only if *all* your income is derived from travel writing. Or *most of it*, at least. Can you show a tax *loss* from your travel writing business?

A CPA explains that if an activity is not engaged in for a profit, no income tax deduction attributable to the activity will be allowed. "An activity is presumed to be entered into for a profit if profits result in three out of five years," he says. "If this requirement is not satisfied, then the activity will be considered a hobby. In that case, losses will only be deductible to the extent of the income."

In other words, if you make a million dollars in a real estate transaction, you can't reduce your tax liability by calling yourself a travel writer and deducting from the real estate profits your expenses from an around-the-world trip if the trip itself doesn't result in travel-writing profits. Or at least you probably can't do it unless your travel-writing business shows a profit three years out of five.

Again, the wise freelancer keeps good records. I was appalled to discover some of my students sending queries without retaining copies, and to discover some of them discarding rejection slips. They were astonished to learn that this negative correspondence might have value. Whether you paper your living room walls with them or keep them in a print or electronic file, evidence of queries and rejection letters may tip the scales in your favor when it comes to convincing IRS that you're *trying* to make travel writing a business, not a hobby.

Another tax expert reminds us, though, that IRS will not necessarily refuse a bona fide deduction just because there was no net profit from travel writing.

So you can see how the answer to the second question, "How much of your travel can you deduct on your income tax?" is also, "It depends."

The variables are many. There are no easy answers to these questions of freebies and tax deductions. There are no foolproof guidelines, either. But careful thought, plus astute selection of a tax expert, will show you how you can, with honor, enjoy some of the fringe benefits of the travel writing profession.

EIGHTEEN

Around the World or Around the Corner– Your Role As a Travel Writer

When Arnold Toynbee called creative use of leisure the "mainspring of civilization," he must have had travel writers in mind. As leisure time increases for people of every age and occupation, travel often becomes the principal leisure time activity, and you, the travel writer, often help determine the quality of this leisure. Will your readers rush to meet adventure, discovering the half-hidden peaks and uncharted beaches you told them existed? Will they hurry to experience the Penguin Parade, the Mardi Gras, the cog railroad ride, the Rhine cruise you promised would delight them? Will they linger longer at the ancient amphitheater, inspect the farthest picture gallery, wait patiently in the safari bus because you suggested they might find more to see?

It's gratifying, isn't it, to enrich the lives of others as well as your own. It's frightening, too. This power carries with it an awesome responsibility. Whether you're digging in the library stacks or surfing the web or sharing a day in the life of an Ozark schoolboy, you'll be careful to interpret the facts with perceptiveness and integrity.

What Do People Want to Read?

You'll be careful, too, to keep in close touch with what your audience wants to read.

I recently asked a large cross-section of people what kind of travel articles they liked to read, in print or online. The group ranged in age from nineteen to ninety, male and female; varied in occupation, interests, educational level, and financial circumstances; and included frequent travelers, infrequent travelers, eager travelers, reluctant travelers, former travelers, and future travelers. Two major threads seemed to emerge:

1. **People want advice, facts, knowledge of how to do it.** "Guides for the green traveler like me," said one. "Realistic details and warnings about pitfalls," said another. "How to save money"; "The basics: where to stay and eat, what to see"; "A knowledgeable traveler who tells the bad as well as the good—no babbling on about gorgeous scenery when the mosquitoes are big as bumblebees!"

2. **People want to hear about people.** "I like stories that humanize the traveler and the people he meets"; "I want to know the things that are unique about a place and its people, and also the things that are the same as at home"; "Tell me about the offbeat, inexpensive trips that pay off in opportunities to meet the locals." Others preferred "a story that gives tantalizing tastes of many areas and the people who live there"; "stories about the people in faraway places—I like to know about them, even if I never get to see them"; and "travel articles that make me feel as though I'm *there*."

When we think about it, we realize that most of the travel articles we consider good, focus on people: those who will be doing the traveling or the people they will see on their trip. Touring monuments is fine—as long as a human being is doing the touring.

The Quest for "Plus Value"

By now you know that the travel article with plus value doesn't begin with sitting down at the keyboard. It begins with the barest glimmer of an idea that you might some day be going to some place.

The preparations, we know, include seeking advance information from many sources and planning ahead for on-trip research, photography, sight-seeing—knowing what to take along and whether to accept special privileges. Your pre-trip market study helps you plan itineraries for your stories. Ahead-of-travel query letters not only sell your article before you write it but also help you define what you want to achieve.

Keeping in mind "What will my reader want to know?" you'll observe, assimilate, and distill. You'll find that all aspects of your research reinforce one another. But don't worry if you want to write about a trip that you took before you'd read the suggestions in this book. These suggestions make it easier, but many are things you've probably done anyway. Though you've omitted some of the steps, you can still write a travel article. And you should. But before your next trip, you can begin at the beginning.

You'll discover that much of what we call "research" doesn't really *feel* like research. As you explore the ambiance of the place, traverse its hidden byways, and talk informally to local people, it may seem less like work than fun. (But remember to note accurately the travel details and record any possible income tax deductions.)

You'll begin your quest for plus value by reading what others have written. Is there a writer in the world who doesn't love to read? Years ago I felt guilty every time I read for an hour—until I heard a very successful writer say, "If you have eight hours a day for writing, spend four hours reading, and if you can only spare two hours a day for writing, spend one of those hours reading." Read for information, for style, for marketing knowledge, for pleasure. Read enough to get different opinions so you'll be able to digest them, and then start off with a fresh approach of your own.

Even more important than reading is thinking. Discuss with yourself what insights you expect to bring home from the trip. Remember, your mission is more than counting cats in Zanzibar.

Change Is the Name of Travel

Prepare yourself for constant change. The travel writer soon finds that the most permanent aspect of travel is change. Prices soar, routes change, hotels open and close. There are detours to accommodate the building of newer, straighter, wider roads; and military barriers to accommodate the take-over by new political forces. There'll be new restrictions and new restraints.

Many places I've loved cannot be visited just now. But there's a happier side to this situation. Other areas previously off-limits are presently available. Perhaps one day worldwide travel will become as commonplace as a trip to the next town.

As technology breeds the kind of changes that may one day have us careening from New York to Los Angeles by underground commuter train in fifty-four minutes, the travel writer needs increasing amounts of discipline—*self*-discipline. As the world grows smaller, its attractions multiply. We're increasingly tempted by the cajoleries of travel: the lures of sun, sand, and surf; the enticements of music and dancing; the persuasions of the champagne-and-caviar circuit. How nice a travel writer's life could be—without the writing. As a journalism professor once told me, "There aren't many people out there who like to write, but the world is full of people who would like to have written." Travel writers who succeed do so because they remember what they're there for and aren't distracted by beguilements.

The Real Journey Is Within

As is often the case in the arts, amateurs don't have the same status as those who have made the effort, withstood the temptations, and mastered the skills to become professionals. But even if you remain an amateur, cultivate the professional attitude. After all, the real journey is within.

Don't be like my neighbor who, after being housebound all winter with sniffles and sinuses and several small children, accompanied me on an errand. "Anything," she said, "to get out of the house!"

"You really should get out more," I told her. "How about a hobby?"

"Well—I signed up for an adult ed art class."

"Great!" I exclaimed, as we drove through spring-green hills punctuated with blossoming apricot trees. Near the ivy-covered dorms of a rural university, canoeing couples courted on a palm-fringed lake, fresh-faced first graders alighted from the yellow school bus, and storybook farm buildings dotted patchwork fields of newborn crops.

"Yes," she replied. "I bought the paint and the canvas and made myself a smock. But I can't seem to get started."

"Why? What's the matter?"

"I just can't think of anything to paint."

Yes, the real journey is within.

Travel Writing Is Alive and Well

If you're moving toward realizing your potential as a travel writer, it's reassuring to know that great opportunity exists. Not only is travel an ever-growing industry, but so is writing. With about 65,000 periodicals published in English, 35,000 of them in the United States, and over 600,000 book titles published each year, over 50,000 in the United States, and with 85 percent of the material being nonfiction, your travel article has a very good chance of finding a home somewhere.

However, this is not a profession for the thin-skinned. Every time you address that query letter, every time you put your manuscript in its big envelope or send off a disk, you're putting yourself in the public eye. Is it good enough? Will they like it? Did I tell it the best way it could be told? All these thoughts buzz around in your head. Your mood may vary from inadequacy (they'll probably send my story back right away!) to belligerence (I'm a great writer, and they're sure to keep my story! If they don't they'll be cheating the world out of viewing my masterpiece!).

Writing is a public profession. You reveal so much of yourself. You may be writing about somebody quite different in a setting far away, but there's always a great deal of you in the story. Your secrets, your mistakes are there for the world to see. This is not a profession for one who takes each rejection slip as an indication of total failure or as a personal insult. And it's not for one who quakes at criticism or takes it out on others when the writing goes badly. I once heard another writer say, "I didn't consider myself a professional when I started getting paid for my writing. That came the first time I didn't cry over a rejection slip."

Nobody likes to see the postman pull from his bag the big envelope that signals rejection, or read the e-mail that begins, "Thank you for sending us your query, but. . .". However, even those experiences can give you a warm glow, as you learn to read between the lines that say, "Not quite good enough, maybe next time" or "Sorry, we have something similar on file. Try us again." There's always "again" and "next time," always the hope that if you keep plugging and do your best, sending it out to market after market on your itinerary, using your salesman's skills, your manuscript *will* eventually find a home.

Keep on "Stretching"

To avoid postpartum depression, when you send something off, be sure you're already at work on your *next* travel story.

Remember, a travel writer has no neon sign, no skyscraper, no inventory. His capital assets are what he has seen and heard, smelled, touched, learned, and loved. And while they might not provide collateral, nobody can steal them, tax them, or appropriate them in any way.

If you feel that, even with strict attention to business, your work compares unfavorably with the professional travel articles you read, don't be discouraged. Everybody has to start someplace. Study and learn as much as you can, attend writing classes, find a capable mentor to help you, and listen carefully to professional criticisms and suggestions. There is only one thing that's required—that you do your very best each time. Don't continually compare your efforts to someone else's (although that can have advantages in a valid learning situation), but measure yourself against yourself. Are you the best travel writer you can possibly be? Are you a better travel writer today than you were six months ago? Where will you be six months from now?

Stretching, I hope. At the second meeting of a small graduate class I was teaching, I asked each student to hand me a note indicating whether the material being covered was too simple, too complex, or about right. Replies were evenly divided between "a little too complex" and "about right." But one young woman put it especially well. "I'm stretching!" she wrote. "But it feels wonderful!"

It does feel wonderful. Stretch to the best that's in you. Reach for your best, and beyond. Reach for the opportunity to write for higher quality markets, and to write higher quality material. Do your best—and then do better. Remember, you can only take from an experience what you bring to it. It is absolutely impossible to write beautifully if you have nothing whatever to say.

As a good travel writer you'll find gratification in creating something that didn't exist before. You'll find satisfaction in knowing you have written something others will read. You'll find pride in noticing the improvement in your own work and pleasure in the interesting ideas, interesting information, and interesting individuals you will encounter.

You may have to make some sacrifices to accomplish this—give up the cajoleries and the beguilements. But you'll never be bored, you'll never be lonely.

If this is what you want to do, and you have faith in yourself, you can do it. If you have a message you want to impart and enthusiasms you want to convey, you can do it.

If you believe you can be a travel writer, you can be one.

Keep your reporter's notebook and your laptop handy, and your tape recorder and camera, too. Put business cards in your pocket and big envelopes in your suitcase, and when the next charter trip leaves for the moon, you'll be ready.

INDEX